all the words on stage
&

A COMPLETE PRONUNCIATION DICTIONARY FOR THE PLAYS OF WILLIAM SHAKESPEARE

Louis Scheeder and Shane Ann Younts

CAREER DEVELOPMENT SERIES

A Smith and Kraus Book

Published by
Smith and Kraus, Inc.
177 Lyme Road, Hanover, New Hampshire 03755
www.SmithKraus.com

Cover and text design by Julia Hill Gignoux, Freedom Hill Design

First edition: March 2002
10 9 8 7 6 5 4 3 2 1

The Library of Congress Cataloging-In-Publication Data
Scheeder, Louis.
All the words on stage : the complete Shakespeare pronunciation dictionary / Louis
Scheeder and Shane Ann Younts. —1st ed.
p. cm. (Career development series)
Includes bibliographical references (p.).
ISBN 1-57525-263-5 (cloth)
ISBN 1-57525-214-7 (pbk.)
1. Shakespeare, William, 1564–1616—Language—Glossaries, etc.
2. English language—Early modern, 1500–1700—Pronunciation—Dictionaries.
I. Younts, Shane Ann. II. Title. III. Series.
PR3081 .S27 2001
822.3'3—dc21
Library of Congress Control Number: 2001020182

contents

ℰ

the contents o'th' story
Cymbeline II, 2, 27

To my *mother, Julia Scheeder*
L.S.

To my *friend, R.N.W.*
S.A.Y.

introduction

&

What's in a name?
Romeo and Juliet II, 2, 43

While *All the Words on Stage* is explicitly a pronunciation dictionary, there is another agenda behind the ostensibly prescriptive notion of the correct pronunciation of the Shakespearean vocabulary. In presenting our work, we hope that it will stir a greater interest on the part of actors and directors, as well as teachers and students, in Shakespeare's handling of language. We believe that a deeper understanding of Shakespeare's verse, specifically the rhythm and variants of the iambic pentameter line, can aid actors in their physical and psychological portrayals of his characters. The suggested pronunciations in this dictionary reflect the interweaving of word and rhythm produced by blank verse in its numerous variants.

In recent years, especially following a number of successful film adaptations, popular interest in Shakespeare has grown enormously. Despite this plethora of visual display, there still exists a major barrier to the plays for many students and actors. That barrier is language. At times, Shakespeare's language fosters intimidation and instills fear. The intent of this book is to assist in the dismantling of the barrier of language and to allow students, actors, and the general audience access not only to an articulation of individual words, but also to the world of these plays, which, after all, exists in and through words. We hope to guide the reader not only through the basic pronunciation of individual words, some of which are no longer in current use, but also through the complexities of how the words work in relation to each other.

In the past, editions of Shakespeare seem to have been created for the reader rather than the actor. However, some editions, like the Pelican, have included markings for stressed "ed" endings in the texts, and others have noted the syllabic divisions of a word in order to respect the rhythm of the verse. The third edition of the Arden series emphasizes the performance aspects of the plays in its introductory essays. Individual editors also suggest pronunciations by including instances of words that elongate (by the addition of a vowel) or shorten (by the deletion of a vowel). There seems to be a growing interest in and attention to the articulation of the plays and their relation to the verse form.

Previous reference works have partially provided what play editions omit. Theodora Irvine's *How to Pronounce the Names in Shakespeare* stems from a survey of leading English actors around 1900. The pronunciations reflect the upper class speech of the Edwardian era. Helge Kökeritz's *Shakespeare's Names: A Pronouncing Dictionary* was the standard work on the pronunciation of character names for many years. The pronunciations tend to be those of English speech with occasional American variants. The book also includes some indications of what Elizabethan pronunciations might have been like. Delbert Spain's *Shakespeare Sounded Soundly* contains much valuable information on the working of the verse. He includes an appendix of some 250 words, giving the stresses for polysyllabic words, though without phonetic transcription. Dale Coye's *Pronouncing Shakespeare's Words* is based primarily on a survey of professors in Britain, Canada, and the U.S. It embraces both names and words but does not include phonetics. Louis Colaianni's *Shakespeare's Names* is a pronunciation guide to the names in the plays, but does not include the rest of the Shakespearean vocabulary nor does it take into account the effects of the iambic pentameter line on pronunciation.

We began this project with a list of words that we had heard actors stumble over in the classroom or in rehearsal. We then added character names, as well as proper, geographic, and mythological names, and included words that seemed unfamiliar to a sampling of undergraduates, graduate students, and professional actors. The final step was the inclusion of words that are changed and altered by the play of the iambic pentameter line. Numerous dictionaries proved invaluable for the determination of the pronunciation of words in prose. The scansion of the verse line was the final arbiter for words in verse.

Invariably, at the beginning of one of our workshops or classes, a talented individual will stand in the performance space and either mangle the name of the character that is about to be portrayed or stumble over an unfamiliar word. Several years ago, one of those students turned and asked, "How come there isn't a book that tells you how to pronounce it?" Our work is an answer to that question.

Our suggested pronunciations are American. We believe that when American actors speak Shakespeare they should sound American. As recently as the 1960s, actors commonly affected English accents in their performances of Shakespeare. Others adopted an indeterminate mid-Atlantic sound. All too often however, such attempts resulted in a phony quality to their speech and, consequently, their acting became unbelievable. On the other hand, we have witnessed productions where the actors' desire to sound natural has led them to be unintelligible.

In order that the actor's voice serves the language, ideas, and world of the play, we believe in the close integration of voice and speech training. To this end, in our private studios and in our individual classes at New York University's Classical Studio and the Graduate Acting Department, we use the methods and techniques developed by Robert Neff Williams at Columbia University and The Juilliard School over the last thirty years. These techniques allow actors to develop voices that are flexible, varied, and expressive enough to convey the nuance, color, and subtle shading of the words that the character uses whether in an intellectual argument or an emotional outburst. We hope that our work on the pronunciation of the Shakespearean vocabulary contributes to this goal.

We have used the International Phonetic Alphabet (IPA) to transcribe the pronunciations in order to be as accurate and precise as possible. However, since many readers will not be familiar with the phonetic alphabet, we have also created a re-spelling system that we trust is clear, simple, and easy to use by both professional and layperson. This system is explained in the pages that follow, along with a brief section that reviews some basic principles of iambic pentameter. We have included sections devoted to Latin and accents, dialects, and foreign languages. We have also provided a section entitled "Afterthoughts," that considers each of Shakespeare's plays in turn. In this section, the reader will find examples of words whose pronunciation is altered by the meter, as well as information on difficult words and puns that are specific to each play. Shakespeare has always served as a measure of challenge and accomplishment for actors, students, and theater artists. We hope that this work will contribute to the growing interest in and increasing emphasis on the complexities of Shakespeare's language, especially his verse, and above all, on the articulation of these texts as performative speech.

acknowledgments

many thousand thanks

Henry VI Part Three III, 2, 56

We would like to thank our students in the Department of Drama and in the Graduate Acting Department at New York University, as well as the students in our private classes. We received invaluable encouragement and advice from colleagues at NYU including Deborah Hecht of Graduate Acting, who willingly shared her vast knowledge of Shakespeare and her point of view about speaking the texts, and Deloss Brown and Donna Germain of the Classical Studio, both of whom provided support, intelligence, and strong opinions. The Reference Librarians and staff at Bobst Library graciously assisted us with numerous tasks. Their help proved crucial.

Ned Jackson provided assistance on the pronunciation of Latin, as did Julie Crosby, who also shared her editorial acumen and grammatical wisdom. We would like to acknowledge Peter Meineck of the Aquila Theatre and Kelly Preston of NYU's Center for Ancient Studies for theoretical conversations and advice in this area.

Numerous friends encouraged and cheered along this lengthy project, including Nancy Kawalek, who was there with early support and thought-provoking questions, Lisa Reardon and Mick Weber, who lent their sharp eyes, keen ears and editorial skills, and J.R. Roessl and Peter Wise, who offered early and enthusiastic feed-back. Simon Opie produced timely assistance and shrewd suggestions, while Peter Webster was unrelenting in his enthusiasm and shared his insights freely. Kristin Stewart assisted in myriad ways. Richard Fitch not only proved to be a good friend throughout, but also a computer whiz with his prompt, efficient, and humorous technical support. Philip Gruber delivered critical eleventh hour aid with his Macintosh skills and creative wizardry. Our agents, Jack Tantleff and Charmaine Ferenczi, championed the book from the beginning and were a key factor in getting it into print.

Marisa Smith and Eric Kraus immediately saw the need for such a book and committed themselves wholeheartedly to the complexities of publishing a work that we trust is both scholarly and accessible. Julia Hill Gignoux was a joy to work with as she guided us through the intricacies of text design. They have our thanks.

For his generous spirit, for many years of friendly debates about speech, and for ongoing conversations about speaking the texts of Shakespeare, Shane Ann would like to thank Andrew Wade, Head of the Voice Department at the Royal Shakespeare Company. She would also like to acknowledge Zelda Fichandler, Chair of New York University's Graduate Acting Department, who has been a source of inspiration for her.

In a casual conversation, Marcia Siegel suggested to Louis that he write a book if he wanted to learn more about a subject. For this, and many other contributions to his intellectual growth, she has his thanks. He would also like to acknowledge the support and encouragement he received from Robert White-head and the late Roger Stevens in past endeavors.

Shane Ann wishes to thank Robert Neff Williams for introducing her to Shakespeare and for sharing his love of the English language. Both of us are grateful and indebted to him for his extensive knowledge about voice, speech, and Shakespeare, and for his unflagging encouragement, extraordinary good taste, and sense of elegance. Finally, we must note that any mistakes and errors in this work are entirely our own.

play titles and abbreviations
&

Show me briefly
Much Ado About Nothing II, 2, 10

All's Well That Ends Well	AW
Antony and Cleopatra	A&C
As You Like It	AYL
The Comedy of Errors	CE
Coriolanus	COR
Cymbeline	CYM
Hamlet	HAM
Henry IV Part One	1HIV
Henry IV Part Two	2HIV
Henry V	HV
Henry VI Part One	1HVI
Henry VI Part Two	2HVI
Henry VI Part Three	3HVI
Henry VIII	HVIII
Julius Caesar	JC
King John	KJ
King Lear	LEAR
Love's Labor's Lost	LLL
Macbeth	MAC
Measure for Measure	MM
The Merchant of Venice	MVEN
The Merry Wives of Windsor	MW
A Midsummer Night's Dream	MID
Much Ado About Nothing	MADO
Othello	OTH
Pericles	PER
Richard II	RII
Richard III	RIII
Romeo and Juliet	R&J
The Taming of the Shrew	SHR
The Tempest	TEMP
Timon of Athens	TIMON
Titus Andronicus	TITUS
Troilus and Cressida	T&C
Twelfth Night	12th
Two Gentlemen of Verona	2GEN
The Two Noble Kinsmen	2NOB
The Winter's Tale	WT

key to pronunciations

Speak the speech, I pray you, as I pronounced it
Hamlet III, 2, 1

The following key gives the pronunciations in two ways—first in a respelled format for those who are not familiar with phonetics, and then phonetically using the IPA (International Phonetic Alphabet). The respelling system is our own invention. The first column contains the respelled sound, the second contains the phonetic symbol, and the third provides examples of the sound as used in a few common words.

RESPELLED	IPA SYMBOL	KEY WORDS
VOWELS		
EE	[i]	as in be, see, tea
I	[ɪ]	as in bit, hid, pin
EH	[ɛ]	as in bet, head, let
AA	[æ]	as in bat, fan, tackle
OO	[u]	as in boot, ooze, zoo
OO	[ʊ]	as in book, foot, put
AW	[ɔ]	as in bought, saw, dawn
AH	[ɑ]	as in father, calm, spa
ER	[ɝ]	as in bird, fur, learn
E(r)	[ɜ]	as in averring, whirring
UH	[ʌ]	as in cup, but, glove

Unstressed Vowels

er	[ɚ]	as in better, modern
uh	[ə]	as in focus, ago, famous

Syllabics

(uh)	[ˌ]	as in mettle, roundel, batten

Diphthongs and Triphthongs

AY	[eɪ]	as in bay, take, say
EYE	[aɪ]	as in bite, high, time
OY	[ɔɪ]	as in boy, avoid, voice
OH	[oʊ]	as in boat, go, sew
OW	[aʊ]	as in how, town, out
YOO	[ɪu]	as in duke, new, tune
EAR	[ɪɚ]	as in beer, hear, fear
AIR	[ɛɚ]	as in bear, hair, fare
OOR	[ʊɚ]	as in tour, sure, poor
AWR	[ɔɚ]	as in bore, four, score
AHR	[ɑɚ]	as in bar, card, part
EYER	[aɪɚ]	as in sire, hire, fire
OWR	[aʊɚ]	as in hour, scour, sour

Consonants

P	[p]	as in pat, puppy, cap
B	[b]	as in bowl, rubbish, cab
T	[t]	as in top, better, cat
D	[d]	as in dip, moody, had
K	[k]	as in car, actor, pick
G	[g]	as in go, agree, hug
M	[m]	as in met, comma, aim
N	[n]	as in no, penny, chain
NG	[ŋ]	as in king, hang, banquet
L	[l]	as in low, salad, bell
R	[r]	as in red, ran, arrive
Y	[j]	as in yet, uniform, use
W	[w]	as in we, word, away
H	[h]	as in have, hid, help

HW	[hw]	as in what, where, wheat
S	[s]	as in soon, ask, toss
Z	[z]	as in zoo, busy, jazz
F	[f]	as in far, affirm, graph
V	[v]	as in vine, even, save
SH	[ʃ]	as in ship, nation, cash
ZH	[ʒ]	as in vision, casual, beige
TH	[θ]	as in thirty, nothing, path
<u>TH</u>	[ð]	as in then, other, breathe
CH	[tʃ]	as in child, future, watch
J	[ʤ]	as in just, fragile, ridge

NOTES ON SYLLABLES AND STRESS

Respellings
- A hyphen (-) separates the syllables.
- A syllable printed in **BOLD CAPITAL LETTERS** has the primary stress.
- A syllable printed in CAPITAL LETTERS has the secondary stress.
- All other syllables are in lower case letters.
- Unstressed vowels are always in lower case letters.
  Example: AY-dree-**AH**-nuh

Phonetics
- Phonetic symbols are surrounded by [brackets].
- Syllables are separated by a hyphen (-).
- ['] in front of a syllable indicates that the primary stress is on the following syllable.
  Example: [eɪ-dri-'ɑ-nə]

A detailed explanation of the respellings and phonetics is included in the next section, "How to Use the Dictionary."

how to use the dictionary

&

Well practiced wise directions
Henry IV Part Two V, 2, 121

"WORDS, WORDS, WORDS"
Hamlet II, 2, 191

All English words in this dictionary, including words absorbed into English from other languages, are listed alphabetically. Latin words and phrases are arranged alphabetically in their own section. We have chosen not to include malaprops or comic blunders. We believe that each actor should be free to develop a pronunciation for these words.

As much as possible, we have made the components of the respelling system reflect the sound that they represent. We have listed the respelled words first and then the phonetic symbols. (See "Key to Pronunciations" page 2.)

We follow the texts of the Pelican Shakespeare. For *The Two Noble Kinsmen* we employed the Arden edition. Occasionally we have used a spelling from another edition if it helps to clarify the pronunciation or if a majority of editions prefer a spelling that differs from the Pelican series:

popingay PAHP-in-gay ['pɑp-ɪn-geɪ] some editions "popin-jay" PAHP-in-jay ['pɑp-ɪn-ʤeɪ]

Sometimes a word that is spelled with a lower case letter is also a proper name. If the pronunciation is the same, these words are listed with the lower case first and the proper name second:

bedlam / Bedlam BEHD-luhm ['bɛd-ləm]

Nouns are listed in their singular form, and verbs are in the present tense, unless the word is used only one time in the plural or past tense form. For example *gallowglasses, gasted, sleeded,* and *smuched* are respelled with their *es* or *ed* endings because they appear only one time.

When an individual word has different spellings in the Pelican series, the variants are listed with a slash between them, followed by the respelling and phonetics:

lower / low'r / lour (to frown) LOWR [lɑʊɚ]

When a multi-syllabic word has more than one pronunciation, the syllables that are unchanged are indicated by a blank line:

scimitar SIM-i-ter ['sɪm-ɪ-tɚ] or ___-___-tahr [___-___-tɑɚ]

If alternate pronunciations are given, we leave the preference to the individual actor. Alternates are separated by the word *or*:

halberd HAAL-berd ['hæl-bɚd] or HAWL-___ ['hɔl-___]

The names of characters which appear in the Cast Lists are followed by the play's abbreviation, the respelling, and the phonetics. Pronunciations, altered by scansion, are given along with the act, scene and line reference. If the scanned version of the pronunciation is used more than one time *e.g.* (for example) precedes the line reference and the @ (at) symbol is placed in front of the act, scene and line:

Antiochus *(PER)* aan-TEYE-uh-kuhs [æn-'taɪ-ə-kəs]
   scans to ___-TEYE-kuhs [__-'taɪ kəs] e.g. @ I, 3, 19

Multiple entries, including family names, proper names of characters in the cast list and characters who are alluded to or mentioned in a play but are not in the cast list, are organized in the following manner: the first line of the main entry gives the basic pronunciation and any variant pronunciations due to scansion. Indented under the main entry, the characters in the cast are listed with their play abbreviation, the line references of variant pronunciations, and the respellings of any additional information. If no line reference is given, then the proper name does not alter in that play:

Katherine KAATH-uh-rin ['kæθ-ə-rɪn] scans to
   KAATH-rin ['kæθ-rɪn]
   Katherine *(HV)*
   Katherine *(HVIII)*
   Katherine *(SHR)* scans @ II, 1, 184, also called
      "Katherina" KAATH-uh-REE-nuh [kæθ-ə-'ri-nə]
      or KAAT-___-___-___ [kæt-___-___-___]
   and "Kate" KAYT [keɪt]

Andronicus aan-DRAHN-i-kuhs [æn-'drɑn-ɪ-kəs]
   Andronicus, Marcus *(TITUS)* MAHR-kuhs ['mɑɚ-kəs]
   Andronicus, Titus *(TITUS)* TEYE-tuhs ['taɪ-təs]

"TAKE NOTE, TAKE NOTE"
Othello III, 3, 377

In order to assist the speaker, we give the syllable divisions and the levels of stress with as much detail as possible. Because most dictionaries are concerned with orthographic division in order to meet the needs of writers, proof readers, and typesetters, the syllable divisions for speakers are usually ignored and the indications of stress are often unclear. To clarify the spoken word, we

7

place a hyphen between every syllable and include three levels of stress — primary, secondary, and unstressed.

The primary stress is the strongest level of emphasis, and it is indicated in the respelling system with **BOLD CAPITAL** letters and in the phonetics with an accent mark preceding the syllable with the primary stress:

lambkins LAAM-kinz ['læm-kɪnz]

In certain multi-syllabic words, a secondary stress is indicated when it clarifies the pronunciation of the word. A secondary stress indicates the syllable that receives an intermediate level of stress and is written in the respelling system in CAPITAL letters without bold face type. For the secondary stress, speakers using the phonetic symbols will need to refer to the respelled version of the word:

palisadoes PAAL-i-SAY-dohz [pæl-ɪ-'seɪ-doʊz]

An unstressed syllable receives the lightest stress and is written in lower case letters:

supplyant suh-**PLEYE**-uhnt [sə-'plaɪ-ənt]

Often the verse demands a variant pronunciation. The variant follows the basic pronunciation. If the variant occurs more than once, the abbreviation *e.g.* precedes a citation:

lamentable luh-MEHN-tuh-b(uh)l [lə-'mɛn-tə-bl̩] scans to
LAAM-uhn-__-__ ['læm-ən-__-__] e.g. @ RII V, 1, 44
character (n) or (v) KAA-rik-ter ['kæ-rɪk-tɚ] scans to
kuh-**RAAK**-___ [kə-'ræk-__] e.g. @ RIII III, 1, 81

If the verse always demands a variant pronunciation, the phrase *always scans to* precedes the respelling and phonetics:

scorpion always scans to SKAWR-pyuhn ['skɔɚ-pjən]
Amazonian always scans to AAM-uh-ZOH-nyuhn
[æm-ə-'zoʊ-njən]

If a word occurs only once in Shakespeare and needs to be elided to fulfill the demands of the meter, then just the elided pronunciation is given. Since the word appears only once, no reference is listed:

contumely scans to KAHN-tyoom-lee ['kɑn-tɪum-li]

The phrase *possibly scans to* precedes a word that might receive an alternate stress:

gallant GAAL-uhnt ['gæl-ənt] possibly scans to
guh-LAHNT [gə-'lɑnt] @ RII V, 3, 15

If the scanned version of the word includes numerous changes, the entire word is respelled:

solemnized SAH-lehm-neyezd ['sɑ-lɛm-naɪzd] scans to
suh-LEHM-neye-zid [sə-'lɛm-naɪ-zɪd] e.g. @ LLL II, 1, 42

When scansion of a verse line indicates that the primary stress of a two syllable word reverses, the word is respelled in its entirety:

complete kuhm-PLEET [kəm-'plit] scans to KAHM-pleet ['kɑm-plit] e.g. @ RIII IV, 4, 190

"The Dictionary" includes many, though not all, words that require an additional syllable to fulfill the demands of the meter. Other examples of these words are listed in "Afterthoughts." When an additional syllable is needed to elongate these words, the necessary metrical beat is indicated by the addition of an *ee* sound. This often combines with *sh*. The *shee* or *ee* syllable is never stressed and should be spoken as lightly as possible:

patrician puh-TRI-shuhn [pə-'trɪ-ʃən] scans to __-__-shee-uhn
[__-__-ʃi-ən] @ COR V, 6, 82
marriage MAA-rij ['mæ-rɪdʒ] scans to MAA-ree-ij ['mæ-ri-ɪdʒ]
e.g. @ R&J IV, 1, 11

One of the most common means of condensing a word to fulfill the demands of the meter is to remove an unstressed, internal vowel. No other sound is added to the remaining syllables:

stomacher STUHM-uh-ker ['stʌm-ə-kɚ] scans to
STUHM-ker ['stʌm-kɚ] @ CYM III, 4, 84

The other common means of condensing a word is to remove the vowel in the penultimate syllable and replace it with *y* so that the two final syllables become one:

calumnious kuh-LUHM-nee-uhs [kə-'lʌm-ni-əs] scans to
__-LUHM-nyuhs [__-'lʌm-njəs] e.g. @ HAM I, 3, 38
perfidious per-FID-ee-uhs [pɚ-'fɪd-i-əs] scans to __-FID-
yuhs [__-'fɪd-jəs] @ TEMP I, 2, 68

To clarify a pronunciation that changes depending on the word's usage, the abbreviations *(adj)* for adjective, *(adv)* for adverb, *(n)* for noun, *(v)* for verb, and *(part)* for participle are included when necessary:

consort (n) KAHN-sort ['kɑn-sɔɚt] scans to kuhn-SAWRT
[kən-'sɔɚt] e.g. @ 2GEN IV, 1, 64
consort (v) kuhn-SAWRT [kən-'sɔɚt]

We offer definitions for apparent homonyms and other select instances:

bow (n) (weapon or collar of a yoke) BOH [bou] e.g. @ LLL
IV, 1, 24 and AYL III, 3, 69
bow (v) (to bend into a curve or to play a stringed instrument with a bow) BOH [bou] @ PER IV, 2, 80
bow (v) (to incline the body) BOW [bɑu] e.g. @ RII I, 3, 47
covent (n) (a religious community) KUH-vehnt ['kʌ-vɛnt]

"DID NOT YOU SPEAK?"
Macbeth II, 2, 16

In this dictionary when the consonant *r* is between vowel sounds, it always indicates the beginning of a syllable. For example *orisons* is respelled **AW**-ri-zuhnz and not **AWR**-i-zuhnz, *Verona* is respelled vuh-**ROH**-nuh and not ver-**OH**-nuh, *environ* is respelled ehn-**VEYE**-ruhn and not ehn-**VEYER**-uhn. This placement of the consonant *r* at the beginning of a syllable gives a clean-cut definition to that syllable and adds clarity when speaking the text.

We have chosen to use the respelling Y$\overline{OO}$ to represent [ɪu]. Those who feel more comfortable using the simple vowel $\overline{OO}$ [u] should substitute it for words that have been respelled using Y$\overline{OO}$ [ɪu].

Syllabic consonants are those that form a syllable with a preceding consonant without the voicing of a vowel between the two. The syllabic is always an unstressed syllable and is indicated by placing the *uh* in parentheses (uh) in the respelled version. A small perpendicular mark is placed under the syllabic consonant in the phonetic version:

mettle MEH-t(uh)l ['mɛ-tl̩]
batten BAA-t(uh)n ['bæ-tn̩]

We give only one pronunciation for words in which the unstressed *i* [ɪ] and the *uh* [ə] are interchangeable, such as the first syllable in *bereft, denay,* and *requital.* Although the *uh* is more common in American speech, the unstressed *i* [ɪ] may be preferable because it has a clear, bright quality.

scanning the verse

Had in them more feet than the verses would bear
As You Like It III, 2, 159

Many of the suggested pronunciations in this dictionary are influenced by Shakespeare's use of iambic pentameter, which was the staple of English poetry from the time of Chaucer until the turn of the last century when free verse (that is, verse written outside of a metrical form) came into play. The verse form and the pronunciation of the Shakespearean vocabulary are intertwined. Shakespeare's verse often demands specific pronunciations, some of which are different than those used in colloquial speech. Pronunciations that respect the verse form can assist the actor not only with meaning and syntax but with acting intentions and emotional clarity.

Beginning students often ask how verse differs from prose. A short answer is that prose follows the rules of grammar, while verse obeys not only grammar but also additional principles, which serve to heighten our attention to the rhythm of the language. A line of iambic pentameter verse, indicated in print by its layout on the page, adheres to a set of metrical principles. An iamb is composed of two syllables, the first unstressed, the second stressed. This is called an iambic foot. A foot is merely a theoretical division of a verse line. Metrical refers to meter. Meter is the organization of the regularity of speech into a strict pattern that can be identified and counted. Pentameter means that there are five metrical units in each line of verse, since *penta* is the Greek word for five. Therefore, iambic pentameter is a line of five iambic feet, which contains ten syllables. For example:

There is no virtue like necessity.
Richard II I, 3, 278

Scansion is the orthographic or written attempt to represent the meter and stress of verse by noting the light and heavy stresses in the line. It seeks to capture the interplay of word and metrical stress. This interplay is often referred to as the rhythm of the language. Rhythm, however, can neither be seen, nor heard, nor read. Rhythm is something that is felt. It is a pulse, a beat, a sense of movement through time. Rhythm is innate, yet invisible. It is a pattern or series of beats that produce energy. Rhythm goes through time as movement goes through space. It is difficult, if not impossible, to portray rhythm on the page, though this is what scansion sets out to do. Capturing rhythm is like trying to capture breath. One can sense the act of breathing, but one does not see the air that is the component of the breath. In order for the audience to sense rhythm, the actor must establish it. And, once established, it must be maintained so that the variants, which heighten the expressiveness of the verse, can be *felt* as opposed to observed or heard. The variants need to be experienced as *variants*. The expressiveness and force of the language often stem from the variants to the iambic pentameter form employed by Shakespeare and his fellow dramatists. In the past, these variants were sometimes dismissed as an example of sloppy craftsmanship or ascribed to misguided typesetters. The actor should use and exploit variation and difference, not homogenize them. An individual line does not stand on its own but must be considered, eventually, both in relation to the other verse lines and to the prose surrounding it. As the variants are discovered and explored, the actor will find that they provide a map or sketch of the thought processes of the character, allowing the actor to create the verse line in the present moment.

It is important to note that Shakespeare and other writers of the period organized the arrangement of particular stresses — the beats and off-beats of the lines — not to fulfill arbitrary standards, but rather to reflect the emotional and psychological state of the character. Shakespeare wrote his plays over an approximately twenty-year period. He and his contemporaries sought to achieve a theatrical reality through the use of language. Consequently, they experimented with iambic pentameter, the English language, and the best theatrical forms for the expression of their ideas. One of his first plays *(Titus Andronicus)* was almost entirely in verse. Some early plays *(The Comedy of Errors, Two Gentlemen of Verona,* and *The Taming of the Shrew)* combine verse and prose. While a few *(Henry VI Part Two, Henry VI Part Three, Richard II,* and *King John)* are completely in verse, others *(Henry IV Part One, Henry IV Part Two, The Merry Wives of Windsor, Much Ado About Nothing,* and *As You Like It)* examine the potential of prose. In some early comedies *(A Midsummer Night's Dream* and *Love's Labor's Lost)* almost half of the play is in rhyming verse. However, a later tragedy *(Antony and Cleopatra)* contains 90 percent blank verse, i.e. verse that does not rhyme. Blank verse then becomes the predominate means of expression in the later tragedies and romances. In addition to these larger categories, Shakespeare investigates changes to the iambic pentameter line in individual plays. He experiments with long lines, epic caesuras, and short and shared lines, which are explained below. He was able to do this because iambic pentameter closely follows the rhythm of spoken English and, thus, has an extraordinary ability to accommodate a host of variations.

The most common variant to the ten syllable line is the longer line, specifically that which contains an eleventh or extra syllable, which is never stressed. (In the past, these line endings were referred to, in a form of literary misogyny, as "feminine" because of their "weak" or unstressed ending.) The most famous line in Shakespeare has an unstressed ending:

> To be or not to be, that is the question
> *Hamlet* III, 1, 55

The line is almost naturalistic in its simplicity, yet the iambic rhythm is present.

Some lines have twelve syllables. This type of line is referred to as either an alexandrine or a hexameter (six metric units to the line). An example is:

> Allow obedience, if you yourselves are old
> *King Lear* II, 4, 186

Whereas the iambic pentameter line of five units cannot divide itself in half, the hexameter line can. Two sections of three feet each give a sense of difference, perhaps a heightening of emotion or crisis in the character. When two characters share a twelve-syllable line, a sense of charged confrontation or heightened exchange exists between them. The twelve syllable line might also be reflective of a heightened emotional state in which the speaker is cramming twelve syllables into the time normally reserved for ten. The twelve-syllable line does something new, perhaps something disturbing, to the established iambic pentameter rhythm that has been set down for us. It is also possible for a hexameter line to have an additional unstressed syllable at the end, resulting in a line of thirteen beats. An example is:

> Yet are they passing cowardly. But, I beseech you
> *Coriolanus* I, 1, 198

Some lines when read appear to have more than ten syllables, but when spoken are actually regular iambic pentameter lines. A reverence for the printed text or a fixed belief in the efficacy of "proper" speech for Shakespearean production often leads actors to attempt to pronounce all the syllables that appear in a given line. Doing so creates havoc with the rhythm of the verse. However, contraction and elision will allow the rhythm to be maintained.

Contraction is the formation of a word by omitting or combining sounds of a longer phrase. Elision is the suppression of a weak, internal vowel or an unstressed syllable. We noted earlier that the verse line sometimes demands a pronunciation that is different than that used in contemporary speech. Conversely, the verse also demands contractions that are quite common in everyday life. The use of *I'm* for *I am* and *you'll* for *you will* often allows the actor to maintain the rhythm while ensuring that the ehm-**FAA**-sis does not fall on the wrong si-**LAA**-buhl. Elisions occur most often with the omission of the "uh" sound, known as the schwa. This is the unstressed sound found in words like *soda, forum,* and *bacon* and is the most common vowel sound in the English language. Given its prevalence in speech, one would expect listeners to be able to perceive the sound even if it is not actually spoken. Its elimination is most common in everyday speech in words like *natural* (**NAACH**–ruhl as opposed to **NAACH**–uh–ruhl) and *general* (**JEHN**–ruhl as opposed to **JEHN**-uh-ruhl). Some other words where this occurs are *liberal, factory, federal,* and *boundary.* This elimination occurs with increasing frequency through the later plays and might reach something of a peak in a line such as Hermione's

The innocent milk in it most innocent mouth

Which, when the unstressed vowels are eliminated, becomes

The inn'cent milk in it most inn'cent mouth
The Winter's Tale III, 2, 99

This elision gives the line greater drive, provides for a stronger point of view, and with the closer antithetical alliteration of *n*'s and *m*'s allows the audience to hear a clearer version of her outrage and grief.

Another type of internal compression occurs when a word has contiguous vowels. Thus words like *glorious* scan to **GLAWR**-yuhs and *happier* scans to **HAAP**-yer. We have found that while actors sometimes find it strange to alter the printed text, once they achieve a certain specificity of action and level of

16

emotional intensity, this elision becomes a part of their approach to the verse.

At times, it becomes necessary to expand a word in order to maintain the verse rhythm. The most common form of this, and one which is almost universally practiced, is pronouncing the *ed* endings to words as "id." This occurs in lines like Juliet's cry:

> Tybalt is dead and Romeo — banished
> That 'banished,' that one word 'banished.'
> *Romeo and Juliet* III, 2, 112–113

Some editions, such as the Pelican series, mark these stresses for the reader. Note also that Romeo with its contiguous vowels scans to two syllables, **ROHM**-yoh.

While contiguous vowels sometimes elide, they also can expand. This is most common with words ending in *ion*. It also occurs with words such as *patience, ocean,* and *marriage.* These syllabic expansions are an area of contention. Some feel that the full articulation of the *ion* ending (probably "ee-uhn" and rendered so in this dictionary) distances the audience from the play, short-circuits the emotional empathy between actor and audience, and thus should never be used. Others advocate the merest suggestion or hint of the extended sound, while still others prefer that the single syllabic sound be elongated to count for two beats. The pronunciation of these words remains anathema to some and controversial to others. We have begun to hear their occurrence in a number of professional productions. The third edition of the Arden series has taken to stating quite clearly that words like *invention* are "pronounced with four syllables" in the Prologue to *Henry V.* Within this Dictionary, we have offered expanded versions of some of these words and noted even more examples in "Afterthoughts" for those who wish to experiment with their usage. A far less controversial form of "stretching" occurs with the addition of a schwa between the existing syllables. With this addition, words like *business, entrance,* and *children,* expand to three syllables.

17

There are words in Shakespeare that can be pronounced with either one or two syllables. Some of the most common are *being, power, hour,* and *fire.* This syllabic variation will also allow the language to fulfill the demands of the meter. Odd as it may seem to those who still hold to an early 20th century elocutionary approach, the verse demands that certain words contract. This is especially true of words which possess a central *v, th,* or *r.* These interior consonants will disappear so that *ever* becomes *e'er* (as it is sometimes printed), *never* becomes *ne'er,* and *even* becomes *e'en. Either* and *whither* elide to monosyllabic *ei'er* and *wh'er.* Some would go so far as to elide *seven* to *se'n,* though this may challenge the comprehension of the audience. In this instance, the solution will be to speak the word quickly so as to give it one beat in the verse line, while still maintaining the *v* sound. Words with a central *r* that elide include *sirrah* and *warrant.*

In many cases, the text will provide instances of contractions, especially with prepositional phrases. Examples are:

> *o'th'* stands for "of the" pronounced as one syllable 'UH<u>TH</u>';
> *in't* stands for "in it" pronounced as one syllable 'INT';
> *to't* stands for "to it" pronounced as one syllable 'T$\overline{OO}$T';
> *i' th* stands for "in the" pronounced as one syllable '<u>ITH</u>';
> *th'other* stands for "the other" pronounced as two syllables '<u>THUHTH</u>-er'.

Elisions already printed in the text occur in words like *know'st, take't,* and *as't* and should be pronounced as one syllable "NOHST," "TAYKT," and "AAST."

Frequently, and especially in the later plays, there will be a line that seems to refuse to scan. Such a line often contains an epic caesura. The epic (or long) caesura is a form of the caesura, which is itself a break in the verse line. The caesura occurs after the fourth or sixth beat and often relates to the syntax of the sentence of which it is a part. While some refer to the caesura as a pause, it is perhaps more helpful to think of it either as a momentary spark of thought or as a shift of gears as the character embarks on a new thought or idea. Examples include:

> To sleep-perchance to dream: ay, there's the rub,
>> *Hamlet* III, 1, 65

in which the caesura appears after the sixth beat, and

> If you have tears, prepare to shed them now,
>> *Julius Caesar* III, 2, 169

and

> Be not afeard: The isle is full of noises,
>> *The Tempest* III, 2, 132

in both of which the caesura occurs after the fourth beat.

The epic (or long) caesura features a definite pause or full break in the line, which follows an extra weak or unstressed syllable in the foot before the break. After this full or deliberate pause, there seems to be a new beginning to the thought of the speaker. Quite often, there is a form of punctuation just before the epic caesura. The pause gives the line of eleven syllables the weight of twelve and allows the line to maintain an iambic rhythm without radically altering the pronunciation of everyday words. Examples are:

> And all the gods go with you. ( ) Upon your sword
>> *Antony and Cleopatra* I, 3, 99

> But for my sport and profit. ( ) I hate the Moor;
>> *Othello* I, 3, 380

Sometimes Shakespeare makes use of a short line which indicates a pause. The syllabic count falls short, but the iambic rhythm remains. The pause should be filled with some sort of non-verbal behavior, which can be either physical activity or silent psychological action, such as Horatio's anticipation of the Ghost's response to him in the first scene of *Hamlet*. On rare occasions, in plays filled with such articulate characters, the pause may reveal a character at a momentary loss for words. The duration of either the psychological action or the physical activity will, ideally, maintain the iambic rhythm of the verse.

At other times a line is shared. The full iambic line of five feet is split between two or more speakers. One character has two or three iambic feet, and another has the balance of the line. In the following, one line serves as an opportunity for two exchanges between the characters:

> LADY
>> I heard the owl scream and the crickets cry.
>> Did not you speak?
> MACBETH   When?
> LADY   Now.
> MACBETH   As I descended?
>> *Macbeth* II, 2, 15–16

Shakespeare occasionally uses both short, shared, and complete pentameter lines in combinations to stunning effect, as in the first scene of *Hamlet*.

Rarely, Shakespeare will employ a "headless" line. One example of this is Richard II casting his truncheon to the ground to stop the trial by combat of Bolingbroke and Mowbray, which prompts the Marshal to cry out:

> (—) Stay! the King hath thrown his warder down.
>> *Richard II* I, 3, 118

The beginning of the line is missing the unstressed syllable that normally precedes a stressed syllable in an iambic foot. The first word thus receives a heavy stress. The text calls for the briefest of pauses, which might allow an actor to register a sudden emotional shift or abrupt change in the scene.

Our attention to rhythm and Shakespeare's use of metrics in the compilation of this dictionary is intended to help the actor speak a living, breathing, supple language, rather than recite a printed text. As obvious as it seems, it might be good to note that the printed text is not the spoken word. The goal should be to experiment with the verse form in order to achieve a spoken language that is heightened yet realistic, thoughtful yet engaging. It is the unseen quality of the verse — its rhythm and the corresponding system of metrics — that gives the words their drive, power, and presence.

Readers who are interested in pursuing their study of Shakespeare's handling of metrics and the use of rhythm in poetic language are encouraged to consult *Shakespeare's Metrical Art* by George T. Wright and *Poetic Rhythm: An Introduction* by Derek Attridge, to whom we are indebted.

the dictionary

A fine volley of words
Two Gentlemen of Verona II, 4, 31

'a (corruption of the pronoun "he") uh [ə] an unstressed sound almost negligible to the ear; some productions substitute "he"

'a' (v) (to have) uh [ə]

a / 'a (prep) ("of" or "on") uh [ə]

Aaron *(TITUS)* **AA**-ruhn [ˈæ-rən] or **EH**-___ [ˈɛ-___]

abate uh-**BAYT** [ə-ˈbeɪt]

Abbess **AAB**-ehs [ˈæb-ɛs] or ___-is [___-ɪs]

Abel **AY**-buhl [ˈeɪ-bəl]

Aberga'ny see "Abergavenny"

Abergavenny, Lord *(HVIII)* **AAB**-er-**GEHN**-ee [æb-ɚ-ˈgɛn-i]

abhor aab-**HAWR** [æb-ˈhɔɚ] or uhb-___ [əb-___]

Abhorson *(MM)* aab-**HAWR**-suhn [æb-ˈhɔɚ-sən]

abject (adj) **AAB**-jehkt [ˈæb-ʤɛkt]

abjects (n) aab-**JEHKTS** [æb-ˈʤɛkts]

abjure aab-**JOOR** [æb-ˈjʊɚ] or uhb-___ [əb-___]

abode uh-**BOHD** [ə-ˈboʊd]

abodements uh-**BOHD**-muhnts [ə-ˈboʊd-mənts]

abominably uh-**BAHM**-i-nuh-blee [ə-ˈbɑm-ɪ-nə-bli]

Abraham **AY**-bruh-haam [ˈeɪ-brə-hæm] scans to **AY**-bruhm [ˈeɪ-brəm] e.g. @ *RIII* IV, 3, 38

Abram **AY**-bruhm [ˈeɪ-brəm]
　　Abram *(R&J)*

abram (light yellow color) **AY**-bruhm [ˈeɪ-brəm]

abroach uh-**BROHCH** [ə-ˈbroʊʧ]

EE i be/ I ɪ bit/ EH ɛ bet/ AA æ bat/ OO u boot / OO ʊ book/ AW ɔ bought/ AH ɑ father/ ER ɝ bird/ UH ʌ cup/ AY eɪ bay/ EYE aɪ bite/ OY ɔɪ boy/ OH oʊ boat/ OW aʊ how/ YOO ɪu duke/ EAR ɪɚ beer/ AIR ɛɚ bear/ OOR ʊɚ tour/ AWR ɔɚ bore/ AHR ɑɚ bar/ NG ŋ king/ SH ʃ ship/ ZH ʒ vision/ TH θ thirty/ TH ð then/ CH ʧ child/ J ʤ just/ For complete list, see Key to Pronunciation p. 2.

25

abrogate AAB-ruh-gayt ['æb-rə-geɪt]

absent (v) aab-SEHNT [æb-'sɛnt]

Absey scans to AYB-see ['eɪb-si]

abstemious aab-STEE-mee-uhs [æb-'sti-mi-əs]

abstract (n) AAB-straakt ['æb-strækt]

Absyrtus uhb-SER-tuhs [əb-'sɝ-təs] or aab-___-___
    [æb-___-___]

aby uh-BEYE [ə-'baɪ]

abysm always scans to uh-BIZM [ə-'bɪzm]

academe AAK-uh-deem ['æk-ə-dim]

a-cap'ring uh-KAYP-ring [ə-'keɪp-rɪŋ]

access aak-SEHS [æk-'sɛs] scans to AAK-sehs ['æk-sɛs]
    @ *HAM* II, 1, 110

accessary (adj) AAK-sehs-uh-ree ['æk-sɛs-ə-ri] or possibly
    scans to AAK-sehs-ree ['æk-sɛs-ri] @ *RIII* I, 2, 191

accessary (n) aak-SEHS-uh-ree [æk-'sɛs-ə-ri] or AAK-sehs-ree
    ['æk-sɛs-ri]

accite aak-SEYET [æk-'saɪt]

accompt uh-KOWNT [ə-'kɑunt] (archaic form of
    "account" stems from Latin "computare" to count)
    Many productions use uh-KAHMPT [ə-'kɑmpt].

accordant uh-KAWR-d(uh)nt [ə-'kɔɚ-dn̩t]

accost uh-KAWST [ə-'kɔst]

accoustrements uh-KUHS-ter-muhnts [ə-'kʌs-tɚ-mənts]

accoutered / accoutred uh-KOO-terd [ə-'ku-tɚd]

accoutrement uh-KOO-truh-muhnt [ə-'ku-trə-mənt]

ache (the letter "H") AYCH [eɪtʃ]

ache (n) (a pain) (v) (to suffer pain) AYK [eɪk]

Acheron AAK-uh-rahn ['æk-ə-rɑn] scans to AAK-rahn ['æk-rɑn] @ *TITUS* IV, 3, 44

aches (pains) (pronounced like the letter "H" by the Elizabethans) AY-chiz ['eɪ-tʃɪz] e.g. @ *TEMP* I, 2, 370

Achilles uh-KIL-eez [ə-'kɪl-iz]
Achilles *(T&C)*

Achitophel uh-KIT-uh-fehl [ə-'kɪt-ə-fɛl]

acknown aak-NOHN [æk-'noʊn]

aconitum AA-kuh-NEYET-uhm [æ-kə-'naɪt-əm]

acquittance uh-KWIT-uhns [ə-'kwɪt-əns]

Actaeon aak-TEE-uhn [æk-'ti-ən]

Actium AAK-tee-uhm ['æk-ti-əm] or possibly scans to AAK-tyuhm ['æk-tjəm]

adage AAD-ij ['æd-ɪdʒ]

Adallas uh-DAAL-uhs [ə-'dæl-əs]

Adam AAD-uhm ['æd-əm]
Adam *(AYL)*
Adam *(SHR)*

adamant AAD-uh-muhnt ['æd-ə-mənt] or ___-___-maant [___-___-mænt]

adder AAD-er ['æd-ɚ]

addle AA-d(uh)l ['æ-dl̩]

addrest uh-DREHST [ə-'drɛst]

adieu uh-DYOO [ə-'dɪu]

EE i be/ I ɪ bit/ EH ɛ bet/ AA æ bat/ OO u boot / OŌ ʊ book/ AW ɔ bought/ AH ɑ father/ ER ɝ bird/
UH ʌ cup/ AY eɪ bay/ EYE aɪ bite/ OY ɔɪ boy/ OH oʊ boat/ OW aʊ how/ YOŌ ɪu duke/ EAR ɪə
beer/ AIR ɛə bear/ OŌR ʊə tour/ AWR ɔɚ bore/ AHR ɑɚ bar/ NG ŋ king/ SH ʃ ship/ ZH ʒ vision/
TH θ thirty/ TH ð then/ CH tʃ child/ J dʒ just/ For complete list, see Key to Pronunciation p. 2.

Admiral AAD-muh-ruhl ['æd-mə-rəl]

Adonis uh-DAHN-is [ə-'dɑn-ɪs] or ___-DOHN-___ [___-'doun-___]

adoptious uh-DAHP-shuhs [ə-'dɑp-ʃəs]

Adrian AY-dree-uhn ['eɪ-dri-ən]
 Adrian *(COR)*
 Adrian *(TEMP)*

Adriana *(CE)* AY-dree-AH-nuh [eɪ-dri-'ɑ-nə]

Adriatic AY-dree-AAT-ik [eɪ-dri-'æt-ɪk]

adverse aad-VERS [æd-'vɝs] scans to AAD-vers ['æd-vɚs] e.g. @ *12th* V, 1, 78

advertise always scans to aad-VER-teyez [æd-'vɝ-taɪz]

advertisement always scans to aad-VER-tiz-muhnt [æd-'vɝ-tɪz-mənt]

Aeacides ee-AAS-i-deez [i-'æs-ɪ-diz]

Aediles *(COR)* EE-deyelz ['i-daɪlz]

Aegles EE-gleez ['i-gliz]

Aemilius *(TITUS)* ee-MIL-ee-uhs [i-'mɪl-i-əs] scans to ___-MIL-yuhs [___-'mɪl-jəs] @ V, 1, 155

Aeneas i-NEE-uhs [ɪ-'ni-əs] or ee-__-__ [i-__-__]
 Aeneas *(T&C)*

Aeolus scans to EE-luhs ['i-ləs]

aery EH-ree ['ɛ-ri]

Aesculapius i-SKYOO-LAY-pee-uhs [ɪ-skju-'leɪ-pi-əs] or EH-__-__-__-__ [ɛ-__-__-__-__] scans to __-__-LAY-pyuhs [__-__-'leɪ-pjəs] @ *PER* III, 2, 111

Aeson EE-suhn ['i-sən]

Aesop EE-sahp ['i-sɑp]

Aetna EHT-nuh ['ɛt-nə]

afeard uh-FEARD [ə-'fɪɚ-d]

affects (n) always scans to uh-FEHKTS [ə-'fɛkts]

affeered uh-FEARD [ə-'fɪɚ-d]

affiance (n) (confidence) uh-FEYE-uhns [ə-'faɪ-əns]

affianced (pl) (betrothed) uh-FEYE-uhnst [ə-'faɪ-ənst]

affined uh-FEYEND [ə'faɪnd]

affray uh-FRAY [ə-'freɪ]

affy uh-FEYE [ə-'faɪ]

Afric AAF-rik ['æf-rɪk]

Agamemnon AAG-uh-MEHM-nahn [æg-ə-'mɛm-nɑn] or
___-___-___-nuhn [___-___-___-nən]
 Agamemnon *(T&C)*

agate AAG-it ['æg-ɪt]

Agenor uh-JEE-nawr [ə-'ʤi-nɔɚ]

Agincourt AAJ-in-kawrt ['æʤ-ɪn-kɔɚt]

aglet AAG-lit ['æg-lɪt]

agnize aag-NEYEZ [æg-'naɪz]

agone uh-GAWN [ə-'gɔn] or __-GAHN [__-'gɑn]

Agrippa uh-GRIP-uh [ə-'grɪp-ə]
 Agrippa *(A&C)*
 Agrippa *(COR)*

ague AY-gyo͞o ['eɪ-gju]

Aguecheek, Sir Andrew *(12th)* AY-gyo͞o-cheek ['eɪ-gju-ʧik]

EE i be/ I ɪ bit/ EH ɛ bet/ AA æ bat/ O͞O u boot / O͞O ʊ book/ AW ɔ bought/ AH ɑ father/ ER ɝ bird/
UH ʌ cup/ AY eɪ bay/ EYE aɪ bite/ OY ɔɪ boy/ OH oʊ boat/ OW aʊ how/ YO͞O ju duke/ EAR ɪɚ
beer/ AIR ɛɚ bear/ O͞OR ʊɚ tour/ AWR ɔɚ bore/ AHR ɑɚ bar/ NG ŋ king/ SH ʃ ship/ ZH ʒ vision/
TH θ thirty/ TH ð then/ CH ʧ child/ J ʤ just/ For complete list, see Key to Pronunciation p. 2.

aidance AY-d(uh)nts [ˈeɪ-dn̩ts]

aidant AY-d(uh)nt [ˈeɪ-dn̩t]

Ajax AY-jaaks [ˈeɪ-dʒæks]
   Ajax *(T&C)*

alablaster AAL-uh-blaas-ter [ˈæl-ə-blæs-tɚ]

alack uh-LAAK [ə-ˈlæk]

Alarbus *(TITUS)* uh-LAHR-buhs [ə-ˈlɑɚ-bəs]

alarum uh-LAH-ruhm [ə-ˈlɑ-rəm] or ___-LAA-___
   [___-ˈlæ-___]

alas uh-LAAS [ə-ˈlæs]

Albans AWL-buhnz [ˈɔl-bənz]

Albany, Duke of *(LEAR)* AWL-buh-nee [ˈɔl-bə-ni] scans to
   AWLB-nee [ˈɔlb-ni] @ I, 1, 66

albeit always scans to awl-BEET [ɔl-ˈbit] except AWL-bee-it
   [ˈɔl-bi-ɪt] @ *KJ* V, 2, 9

Albion AAL-bee-uhn [ˈæl-bi-ən] scans to AAL-byuhn
   [ˈæl-bjən] e.g. @ *2HVI* I, 3, 43

Al'ce AALS [æls]

alchemy AAL-kuh-mee [ˈæl-kə-mi]

Alcibiades *(TIMON)* AAL-si-BEYE-uh-deez [æl-sɪ-ˈbaɪ-ə-diz]

Alcides aal-SEYE-deez [æl-ˈsaɪ-diz]

alderliefest AWL-der-leef-ist [ˈɔl-dɚ-lif-ɪst]

Alderman AWL-der-muhn [ˈɔl-dɚ-mən]

Alecto uh-LEHK-toh [ə-ˈlɛk-toʊ]

Alencon uh-LEHN-suhn [ə-ˈlɛn-sən] scans to AAL-uhn-__
   [ˈæl-ən-__]
   Alencon, Duke of *(1HVI)* scans @ I, 1, 95

Aleppo uh-LEHP-oh [ə-ˈlɛp-oʊ]

Alexander AAL-ig-ZAAN-der [æl-ɪg-ˈzæn-dɚ]
   Alexander *(T&C)*

Alexandria AAL-ig-ZAAN-dree-uh [æl-ɪg-ˈzæn-dri-ə] scans
   to __-__-ZAAN-druh [__-__-ˈzæn-drə] @ *A&C* IV, 8, 30

Alexandrian always scans to AAL-ig-ZAAN-druhn
   [æl-ɪg-ˈzæn-drən]

Alexas *(A&C)* uh-LEHKS-uhs [ə-ˈlɛks-əs]

Alice AA-lis [ˈæ-lɪs]
   Alice *(HV)* ah-LEES [ɑ-ˈlis] (since her name is only
      spoken by Katherine, a native speaker of French)

Aliena AY-li-EE-nuh [eɪ-lɪ-ˈi-nə] possibly scans to
   uh-LEE-uh-nuh [ə-ˈli-ə-nə] @ *AYL* I, 3, 124 if "Celia" is
   SEE-lyuh [ˈsi-ljə]

Alisander AAL-i-SAAN-der [æl-ɪ-ˈsæn-dɚ]

allay uh-LAY [ə-ˈleɪ]

allayment uh-LAY-muhnt [ə-ˈleɪ-mənt]

allegiant uh-LEE-juhnt [ə-ˈli-ʤənt]

Allhallond-Eve awl-HAAL-uhnd-eev [ɔl-ˈhæl-ənd-iv]

Allhallowmas awl-HAAL-oh-muhs [ɔl-ˈhæl-oʊ-məs]

Allhallown awl-HAAL-ohn [ɔ-ˈhæl-oʊn]

allicholy AAL-i-kahl-ee [ˈæl-ɪ-kɑl-i]

alligant AAL-uh-guhnt [ˈæl-ə-gənt]

allottery uh-LAHT-uh-ree [ə-ˈlɑt-ə-ri]

All-seer awl-SEE-er [ɔl-ˈsi-ɚ]

EE i be/ I ɪ bit/ EH ɛ bet/ AA æ bat/ OO u boot / OO ʊ book/ AW ɔ bought/ AH ɑ father/ ER ɝ bird/
UH ʌ cup/ AY eɪ bay/ EYE aɪ bite/ OY ɔɪ boy/ OH oʊ boat/ OW aʊ how/ YOO ɪu duke/ EAR ɪə
beer/ AIR ɛə bear/ OOR ʊə tour/ AWR ɔə bore/ AHR ɑə bar/ NG ŋ king/ SH ʃ ship/ ZH ʒ vision/
TH θ thirty/ TH ð then/ CH ʧ child/ J ʤ just/ For complete list, see Key to Pronunciation p. 2.

ally (n) always scans to uh-LEYE [ə-'laɪ]

Almain AHL-mayn ['ɑl-meɪn]

almost AWL-mohst ['ɔl-moʊst] scans to awl-MOHST [ɔl-'moʊst] e.g. @ *MID* II, 2, 154

alms AHMZ [ɑmz]

Alonso *(TEMP)* uh-LAHN-zoh [ə-'lɑn-zoʊ]

Alow see "George Alow"

Althaea aal-THEE-uh [æl-'θi-ə]

Alton AWL-tuhn ['ɔl-tən]

Amaimon / Amamon uh-MAY-mahn [ə-'meɪ-mɑn]

amain uh-MAYN [ə-'meɪn]

Amazonian always scans to AAM-uh-ZOH-nyuhn [æm-ə-'zoʊ-njən]

ambuscadoes AAM-buh-SKAY-dohz [æm-bə-'skeɪ-doʊz]

amerce uh-MERS [ə-'mɝs]

ames-ace AAMZ-ays ['æmz-eɪs] or possibly aamz-AYS [æmz-'eɪs]

Amiens *(AYL)* scans to AAM-yuhnz ['æm-jənz]

amiss uh-MIS [ə-'mɪs]

amity AAM-i-tee ['æm-ɪ-ti]

amort uh-MAWRT [ə-'mɔɚt]

Amphimachus aam-FIM-uh-kuhs [æm-'fɪm-ə-kəs]

Ampthill AAM-t(uh)l ['æm-tl̩]

Amurath AA-muh-raat ['æ-mə-ræt] or __-__-raath [__-__-ræθ]

Amyntas uh-MIN-tuhs [ə-'mɪn-təs]

anathomize / anatomize uh-NAAT-uh-meyez [ə-'næt-ə-maɪz] possibly __-NOHT-__-__ [__-'nout-__-__] @ *LLL* IV, 1, 68

Anchises aan-KEYE-seez [æn-'kaɪ-siz]

ancientry AYN-shuhn-tree ['eɪn-ʃən-tri]

Ancus Marcius AANG-kuhs MAHR-shuhs ['æŋ-kəs] ['mɑɚ-ʃəs]

andirons AAND-eyernz ['ænd-aɪɚnz]

Andren AAN-druhn ['æn-drən]

Andromache *(T&C)* aan-DRAHM-uh-kee [æn-'drɑm-ə-ki] scans to __-DRAHM-kee [__-'drɑm-ki] @ V, 3, 84

Andronici aan-DRAHN-i-seye [æn-'drɑn-ɪ-saɪ]

Andronicus aan-DRAHN-i-kuhs [æn-'drɑn-ɪ-kəs]
Andronicus, Marcus *(TITUS)* MAHR-kuhs ['mɑɚ-kəs]
Andronicus, Titus *(TITUS)* TEYE-tuhs ['taɪ-təs]

Angelica aan-JEHL-i-kuh [æn-'dʒɛl-ɪ-kə]

Angelo AAN-ji-loh ['æn-dʒɪ-lou] scans to AANJ-loh ['ændʒ-lou]
Angelo *(CE)*
Angelo *(MM)* scans @ II, 1, 266

Angiers AAN-jearz ['æn-dʒɪɚz] scans to aan-JEARZ [æn-'dʒɪɚz] @ *KJ* II, 1, 1

Angus *(MAC)* AANG-guhs ['æŋ-gəs]

anhungry aan-HUHNG-gree [æn-'hʌŋ-gri]

Anjou aan-JOO [æn-'dʒu] scans to AAN-joo ['æn-dʒu] e.g. @ *1HVI* V, 3, 95

Anne, Lady *(RIII)* AAN [æn]

EE i be/ I ɪ bit/ EH ɛ bet/ AA æ bat/ OO u boot / OO ʊ book/ AW ɔ bought/ AH ɑ father/ ER ɝ bird/ UH ʌ cup/ AY eɪ bay/ EYE aɪ bite/ OY ɔɪ boy/ OH ou boat/ OW ɑu how/ YOO ɪu duke/ EAR ɪɚ beer/ AIR eɚ bear/ OOR ʊɚ tour/ AWR ɔɚ bore/ AHR ɑɚ bar/ NG ŋ king/ SH ʃ ship/ ZH ʒ vision/ TH θ thirty/ TH ð then/ CH tʃ child/ J dʒ just/ For complete list, see Key to Pronunciation p. 2.

33

annexment uh-NEHKS-muhnt [ə-'nɛks-mənt]

anon uh-NAHN [ə-'nɑn]

Anselmo aan-SEHL-moh [æn-'sɛl-moʊ]

an't AANT [ænt]

Antenonidus AAN-ti-NOH-ni-duhs [æn-tɪ-'noʊ-nɪ-dəs]
some editions "Antenorides" AAN-ti-NAW-ri-deez
[æn-tɪ-'nɔ-rɪ-diz]

Antenor *(T&C)* aan-TEE-nawr [æn-'ti-nɔɚ]

anters AAN-terz ['æn-tɚz]

Anthropophagi AAN-thruh-PAHF-uh-jeye [æn-θrə-'pɑf-ə-ʤaɪ]

Anthropophaginian aan-thruh-PAHF-uh-JIN-ee-uhn
[æn-θrə-pɑf-ə-'ʤɪn-i-ən]

Antiates AAN-shee-ayts ['æn-ʃi-eɪts] possibly scans to
AAN-shyayts ['æn-ʃjeɪts] @ *COR* I, 6, 59

antic (n) or (v) or (adj) AAN-tik ['æn-tɪk]

Antigonus *(WT)* aan-TIG-uh-nuhs [æn-'tɪg-ə-nəs]

Antioch AAN-tee-ahk ['æn-ti-ɑk] scans to AAN-tyahk
['æn-tjɑk] e.g. @ *PER* I, Cho, 17

Antiochus *(PER)* aan-TEYE-uh-kuhs [æn-'taɪ-ə-kəs] scans
to ___-TEYE-kuhs [___-'taɪ-kəs] e.g. @ I, 3, 19

Antiopa aan-TEYE-uh-puh [æn-'taɪ-ə-pə]

Antipholus aan-TIF-uh-luhs [æn-'tɪf-ə-ləs]
Antipholus of Ephesus *(CE)* EHF-i-suhs ['ɛf-ɪ-səs]
Antipholus of Syracuse *(CE)* SI-ruh-kyōōz ['sɪ-rə-kjuz]

Antipodes aan-TIP-uh-deez [æn-'tɪp-ə-diz]

antiquary AAN-ti-kweh-ree ['æn-tɪ-kwɛ-ri]

antique (n) (a buffoon) AAN-tik ['æn-tɪk] (sometimes
spelled "antic")

antique (adj) (old or resembling antiquity) always scans to
AAN-teek ['æn-tik]

Antium AAN-tee-uhm ['æn-ti-əm] scans to AAN-tyuhm
['æn-tjəm] or AAN-shee-uhm ['æn-ʃi-əm] scans to
AAN-shyuhm ['æn-ʃjəm] e.g. @ COR III, 1, 11

Antoniad aan-TOH-nee-aad [æn-'tou-ni-æd]

Antonio aan-TOH-nee-oh [æn-'tou-ni-ou] scans to
___-TOH-nyoh [___-'tou-njou]
Antonio (MADO)
Antonio (MVEN) scans e.g. @ II, 8, 10
Antonio (TEMP) scans e.g. @ I, 2, 129
Antonio (12th) scans e.g. @ IV, 3, 4
Antonio (2GEN) seems to scan @ II, 4, 51

Antonius, Marcus aan-TOH-nee-uhs [æn-'tou-ni-əs]
scans to ___-TOH-nyuhs [___-'tou-njəs] MAHR-kuhs
['maɚ-kəs]
Marcus Antonius (JC) also called "Mark Antony"
MAHRK AAN-tuh-nee [maɚk] ['æn-tə-ni] scans to
AANT-nee ['ænt-ni] e.g. @ II, 2, 52 (for the name in
A&C, see "Mark Antony")

Apemantus (TIMON) AAP-uh-MAAN-tuhs [æp-ə-'mæn-təs]

Apennines AAP-uh-neyenz ['æp-ə-naɪnz]

apish AY-pish ['eɪ-pɪʃ]

Apollo uh-PAHL-oh [ə-'pɑl-ou]

Apollodorus uh-PAHL-uh-DAW-ruhs [ə-pɑl-ə-'dɔ-rəs]

apoplexed AA-puh-plehkst ['æ-pə-plɛkst]

apoplexy AAP-uh-plehk-see ['æp-ə-plɛk-si] possibly scans to
AAP-plehk-__ ['æp-plɛk-__] @ 2HIV IV, 4, 130

EE i be/ I ɪ bit/ EH ɛ bet/ AA æ bat/ OO u boot / OO ʊ book/ AW ɔ bought/ AH ɑ father/ ER ɝ bird/
UH ʌ cup/ AY eɪ bay/ EYE aɪ bite/ OY ɔɪ boy/ OH ou boat/ OW aʊ how/ YOO ɪu duke/ EAR ɪɚ
beer/ AIR ɛɚ bear/ OOR ʊɚ tour/ AWR ɔɚ bore/ AHR ɑɚ bar/ NG ŋ king/ SH ʃ ship/ ZH ʒ vision/
TH θ thirty/ TH ð then/ CH tʃ child/ J ʤ just/ For complete list, see Key to Pronunciation p. 2.

35

apostrophus uh-PAHS-truh-fuhs [ə-'pɑs-trə-fəs]

apothecary uh-PAHTH-uh-KEH-ree [ə-'paθ-ə-kɛ-ri]
   Apothecary *(R&J)*

appal uh-PAWL [ə-'pɔl]

appeach uh-PEECH [ə-'pitʃ]

appellant uh-PEHL-uhnt [ə-'pɛl-ənt] possibly scans to
   AA-pehl-___ ['æ-pɛl-___] @ *RII* IV, 1, 104

apperil uh-PEH-ruhl [ə-'pɛ-rəl]

appertinent uh-PER-ti-nuhnt [ə-'pɝ-tɪ-nənt]

approbation AA-pruh-BAY-shuhn [æ-prə-'beɪ-ʃən] scans to
   __-__-__-shee-uhn [__-__-__-ʃi-ən] e.g. @ *HV* I, 2, 19

approof uh-PROOF [ə-'pruf]

appurtenance uh-PER-t(uh)n-uhns [ə-'pɝ-tn̩-əns]

apricock AA-pri-kahk ['æ-prɪ-kɑk]

aptest AAPT-ist ['æpt-ɪst]

aqua vitae AH-kwuh VEE-teye or VEYE-tee ['ɑ-kwə]
   ['vi-taɪ] or ['vaɪ-ti]

Aquilon AAK-wi-lahn ['æk-wɪ-lɑn]

Aquitaine AAK-wi-tayn ['æk-wɪ-teɪn]

Arabia uh-RAY-bee-uh [ə-'reɪ-bi-ə] scans to ___-RAY-byuh
   [___-'reɪ-bjə] e.g. @ *COR* IV, 2, 24

Arabian always scans to uh-RAY-byuhn [ə-'reɪ-bjən]

araise uh-RAYZ [ə-'reɪz]

arbitrament / arbitrement ahr-BI-truh-muhnt [ɑɚ-'bɪ-trə-mənt]

Arcas AHR-kuhs ['ɑɚ-kəs]

Archbishop ahrch-BISH-uhp [ɑɚtʃ-'bɪʃ-əp] scans to
   AHRCH-bish-__ ['ɑɚtʃ-bɪʃ-__] e.g. @ *2HIV* I, 1, 189

archbishopric scans to AHRCH-bish-uhp-rik [ˈɑɚ tʃ bɪʃ-ɔp-rɪk]

Archelaus AHR-ki-LAY-uhs [ɑɚ-kɪ-ˈleɪ-əs]

Archibald, Earl of Douglas *(1HIV)* AHR-chi-bawld
DUHG-luhs [ˈɑɚ-tʃɪ-bɔld] [ˈdʌg-ləs] scans to
DUHG-uh-luhs [ˈdʌg-ə-ləs] @ V, 2, 32

Archidamus *(WT)* AHR-ki-DAY-muhs [ɑɚ-kɪ-ˈdeɪ-məs]

Arcite *(2NOB)* AHR-seyet [ˈɑɚ-saɪt]

Arde AHRD [ɑɚd]

Arden AHR-duhn [ˈɑɚ-dən]

argentine AHR-jin-teyen [ˈɑɚ-dʒɪn-taɪn]

Argier ahr-JEAR [ɑɚ-ˈdʒɪɚ]

argo AHR-goh [ˈɑɚ-goʊ]

argosy AHR-guh-see [ˈɑɚ-gə-si]

Argus AHR-guhs [ˈɑɚ-gəs]

Ariachne AA-ree-AAK-nee [æ-ri-ˈæk-ni]

Ariadne AA-ree-AAD-nee [æ-ri-ˈæd-ni] or EH-___-___-___
[ɛ-___-___-___]

Ariel *(TEMP)* EH-ree-uhl [ˈɛ-ri-əl] scans to EH-ryuhl
[ˈɛ-rjəl] e.g. @ IV, 1, 57

Aries EH-reez [ˈɛ-riz]

Arion uh-REYE-uhn [ə-ˈraɪ-ən]

Aristotle AA-ri-STAH-t(uh)l [æ-rɪ-ˈstɑ-tl̩]

arithmetician uh-RITH-muh-TI-shuhn [ə-ˈrɪθ-mə-tɪ-ʃən] or
scans to __-__-__-__-shee-uhn [__-__-__-__-ʃi-ən]

EE i be/ I ɪ bit/ EH ɛ bet/ AA æ bat/ OO u boot / OO ʊ book/ AW ɔ bought/ AH ɑ father/ ER ɝ bird/
UH ʌ cup/ AY eɪ bay/ EYE aɪ bite/ OY ɔɪ boy/ OH oʊ boat/ OW aʊ how/ YOO ɪu duke/ EAR ɪɚ
beer/ AIR ɛɚ bear/ OOR ʊɚ tour/ AWR ɔɚ bore/ AHR ɑɚ bar/ NG ŋ king/ SH ʃ ship/ ZH ʒ vision/
TH θ thirty/ TH ð then/ CH tʃ child/ J dʒ just/ For complete list, see Key to Pronunciation p. 2.

armado ahr-MAH-doh [aɚ-'mɑ-doʊ]

Armagnac AHRM-uhn-yaak ['aɚm-ən-jæk]

Armenia ahr-MEE-nee-uh [aɚ-'mi-ni-ə] possibly scans to
___-MEE-nyuh [___-'mi-njə] @ *A&C* III, 6, 35

Armigero ahr-MIJ-uh-roh [aɚ-'mɪdʒ-ə-roʊ]

armipotent ahr-MI-puh-tuhnt [aɚ-'mɪ-pə-tənt]

aroint uh-ROYNT [ə-'rɔɪnt]

Arragon, Prince of *(MVEN)* AA-ruh-gahn ['æ-rə-gɑn]

arraign uh-RAYN [ə-'reɪn]

arrant AA-ruhnt ['æ-rənt]

arras AA-ruhs ['æ-rəs]

array uh-RAY [ə-'reɪ]

arrearages uh-RI-rij-iz [ə-'rɪ-rɪdʒ-ɪz]

arrivance uh-REYE-vuhns [ə-'raɪ-vəns]

arrogancy AA-ruh-guhn-see ['æ-rə-gən-si]

Artemidorus *(JC)* AHR-tuh-mi-DAW-ruhs [aɚ-tə-mɪ-'dɔ-rəs]

artere scans to AHR-ter ['aɚ-tɚ]

Artesius *(2NOB)* ahr-TEE-zhuhs [aɚ-'ti-ʒəs] or __-__-zyuhs
[__-__- zjəs]

Arthur, Duke of Britain *(KJ)* AHR-ther ['aɚ-θɚ]

artificer ahr-TIF-i-ser [aɚ-'tɪf-ɪ-sɚ]

Artois ahr-TOYZ [aɚ-'tɔɪz]

Arundel, Earl of AA-ruhn-d(uh)l ['æ-rən-dl̩]

Arviragus / Cadwal *(CYM)* AHR-vi-RAH-guhs [aɚ-vɪ-'rɑ-gəs]
or __-__-RAY-__ [__-__-'reɪ-__] called **KAAD**-wawl
['kæd-wɔl]

Ascanius aas-KAYN-yuhs [æs-'keɪn-jəs]

ascribe uh-SKREYEB [ə-'skraɪb]

Asher AA-sher ['æ-ʃɚ]

Ashford AASH-ferd ['æʃ-fɚd]

Asia AY-zhuh ['eɪ-ʒə] scans to AY-zhee-uh ['eɪ-ʒi-ə]
  e.g. @ *CE* I, 1, 133

asinico AAS-i-NEE-koh [æs-ɪ-'ni-koʊ]

askant uh-SKAANT [ə-'skænt]

Asnath AAZ-nuhth ['æz-nəθ] some editions "Asmath"
  AAZ-muhth ['æz-məθ]

aspect always scans to aas-PEHKT [æs-'pɛkt]

aspic AAS-pik ['æs-pɪk]

asquint uh-SKWINT [ə-'skwɪnt]

assay (n) AA-say ['æ-seɪ] or aa-SAY [æ-'seɪ] in prose; always
  scans to aa-SAY [æ-'seɪ] in verse e.g. @ *MAC* IV, 3, 143

assay (v) AA-say ['æ-seɪ] scans to aa-SAY [æ-'seɪ]
  e.g. @ *AW* III, 7, 44

assembly uh-SEHM-blee [ə-'sɛm-bli] scans to __-__-buh-lee
  [__-__-bə-li] e.g. @ *MADO* V, 4, 34

assigns uh-SEYENZ [ə-'saɪnz]

assubjugate uh-SUHB-juh-gayt [ə-'sʌb-ʤə-geɪt]

Assyrian always scans to uh-SI-ryuhn [ə-'sɪ-rjən]

Astraea aas-TREE-uh [æs-'tri-ə]

asunder uh-SUHN-der [ə-'sʌn-dɚ]

Atalanta AA-tuh-LAAN-tuh [æ-tə-'læn-tə]

atasked uh-TAASKT [ə-'tæskt]

Ate AH-tay ['ɑ-teɪ] or AY-tee ['eɪ-ti]

Athenian (n) or (adj) uh-THEE-nee-uhn [ə-'θi-ni-ən] scans to __-THEE-nyuhn [__-'θi-njən] e.g. @ *MID* I, 1, 162

Athol AA-thuhl ['æ-θəl]

athwart uh-THWAWRT [ə-'θwɔɹt]

atomy AAT-uh-mee ['æt-ə-mi]

Atropos AA-truh-pahs ['æ-trə-pɑs] or __-__-puhs [__-__-pəs]

attainder uh-TAYN-der [ə-'teɪn-dɚ]

attainture uh-TAYN-cher [ə-'teɪn-tʃɚ]

attendure uh-TEHN-der [ə-'tɛn-dɚ]

attent uh-TEHNT [ə-'tɛnt]

attributive uh-TRIB-yuh-tiv [ə-'trɪb-jə-tɪv]

atwain uh-TWAYN [ə-'tweɪn]

Aubrey Vere AW-bree VEAR ['ɔ-bri] [vɪɚ]

Audrey *(AYL)* AW-dree ['ɔ-dri]

Aufidius See "Tullus Aufidius"

auger AW-ger ['ɔ-gɚ]

aught AWT [ɔt]

augurer AW-guh-rer ['ɔ-gə-rɚ] or __-gyuh-__ [__-gjə-__]

augures AW-gerz ['ɔ-gɚz]

augury AW-gyuh-ree ['ɔ-gjə-ri]

Augustus aw-GUHS-tuhs [ɔ-'gʌs-təs]

auld AWLD [ɔld]

Aulis AW-lis ['ɔ-lɪs]

Aumerle, Duke of *(RII)* oh-MERL [ou-'mɝl]

auricular aw-RIK-yuh-ler [ɔ-'rɪk-jə-lɚ]

Aurora uh-RAW-ruh [ə-'rɔ-rə]

Autolycus *(WT)* aw-TAHL-uh-kuhs [ɔ-'tɑl-ə-kəs]

Auvergne, Countess of *(1HVI)* oh-VAIRN [ou-'vɛɚn] or
__-VERN [_-'vɝn]

avaunt uh-VAWNT [ə-'vɔnt]

Ave Maries AH-vee or __-vay MEH-reez ['ɑ-vi] or [_-veɪ]
['mɛ-riz]

averring uh-VE(r)-ring [ə-'vɝ-rɪŋ]

aves AH-vayz ['ɑ-veɪz]

avised uh-VEYEZD [ə-'vaɪzd]

avoirdupois aav-er-duh-POYZ [æv-ɚ-də-'pɔɪz]

avouch uh-VOWCH [ə-'vauʧ]

aweary uh-WI-ree [ə-'wɪ-ri]

awl AWL [ɔl]

awry uh-REYE [ə-'raɪ]

ay (yes) EYE [aɪ]

aye (ever) AY [eɪ]

azure AAZH-er ['æʒ-ɚ]

ba / baa BAA [bæ] or BAH [bɑ]

EE i be/ I ɪ bit/ EH ɛ bet/ AA æ bat/ O͞O u boot / O͝O ʊ book/ AW ɔ bought/ AH ɑ father/ ER ɝ bird/
UH ʌ cup/ AY eɪ bay/ EYE aɪ bite/ OY ɔɪ boy/ OH ou boat/ OW au how/ YO͞O ɪu duke/ EAR ɪɚ
beer/ AIR ɛɚ bear/ O͞OR ʊɚ tour/ AWR ɔɚ bore/ AHR ɑɚ bar/ NG ŋ king/ SH ʃ ship/ ZH ʒ vision/
TH θ thirty/ T̲H̲ ð then/ CH ʧ child/ J ʤ just/ For complete list, see Key to Pronunciation p. 2.

41

baboon baa-BOON [bæ-'bun] scans to BAA-boon ['bæ-bun]
 e.g. @ *MAC IV*, 1, 37

Babylon BAA-bi-lahn ['bæ-bɪ-lɑn] or __-__-luhn [__-__-lən]

Bacchanals BAAK-uh-naalz ['bæk-ə-nælz] or ___-___-nahlz
 [___-___-nɑlz]

Bacchus BAAK-uhs ['bæk-əs] or BAHK-___ ['bɑk-___]

backare (false Latin for "back-off") possibly BAAK-uh-ray
 ['bæk-ə-reɪ] or baak-AH-___ [bæk-'ɑ-___]

bad'st BAADST [bædst]

bade BAAD [bæd]

baes BAAZ [bæz] or BAHZ [bɑz]

Bagot *(RII)* BAAG-uht ['bæg-ət]

Bajazet baa-juh-ZEHT [bæ-ʤə-'zɛt]

baldrick BAWL-drik ['bɔl-drɪk]

bale BAYL [beɪl]

ballast BAAL-uhst ['bæl-əst]

ballet (a ballad) BAAL-it ['bæl-ɪt]

ballet-mongers BAAL-it-MUHNG-gerz ['bæl-ɪt-mʌŋ-gɚz]
 or ___-___-MAHNG-___ [___-___-mɑŋ-___]

balsamum BAWL-suh-muhm ['bɔl-sə-məm]

Balthasar / Balthazar BAAL-thuh-zahr ['bæl-θə-zɑɚ]
 Balthasar *(MVEN)*
 Balthasar *(MADO)*
 Balthasar *(R&J)*
 Balthazar *(CE)*

Banbury BAAN-buh-ree ['bæn-bə-ri]

banditto baan-DEE-toh [bæn-'di-toʊ]

bandogs BAAN-dawgz [ˈbæn-dɔgz]

bane BAYN [beɪn]

Banister BAAN-is-ter [ˈbæn-ɪs-tɚ]

bankrout BAANGK-rowt [ˈbæŋk-raʊt]

bannerets BAAN-uh-rehts [ˈbæn-ə-rɛts]

banning BAAN-ing [ˈbæn-ɪŋ]

banns BAANZ [bænz]

Banquo *(MAC)* BAANG-kwoh [ˈbæŋ-kwoʊ]

Baptista baap-TIS-tuh [bæp-ˈtɪs-tə] or __-TEES-__ [__-ˈtis-__]
Baptista Minola *(SHR)* MIN-uh-luh [ˈmɪn-ə-lə]

Bar BAHR [baɚ]

Barabbas scans to BAA-ruh-buhs [ˈbæ-rə-bəs]

Barbary BAHR-buh-ree [ˈbaɚ-bə-ri] scans to BAHR-bree
[ˈbaɚ-bri] @ *RII* V, 5, 81

Barbason BAHR-buh-suhn [ˈbaɚ-bə-sən]

barbermonger BAHR-ber-MUHNG-ger [ˈbaɚ-bɚ-mʌŋ-gɚ]
or ___-___-MAHNG-___ [___-___-mɑŋ-___]

bard BAHRD [baɚd]

Bardolph BAHR-dahlf [ˈbaɚ-dɑlf]
Bardolph *(1HIV, 2HIV, HV, MW)* possibly BAHR-d(uh)l
[ˈbaɚ-dl̩] based on spelling of "Bardol" in Quarto of 1HIV
Bardolph, Lord *(2HIV)*

Bargulus BAHR-guh-luhs [ˈbaɚ-gə-ləs]

baring BEH-ring [ˈbɛ-rɪŋ]

EE i be/ I ɪ bit/ EH ɛ bet/ AA æ bat/ O͞O u boot / OͦO ʊ book/ AW ɔ bought/ AH ɑ father/ ER ɝ bird/
UH ʌ cup/ AY eɪ bay/ EYE aɪ bite/ OY ɔɪ boy/ OH oʊ boat/ OW aʊ how/ YO͞O ɪu duke/ EAR ɪɚ
beer/ AIR ɛɚ bear/ OͦOR ʊɚ tour/ AWR ɔɚ bore/ AHR ɑɚ bar/ NG ŋ king/ SH ʃ ship/ ZH ʒ vision/
TH θ thirty/ T̲H̲ ð then/ CH ʧ child/ J ʤ just/ For complete list, see Key to Pronunciation p. 2.

43

Barkloughly bahrk-LOH-lee [baɚk-'loʊ-li] or possibly scans to **BAHRK**-loh-___ ['baɚk-loʊ-___] @ *RII* III, 2, 1

barm BAHRM [baɚm]

Barnardine *(MM)* **BAHR**-ner-deen ['baɚ-nɚ-din] possibly scans to ber-**NAHR**-__ [bɚ-'naɚ-__] @ IV, 2, 60

barne BAHRN [baɚn]

Barnet BAHR-nit ['baɚ-nɪt]

barony BAA-ruhn-ee ['bæ-rən-i]

barr'st BAHRST [baɚst]

barricado BAA-ri-KAY-doh [bæ-rɪ-'keɪ-doʊ] or __-__-KAH-__ [__-__-'ka-__]

Barson BAHR-s(uh)n ['baɚ-sn̩]

Barthol'mew *(SHR)* **BAHRTH**-uhl-myoo ['baɚθ-əl-mju] or **BAHR**-t(uh)l-___ ['baɚ-tl̩-___]

Bartholomew bahr-THAHL-uh-myoo [baɚ-'θal-ə-mju] or **BAHR**-t(uh)l-___ ['baɚ-tl̩-___] @ *HV* V, 2, 297

Basan BAY-suhn ['beɪ-sən]

Basilisco BAAS-i-LIS-koh [bæs-ɪ-'lɪs-koʊ] or BAAZ-__-__-__ [bæz-__-__-__]

basilisk BAAS-i-lisk ['bæs-ɪ-lɪsk] or **BAAZ**-__-__ ['bæz-__-__]

Basingstoke BAY-zing-stohk ['beɪ-zɪŋ-stoʊk]

Bassanio *(MVEN)* always scans to buh-SAH-nyoh [bə-'sa-njoʊ] possibly buh-SAH-nee-oh [bə-'sa-ni-oʊ] in prose

Basset *(1HVI)* BAAS-it ['bæs-ɪt]

Bassianus *(TITUS)* BAA-see-AY-nuhs [bæ-si-'eɪ-nəs]

basta BAHS-tuh ['bas-tə]

Bastard of Orleans *(1HVI)* AWR-lee-uhnz ['ɔɚ-li-ənz] scans to awr-LEENZ [ɔɚ-'linz] e.g. @ I, 1, 93

bastinado BAAS-tuh-NAY-doh [bæs-tə-'neɪ-dou] or __-__-NAH-__ [__-__-'nɑ-__]

bate BAYT [beɪt]

Bates, John *(HV)* BAYTS [beɪts]

batler BAAT-ler ['bæt-lɚ]

battalia buh-TAYL-yuh [bə-'teɪl-jə] or __-TAHL-__ [__-'tɑl-__]

batten BAA-t(uh)n ['bæ-tn̩]

bauble BAW-b(uh)l ['bɔ-bl̩]

Bavian BAY-vee-uhn ['beɪ-vi-ən]

bavin BAAV-in ['bæv-ɪn]

bawcock BAW-kahk ['bɔ-kɑk]

bawd / Bawd *(PER)* BAWD [bɔd]

bawdry BAW-dree ['bɔ-dri]

Baynard BAY-nerd ['beɪ-nɚd]

Bayonne bay-OHN [beɪ-'oun]

be'st see "beest (v)"

beadle / Beadle BEE-d(uh)l ['bi-dl̩]

bearherd BE(r)-rerd ['bɜ-rɚd]

Beatrice *(MADO)* BEE-uh-tris ['bi-ə-trɪs] scans to BEE-tris ['bi-trɪs] e.g. @ III, 1, 21

EE i be/ I ɪ bit/ EH ɛ bet/ AA æ bat/ OO u boot / OO ʊ book/ AW ɔ bought/ AH ɑ father/ ER ɝ bird/ UH ʌ cup/ AY eɪ bay/ EYE aɪ bite/ OY ɔɪ boy/ OH oʊ boat/ OW aʊ how/ YOO ɪu duke/ EAR ɪɚ beer/ AIR ɛɚ bear/ OOR ʊɚ tour/ AWR ɔɚ bore/ AHR ɑɚ bar/ NG ŋ king/ SH ʃ ship/ ZH ʒ vision/ TH θ thirty/ TH ð then/ CH tʃ child/ J dʒ just/ For complete list, see Key to Pronunciation p. 2.

Beauchamp, Richard, Earl of Warwick *(1HVI)* BOH-chaamp ['boʊ-tʃæmp] WAW-rik ['wɔ-rɪk] or WAH-__ ['wɑ-__]

Beaufort BOH-fert ['boʊ-fɚt]
    Beaufort, Cardinal Henry, Bishop of Winchester *(1HVI,*
       2HVI) WIN-chehs-ter ['wɪn-tʃɛs-tɚ]
    Beaufort, Edmund, Duke of Somerset *(1HVI, 2HVI)*
       SUHM-er-seht ['sʌm-ɚ-sɛt] scans to SUHM-seht
       ['sʌm-sɛt]
    Beaufort, Henry, Duke of Somerset *(1HVI)*
    Beaufort, John, Duke of Somerset *(1HVI)*
    Beaufort, Thomas, Duke of Exeter *(1HVI)* EHK-si-ter
       ['ɛk-sɪ-tɚ]
    Beaufort, Thomas, Duke of Exeter *(3HVI)*

Beaumond BOH-muhnd ['boʊ-mənd]

Beaumont BOH-mahnt ['boʊ-mɑnt] possibly scans to
    boh-**MAHNT** [boʊ-'mɑnt] e.g. @ *HV* III, 5, 44

Bedford BEHD-ferd ['bɛd-fɚd]
    Bedford, Duke of, John *(HV, 1HVI)*

bedlam / Bedlam BEHD-luhm ['bɛd-ləm]

bedrid BEHD-rid ['bɛd-rɪd]

bedtime always scans to behd-**TEYEM** [bɛd-'taɪm]

bedward BEHD-werd ['bɛd-wɚd]

beest / be'st (v) BEEST [bist]

beest (n) BEEST [bist]

beget bi-GEHT [bɪ-'gɛt]

begot bi-GAHT [bɪ-'gɑt]

beguile bi-GEYEL [bɪ-'gaɪl]

behoof bi-HOOF [bɪ-'huf]

behoove bi-HOOV [bɪ-'huv]

behove bi-HOHV [bɪ-ˈhoʊv]

Bel BAYL [beɪl] or BEHL [bɛl]

Belarius / Morgan *(CYM)* bi-LEH-ree-uhs [bɪ-ˈlɛ-ri-əs] called MAWR-guhn [ˈmɔɚ-gən]

Belch, Sir Toby *(12th)* BEHLCH TOH-bee [bɛltʃ] [ˈtoʊ-bi]

beldam / beldame BEHL-daam [ˈbɛl-dæm] or ___- duhm [___- dəm]

belee'd bi-LEED [bɪ-ˈlid]

Belgia BEHL-juh [ˈbɛl-dʒə] scans to BEHL-jee-uh [ˈbɛl-dʒi-ə] @ *3HVI* IV, 3, 1

belie bi-LEYE [bɪ-ˈlaɪ]

belike bi-LEYEK [bɪ-ˈlaɪk]

Bellario buh-LAH-ree-oh [bə-ˈlɑ-ri-oʊ] scans to __-LAH-ryoh [__-ˈlɑ-rjoʊ] e.g. @ *MVEN* IV, 1, 164

Bellona beh-LOH-nuh [bɛ-ˈloʊ-nə]

bell-wether BEHL-wehth-er [ˈbɛl-wɛð-ɚ]

Belzebub BEHL-zuh-buhb [ˈbɛl-zə-bəb]

bemadding bi-MAAD-ing [bɪ-ˈmæd-ɪŋ]

bemete bi-MEET [bɪ-ˈmit]

bemock bi-MAHK [bɪ-ˈmɑk]

bemoiled bi-MOYLD [bɪ-ˈmɔɪld]

bemonster bi-MAHNS-ter [bɪ-ˈmɑns-tɚ]

Benedick *(MADO)* BEHN-uh-dik [ˈbɛn-ə-dɪk] or ___-i-___ [___-ɪ-___]

EE i be/ I ɪ bit/ EH ɛ bet/ AA æ bat/ OO u boot / OO ʊ book/ AW ɔ bought/ AH ɑ father/ ER ɝ bird/ UH ʌ cup/ AY eɪ bay/ EYE aɪ bite/ OY ɔɪ boy/ OH oʊ boat/ OW aʊ how/ YOO ɪu duke/ EAR ɪɚ beer/ AIR ɛɚ bear/ OOR ʊɚ tour/ AWR ɔɚ bore/ AHR ɑɚ bar/ NG ŋ king/ SH ʃ ship/ ZH ʒ vision/ TH θ thirty/ TH ð then/ CH tʃ child/ J dʒ just/ For complete list, see Key to Pronunciation p. 2.

47

benefice BEHN-i-fis ['bɛn-ɪ-fɪs]

benetted bi-NEHT-id [bɪ-'nɛt-ɪd]

benign scans to BEE-neyen ['bi-naɪn]

benison BEHN-i-suhn ['bɛn-ɪ-sən] or ___-___-zuhn
[___-___- zən]

Bentii BEHN-shee-eye ['bɛn-ʃi-aɪ]

Bentivolii BEHN-ti-VOH-lee-eye [bɛn-tɪ-'voʊ-li-aɪ]

Benvolio *(R&J)* behn-VOH-lee-oh [bɛn-'voʊ-li-oʊ] scans to
___-VOH-lyoh [___-'voʊ-ljoʊ]

bequeath bi-KWEE<u>TH</u> [bɪ-'kwið] or __-KWEETH [__-'kwiθ]

berard BEH-rerd ['bɛ-rɚd]

bereft bi-REHFT [bɪ-'rɛft]

Bergamo BER-guh-moh ['bɝ-gə-moʊ]

Bergomask BER-guh-maask ['bɝ-gə-mæsk]

Berkeley (the name of a place in *1HIV* and RII) BAHRK-lee
['bɑɚk-li] scans to BAHRK-uh-lee ['bɑɚk-ə-li] or BERK-lee
['bɝk-li] scans to BERK-uh-lee ['bɝk-ə-li] @ *RII* II, 2, 119

Berkeley *(RIII)* BAHRK-lee ['bɑɚk-li] or BERK-lee ['bɝk-li]

Berkeley, Lord *(RII)* BAHRK-lee ['bɑɚk-li] or BERK-lee
['bɝk-li]

Bermoothes ber-M<u>OO</u>TH-iz [bɚ-'muð-ɪz]

Bernardo *(HAM)* ber-NAHR-doh [bɚ-'nɑɚ-doʊ]

Berowne *(LLL)* bi-R<u>OO</u>N [bɪ-'run] possibly scans to
BR<u>OO</u>N [brun] @ II, 1, 213

Berri BEH-ree ['bɛ-ri]

berrord BEH-rerd ['bɛ-rɚd]

Bertram see "Rossillion"

Berwick BEH-rik ['bɛ-rɪk]

beseech bi-SEECH [bɪ-'sitʃ]

beshrew bi-SHR$\overline{OO}$ [bɪ-'ʃru]

beshrow bi-SHROH [bɪ-'ʃroʊ]

besom BEE-zuhm ['bi-zəm]

Besonian scans to bi-ZOH-nyuhn [bɪ-'zoʊ-njən]

bestead bi-STEHD [bɪ-'stɛd]

bestial BEHS-chuhl ['bɛs-tʃəl]

bestraught bi-STRAWT [bɪ-'strɔt]

bestrid bi-STRID [bɪ-'strɪd]

betid bi-TID [bɪ-'tɪd]

betide bi-TEYED [bɪ-'taɪd]

betroth bi-TRO<u>H</u> [bɪ-'troʊð] or __-TROHTH [__-'troʊθ]

Bevis BEHV-is ['bɛv-ɪs] or BEEV-___ ['biv-___]

bevy BEHV-ee ['bɛv-i]

bewet bi-WEHT [bɪ-'wɛt]

bewray bi-RAY [bɪ-'reɪ]

bezonians bi-ZOH-nee-uhnz [bɪ-'zoʊ-ni-ənz]

Bianca bee-AHNG-kuh [bi-'ɑŋ-kə] or __-AANG-__ [__-'æŋ-__]
    Bianca *(OTH)*
    Bianca *(SHR)*

bier BEAR [bɪɚ]

EE i be/ I ɪ bit/ EH ɛ bet/ AA æ bat/ $\overline{OO}$ u boot / $\overline{OO}$ ʊ book/ AW ɔ bought/ AH ɑ father/ ER ɝ bird/ UH ʌ cup/ AY eɪ bay/ EYE aɪ bite/ OY ɔɪ boy/ OH oʊ boat/ OW ɑʊ how/ Y$\overline{OO}$ ɪu duke/ EAR ɪɚ beer/ AIR ɛɚ bear/ $\overline{OO}$R ʊɚ tour/ AWR ɔɚ bore/ AHR ɑɚ bar/ NG ŋ king/ SH ʃ ship/ ZH ʒ vision/ TH θ thirty/ <u>TH</u> ð then/ CH tʃ child/ J dʒ just/ For complete list, see Key to Pronunciation p. 2.

49

biggen BIG-in ['bɪg-ɪn]

Bigot, Lord *(KJ)* BIG-uht ['bɪg-ət]

bilberry BIL-buh-ree ['bɪl-bə-ri]

bilbo BIL-boh ['bɪl-boʊ]

billeted BIL-i-tid ['bɪl-ɪ-tɪd]

billets BIL-its ['bɪl-ɪts]

Biondello *(SHR)* bee-uhn-DEHL-oh [bi-ən-'dɛl-oʊ] possibly scans to byuhn-DEHL-__ [bjən-'dɛl-__] @ I, 2, 223

Birnam Wood BER-nuhm WŌOD ['bɝ-nəm] [wʊd]

bisson BIS-uhn ['bɪs-ən]

bitumed BI-tyōomd ['bɪ-tɪumd]

blackamoor BLAAK-uh-mōor ['blæk-ə-mʊɚ]

Blackfriars scans to blaak-FREYERZ [blæk-'fraɪɚz]

Blackheath scans to blaak-HEETH [blæk-'hiθ]

Blackmere BLAAK-mear ['blæk-mɪɚ]

blains BLAYNZ [bleɪnz]

Blanch BLAANCH ['blæntʃ]
Blanch *(KJ)*

blaspheme blaas-FEEM [blæs-'fim]

blastments BLAAST-muhnts ['blæst-mənts]

blazon BLAY-z(uh)n ['bleɪ-zn̩]

blench BLEHNCH [blɛntʃ]

blent BLEHNT [blɛnt]

blithe BLEYE<u>TH</u> [blaɪð] or BLEYETH [blaɪθ]

blither (happier) BLEYE<u>TH</u>-er ['blaɪð-ɚ]

Blithild BLITH-ild ['blɪθ-ɪld] or BLITH-__ ['blɪð __]

Blois BLOYZ [blɔɪz]

blowse BLOWZ [blɑʊz]

Blunt BLUHNT [blʌnt]
Blunt, Sir James *(RIII)*
Blunt, Sir John *(2HIV)*
Blunt, Sir Walter *(1HIV)*

boatswain / Boatswain *(TEMP)* BOH-s(uh)n ['boʊ-sn̩]

Bocchus BAHK-uhs ['bɑk-əs]

bode BOHD [boʊd]

bodements BOHD-muhnts ['boʊd-mənts]

bodged BAHJD [bɑʤd]

bodkin BAHD-kin ['bɑd-kɪn]

bodykins BAH-dee-kinz ['bɑ-di-kɪnz]

boggle BAHG-uhl ['bɑg-əl]

boggler BAH-guh-ler ['bɑ-gə-lɚ]

Bohemia boh-HEE-mee-uh [boʊ-'hi-mi-ə] scans to
__-HEE-myuh [__-'hi-mjə] e.g. @ *WT* I, 2, 333

Bohun BOON [bun]

Bolingbroke BAH-ling-brook ['bɑ-lɪŋ-brʊk] or BOH-__-__
['boʊ-__-__] or BOO-__-__ ['bʊ-__-__]
Bolingbroke, Henry, Duke of Hereford, afterward Henry IV
(RII) HER-ferd ['hɝ-fɚd]
Bolingbroke, Roger

bolins BOH-linz ['boʊ-lɪnz]

EE i be/ I ɪ bit/ EH ɛ bet/ AA æ bat/ OO u boot / OO ʊ book/ AW ɔ bought/ AH ɑ father/ ER ɝ bird/
UH ʌ cup/ AY eɪ bay/ EYE aɪ bite/ OY ɔɪ boy/ OH oʊ boat/ OW ɑʊ how/ YOO ɪu duke/ EAR ɪɚ
beer/ AIR ɛɚ bear/ OOR ʊɚ tour/ AWR ɔɚ bore/ AHR ɑɚ bar/ NG ŋ king/ SH ʃ ship/ ZH ʒ vision/
TH θ thirty/ TH ð then/ CH ʧ child/ J ʤ just/ For complete list, see Key to Pronunciation p. 2.

51

bombard BAHM-berd ['bɑm-bɚd]

bombast BAHM-baast ['bɑm-bæst]

Bona *(3HVI)* BOH-nuh ['boʊ-nə]

bona-robas BOH-nuh-roh-buhz ['boʊ-nə-roʊ-bəz]

bonny BAHN-ee ['bɑn-i]

Bonville BAHN-vil ['bɑn-vɪl]

boon BOŌN [bun]

boor BOŌR [bʊɚ]

booteless BOŌT-uh-luhs ['but-ə-ləs] scans to boō-TUH-luhs [bu-'tʌ-ləs] @ *1HIV* III, 1, 67

Borachio *(MADO)* boh-RAH-chee-oh [boʊ-'rɑ-ʧi-oʊ]

Bordeaux scans to BAWR-doh ['bɔɚ-doʊ]

Boreas scans to BAWR-yuhs ['bɔɚ-jəs]

boresprit BAWR-sprit ['bɔɚ-sprɪt]

borne BAWRN [bɔɚn]

borough BUH-roh ['bʌ-roʊ]

bosky BAHS-kee ['bɑs-ki]

Bosworth BAHZ-werth ['bɑz-wɚθ]

botcher BAHCH-er ['bɑʧ-ɚ]

botchy BAHCH-ee ['bɑʧ-i]

bots BAHTS [bats]

Bottom, Nick / Pyramus *(MID)* BAH-tuhm ['bɑ-təm] PI-ruh-muhs ['pɪ-rə-məs]

Bouciqualt BOŌ-si-kawlt ['bu-sɪ-kɔlt]

bough BOW [baʊ]

Boult *(PER)* BOHLT [boʊlt]

bounden BOWN-duhn [ˈbaʊn-dən]

Bourbon BŌOR-buhn [ˈbʊɚ-bən] or BER-___ [ˈbɝ-___]
Bourbon, Duke of *(HV)*

Bourchier, Cardinal, Archbishop of Canterbury *(RIII)*
BOW-cher [ˈbaʊ-tʃɚ]

bourn BAWRN [bɔɚn] or BŌORN [bʊɚn]

bow (n) (weapon or collar of a yoke) BOH [boʊ] e.g. @
LLL IV, 1, 24 and *AYL* III, 3, 69

bow (v) (to bend into a curve or to play a stringed instrument
with a bow) BOH [boʊ] @ *PER* IV, 2, 80

bow (v) (to incline the body) BOW [baʊ] e.g. @ *RII* I, 3, 47

Boyet *(LLL)* boy-EHT [bɔɪ-ˈɛt]

Brabant BRAA-buhnt [ˈbræ-bənt]

Brabantio *(OTH)* bruh-BAHN-shyoh [brə-ˈbɑn-ʃjoʊ] or
__-BAAN-__ [__-ˈbæn-__] possibly scans to __-__-shee-oh
[__-__-ʃi-oʊ] @ I, 2, 78

brabbler / Brabbler BRAAB-ler [ˈbræb-lɚ]

brach BRAACH [brætʃ]

braggardism scans to BRAAG-er-dizm [ˈbræg-ɚ-dɪzm]

braggart BRAAG-ert [ˈbræg-ɚt]

Brainford BRAYN-ferd [ˈbreɪn-fɚd]

Brakenbury, Sir Robert *(RIII)* BRAAK-uhn-buh-ree
[ˈbræk-ən-bə-ri] or ___-___-beh-___ [___-___-bɛ-___]

brandish BRAAN-dish [ˈbræn-dɪʃ]

EE i be/ I ɪ bit/ EH ɛ bet/ AA æ bat/ ŌO u boot / ŌO ʊ book/ AW ɔ bought/ AH ɑ father/ ER ɝ bird/
UH ʌ cup/ AY eɪ bay/ EYE aɪ bite/ OY ɔɪ boy/ OH oʊ boat/ OW aʊ how/ YŌO ɪu duke/ EAR ɪɚ
beer/ AIR ɛɚ bear/ ŌOR ʊɚ tour/ AWR ɔɚ bore/ AHR ɑɚ bar/ NG ŋ king/ SH ʃ ship/ ZH ʒ vision/
TH θ thirty/ TH ð then/ CH tʃ child/ J ʤ just/ For complete list, see Key to Pronunciation p. 2.

Brandon BRAAN-duhn ['bræn-dən]
Brandon *(HVIII)*
Brandon, Sir William *(RIII)*

bray BRAY [breɪ]

brazed BRAYZD [breɪzd]

brazier BRAY-zher ['breɪ-ʒɚ]

breach BREECH [britʃ]

Brecknock BREHK-nuhk ['brɛk-nək]

breech (n) (leg covering) BRICH [brɪtʃ] or BREECH [britʃ] usually in the plural BRICH-iz ['brɪtʃ-ɪz] or BREECH-___ ['britʃ-___]

breech (v) (to sheathe or to flog) BREECH [britʃ]

breedbate BREED-bayt ['brid-beɪt]

breese BREEZ [briz]

Bretagne BREHT-uhn ['brɛt-ən] possibly scans to breh-**TAHN** [brɛ-'tɑn]

brethren BRE**HTH**-rehn ['brɛð-rɛn] scans to BREH-<u>th</u>uh-rehn ['brɛ-ðə-rɛn] e.g. @ *TITUS* I, 1, 92

Briareus breye-AH-ree-uhs [braɪ-'ɑ-ri-əs] or ___-**EH**-___-___ [___-'ɛ-___-___]

Bridget BRIJ-it ['brɪdʒ-ɪt]

brinded BRIND-id ['brɪnd-ɪd]

brinish BREYEN-ish ['braɪn-ɪʃ]

Bristol BRIS-t(uh)l ['brɪs-tl̩]

Bristow BRIS-toh ['brɪs-toʊ]

Britaine bri-TAYN [brɪ-'teɪn]

Britaine, Duke of *(KJ)* BRI-t(uh)n ['brɪ-tn̩]

Briton BRI-t(uh)n ['brɪ-tn̩]

Brittaine BRI-t(uh)n-ee ['brɪ-tn̩-i]

Brittany BRI-t(uh)n-ee ['brɪ-tn̩-i]

broach BROHCH [broʊtʃ]

Brocas BRAHK-uhs ['brɑk-əs] or BROHK-__ ['broʊk-__]

brogues BROHGZ [broʊgz]

brooch BROHCH [broʊtʃ]

brothel BRAHTH-uhl ['brɑθ-əl]

Brownist BROWN-ist ['braʊn-ɪst]

bruit BR$\overline{OO}$T [brut]

Brundusium bruhn-DY$\overline{OO}$-zee-uhm [brən-'dɪu-zi-əm]

Brutus BR$\overline{OO}$-tuhs ['bru-təs]
    Brutus, Decius *(JC)* DEE-shee-uhs ['di-ʃi-əs] scans to
    DEE-shuhs ['di-ʃəs] e.g. @ I, 3, 148
    Brutus, Marcus *(JC)* MAHR-kuhs ['mɑɚ-kəs]

bubukles BY$\overline{OO}$-buh-kuhlz ['bju-bə-kəlz]

Buckingham BUHK-ing-uhm ['bʌk-ɪŋ-əm]
    Buckingham, Duke of *(2HVI)*
    Buckingham, Duke of *(HVIII)*
    Buckingham, Duke of *(RIII)*

Bucklersbury BUHK-lerz-buh-ree ['bʌk-lɚz-bə-ri]

buckram BUHK-ruhm ['bʌk-rəm]

buffet (n) (a blow) BUHF-it ['bʌf-ɪt]

buffet (v) (to hit) BUHF-it ['bʌf-ɪt]

bull-beeves b$\overline{oo}$l-BEEVZ [bʊl-'bivz]

EE i be/ I ɪ bit/ EH ɛ bet/ AA æ bat/ $\overline{OO}$ u boot / $\overline{OO}$ ʊ book/ AW ɔ bought/ AH ɑ father/ ER ɝ bird/
UH ʌ cup/ AY eɪ bay/ EYE aɪ bite/ OY ɔɪ boy/ OH oʊ boat/ OW aʊ how/ Y$\overline{OO}$ ɪu duke/ EAR ɪə
beer/ AIR ɛə bear/ $\overline{OO}$R ʊɚ tour/ AWR ɔɚ bore/ AHR ɑɚ bar/ NG ŋ king/ SH ʃ ship/ ZH ʒ vision/
TH θ thirty/ <u>TH</u> ð then/ CH tʃ child/ J dʒ just/ For complete list, see Key to Pronunciation p. 2.

55

Bullcalf, Peter *(2HIV)* BŌOL-kaaf [ˈbʊl-kæf]

Bullen, Anne *(HVIII)* BŌOL-in [ˈbʊl-ɪn]

bullock BŌOL-uhk [ˈbʊl-ək]

Bulmer BŌOL-mer [ˈbʊl-mɚ]

bulwark BŌOL-werk [ˈbʊl-wɚk]

bunghole BUHNG-hohl [ˈbʌŋ-hoʊl]

burbolt BER-bohlt [ˈbɝ-boʊlt]

burgher BER-ger [ˈbɝ-gɚ]

burgomasters BER-guh-maas-terz [ˈbɝ-gə-mæs-tɚz]

burgonet BER-guh-neht [ˈbɝ-gə-nɛt]

Burgundy, Duke of BER-guhn-dee [ˈbɝ-gən-di]
  Burgundy, Duke of *(HV, 1HVI)*
  Burgundy, Duke of *(LEAR)*

burnet BER-neht [ˈbɝ-nɛt] or ___-nuht [___-nət]

burthen BER-thuhn [ˈbɝ-ðən]

Burton-heath BER-t(uh)n-heeth [ˈbɝ-tn̩-hiθ]

Bury BEH-ree [ˈbɛ-ri]

Bushy *(RII)* BŌOSH-ee [ˈbʊʃ-i]

business BIZ-niz [ˈbɪz-nɪs] scans to BIZ-uh-nis [ˈbɪz-ə-nɪs]
  e.g. @ *WT* IV, 4, 403

buskined BUHS-kind [ˈbʌs-kɪnd]

buss BUHS [bʌs]

Butts, Doctor *(HVIII)* BUHTS [bʌts]

by'r BEYER [baɪɚ]

Byzantium bi-ZAAN-tee-uhm [bɪ-ˈzæn-ti-əm] or __-__-shee-__
  [__-__-ʃi-__]

cabileros KAA-bi-LEH-rohz [kæ-bɪ-'lɛ-roʊz]

cacodemon KAA-kuh-dee-muhn ['kæ-kə-di-mən]

caddis KAAD-is ['kæd-ɪs]

Cade, Jack *(2HVI)* KAYD [keɪd]

cadent KAY-d(uh)nt ['keɪ-dn̩t]

Cadmus KAAD-muhs ['kæd-məs]

caduceus kuh-DYOO-see-uhs [kə-'dɪu-si-əs] or __-__-shee-__
  [__-__-ʃi-__]

Cadwallader kaad-WAWL-uh-der [kæd-'wɔl-ə-dɚ]

Caelius scans to SEEL-yuhs ['sil-jəs]

Caesar SEE-zer ['si-zɚ]

Caesarion always scans to si-ZEH-ryuhn [sɪ-'zɛ-rjən] or see-
  ___-___ [si-___-___]

Cain KAYN [keɪn]

Caithness *(MAC)* KAYTH-nehs ['keɪθ-nɛs]

caitiff KAY-tif ['keɪ-tɪf]

Caius KEYE-uhs ['kaɪ-əs] or possibly KAY-___ ['keɪ-___]
  Caius *(TITUS)*
  Caius Lucius *(CYM)* LOO-shuhs ['lu-ʃəs] scans to
    LOO-see-uhs ['lu-si-əs] @ II, 3, 55
  Caius Marcius Coriolanus *(COR)* MAHR-shuhs ['mɑɚ-ʃəs]
    scans to MAHR-shee-uhs ['mɑɚ-ʃi-əs] e.g. @ III, 1, 195
    KAW-ree-oh-LAY-nuhs [kɔ-ri-oʊ-'leɪ-nəs] scans to
    KAWR-yoh-LAY-nuhs [kɔɚ-joʊ-'leɪ-nəs] e.g. @ II, 2, 65

Caius, Doctor *(MW)* KEEZ [kiz] possibly scans to KAY-uhs
  ['keɪ-əs] or KEE-___ ['ki-___] @ IV, 6, 27

Calaber KAAL-uh-ber ['kæl-ə-bɚ] or scans to KAAL-ber ['kæl-bɚ]

Calais KAA-lis ['kæ-lɪs] (if French pronunciation is preferred in prose kaa-LAY [kæ-'leɪ])

Calchas *(T&C)* KAAL-kuhs ['kæl-kəs]

Caliban *(TEMP)* KAAL-i-baan ['kæl-ɪ-bæn]

Calipolis kuh-LIP-uh-lis [kə-'lɪp-ə-lɪs]

caliver KAAL-i-ver ['kæl-ɪ-vɚ]

calkin KAW-kin ['kɔ-kɪn]

callet KAAL-it ['kæl-ɪt]

Calphurnia *(JC)* kaal-PER-nee-uh [kæl-'pɝ-ni-ə] scans to ___-PER-nyuh [___-'pɝ-njə] e.g. @ I, 2, 7

calumniate kuh-LUHM-nee-ayt [kə-'lʌm-ni-eɪt]

calumniating kuh-LUHM-nee-AYT-ing [kə-'lʌm-ni-eɪt-ɪŋ]

calumnious kuh-LUHM-nee-uhs [kə-'lʌm-ni-əs] scans to ___-LUHM-nyuhs [___-'lʌm-njəs] e.g. @ *HAM* I, 3, 38

calumny KAAL-uhm-nee ['kæl-əm-ni]

Calydon KAAL-i-duhn ['kæl-ɪ-dən] or __-__-dahn [__-__-dɑn]

Cambio see "Lucentio"

Cambria KAAM-bree-uh ['kæm-bri-ə] scans to KAAM-bryuh ['kæm-brjə] @ *CYM* V, 5, 17

cambric KAAM-brik ['kæm-brɪk] or KAYM-___ ['keɪm-___]

Cambridge KAYM-brij ['keɪm-brɪʤ]
   Cambridge, Earl of *(HV)*

Cambyses kaam-BEYE-seez [kæm-'baɪ-siz]

Camelot KAAM-uh-laht ['kæm-ə-lɑt]

Camillo *(WT)* kuh-MIL-oh [kə-'mɪl-oʊ]

camomile KAAM-uh-meyel ['kæm-ə-maɪl] or ___-___-meel [___-___-mil]

Campeius, Cardinal *(HVIII)* kaam-PEE-uhs [kæm-'pi-əs]

canakin KAA-nuh-kin ['kæ-nə-kɪn]

canary (a sweet wine or a dance) kuh-NEH-ree [kə-'nɛ-ri]

Canidius *(A&C)* kuh-NID-ee-uhs [kə-'nɪd-i-əs] scans to ___-NI-dyuhs [___-'nɪ-djəs] @ IV, 6, 16 if Epic Caesura

canker KAANG-ker ['kæŋ-kɚ]

cannibally KAAN-i-buh-lee ['kæn-ɪ-bə-li]

cannoneer kaa-nuh-NEAR [kæ-nə-'nɪɚ]

canonized KAA-nuhn-eyezd ['kæ-nən-aɪzd] scans to kuh-NUHN-___ [kə-'nʌn-___] e.g. @ *HAM* I, 4, 47

canstick KAAN-stik ['kæn-stɪk]

Canterbury KAAN-tuh-buh-ree ['kæn-tə-bə-ri] scans to ___-tuh-bree [___-tə-bri]
Canterbury, Archbishop of *(HV)*

cantle KAAN-t(uh)l ['kæn-tl̩]

canton KAAN-tuhn ['kæn-tən]

canvass (v) KAAN-vuhs ['kæn-vəs]

canzonet kaan-zuh-NEHT [kæn-zə-'nɛt]

Capaneus KAAP-uh-NEE-uhs [kæp-ə-'ni-əs]

cap-a-pe kaap-uh-PEE [kæp-ə-'pi] or KAAP-uh-pee ['kæp-ə-pi]

caparison kuh-PAA-ri-suhn [kə-'pæ-rɪ-sən]

Capel KAA-p(uh)l ['kæ-pl̩]

EE i be/ I ɪ bit/ EH ɛ bet/ AA æ bat/ OO u boot / OO ʊ book/ AW ɔ bought/ AH ɑ father/ ER ɝ bird/ UH ʌ cup/ AY eɪ bay/ EYE aɪ bite/ OY ɔɪ boy/ OH oʊ boat/ OW aʊ how/ YOO ɪu duke/ EAR ɪɚ beer/ AIR ɛɚ bear/ OOR ʊɚ tour/ AWR ɔɚ bore/ AHR ɑɚ bar/ NG ŋ king/ SH ʃ ship/ ZH ʒ vision/ TH θ thirty/ TH ð then/ CH tʃ child/ J dʒ just/ For complete list, see Key to Pronunciation p. 2.

Capet KAY-pit ['keɪ-pɪt] or **KAA-___** ['kæ-___]

Caphis *(TIMON)* KAY-fis ['keɪ-fɪs]

Capilet KAAP-uh-lit ['kæp-ə-lɪt]
  Capilet, Widow of Florence *(AW)* FLAW-rehns ['flɔ-rɛns]
  or **FLAH-___** ['flɑ-___]

capitulate kuh-PICH-uh-layt [kə-'pɪtʃ-ə-leɪt]

capocchia kuh-POH-kee-uh [kə-'poʊ-ki-ə]

capon KAY-pahn ['keɪ-pɑn] or **___-puhn** [___-pən]

Cappadocia KAAP-uh-DOH-shuh [kæp-ə-'doʊ-ʃə]

capriccio scans to kuh-PREE-chyoh [kə-'pri-tʃjoʊ]

capricious kuh-PRISH-uhs [kə-'prɪʃ-əs]

Captain *(Various)*
  The Captains Dumain *(AW)* dyoo-MAYN [dɪu-'meɪn]

captious KAAP-shuhs ['kæp-ʃəs]

captivate KAAP-ti-vayt ['kæp-tɪ-veɪt]

Capuchius *(HVIII)* kuh-PYOO-shuhs [kə-'pju-ʃəs]

Capulet KAAP-yoo-lit ['kæp-ju-lɪt]
  Capulet *(R&J)*
  Capulet, Lady *(R&J)*

carack / carrack KAA-rik ['kæ-rɪk]

caracts KAA-rikts ['kæ-rɪkts]

caraways KAA-ruh-wayz ['kæ-rə-weɪz]

carbonado KAHR-buh-NAH-doh [kɑɚ-bə-'nɑ-doʊ] or
  ___-___- NAY-___ [___-___-'neɪ-___]

carbuncle KAHR-buhng-kuhl ['kɑɚ-bəŋ-kəl]

carcanet KAHR-kuh-neht ['kɑɚ-kə-nɛt]

carcase / carcass KAHR-kuhs ['kɑɚ-kəs]

cardecue KAHR-duh-kyōō [ˈkɑɚ-də-kju]

cardinal / Cardinal KAHR-di-nuhl [ˈkɑɚ-dɪ-nəl] scans to KAHRD-nuhl [ˈkɑɚd-nəl] e.g. @ *1HVI* I, 3, 36

carduus benedictus KAHR-jōō-uhs BEHN-i-DIK-tuhs [ˈkɑɚ-ʤu-əs] [bɛn-ɪ-ˈdɪk-təs]

Carlisle, Bishop of *(RII)* kahr-LEYEL [kɑɚ-ˈlaɪl]

carlot KAHR-luht [ˈkɑɚ-lət]

carman KAHR-maan [ˈkɑɚ-mæn]

Carnarvonshire kahr-NAHR-vuhn-sher [kɑɚ-ˈnɑɚ-vən-ʃɚ] or ___-___-___-shear [___-___-___-ʃɪɚ]

carouse (n) (a hearty drink) kuh-ROWZ [kə-ˈrɑuz]

carpet-monger KAHR-pit-MUHNG-ger [ˈkɑɚ-pɪt-mʌŋ-gɚ] or ___-___-MAHNG-___ [___-___-mɑŋ-___]

carriage KAA-rij [ˈkæ-rɪʤ] scans to KAA-ree-ij [ˈkæ-ri-ɪʤ] e.g. @ *R&J* I, 4, 94

carrion KAA-ree-uhn [ˈkæ-ri-ən] scans to KAA-ryuhn [ˈkæ-rjən] e.g. @ *2HVI* V, 2, 11

carters KAHR-terz [ˈkɑɚ-tɚz]

Carthage KAHR-thij [ˈkɑɚ-θɪʤ]

Casca *(JC)* KAAS-kuh [ˈkæs-kə]

casement KAYS-muhnt [ˈkeɪs-mənt]

casketed KAAS-ki-tid [ˈkæs-kɪ-tɪd]

casque KAASK [kæsk]

Cassandra *(T&C)* kuh-SAAN-druh [kə-ˈsæn-drə]

Cassibelan kaa-SIB-uh-luhn [kæ-ˈsɪb-ə-lən]

EE i be/ I ɪ bit/ EH ɛ bet/ AA æ bat/ OͦO u boot / OO ʊ book/ AW ɔ bought/ AH ɑ father/ ER ɝ bird/ UH ʌ cup/ AY eɪ bay/ EYE aɪ bite/ OY ɔɪ boy/ OH oʊ boat/ OW ɑʊ how/ YOO ɪu duke/ EAR ɪɚ beer/ AIR ɛɚ bear/ OͦOR ʊɚ tour/ AWR ɔɚ bore/ AHR ɑɚ bar/ NG ŋ king/ SH ʃ ship/ ZH ʒ vision/ TH θ thirty/ TH ð then/ CH ʧ child/ J ʤ just/ For complete list, see Key to Pronunciation p. 2.

61

Cassio *(OTH)* KAAS-ee-oh ['kæs-i-oʊ] scans to KAASH-yoh ['kæʃ-joʊ] e.g. @ V, 2, 319

Cassius KAASH-uhs ['kæʃ-əs] scans to KAASH-ee-uhs ['kæʃ-i-əs] or KAAS-yuhs ['kæs-jəs] scans to KAAS-ee-uhs ['kæs-i-əs]
Cassius *(JC)* scans e.g. @ I, 2, 182

cassocks KAAS-uhks ['kæs-əks]

Castilian King-Urinal kaa-STIL-yuhn king-YOŌ-ri-nuhl [kæ-'stɪl-jən] [kɪŋ-'jʊ-rɪ-nəl]

Castor KAAS-ter ['kæs-tɚ]

Cataian kuh-TAY-uhn [kə-'teɪ-ən]

cataplasm scans to KAAT-uh-plaazm ['kæt-ə-plæzm]

catarrhs kuh-TAHRZ [kə-'tɑɚz]

catechise / catechize KAAT-i-keyez ['kæt-ɪ-kaɪz]

catechism KAAT-uh-kiz-uhm ['kæt-ə-kɪz-əm]

cate-log KAYT-lahg ['keɪt-lɑg]

cater-cousins KAY-ter-KUHZ-inz ['keɪ-tɚ-kʌz-ɪnz]

caterwauling KAAT-er-wawl-ing ['kæt-ɚ-wɔl-ɪŋ]

cates KAYTS [keɪts]

Catesby, Sir William *(RIII)* KAYTS-bee ['keɪts-bi] scans to KAY-tis-bee ['keɪ-tɪs-bi] or KAATS-bee ['kæts-bi] scans to KAA-tis-bee ['kæ-tɪs-bi] e.g. @ III, 7, 83

catlings KAAT-lingz ['kæt-lɪŋz]

Cato KAY-toh ['keɪ-toʊ]

Caucasus KAW-kuh-suhs ['kɔ-kə-səs]

caudle KAW-d(uh)l ['kɔ-dl̩]

cautel KAW-t(uh)l ['kɔ-tl̩]

cautelous KAW-tuh-luhs ['kɔ-tə-ləs] scans to KAWT-luh̩s ['kɔt-ləs] @ *COR* IV, 1, 33

Cavalery KAA-vuh-LI-ree [kæ-və-'lɪ-ri]

Cavaliero KAA-vuh-LEE-roh [kæ-və-'li-roʊ]

cavalleria KAA-vuh-LEH-ree-uh [kæ-və-'lɛ-ri-ə]

caviary KAAV-ee-eh-ree ['kæv-i-ɛ-ri]

cavil KAA-vuhl ['kæ-vəl]

Cawdor KAW-dawr ['kɔ-dɔ˞] or ___-der [___-də˞]

Cedius SEE-dee-uhs ['si-di-əs] or scans to SEE-dyuhs ['si-djəs]

ceinture SEHN-cher ['sɛn-ʧə˞]

celerity si-LEH-ri-tee [sɪ-'lɛ-rɪ-ti]

Celia *(AYL)* SEE-lee-uh ['si-li-ə] possibly scans to SEE-lyuh ['si-ljə] @ I, 3, 124 if "Aliena" scans to uh-LEE-uh-nuh [ə-'li-ə-nə]

cellarage SEH-luh-rij ['sɛ-lə-rɪʤ]

cement (n) or (v) always scans to SEE-mehnt ['si-mɛnt]

censer SEHN-ser ['sɛn-sə˞]

Censorinus SEHN-suh-REYE-nuhs [sɛn-sə-'raɪ-nəs]

censure SEHN-sher ['sɛn-ʃə˞]

Centaur SEHN-tawr ['sɛn-tɔ˞]

centry SEHN-tree ['sɛn-tri]

ceunturions sehn-TYOO-ree-uhnz [sɛn-'tjʊ-ri-ənz]

Cerberus SER-buh-ruhs ['sɝ-bə-rəs] scans to SER-bruhs ['sɝ-brəs] e.g. @ *TITUS* II, 4, 51

EE i be/ I ɪ bit/ EH ɛ bet/ AA æ bat/ O͞O u boot / O͞O ʊ book/ AW ɔ bought/ AH ɑ father/ ER ɝ bird/ UH ʌ cup/ AY eɪ bay/ EYE aɪ bite/ OY ɔɪ boy/ OH oʊ boat/ OW aʊ how/ YO͞O ɪu duke/ EAR ɪə˞ beer/ AIR ɛə˞ bear/ O͞OR ʊə˞ tour/ AWR ɔə˞ bore/ AHR ɑə˞ bar/ NG ŋ king/ SH ʃ ship/ ZH ʒ vision/ TH θ thirty/ TH̱ ð then/ CH ʧ child/ J ʤ just/ For complete list, see Key to Pronunciation p. 2.

cere SEAR [sɪɚ]

cerecloth SEAR-klawth ['sɪɚ-klɔθ]

cerements SEAR-muhnts ['sɪɚ-mənts]

Ceres SI-reez ['sɪ-riz]
Ceres *(TEMP)*

Cerimon SEH-ri-mahn ['sɛ-rɪ-mɑn]

certes SER-teez ['sɝ-tiz] scans to SERTS [sɝts] e.g. @ *HVIII*
I, 1, 48

Cesario suh-ZAH-ree-oh [sə-'zɑ-ri-ou] scans to __-ZAH-
ryoh [__-'zɑ-rjou] e.g. @ *12th* II, 4, 2

cess / cesse SEHS [sɛs]

chafe CHAYF [tʃeɪf]

chaff CHAAF [tʃæf]

chaffy CHAAF-ee ['tʃæf-i]

chalice (n) CHAA-lis ['tʃæ-lɪs]

Cham KAAM [kæm]

Chamberlain CHAYM-ber-lin ['tʃeɪm-bɚ-lɪn]
Chamberlain *(1HIV)*
Chamberlain, Lord *(HVIII)*

chamblet KAAM-blit ['kæm-blɪt] some editions "camlet"
KAAM-lit ['kæm-lɪt]

chameleon kuh-MEEL-yuhn [kə-'mil-jən] scans to KAA-
mee-leye-uhn ['kæ-mi-laɪ-ən] @ *3HVI* 3, 2, 191

Champagne shaam-PAYN [ʃæm-'peɪn]

champain CHAAM-payn ['tʃæm-peɪn]

champian CHAAM-pee-uhn ['tʃæm-pi-ən] or CHAAM-
payn ['tʃæm-peɪn]

Chancellor CHAAN-suh-ler [ˈʧæn-sə-lɚ]
Chancellor, Lord *(HVIII)*

changeling CHAYNJ-ling [ˈʧeɪnʤ-lɪŋ] scans to CHAYNJ-uh-ling [ˈʧeɪnʤ-ə-lɪŋ] @ *MID* II, 1, 23

chanson shahn-SOHN [ʃɑn-ˈsoʊn] or CHAAN-suhn [ˈʧæn-sən]

chanticleer CHAAN-tuh-klear [ˈʧæn-tə-klɪɚ] or SHAAN-___-___ [ˈʃæn-___-___]

chantry CHAAN-tree [ˈʧæn-tri]

chape CHAYP [ʧeɪp]

chapeless CHAYP-lis [ˈʧeɪp-lɪs]

chapfall'n CHAAP-fawln [ˈʧæp-fɔln]

chaplet CHAAP-lit [ˈʧæp-lɪt]

chapmen CHAAP-mehn [ˈʧæp-mɛn]

character (n) or (v) KAA-rik-ter [ˈkæ-rɪk-tɚ] scans to kuh-RAAK-___ [kə-ˈræk-___] e.g. @ *RIII* III, 1, 81

characterless scans to kuh-RAAK-ter-lis [kə-ˈræk-tɚ-lɪs]

charactery always scans to kuh-RAAK-tuh-ree [kə-ˈræk-tə-ri]

Charbon SHAHR-bahn [ˈʃɑɚ-bɑn]

chare CHAIR [ʧɛɚ]

chariest scans to CHEH-ryuhst [ˈʧɛ-rjəst]

chariness CHEH-ree-nuhs [ˈʧɛ-ri-nəs]

Charing Cross CHEH-ring KRAWS [ˈʧɛ-rɪŋ] [krɔs]

Charlemain SHAHR-luh-mayn [ˈʃɑɚ-lə-meɪn]

EE i be/ I ɪ bit/ EH ɛ bet/ AA æ bat/ O͞O u boot / O͝O ʊ book/ AW ɔ bought/ AH ɑ father/ ER ɝ bird/ UH ʌ cup/ AY eɪ bay/ EYE aɪ bite/ OY ɔɪ boy/ OH oʊ boat/ OW aʊ how/ YO͞O ɪu duke/ EAR ɪɚ beer/ AIR ɛɚ bear/ O͞OR ʊɚ tour/ AWR ɔɚ bore/ AHR ɑɚ bar/ NG ŋ king/ SH ʃ ship/ ZH ʒ vision/ TH θ thirty/ TH̲ ð then/ CH ʧ child/ J ʤ just/ For complete list, see Key to Pronunciation p. 2.

Charles CHAHRLZ [ʧɑɚlz] scans to **CHAH**-ruhlz ['ʧɑ-rəlz]
Charles *(AYL)*
Charles VI *(HV)*
Charles, Dauphin *(1HVI)* scans @ IV, 4, 26

Charmian *(A&C)* **CHAHR**-mee-uhn ['ʧɑɚ-mi-ən] scans to
CHAHR-myuhn ['ʧɑɚ-mjən] or **SHAHR**-__-__
['ʃɑɚ-__-__] scans to **SHAHR**-__ ['ʃɑɚ-__] or **KAHR**-__-__
['kɑɚ-__-__] scans to **KAHR**-__ ['kɑɚ-__] e.g. @ I, 3, 15

charneco shahr-**NAY**-koh [ʃɑɚ-'neɪ-koʊ] or **CHAHR**-ni-___
['ʧɑɚ-nɪ-___]

charnel CHAHR-nuhl ['ʧɑɚ-nəl]

Charolois SHAA-ruh-loyz ['ʃæ-rə-lɔɪz]

Charon KEH-ruhn ['kɛ-rən] or KAA-___ ['kæ-___]

Chartreux SHAHR-trōō ['ʃɑɚ-tru]

Charybdis kuh-**RIB**-dis [kə-'rɪb-dɪs]

chastise always scans to **CHAAS**-teyez ['ʧæs-taɪz] except
possibly chaas-**TEYEZ** [ʧæs-'taɪz] @ *T&C* V, 5, 4

chastisement CHAAS-tiz-muhnt ['ʧæs-tɪz-mənt]

Chatillion *(KJ)* shaa-**TIL**-yuhn [ʃæ-'tɪl-jən] scans to __-__-ee-uhn
[__-__-i-ən] @ I, 1, 30

Chatillon SHAA-til-yuhn ['ʃæ-tɪl-jən] if "Jacques" is JAYKS
[ʤeɪks] or JAAKS [ʤæks] or shaa-**TIL**-yuhn [ʃæ-'tɪl-jən]
if "Jacques" is JAY-kweez ['ʤeɪ-kwiz] @ *HV* III, 5, 43

chattels CHAA-t(uh)lz ['ʧæ-t̩z]

Chaucer CHAW-ser ['ʧɔ-sɚ]

chaudron CHAW-druhn ['ʧɔ-drən]

chaunt CHAANT [ʧænt]

chawed CHAWD [ʧɔd]

checkins CHEH-kinz ['tʃɛ-kɪnz]

cheerly CHEAR-lee ['tʃɪɚ-li]

Chertsey CHERT-see ['tʃɝt-si]

cherubin CHEH-ruh-bin ['tʃɛ-rə-bɪn]

Chetas KEE-tuhs ['ki-təs]

chev'ril SHEHV-ruhl ['ʃɛv-rəl]

chevalier sheh-vuh-LEAR [ʃɛ-və-'lɪɚ]

cheveril SHEHV-uh-ruhl ['ʃɛv-ə-rəl] scans to SHEHV-ruhl ['ʃɛv-rəl] @ *HVIII* II, 3, 32

chewet CHOO-it ['tʃu-ɪt]

chid CHID [tʃɪd]

chidden CHI-d(uh)n ['tʃɪ-dn̩]

chide CHEYED [tʃaɪd]

chiders CHEYED-erz ['tʃaɪd-ɚz]

Chief Justice, Lord *(2HIV)* CHEEF JUHS-tis [tʃif] ['dʒʌs-tɪs]

Childeric CHIL-duh-rik ['tʃɪl-də-rɪk]

children CHIL-drehn ['tʃɪl-drɛn] or __-druhn [__-drən] scans to CHIL-duh-rehn ['tʃɪl-də-rɛn] or CHIL-duh-ruhn ['tʃɪl-də-rən] e.g. @ *CE* V, 1, 361

chine CHEYEN [tʃaɪn]

chink CHINGK [tʃɪŋk]

Chiron *(TITUS)* KEYE-ruhn ['kaɪ-rən] or __-rahn [__-rɑn]

chirurgeonly keye-RER-juhn-lee [kaɪ-'rɝ-dʒən-li]

Chitopher CHIT-uh-fer ['tʃɪt-ə-fɚ] or KIT-__-__ ['kɪt-__-__]

EE i be/ I ɪ bit/ EH ɛ bet/ AA æ bat/ OO u boot/ OO ʊ book/ AW ɔ bought/ AH ɑ father/ ER ɝ bird/ UH ʌ cup/ AY eɪ bay/ EYE aɪ bite/ OY ɔɪ boy/ OH oʊ boat/ OW aʊ how/ YOO ɪu duke/ EAR ɪɚ beer/ AIR ɛɚ bear/ OOR ʊɚ tour/ AWR ɔɚ bore/ AHR ɑɚ bar/ NG ŋ king/ SH ʃ ship/ ZH ʒ vision/ TH θ thirty/ <u>TH</u> ð then/ CH tʃ child/ J dʒ just/ For complete list, see Key to Pronunciation p. 2.

choler KAHL-er ['kɑl-ɚ]

choleric KAH-luh-rik ['kɑ-lə-rɪk] scans to KAHL-rik ['kɑl-rɪk] e.g. @ *MM* II, 2, 130

chopine choh-PEEN [tʃoʊ-'pin]

chopt CHAHPT [tʃɑpt]

Chorus KAW-ruhs ['kɔ-rəs]
  Chorus *(HV)*
  Chorus *(R&J)*
  Chorus *(WT)*

chough CHUHF [tʃʌf]

christen KRIS-uhn ['krɪs-ən]

christendom / Christendom KRIS-uhn-duhm ['krɪs-ən-dəm] scans to KRIS-duhm ['krɪs-dəm] @ *HVIII* III, 2, 67

christom KRIZ-uhm ['krɪz-əm]

Christophero kris-TAHF-uh-roh [krɪs-'tɑf-ə-roʊ] scans to __-TAHF-roh [__-'tɑf-roʊ] @ *SHR* Ind, 2, 71

chrysolite KRIS-uh-leyet ['krɪs-ə-laɪt]

chuffs CHUHFS [tʃʌfs]

churl CHERL [tʃɝl]

Chus KUHS [kʌs] or KUHSH [kʌʃ]

cicatrice SI-kuh-tris ['sɪ-kə-trɪs]

Cicely always scans to SIS-lee ['sɪs-li]

Cicero *(JC)* SIS-uh-roh ['sɪs-ə-roʊ] scans to SIS-roh ['sɪs-roʊ] @ IV, 3, 178

Ciceter SIS-i-ter ['sɪs-ɪ-tɚ]

Cilicia scans to si-LI-shuh [sɪ-'lɪ-ʃə]

Cimber, Metellus *(JC)* See "Metellus Cimber"

Cimmerian si-MI-ree-uhn [sɪ-'mɪ-ri-ən]

Cinna SIN-uh ['sɪn-ə]
    Cinna *(JC)*
    Cinna, a Poet *(JC)*

cinque-pace SINGK-uh-pays ['sɪŋk-ə-peɪs] or SINGK-pays ['sɪŋk-peɪs]

Cinque-Ports singk-PAWRTS [sɪŋk-'pɔɚts]

cinque-spotted singk-SPAHT-id [sɪŋk-'spɑt-ɪd]

cipher SEYE-fer ['saɪ-fɚ]

Circe SER-see ['sɝ-si]

circummured SER-kuhm-myōōrd ['sɝ-kəm-mjʊɚd]

cistern SIS-tern ['sɪs-tɚn]

cital SEYE-t(uh)l ['saɪ-tl̩]

cittern-head SIT-ern-hehd ['sɪt-ɚn-hɛd]

civet SIV-it ['sɪv-ɪt]

clamber KLAAM-ber ['klæm-bɚ]

clangor KLAANG-er ['klæŋ-ɚ] or ___-ger [___-gɚ]

Clare KLAIR [klɛɚ]

Clarence KLAA-ruhns ['klæ-rəns]

claret KLAA-rit ['klæ-rɪt]

Claribel KLAA-ri-behl ['klæ-rɪ-bɛl]

Claudio KLAW-dee-oh ['klɔ-di-oʊ] scans to KLAW-dyoh ['klɔ-djoʊ]
    Claudio *(MM)* scans @ III, 1, 74
    Claudio *(MADO)* scans @ I, 1, 264

EE i be/ I ɪ bit/ EH ɛ bet/ AA æ bat/ OŌ u boot / OŌ ʊ book/ AW ɔ bought/ AH ɑ father/ ER ɝ bird/
UH ʌ cup/ AY eɪ bay/ EYE aɪ bite/ OY ɔɪ boy/ OH oʊ boat/ OW aʊ how/ YOŌ ɪu duke/ EAR ɪɚ
beer/ AIR ɛɚ bear/ OŌR ʊɚ tour/ AWR ɔɚ bore/ AHR ɑɚ bar/ NG ŋ king/ SH ʃ ship/ ZH ʒ vision/
TH θ thirty/ TH ð then/ CH ʧ child/ J ʤ just/ For complete list, see Key to Pronunciation p. 2.

Claudius KLAW-dee-uhs [ˈklɔ-di-əs] scans to **KLAW**-dyuhs
    [ˈklɔ-djəs]
    Claudius *(HAM)*
    Claudius *(JC)* scans @ IV, 3, 242

cleft KLEHFT [klɛft]

Cleitus KLEYE-tuhs [ˈklaɪ-təs]

clement KLEHM-uhnt [ˈklɛm-ənt]

Cleomenes *(WT)* klee-**AHM**-i-neez [kli-ˈɑm-ɪ-niz]

Cleon *(PER)* KLEE-ahn [ˈkli-ɑn]

Cleopatra KLEE-uh-**PAA**-truh [kli-ə-ˈpæ-trə]
    Cleopatra *(A&C)* possibly scans to klee-**PAA**-___
        [kli-ˈpæ-___] e.g. @ V, 2, 124

clepe KLEEP [klip]

clepeth KLEEP-ith [ˈklip-ɪθ]

clept KLEHPT [klɛpt]

clerestories KLEAR-staw-reez [ˈklɪɚ-stɔ-riz]

clerk KLERK [klɝk] possibly KLAHRK [klɑɚk] in *MVEN*
    to follow rhyme scheme in final speech

Clerk of Chartham *(2HVI)* CHAA-tuhm [ˈtʃæ-təm] or
    CHAHR-tuhm [ˈtʃɑɚ-təm]

clew KLOO [klu]

Clifford KLIF-erd [ˈklɪf-ɚd]
    Clifford, Lord John *(3HVI)*
    Clifford, Lord Thomas *(2HVI)*

climatures KLEYE-muh-cherz [ˈklaɪ-mə-tʃɚz]

clime KLEYEM [klaɪm]

clinquant KLING-kuhnt [ˈklɪŋ-kənt]

Clitus *(JC)* KLEYE-tuhs [ˈklaɪ-təs]

70

clo'es KLOHZ [kloʊz]

clodpoll KLAHD-pohl ['klɑd-poʊl]

cloistress KLOY-stris ['klɔɪ-strɪs]

close (adj) or (adv) KLOHS [kloʊs]

close (n) or (v) KLOHZ [kloʊz]

close-stool KLOHS-stool ['kloʊs-stul]

Cloten *(CYM)* KLAH-t(uh)n ['klɑ-tn̩] or KLOH-___ ['kloʊ-___]

Clothair KLOH-thair ['kloʊ-θɛɚ] or ___-tair [___-tɛɚ]

Clotharius kloh-<u>TH</u>EH-ree-uhs [kloʊ-'ðɛ-ri-əs] or __-TEH-__-__ [__-'tɛ-__-__]

clothier KLOH-<u>th</u>ee-er ['kloʊ-ði-ɚ] scans to KLOH<u>TH</u>-yer ['kloʊð-jɚ] @ *HVIII* I, 2, 31

clotpoll KLAHT-pohl ['klɑt-poʊl]

clout KLOWT [klaʊt]

cloven KLOH-vuhn ['kloʊ-vən]

Clowder KLOW-der ['klɑʊ-dɚ]

cloyment KLOY-muhnt ['klɔɪ-mənt]

clyster KLIS-ter ['klɪs-tɚ]

Cobham KAH-buhm ['kɑ-bəm]
    Cobham, Eleanor, Duchess of Gloucester *(2HVI)* EHL-i-nawr ['ɛl-ɪ-nɔɚ] or __-__-ner [__-__-nɚ] scans to EHL-nawr ['ɛl-nɔɚ] or __-ner [__-nɚ] e.g. @ II, 3, 1

cobloaf KAHB-lohf ['kɑb-loʊf]

Cobweb *(MID)* KAHB-wehb ['kɑb-wɛb]

EE i be/ I ɪ bit/ EH ɛ bet/ AA æ bat/ OO u boot / OO ʊ book/ AW ɔ bought/ AH ɑ father/ ER ɝ bird/ UH ʌ cup/ AY eɪ bay/ EYE aɪ bite/ OY ɔɪ boy/ OH oʊ boat/ OW aʊ how/ YOO ɪu duke/ EAR ɪɚ beer/ AIR ɛɚ bear/ OOR ʊɚ tour/ AWR ɔɚ bore/ AHR ɑɚ bar/ NG ŋ king/ SH ʃ ship/ ZH ʒ vision/ TH θ thirty/ <u>TH</u> ð then/ CH tʃ child/ J ʤ just/ For complete list, see Key to Pronunciation p. 2.

cock'rel KAHK-ruhl [ˈkɑk-rəl]

cockatrice KAHK-uh-tris [ˈkɑk-ə-trɪs]

cockle KAHK-uhl [ˈkɑk-əl]

Cocytus koh-SEYE-tuhs [koʊ-ˈsaɪ-təs]

codding KAHD-ing [ˈkɑd-ɪŋ]

Coeur-de-Lion KAWR-duh-leye-uhn [ˈkɔɚ-də-laɪ-ən] or
   KER-__-lee-__ [ˈkɝ-__-li-__]

coffer KAW-fer [ˈkɔ-fɚ] or KAH-___ [ˈkɑ-___]

cognizance KAHG-ni-zuhns [ˈkɑg-nɪ-zəns]

cohere koh-HEAR [koʊ-ˈhɪɚ]

cohorts KOH-hawrts [ˈkoʊ-hɔɚts]

coign KOYN [kɔɪn]

Coint, Francis KOYNT [kɔɪnt] some editions "Quoint"
   KWOYNT [kwɔɪnt]

coistrel KOYS-truhl [ˈkɔɪs-trəl]

Colbrand / Colebrand KOHL-braand [ˈkoʊl-brænd]

Colchos KAHL-kis [ˈkɑl-kɪs]

Colebrook KOHL-brŏŏk [ˈkoʊl-brʊk]

Coleville, Sir John *(2HIV)* KOHL-vil [ˈkoʊl-vɪl] scans to
   KOHL-uh-vil [ˈkoʊl-ə-vɪl] e.g. @ IV, 3, 70

colic KAHL-ik [ˈkɑl-ɪk]

colleagued kuh-LEE-gid [kə-ˈli-gɪd]

collied KAH-leed [ˈkɑ-lid]

collier KAHL-yer [ˈkɑl-jɚ]

collop KAHL-uhp [ˈkɑl-əp]

Colmekill KOHM-kil [ˈkoʊm-kɪl]

Colme's Inch KAHL-meez INCH ['kɑl-miz] [ɪntʃ]

coloquintida KAH-luh-**KWIN**-ti-duh [kɑ-lə-'kwɪn-tɪ-də]

colossus / Colossus kuh-**LAH**-suhs [kə-'lɑ-səs]

columbine KAHL-uhm-beyen ['kɑl-əm-baɪn]

Comagene KAHM-uh-jeen ['kɑm-ə-ʤin]

comart koh-**MAHRT** [koʊ-'mɑɚt]

combat (n) KAHM-baat ['kɑm-bæt]

combat (v) KAHM-baat ['kɑm-bæt] possibly scans to
kuhm-**BAAT** [kəm-'bæt] @ *1HVI* I, 1, 54

combatants always scans to KAHM-buh-tuhnts
['kɑm-bə-tənts]

combated (pl) KAHM-buh-tid ['kɑm-bə-tɪd] or __-baa-__
[__-bæ-__]

combating KAHM-baat-ing ['kɑm-bæt-ɪŋ]

combinate KAHM-bi-nit ['kɑm-bɪ-nɪt]

Comfect KAHM-fehkt ['kɑm-fɛkt]

comfit-maker KUHM-fit-may-ker ['kʌm-fɪt-meɪ-kɚ]

comfortable KUHMF-ter-b(uh)l ['kʌmf-tɚ-bl̩] scans to
KUHM-fer-tuh-b(uh)l ['kʌm-fɚ-tə-bl̩] e.g. @ *RIII* IV, 4, 174

Cominius *(COR)* kuh-**MIN**-ee-uhs [kə-'mɪn-i-əs] scans to
__-**MIN**-yuhs [__-'mɪn-jəs] e.g. @ I, 1, 232

commandement kuh-**MAAN**-duh-munt [kə-'mæn-də-mənt]

commeddled koh-**MEH**-d(uh)ld [koʊ-'mɛ-dl̩d]

commend (n) kuh-**MEHND** [kə-'mɛnd]

EE i be/ I ɪ bit/ EH ɛ bet/ AA æ bat/ OO u boot / OO ʊ book/ AW ɔ bought/ AH ɑ father/ ER ɝ bird/
UH ʌ cup/ AY eɪ bay/ EYE aɪ bite/ OY ɔɪ boy/ OH oʊ boat/ OW aʊ how/ YOO ɪu duke/ EAR ɪɚ
beer/ AIR ɛɚ bear/ OOR ʊɚ tour/ AWR ɔɚ bore/ AHR ɑɚ bar/ NG ŋ king/ SH ʃ ship/ ZH ʒ vision/
TH θ thirty/ TH ð then/ CH tʃ child/ J ʤ just/ For complete list, see Key to Pronunciation p. 2.

commendable always scans to **KAH**-mehn-duh-b(uh)l
['kɑ-mɛn-də-bļ] except possibly kuh-**MEHN**-__-__
[kə-'mɛn-__-__] @ *MVEN* I, 1, 111

commerce **KAH**-mers ['kɑ-mɚs] scans to kah-**MERS**
[kɑ-'mɝs] e.g. @ *T&C* III, 3, 205

commit kuh-**MIT** [kə-'mɪt] scans to **KOH**-mit ['koʊ-mɪt]
@ *TIMON* III, 5, 72

commix kuh-**MIKS** [kə-'mɪks]

commixtion kuh-**MIKS**-chuhn [kə-'mɪks-tʃən]

commixture koh-**MIKS**-cher [koʊ-'mɪks-tʃɚ]

commonalty **KAHM**-uh-nuhl-tee ['kɑm-ə-nəl-ti] scans to
KAHM-nuhl-___ ['kɑm-nəl-___] @ *HVIII* I, 2, 170

commonweal **KAHM**-uhn-weel ['kɑm-ən-wil]

commune (v) **KAH**-myo͞on ['kɑ-mjun] possibly scans to
kuh-**MYO͞ON** [kə-'mjun] @ *WT* II, 1, 162

commutual scans to kuh-**MYO͞O**-chuhl [kə-'mju-tʃəl]

compact (n) or (adj) kuhm-**PAAKT** [kəm-'pækt] scans to
KAHM-paakt ['kɑm-pækt] @ *1HVI* V, 4, 163

compact (v) **KAHM**-paakt ['kɑm-pækt]

compeers kuhm-**PEARZ** [kəm-'pɪɚz]

compel kuhm-**PEHL** [kəm-'pɛl] scans to **KAHM**-pehl
['kɑm-pɛl] e.g. @ *2NOB* III, 1, 68

complete kuhm-**PLEET** [kəm-'plit] scans to **KAHM**-pleet
['kɑm-plit] e.g. @ *RIII* IV, 4, 190

complices **KAHM**-plis-iz ['kɑm-plɪs-ɪz]

complot (n) **KAHM**-plaht ['kɑm-plɑt] scans to kuhm-
PLAHT [kəm-'plɑt] e.g. @ *RIII* III, 1, 192

complot (v) kuhm-**PLAHT** [kəm-'plɑt] scans to **KAHM**-plaht ['kɑm-plɑt] @ *RII* I, 3, 189

composture kuhm-**PAHS**-tyer [kəm-'pɑs-tjɚ] or __-__-cher [__-__-tʃɚ]

compremise **KAHM**-pruh-meyez ['kɑm-prə-maɪz]

compt **KOWNT** [kaʊnt] (archaic form of "count" stems from Latin "computare" to count) Many productions use **KAHMPT** [kɑmpt].

comptible **KOWNT**-uh-b(uh)l ['kaʊnt-ə-bl̩] (archaic form of "count" stems from Latin "computare" to count) Many productions use **KAHMP**-tuh-b(uh)l ['kɑmp-tə-bl̩].

comptroller kuhn-**TROH**-ler [kən-'troʊ-lɚ] or kuhmp-__-__ [kəmp-__-__]

compunctious kuhm-**PUHNGK**-shuhs [kəm-'pʌŋk-ʃəs]

comrade **KAHM**-raad ['kɑm-ræd] scans to kahm-**RAAD** [kɑm-'ræd] @ *1HIV* IV, 1, 96

concavities kahn-**KAAV**-i-teez [kɑn-'kæv-ɪ-tiz]

conceal kuhn-**SEEL** [kən-'sil] scans to **KAHN**-seel ['kɑn-sil] e.g. @ *R&J* III, 3, 98

concernancy **KAHN**-ser-nuhn-see ['kɑn-sɚ-nən-si]

concubine **KAHNG**-kyo͞o-beyen ['kɑŋ-kju-baɪn]

Concolinel (unexplained lyric or title) possibly kahn-**KAH**-li-nehl [kɑn-'kɑ-lɪ-nɛl]

concupiscible scans to kuhn-**KYO͞OP**-si-b(uh)l [kən-'kjup-sɪ-bl̩] with "intemperate" as three syllables @ *MM* V, 1, 98

concupy **KAHN**-kyo͞o-peye ['kɑn-kju-paɪ]

EE i be/ I ɪ bit/ EH ɛ bet/ AA æ bat/ O͞O u boot / O͞O ʊ book/ AW ɔ bought/ AH ɑ father/ ER ɝ bird/ UH ʌ cup/ AY eɪ bay/ EYE aɪ bite/ OY ɔɪ boy/ OH oʊ boat/ OW aʊ how/ YO͞O ɪu duke/ EAR ɪɚ beer/ AIR ɛɚ bear/ OOR ʊɚ tour/ AWR ɔɚ bore/ AHR ɑɚ bar/ NG ŋ king/ SH ʃ ship/ ZH ʒ vision/ TH θ thirty/ <u>TH</u> ð then/ CH tʃ child/ J dʒ just/ For complete list, see Key to Pronunciation p. 2.

condemn kuhn-DEHM [kən-'dɛm] scans to KAHN-dehm ['kɑn-dɛm] e.g. @ *A&C* I, 3, 49

condign kuhn-DEYEN [kən-'daɪn] scans to KAHN-deyen ['kɑn-daɪn] @ *2HVI* III, 1, 130

condole kuhn-DOHL [kən-'doʊl]

condolements kuhn-DOHL-muhnts [kən-'doʊl-mənts]

conduce kuhn-DYŌŌS [kən-'dɪus]

conduct (n) KAHN-duhkt ['kɑn-dəkt] scans to kuhn-DUHKT [kən-'dʌkt] @ *TITUS* IV, 4, 64

conduit KAHN-dyōō-it ['kɑn-dɪu-ɪt] scans to KAHN-dit ['kɑn-dɪt] or KAHN-dwit ['kɑn-dwɪt] e.g. @ *COR* II, 3, 237

confessor kuhn-FEHS-er [kən-'fɛs-ɚ] scans to KAHN-fehs-er ['kɑn-fɛs-ɚ] e.g. @ *HVIII* I, 1, 218

confine (n) KAHN-feyen ['kɑn-faɪn] scans to kuhn-FEYEN [kən-'faɪn] e.g. @ *HAM* I, 1, 155

confiners KAHN-feyen-erz ['kɑn-faɪn-ɚz]

confirm kuhn-FERM [kən-'fɝm] scans to KAHN-ferm ['kɑn-fɚm] e.g. @ *MADO* V, 4, 17

confiscate KAHN-fi-skayt ['kɑn-fɪ-skeɪt] scans to kuhn-FI-___ [kən-'fɪ-___] e.g. @ *CE* I, 1, 20

conflux scans to kahn-FLUHKS [kɑn-'flʌks]

conformable kuhn-FAWR-muh-b(uh)l [kən-'fɔɚ-mə-bl̩]

conger (an eel) KAHNG-ger ['kɑŋ-gɚ]

congied KAHN-jeed ['kɑn-ʤid]

congreeing kuhn-GREE-ing [kən-'gri-ɪŋ]

congreeted kuhn-GREET-id [kən-'grit-ɪd]

congruing KAHN-grōō-ing ['kɑn-gru-ɪŋ]

conjoin kuhn-JOYN [kən-'ʤɔɪn]

conjointly kuhn-JOYNT-lee [kən-'ʤɔɪnt-li]

conjunct kuhn-JUHNGKT [kən-'ʤʌŋkt]

conjunctive kuhn-JUHNGK-tiv [kən-'ʤʌŋk-tɪv]

conjuration KAHN-juh-RAY-shuhn [kɑn-ʤə-'reɪ-ʃən]

conjure KAHN-jer ['kɑn-ʤɚ] scans to kuhn-JOOR [kən-'ʤʊɚ] e.g. @ *R&J* II, 1, 26

Conrade *(MADO)* KAHN-raad ['kɑn-ræd]

consanguineous KAHN-saang-GWIN-ee-uhs [kɑn-sæŋ-'gwɪn-i-əs]

consanguinity KAHN-saang-GWIN-i-tee [kɑn-sæŋ-'gwɪn-ɪ-ti]

consecrate KAHN-si-krayt ['kɑn-sɪ-kreɪt]

conserves (n) KAHN-servz ['kɑn-sɚvz] scans to kuhn-SERVZ [kən-'sɝvz] @ *SHR* Ind, 2, 3

consign kuhn-SEYEN [kən-'saɪn] scans to KAHN-seyen ['kɑn-saɪn] @ *T&C* IV, 4, 44

consistory KAHN-sis-taw-ree ['kɑn-sɪs-tɔ-ri] possibly scans to ___-sis-tree [___-sɪs-tri] e.g. @ *HVIII* II, 4, 91

consolate KAHN-suh-layt ['kɑn-sə-leɪt]

consonancy KAHN-suh-nuhn-see ['kɑn-sə-nən-si]

consort (n) KAHN-sawrt ['kɑn-sɔɚt] scans to kuhn-SAWRT [kən-'sɔɚt] e.g. @ *2GEN* IV, 1, 64

consort (v) kuhn-SAWRT [kən-'sɔɚt]

conspectuities kuhn-SPEHK-TYOO-i-teez [kən-spɛk-'tɪu-ɪ-tiz] or kahn-__-__-__-__ [kɑn-__-__-__-__]

EE i be/ I ɪ bit/ EH ɛ bet/ AA æ bat/ OO u boot / OO ʊ book/ AW ɔ bought/ AH ɑ father/ ER ɝ bird/
UH ʌ cup/ AY eɪ bay/ EYE aɪ bite/ OY ɔɪ boy/ OH oʊ boat/ OW aʊ how/ YOO ɪu duke/ EAR ɪɚ
beer/ AIR ɛɚ bear/ OOR ʊɚ tour/ AWR ɔɚ bore/ AHR ɑɚ bar/ NG ŋ king/ SH ʃ ship/ ZH ʒ vision/
TH θ thirty/ TH ð then/ CH tʃ child/ J ʤ just/ For complete list, see Key to Pronunciation p. 2.

conspirant kuhn-SPEYE-ruhnt [kən-'spaɪ-rənt]

Constable of France *(HV)* KAHN-stuh-b(uh)l ['kɑn-stə-bl̩]

Constance *(KJ)* KAHN-stuhns ['kɑn-stəns]

Constantine KAHN-stuhn-teen ['kɑn-stən-tin]

Constantinople KAHN-staan-ti-NOH-p(uh)l
    [kɑn-stæn-tɪ-'noʊ-pl̩]

conster KAHN-ster ['kɑn-stɚ]

constringed kuhn-STRINJD [kən-'strɪndʒd]

consul KAHN-suhl ['kɑn-səl]

contagion kuhn-TAY-juhn [kən-'teɪ-dʒən] scans to __-__-jee-uhn
    [__-__-dʒi-ən] @ *CE* II, 2, 143 if "being" is one syllable

contemn kuhn-TEHM [kən-'tɛm]

contemplative kuhn-TEHM-pluh-tiv [kən-'tɛm-plə-tɪv]

contents (n) KAHN-tehnts ['kɑn-tɛnts] scans to kuhn-
    TEHNTS [kən-'tɛnts] e.g. @ *AYL* IV, 3, 9

contestation KAHN-teh-STAY-shuhn [kɑn-tɛ-'steɪ-ʃən]

continency KAHN-tuh-nuhn-see ['kɑn-tə-nən-si]

continuance kuhn-TIN-yo͞o-uhns [kən-'tɪn-ju-əns] scans to
    __-TIN-yuhns [__-'tɪn-jəns] e.g. @ *R&J* Pro, 10

continuantly kuhn-TIN-YO͞O-uhnt-lee [kən-'tɪn-ju-ənt-li]

continuate always scans to kuhn-TIN-wit [kən-'tɪn-wɪt]

contract (n) KAHN-traakt ['kɑn-trækt] scans to kuhn-
    TRAAKT [kən-'trækt] e.g. @ *1HVI* III, 1, 143

contrariety KAHN-truh-REYE-i-tee [kɑn-trə-'raɪ-ɪ-ti]

contrarious always scans to kuhn-TRAIR-yuhs [kən-'trɛɚ-jəs]

contrary (adj) KAHN-treh-ree ['kɑn-trɛ-ri] scans to kuhn-
    TREH-__ [kən-'trɛ-__] e.g. @ *KJ* IV, 2, 198

contrary (n) KAHN-treh-ree ['kɑn-trɛ-ri]

contrary (v) kuhn-TREH-ree [kən-'trɛ-ri]

contumelious KAHN-tyo͞o-MEE-li-uhs [kɑn-tɪu-'mi-lɪ-əs]
scans to ___-___-MEEL-yuhs [___-___-'mil-jəs]
e.g. @ *1HVI* I, 4, 39

contumeliously scans to KAHN-tyo͞o-MEEL-yuhs-lee
[kɑn-tɪu-'mil-jəs-li]

contumely scans to KAHN-tyo͞om-lee ['kɑn-tɪum-li]

convent (v) (to summon) kuhn-VEHNT [kən-'vɛnt]

conventicles scans to KAHN-vehn-ti-k(uh)lz ['kɑn-vɛn-tɪ-kl̩z]

conversant KAHN-ver-suhnt ['kɑn-və˞-sənt]

converse (n) kuhn-VERS [kən-'vɝs]

convertite KAHN-ver-teyet ['kɑn-və˞-taɪt]

convive kuhn-VEYEV [kən-'vaɪv]

cony KOH-nee ['koʊ-ni]

copatain KAHP-uh-tayn ['kɑp-ə-teɪn]

coped KOHPT [koʊpt]

Cophetua koh-FEH-tyo͞o-uh [koʊ-'fɛ-tɪu-ə] scans to ___-FEH-
tyuh [___-'fɛ-tjə] e.g. @ *R&J* II, 1, 14

copped KAHPT [kɑpt]

coppice KAHP-is ['kɑp-ɪs]

cop'st KOHPST [koʊpst]

copulatives KAH-pyo͞o-lay-tivz ['kɑ-pju-leɪ-tɪvz]

coragio kuh-RAH-zhoh [kə-'rɑ-ʒoʊ]

Coram KOH-ruhm ['koʊ-rəm]

Corambus koh-RAAM-buhs [koʊ-'ræm-bəs]

coranto kuh-RAHN-toh [kə-'rɑn-toʊ]

Cordelia *(LEAR)* kawr-DEE-lyuh [kɔɚ-'di-ljə] scans to ___-___-lee-uh [__-__-li-ə] @ V, 3, 272 first citation

Cordelion KAWR-duh-leye-uhn ['kɔɚ-də-laɪ-ən] some editions use French spelling "Coeur de Lion" KAWR-duh-leye-uhn ['kɔɚ-də-laɪ-ən] or KER-___-lee-___ ['kɝ-__-li-__]

cordial (adj) KAWR-juhl ['kɔɚ-dʒəl] scans to KAWR-jee-uhl ['kɔɚ-dʒi-əl] @ CYM IV, 2, 327

cordial (n) KAWR-juhl ['kɔɚ-dʒəl]

Corin KAW-rin ['kɔ-rɪn]
   Corin *(AYL)*

Corinth KAW-rinth ['kɔ-rɪnθ]

Corinthian kuh-RIN-thee-uhn [kə-'rɪn-θi-ən]

Coriolanus KAW-ree-oh-LAY-nuhs [kɔ-ri-oʊ-'leɪ-nəs]   scans to KAW-ryoh-LAY-___ [kɔ-rjoʊ-'leɪ-___]
   Coriolanus *(COR)* see "Caius Marcius Coriolanus"
   Coriolanus scans @ *TITUS* IV, 4, 67

Corioles kuh-REYE-uh-luhs [kə-'raɪ-ə-ləs] scans to ___-REYE-luhs [___-'raɪ-ləs] e.g. @ COR V, 3, 179

cormorant KAWR-muh-raant ['kɔɚ-mə-rænt] scans to KAWRM-raant ['kɔɚm-rænt] or __-__- ruhnt [__-__-rənt] scans to __-ruhnt [__-rənt] e.g. @ *T&C* II, 2, 6

Cornelia kawr-NEE-lyuh [kɔɚ-'ni-ljə] scans to __-__-lee-uh [__-__-li-ə] @ *TITUS* IV, 2, 141

Cornelius kawr-NEE-lyuhs [kɔɚ-'ni-ljəs]
   Cornelius *(CYM)*
   Cornelius *(HAM)*

cornets KAWR-nets ['kɔɚ-nɛts] or ____-nits [___-nɪts]

cornuto kawr-NOO-toh [kɔɚ-'nu-toh] or __-NYOO-__ [__-'nɪu-__]

Cornwall, Duke of *(LEAR)* KAWRN-wawl ['kɔɚn-wɔl]

corollary KAW-ruh-leh-ree ['kɔ-rə-lɛ-ri]

coronet KAW-ruh-neht ['kɔ-rə-nɛt] scans to KAWR-neht ['kɔɚ-nɛt] e.g. @ *LEAR* I, 1, 139

corrival kuh-REYE-vuhl [kə-'raɪ-vəl] or koh-___-___ [kou-___-___]

corroborate kuh-RAHB-uh-rit [kə-'rɑb-ə-rɪt]

corrosive (n) or (adj) always scans to KAW-ruh-siv ['kɔ-rə-sɪv]

corslet KAWRS-lit ['kɔɚs-lɪt]

Cosmo KAHZ-moh ['kɑz-mou]

costard / Costard *(LLL)* KAHS-terd ['kɑs-tɚd]

costermonger KAHS-ter-MUHNG-ger ['kɑs-tə-mʌŋ-gɚ] or ___-___-MAHNG-___ [___-___-mɑŋ-___]

cote (n) KOHT [kout]

coted KOHT-id ['kout-ɪd]

Cotsall KAHT-s(uh)l ['kɑt-sl̩]

Cotswold KAHTS-wohld ['kɑts-woʊld]

Cotus KOH-tuhs ['kou-təs]

coulter KOHL-ter ['koʊl-tɚ]

counterpoise KOWN-ter-poyz ['kaʊn-tɚ-pɔɪz]

countervail KOWN-ter-vayl ['kaʊn-tɚ-veɪl]

EE i be/ I ɪ bit/ EH ɛ bet/ AA æ bat/ OO u boot / OO ʊ book/ AW ɔ bought/ AH ɑ father/ ER ɝ bird/ UH ʌ cup/ AY eɪ bay/ EYE aɪ bite/ OY ɔɪ boy/ OH oʊ boat/ OW aʊ how/ YOO ɪu duke/ EAR ɪɚ beer/ AIR ɛɚ bear/ OOR ʊɚ tour/ AWR ɔɚ bore/ AHR ɑɚ bar/ NG ŋ king/ SH ʃ ship/ ZH ʒ vision/ TH θ thirty/ TH ð then/ CH tʃ child/ J dʒ just/ For complete list, see Key to Pronunciation p. 2.

County KOWN-tee ['kɑʊn-ti]

courage (n) (bravery) **KE(r)**-rij ['kɜ-rɪʤ] or KUH-__ ['kʌ-__]

courage (n) (a fiery young person) kuh-**RAHJ** [kə-'rɑʤ]

courier KŌŌ-ree-er ['kʊ-ri-ɚ] scans to KŌŌR-yer ['kʊɚ-jɚ]
@ *MAC* I, 7, 23

courser KAWR-ser ['kɔɚ-sɚ]

coursing KAWR-sing ['kɔɚ-sɪŋ]

Court, Alexander KAWRT AAL-ig-ZAAN-der [kɔɚt]
[æl-ɪg-'zæn-dɚ]

court'sy (contraction of "courtesy") **KERT**-see ['kɜt-si]

courtesan KAWR-tuh-zuhn ['kɔɚ-tə-zən]
Courtesan *(CE)*

courtier KAWR-tee-er ['kɔɚ-ti-ɚ] scans to KAWR-tyer
['kɔɚ-tjɚ] e.g. @ *2HVI* IV, 4, 36

covent (n) (a religious community) KUH-vehnt ['kʌ-vɛnt]

Coventry KUHV-uhn-tree ['kʌv-ən-tri]

covert (adj) KOH-vert ['koʊ-vɚt] or KUHV-ert ['kʌv-ɚt]

covert (n) KUHV-ert ['kʌv-ɚt] or KOH-vert ['koʊ-vɚt]

covertly (adv) koh-**VERT**-lee [koʊ-'vɝt-li] or KUHV-ert-lee
['kʌv-ɚt-li]

coverture KUHV-er-cher ['kʌv-ɚ-ʧɚ]

covetousness KUHV-i-tuhs-nuhs ['kʌv-ɪ-təs-nəs]

cowish KOW-ish ['kɑʊ-ɪʃ]

cowl-staff KOWL-staaf ['kɑʊl-stæf]

cowslip KOW-slip ['kɑʊ-slɪp]

coxcomb KAHKS-kohm ['kɑks-koʊm]

coz KUHZ [kʌz]

coz'nage KUHZ-nij [ˈkʌz-nɪʤ]

cozenage KUHZ-uh-nij [ˈkʌz-ə-nɪʤ]

cozener KUHZ-uhn-er [ˈkʌz-ən-ɚ]

coziers KOH-zherz [ˈkou-ʒɚz]

Crab KRAAB [kræb]

Cranmer, Archbishop of Canterbury *(HVIII)* KRAAN-mer [ˈkræn-mɚ]

crants KRAANTS [krænts]

crare KRAIR [krɛɚ]

crasing KRAYZ-ing [ˈkreɪz-ɪŋ] some editions "crazing" KRAYZ-ing [ˈkreɪz-ɪŋ] or "grazing" GRAYZ-ing [ˈgreɪz-ɪŋ]

Crassus KRAAS-uhs [ˈkræs-əs]

craven KRAY-vuhn [ˈkreɪ-vən]

Crécy KREHS-ee [ˈkrɛs-i]

credence KREE-d(uh)nts [ˈkri-dn̩ts]

credent KREE-d(uh)nt [ˈkri-dn̩t]

credulity kruh-DYOO-li-tee [krə-ˈdɪu-lɪ-ti]

Creon KREE-ahn [ˈkri-ɑn]

crept KREHPT [krɛpt]

crescent KREHS-uhnt [ˈkrɛs-ənt] (KREHS-kint [ˈkrɛs-kɪnt] is sometimes heard)

crescive KREH-siv [ˈkrɛ-sɪv]

cressets KREH-sits [ˈkrɛ-sɪts]

EE i be/ I ɪ bit/ EH ɛ bet/ AA æ bat/ OO u boot / OO ʊ book/ AW ɔ bought/ AH ɑ father/ ER ɝ bird/ UH ʌ cup/ AY eɪ bay/ EYE aɪ bite/ OY ɔɪ boy/ OH ou boat/ OW aʊ how/ YOO ɪu duke/ EAR ɪɚ beer/ AIR ɛɚ bear/ OOR ʊɚ tour/ AWR ɔɚ bore/ AHR ɑɚ bar/ NG ŋ king/ SH ʃ ship/ ZH ʒ vision/ TH θ thirty/ TH ð then/ CH ʧ child/ J ʤ just/ For complete list, see Key to Pronunciation p. 2.

Cressid KREHS-id [ˈkrɛs-ɪd]

Cressida KREHS-i-duh [ˈkrɛs-ɪ-də]
    Cressida *(T&C)* also called "Cressid" KREHS-id [ˈkrɛs-ɪd]

Cretan KREE-t(uh)n [ˈkri-tn̩]

Crete KREET [krit]

Crispian KRIS-pee-uhn [ˈkrɪs-pi-ən]

Crispianus KRIS-pee-AY-nuhs [krɪs-pi-ˈeɪ-nəs]

Crispin KRIS-pin [ˈkrɪs-pɪn]

Cromer KROH-mer [ˈkroʊ-mɚ]

Cromwell *(HVIII)* KRAHM-wehl [ˈkrɑm-wɛl] or
    ____-wuhl [__-wəl]

crotchets KRAH-chits [ˈkrɑ-ʧɪts]

crownet KROW-nit [ˈkrɑʊ-nɪt]

crudy KROO-dee [ˈkru-di]

crupper KRUHP-er [ˈkrʌp-ɚ]

crusadoes kroo-SAH-dohz [kru-ˈsɑ-doʊz]

cubiculo kyoo-BIK-yuh-loh [kju-ˈbɪk-jə-loʊ]

cuckold KUHK-uhld [ˈkʌk-əld]

cudgel KUHJ-uhl [ˈkʌʤ-əl]

cull KUHL [kʌl]

cullion KUHL-yuhn [ˈkʌl-jən] scans to KUHL-ee-uhn
    [ˈkʌl-i-ən] @ *SHR* IV, 2, 20

culverin KUHL-vuh-rin [ˈkʌl-və-rɪn]

cumber KUHM-ber [ˈkʌm-bɚ]

Cumberland KUHM-ber-luhnd [ˈkʌm-bɚ-lənd]

Curan *(LEAR)* KUH-ruhn [ˈkʌ-rən] or KE(r)-__ [ˈkɜ-__]

curate KYOO-rit ['kjʊ-rɪt]

Curio *(12th)* KYOO-ree-oh ['kjʊ-ri-oʊ]]

currance KUH-ruhns ['kʌ-rəns]

currish KUH-rish ['kʌ-rɪʃ]

cursitory KER-si-taw-ree ['kɝ-sɪ-tɔ-ri]

curst KERST [kɝst]

cursy KER-see ['kɝ-si]

curtail (v) ker-TAYL [kɚ-'teɪl] scans to KER-tayl ['kɝ-teɪl] @ *RIII* I, 1, 18

curtal / Curtal KER-t(uh)l ['kɝ-tl̩]

Curtis *(SHR)* KER-tis ['kɝ-tɪs]

curtle-axe KER-t(uh)l-aaks ['kɝ-tl̩-æks]

curvet ker-VEHT [kɚ-'vɛt]

cushes KOOSH-iz ['kʊʃ-ɪz]

Cyclops SEYE-klahps ['saɪ-klɑps]

Cydnus SID-nuhs ['sɪd-nəs]

cygnet SIG-nit ['sɪg-nɪt]

Cymbeline *(CYM)* SIM-buh-leen ['sɪm-bə-lin]

Cynthia always scans to SIN-thyuh ['sɪn-θjə]

Cyprus SEYE-pruhs ['saɪ-prəs]

Cyrus SEYE-ruhs ['saɪ-rəs]

Cytherea SITH-uh-REE-uh [sɪθ-ə-'ri-ə]

d. (abbreviation for "pence") PEHNS [pɛns]

EE i be/ I ɪ bit/ EH ɛ bet/ AA æ bat/ OO u boot / OO ʊ book/ AW ɔ bought/ AH ɑ father/ ER ɝ bird/ UH ʌ cup/ AY eɪ bay/ EYE aɪ bite/ OY ɔɪ boy/ OH oʊ boat/ OW aʊ how/ YOO ɪu duke/ EAR ɪɚ beer/ AIR ɛɚ bear/ OOR ʊɚ tour/ AWR ɔɚ bore/ AHR ɑɚ bar/ NG ŋ king/ SH ʃ ship/ ZH ʒ vision/ TH θ thirty/ <u>TH</u> ð then/ CH tʃ child/ J dʒ just/ For complete list, see Key to Pronunciation p. 2.

Daedalus DEHD-uh-luhs ['dɛd-ə-ləs]

daff DAAF [dæf]

daffadilly DAAF-uh-dil-ee ['dæf-ə-dɪl-i]

Dagonet DAA-goh-neht ['dæ-gou-nɛt] or ___-guh-nit [___-gə-nɪt]

Daintry DAYN-tree ['deɪn-tri]

dalliance DAAL-ee-uhns ['dæl-i-əns] scans to DAAL-yuhns ['dæl-jəns] e.g. @ *HAM* I, 3, 50

Dalmatians daal-MAY-shunz [dæl-'meɪ-ʃənz] scans to ___-___-shee-uhnz [___-___-ʃi-ənz] @ *CYM* III, 7, 3

dam DAAM [dæm]

Damascus duh-MAAS-kuhs [də-'mæs-kəs]

damask DAAM-uhsk ['dæm-əsk]

damned DAAMD [dæmd] scans to DAAM-nid ['dæm-nɪd] e.g. @ *RIII* II, 4, 64

Damon DAY-muhn ['deɪ-mən]

damosella daam-oh-ZEHL-uh [dæm-ou-'zɛl-ə]

damsons DAAM-zuhnz ['dæm-zənz] or ___-suhnz [___-sənz]

dandle DAAN-d(uh)l ['dæn-dl̩]

Daniel DAAN-yuhl ['dæn-jəl] scans to DAAN-ee-uhl ['dæn-i-əl] @ *MVEN* IV, 1, 331 first citation

Danskers DAANSK-erz ['dænsk-ɚz]

Daphne DAAF-nee ['dæf-ni]

dar'st DAIRST [dɛɚst]

Dardan DAHR-d(uh)n ['dɑɚ-dn̩]

Dardanian scans to dahr-DAY-nyuhn [dɑɚ-'deɪ-njən]

Dardanius *(JC)* dahr-DAY-nee-uhs [dɑɚ-'dɑɪ-ni-əs]

Darius duh-REYE-uhs [də-'raɪ-əs]

darnel DAHR-nuhl ['dɑɚ-nəl]

darraign di-RAYN [dɪ-'reɪn]

dastard DAAS-terd ['dæs-tɚd]

Datchet Mead DAACH-it MEED ['dætʃ-ɪt] [mid]

daub DAWB [dɔb]

daubery DAWB-uh-ree ['dɔb-ə-ri]

Daughter of Antiochus *(PER)* aan-TEYE-uh-kuhs [æn-'taɪ-ə-kəs]

daunt DAWNT [dɔnt]

Dauphin DAW-fin ['dɔ-fɪn]

Daventry DAAV-uhn-tree ['dæv-ən-tri]

Davy DAY-vee ['deɪ-vi]
   Davy *(2HIV)*

daw DAW [dɔ]

de Armado, Don Adriano *(LLL)* duh-ahr-MAH-doh DAHN AY-dree-AH-noh [də-ɑɚ-'mɑ-dou] [dɑn] [eɪ-dri-'ɑ-nou]

de Burgh, Hubert *(KJ)* duh-BERG HYOO-bert [də-'bɝg] ['hju-bɚt]

de Champ dyoo-CHAAMP [dɪu-'tʃæmp]

de la Car deh-luh-KAHR [dɛ-lə-'kɑɚ]

de la Pole, William, Earl afterward Duke of Suffolk *(1HVI, 2HVI)* deh-luh-POHL [dɛ-lə-'poul] or __-__-POOL [__-__'pul] SUHF-uhk ['sʌf-ək]

---

de Pucelle, Joan *(1HVI)* duh-poo-SEHL [də-pu-'sɛl] scans to
__-PUH-suhl [__-'pʌ-səl] or __-PUH-zuhl [__-'pʌ-zəl]
e.g. @ I, 6, 3

de Vere, John, Earl of Oxford duh-VEAR [də-'vɪɚ]
de Vere, John, Earl of Oxford *(3HVI, RIII)*

dearth DERTH [dɝθ]

debile DEH-buhl ['dɛ-bəl] or DEE-beyel ['di-baɪl]

Deborah DEHB-uh-ruh ['dɛb-ə-rə]

deboshed di-BAHSHT [dɪ-'baʃt]

decimation DEH-si-MAY-shuhn [dɛ-sɪ-'meɪ-ʃən]

decoct dee-KAHKT [di-'kɑkt]

Decretas *(A&C)* duh-KREE-tuhs [də-'kri-təs] scans to
DEHK-ruh-__ ['dɛk-rə-__] @ V, 1, 5 if "I am" elides; some
editions "Dercetas" der-SEE-tuhs [dɚ-'si-təs]

defunction di-FUHNGK-shuhn [dɪ-'fʌŋk-ʃən]

deign DAYN [deɪn]

deifying DEE-uh-feye-ing ['di-ə-faɪ-ɪŋ]

Deiphobus *(T&C)* dee-IF-uh-buhs [di-'ɪf-ə-bəs]

deity DEE-i-tee ['di-ɪ-ti] scans to DEE-tee ['di-ti]
e.g. @ *12th* V, 1, 219

Delabreth DEH-luh-brehth ['dɛ-lə-brɛθ]

delated di-LAY-tid [dɪ-'leɪ-tɪd]

delectable scans to DEE-lehk-tuh-b(uh)l ['di-lɛk-tə-bl̩] possibly the same in prose

Delphos DEHL-fahs ['dɛl-fɑs] or ___-fuhs [___-fəs]

deluge DEHL-yooj ['dɛl-judʒ]

Delver DEHL-ver ['dɛl-vɚ]

demesnes di-MAYNZ [dɪ-'mɛɪnz]

Demetrius di-MEE-tree-uhs [dɪ-'mi-tri-əs] scans to
    __-MEE-truhs [__-'mi-trəs]
    Demetrius *(A&C)*
    Demetrius *(MID)* scans e.g. @ I, 1, 52
    Demetrius *(TITUS)*

demise di-MEYEZ [dɪ-'maɪz]

demonstrable scans to DEHM-uhn-struh-b(uh)l
    ['dɛm-ən-strə-bl̩]

demonstrate DEH-muhn-strayt ['dɛ-mən-streɪt] scans to
    duh-MAHN-___ [də-'mɑn-___] e.g. @ *TIMON* I, 1, 91

denay di-NAY [dɪ-'neɪ]

denier di-NEAR [dɪ-'nɪɚ]

Dennis DEHN-is ['dɛn-ɪs]

Denny, Sir Anthony *(HVIII)* DEHN-ee ['dɛn-i]

depart (n) di-PAHRT [dɪ-'pɑɚt]

depositaries di-PAHZ-i-TEH-reez [dɪ-'pɑz-ɪ-tɛ-riz]

deputation DEHP-yuh-TAY-shuhn [dɛp-jə-'teɪ-ʃən]

depute di-PYOOT [dɪ-'pjut]

deracinate di-RAAS-in-ayt [dɪ-'ræs-ɪn-eɪt]

Derby DAHR-bee ['dɑɚ-bi] or DER-___ ['dɝ-___]

dern DERN [dɝn]

derogate (v) DEH-ruh-gayt ['dɛ-rə-geɪt]

derogate (adj) scans to DAIR-guht ['dɛɚ-gət]

derogately DEH-roh-gayt-lee ['dɛ-roʊ-geɪt-li]

EE i be/ I ɪ bit/ EH ɛ bet/ AA æ bat/ OO u boot / OO ʊ book/ AW ɔ bought/ AH ɑ father/ ER ɝ bird/
UH ʌ cup/ AY eɪ bay/ EYE aɪ bite/ OY ɔɪ boy/ OH oʊ boat/ OW aʊ how/ YOO ɪu duke/ EAR ɪɚ
beer/ AIR ɛɚ bear/ OOR ʊɚ tour/ AWR ɔɚ bore/ AHR ɑɚ bar/ NG ŋ king/ SH ʃ ship/ ZH ʒ vision/
TH θ thirty/ TH ð then/ CH tʃ child/ J dʒ just/ For complete list, see Key to Pronunciation p. 2.

89

derogation DEH-roh-**GAY**-shuhn [dɛ-rou-'geɪ-ʃən]

descant DEHS-kaant ['dɛs-kænt]

descension di-SEHN-shuhn [dɪ-'sɛn-ʃən]

descry (n) or (v) di-SKREYE [dɪ-'skraɪ]

Desdemona *(OTH)* DEHZ-di-**MOH**-nuh [dɛz-dɪ-'mou-nə]
 also called "Desdemon" **DEHZ**-di-mohn ['dɛz-dɪ-moun]

desert (an uninhabited land) **DEH**-zert ['dɛ-zɚt] e.g. @ *WT*
 III, 3, 2

desert (that which is due to a person) di-**ZERT** [dɪ-'zɝt]
 e.g. @ *3HVI* III, 3, 192

designment di-**ZEYEN**-muhnt [dɪ-'zaɪn-mənt]

desist di-SIST [dɪ-'sɪst] or ___-ZIST [___-'zɪst]

despised di-SPEYEZD [dɪ-'spaɪzd] scans to DIS-peyezd
 ['dɪs-paɪzd] @ *HAM* III, 1, 72

despite di-SPEYET [dɪ-'spaɪt]

detestable always scans to DEE-tehs-tuh-b(uh)l
 ['di-tɛs-tə-bl̩]

Deucalion dyōō-KAY-lee-uhn [dɪu-'keɪ-li-ən] scans to
 __-KAY-lyuhn [__-'keɪ-ljən] @ *WT* IV, 4, 424

devesting di-VEHST-ing [dɪ-'vɛst-ɪŋ]

Devonshire DEHV-uhn-sher ['dɛv-ən-ʃɚ] or ___-___-shear
 [___-___-ʃɪɚ]

dewlap DYŌŌ-laap ['dɪu-læp]

dexter DEHK-ster ['dɛk-stɚ]

dexteriously dehk-STEH-ree-uhs-lee [dɛk-'stɛ-ri-əs-li]

diadem DEYE-uh-dehm ['daɪ-ə-dɛm] scans to DEYE-dehm
 ['daɪ-dɛm] e.g. @ *HAM* III, 4, 101

dial DEYE-uhl [ˈdaɪ̯l] scans to DEYE-uhl [ˈdaɪ-əl] e.g. @ *3HVI* II, 5, 24

diamond DEYE-muhnd [ˈdaɪ-mənd] scans to DEYE-uh-muhnd [ˈdaɪ-ə-mənd] e.g. @ *CE* IV, 3, 64

Dian DEYE-uhn [ˈdaɪ-ən]

Diana deye-AAN-uh [daɪ-ˈæn-ə]
Diana *(AW)*
Diana *(PER)*

dibble DIB-uhl [ˈdɪb-əl]

dich DICH [dɪtʃ]

Dickon DIK-uhn [ˈdɪk-ən]

Dictynna dik-TIN-uh [dɪk-ˈtɪn-ə]

diddest DID-dist [ˈdɪd-dɪst]

Dido DEYE-doh [ˈdaɪ-doʊ]

different DIF-uh-ruhnt [ˈdɪf-ə-rənt] possibly scans to di-FE(r)-ruhnt [dɪ-ˈfɜ-rənt] @ *CE* V, 1, 46

Dighton DEYE-t(uh)n [ˈdaɪ-tn̩]

dilatory DIL-uh-taw-ree [ˈdɪl-ə-tɔ-ri]

dild DEELD [dild]

diminitives di-MIN-i-tivz [dɪ-ˈmɪn-ɪ-tɪvz]

diminution DIM-i-NYOO-shuhn [dɪm-ɪ-ˈnɪu-ʃən]

din DIN [dɪn]

dint DINT [dɪnt]

Diomede DEYE-uh-meed [ˈdaɪ-ə-mid]

EE i be/ I ɪ bit/ EH ɛ bet/ AA æ bat/ O͞O u boot / O͞O ʊ book/ AW ɔ bought/ AH ɑ father/ ER ɝ bird/ UH ʌ cup/ AY eɪ bay/ EYE aɪ bite/ OY ɔɪ boy/ OH oʊ boat/ OW aʊ how/ YO͞O ɪu duke/ EAR ɪɚ beer/ AIR ɛɚ bear/ O͞OR ʊɚ tour/ AWR ɔɚ bore/ AHR ɑɚ bar/ NG ŋ king/ SH ʃ ship/ ZH ʒ vision/ TH θ thirty/ T͟H ð then/ CH tʃ child/ J ʤ just/ For complete list, see Key to Pronunciation p. 2.

Diomedes DEYE-uh-MEE-deez [daɪ-ə-ˈmi-diz] also called "Diomed" **DEYE**-uh-mehd [ˈdaɪ-ə-mɛd] scans to **DEYE**-mehd [ˈdaɪ-mɛd]
    Diomedes *(A&C)* scans @ IV, 14, 116
    Diomedes *(T&C)* scans @ V, 2, 133

Dion *(WT)* DEYE-ahn [ˈdaɪ-ɑn] or ___-uhn [___-ən]

Dionyza *(PER)* DEYE-uh-**NEYE**-zuh [daɪ-ə-ˈnaɪ-zə]

dire DEYER [daɪɚ]

direct (adj) di-**REHKT** [dɪ-ˈrɛkt] scans to **DEYE**-rehkt [ˈdaɪ-rɛkt] e.g. @ *OTH* I, 2, 86

directitude di-**REHK**-ti-tyōōd [dɪ-ˈrɛk-tɪ-tɪud]

dirge DERJ [dɝʤ]

Dis DIS [dɪs]

disannul dis-uh-**NUHL** [dɪs-ə-ˈnʌl]

discandying scans to dis-**KAAN**-dying [dɪs-ˈkæn-djɪŋ]

discomfit dis-**KUHM**-fit [dɪs-ˈkʌm-fɪt]

discomfiture dis-**KUHM**-fi-chōōr [dɪs-ˈkʌm-fɪ-ʧʊɚ] or ___-___-___-cher [___-___-___-ʧɚ]

discourse (n) DIS-kawrs [ˈdɪs-kɔɚs] scans to dis-**KAWRS** [dɪs-ˈkɔɚs] e.g. @ *R&J* III, 5, 53

disedged dis-**EHJD** [dɪs-ˈɛʤd]

disgest dis-**JEHST** [dɪs-ˈʤɛst]

dishclout DISH-klowt [ˈdɪʃ-klɑʊt]

disinsanity DIS-in-**SAAN**-i-tee [dɪs-ɪn-ˈsæn-ɪ-ti]

dislimns dis-**LIMZ** [dɪs-ˈlɪmz]

dismes DEYEMZ [daɪmz]

dismission dis-**MISH**-uhn [dɪs-ˈmɪʃ-ən]

dispatch (n) dis-PAACH [dɪs-'pætʃ]

displant dis-PLAANT [dɪs-'plænt]

disponge di-SPUHNJ [dɪ-'spʌndʒ]

disport di-SPAWRT [dɪ-'spɔɚt]

dispose di-SPOHZ [dɪ-'spoʊz]

disputation dis-pyōō-TAY-shuhn [dɪs-pju-'teɪ-ʃən] scans to
__-__-__-shee-uhn [__-__-__-ʃi-ən] @ *1HIV* II, 1, 203

disseat dis-SEET [dɪs-'sit]

dissemble di-SEHM-b(uh)l [dɪ-'sɛm-bl̩]

dissentious di-SEHN-shuhs [dɪ-'sɛn-ʃəs]

dissever dis-SEHV-er [dɪs-'sɛv-ɚ]

distaff DIS-taaf ['dɪs-tæf]

distain di-STAYN [dɪ-'steɪn]

distemperature dis-TEHM-pruh-chōōr [dɪs-'tɛm-prə-tʃʊɚ]
or ___-___-___-cher [___-___-___-tʃɚ]

distinct dis-TINGKT [dɪs-'tɪŋkt] scans to DIS-tingkt
['dɪs-tɪŋkt] e.g. @ *T&C* IV, 4, 44

distrain dis-TRAYN [dɪs-'treɪn]

distressed dis-TREHST [dɪs-'trɛst] scans to DIS-trehst
['dɪs-trɛst] @ *1HVI* IV, 3, 30

diurnal deye-ER-nuhl [daɪ-'ɝ-nəl]

divers DEYE-verz ['daɪ-vɚz]

Dives DEYE-veez ['daɪ-viz]

dividable scans to DI-vi-duh-b(uh)l ['dɪ-vɪ-də-bl̩]

---

dividant di-VEYE-duhnt [dɪ-ˈvaɪ-dənt]

dividual di-VIJ-o͞o-uhl [dɪ-ˈvɪʤ-u-əl]

divination DIV-uh-NAY-shuhn [dɪv-ə-ˈneɪ-ʃən]

Dobbin DAHB-in [ˈdɑb-ɪn]

do'ee DO͞O-ee [ˈdu-i]

doers DO͞O-erz [ˈdu-ɚ-z]

doff DAWF [dɔf] or DAHF [daf]

Dogberry *(MADO)* DAWG-beh-ree [ˈdɔg-bɛ-ri]

doit / Doit DOYT [dɔɪt]

Dolabella *(A&C)* DAH-luh-BEH-luh [dɑ-lə-ˈbɛ-lə]

dolor / dolour DOH-ler [ˈdoʊ-lɚ]

dolorous DOH-luh-ruhs [ˈdoʊ-lə-rəs]

dolphin / Dolphin DAHL-fin [ˈdɑl-fɪn]

dolt DOHLT [doʊlt]

Dombledon DUHM-uhl-duhn [ˈdʌm-əl-dən]

Domine DAH-min-ee [ˈdɑ-mɪn-i]

dominical duh-MIN-i-k(uh)l [də-ˈmɪn-ɪ-kl̩]

dominie DAH-min-ee [ˈdɑ-mɪn-i]

Domitius Enobarbus *(A&C)* always scans to doh-MI-shuhs
  [doʊ-ˈmɪ-ʃəs] or duh-__-__ [də-__-__] EE-nuh-BAHR-buhs
  [i-nə-ˈbɑɚ-bəs] scans to een-BAHR-buhs [in-ˈbɑɚ-bəs]
  e.g. @ III, 13, 1; also called "Enobarb" EE-nuh-barb
  [ˈi-nə-bɑɚ-b] @ II, 7, 121

Don Alphonso DAHN aal-FAHN-zoh [dɑn] [æl-ˈfɑn-zoʊ]

Donalbain *(MAC)* DAHN-uhl-bayn [ˈdɑn-əl-beɪn]

Doncaster DAHNG-kuhs-ter [ˈdɑŋ-kəs-tɚ]

donned DAHND [dɑnd]

Dorcas *(WT)* DAWR-kuhs ['dɔɚ-kəs]

Doreus scans to DAWR-yuhs ['dɔɚ-jəs]

Doricles DAW-ri-kleez ['dɔ-rɪ-kliz]

Dorset, Marquess of *(RIII)* DAWR-sit ['dɔɚ-sɪt]

Dorsetshire DAWR-sit-sher ['dɔɚ-sɪt-ʃɚ] or ___-___-shear [__-__-ʃɪɚ]

dost DUHST [dʌst]

dotage DOH-tij ['dou-tɪdʒ]

dotant DOH-tuhnt ['dou-tənt]

dotard DOH-terd ['dou-tɚd]

dote DOHT [dout]

doth DUHTH [dʌθ]

doublet DUHB-lit ['dʌb-lɪt]

doubly DUHB-lee ['dʌb-li]

doughty-handed DOW-tee-HAAND-id ['dɑu-ti-hænd-ɪd]

dout DOWT [dɑut]

dovecote DUHV-koht ['dʌv-kout]

Dover DOH-ver ['dou-vɚ]

dowager DOW-uh-jer ['dɑu-ə-dʒɚ]

dower DOW-er ['dɑu-ɚ] scans to DOWR [dɑuɚ] e.g. @ *LEAR* I, 1, 128

dowlas DOW-luhs ['dɑu-ləs]

EE i be/ I ɪ bit/ EH ɛ bet/ AA æ bat/ OO u boot / OO ʊ book/ AW ɔ bought/ AH ɑ father/ ER ɝ bird/
UH ʌ cup/ AY eɪ bay/ EYE aɪ bite/ OY ɔɪ boy/ OH ou boat/ OW ɑu how/ YOO ɪu duke/ EAR ɪɚ
beer/ AIR ɛɚ bear/ OOR ʊɚ tour/ AWR ɔɚ bore/ AHR ɑɚ bar/ NG ŋ king/ SH ʃ ship/ ZH ʒ vision/
TH θ thirty/ TH ð then/ CH tʃ child/ J dʒ just/ For complete list, see Key to Pronunciation p. 2.

95

dowle DOWL [daʊl]

Dowsabel DOW-suh-behl [ˈdaʊ-sə-bɛl] or ___-zuh-___ [___-zə-___]

dowset DOW-sit [ˈdaʊ-sɪt]

doxy DAHK-see [ˈdak-si]

dozy DOH-zee [ˈdoʊ-zi]

drab DRAAB [dræb]

drachma DRAAK-muh [ˈdræk-mə]

draff DRAAF [dræf]

dram DRAAM [dræm]

draught DRAAFT [dræft]

drave DRAYV [dreɪv]

drawer (waiter / tapster) DRAW-er [ˈdrɔ-ɚ]

drayman DRAY-muhn [ˈdreɪ-mən]

Dromio DROH-mee-oh [ˈdroʊ-mi-oʊ] scans to DROH-myoh [ˈdroʊ-mjoʊ]
　Dromio of Ephesus *(CE)* scans e.g. @ I, 2, 68 EHF-i-suhs [ˈɛf-ɪ-səs]
　Dromio of Syracuse *(CE)* scans e.g. @ I, 2, 10 SI-ruh-kyōōz [ˈsɪ-rə-kjuz]

dross DRAWS [drɔs] or DRAHS [dras]

drossy DRAWS-ee [ˈdrɔs-i] or DRAHS-__ [ˈdras-__]

drouth DROWTH [draʊθ]

drovier DROHV-er [ˈdroʊv-ɚ]

drudge DRUHJ [drʌʤ]

drumble DRUHM-b(uh)l [ˈdrʌm-bl̩]

ducat DUHK-it [ˈdʌk-ɪt]

ducdame (a nonsense word) possibly duhk DAH may
['dək-'dɑ-meɪ]

duchy DUHCH-ee ['dʌtʃ-i]

dudgeon DUHJ-uhn ['dʌdʒ-ən]

duello dyo͞o-EHL-oh [dɪu-'ɛl-ou]

duer DYO͞O-er ['dɪu-ɚ]

Duff DUHF [dʌf]

Duke DYO͞OK [dɪuk]
    Duke Frederick *(AYL)* FREH-duh-rik ['frɛ-də-rɪk] scans
      to FREH-drik ['frɛ-drɪk] @ V, 4, 148
    Duke Senior *(AYL)* SEEN-yer ['sin-jɚ]

dukedom DYO͞OK-duhm ['dɪuk-dəm]

dulcet DUHL-sit ['dʌl-sɪt]

Dull *(LLL)* DUHL [dʌl]

Dumaine *(LLL)* dyo͞o-MAYN [dɪu-'meɪn]

Dumbe DUHM [dʌm]

dun DUHN [dʌn]

Dun Adramadio DUHN AH-drah-MAH-dee-oh [dʌn]
[ɑ-drɑ-'mɑ-di-ou]

Duncan *(MAC)* DUHNG-kuhn ['dʌŋ-kən]

dungy DUHNG-ee ['dʌŋ-i]

Dunsinane Hill DUHN-si-nayn ['dʌn-sɪ-neɪn] scans to
    duhn-SI-nayn [dən-'sɪ-neɪn] @ *MAC* IV, 1, 93

Dunsmore DUHNZ-mawr ['dʌnz-mɔɚ]

Dunstable DUHN-stuh-b(uh)l ['dʌn-stə-bl̩]

EE i be/ I ɪ bit/ EH ɛ bet/ AA æ bat/ O͞O u boot / O͞O ʊ book/ AW ɔ bought/ AH ɑ father/ ER ɝ bird/
UH ʌ cup/ AY eɪ bay/ EYE aɪ bite/ OY ɔɪ boy/ OH ou boat/ OW aʊ how/ YO͞O ɪu duke/ EAR ɪɚ
beer/ AIR ɛɚ bear/ O͞OR ʊɚ tour/ AWR ɔɚ bore/ AHR ɑɚ bar/ NG ŋ king/ SH ʃ ship/ ZH ʒ vision/
TH θ thirty/ TH ð then/ CH tʃ child/ J dʒ just/ For complete list, see Key to Pronunciation p. 2.

dupped DUHPT [dʌpt]

durance DYŌŌ-ruhns ['djʊ-rəns]

dure DYŌŌR [djʊɚ]

durst DERST [dɝst]

duteous DYŌŌ-tee-uhs ['dɪu-ti-əs]

e'en EEN [in]

e'er AIR [ɛɚ]

ean EEN [in]

eanling EEN-ling ['in-lɪŋ]

earing (cultivating or plowing) I-ring ['ɪ-rɪŋ]

Eastcheap EEST-cheep ['ist-tʃip]

eat EHT [ɛt] (archaic form of "eaten")

ebon EHB-uhn ['ɛb-ən]

eche EECH [itʃ]

Edgar *(LEAR)* EHD-ger ['ɛd-gɚ]

edict EE-dikt ['i-dɪkt] scans to ee-**DIKT** [i-'dɪkt]
  e.g. @ *MID* I, 1, 151

Edmund EHD-muhnd ['ɛd-mənd]
  Edmund *(LEAR)*
  Edmund of Langley, Duke of York *(RII)* **LAANG**-lee
    ['læŋ-li]
  Edmund, Earl of Rutland *(3HVI)* **RUHT**-luhnd ['rʌt-lənd]

Edmundsbury EHD-muhndz-buh-ree ['ɛd-məndz-bə-ri]

Edward EHD-werd ['ɛd-wɚd]
  Edward IV *(3HVI, RIII)*
  Edward, Earl of March *(1HIV)* MAHRCH [maɚtʃ]
  Edward, Prince of Wales *(3HVI)*
  Edward, Prince of Wales, afterward Edward V *(RIII)*

effigies scans to i-FI-jeez [ɪ-'fɪ-ʤiz]

effuse i-FYOOZ [ɪ-'fjuz] or __-FYOOS [__-'fjus]

eftsoons ehft-SOONZ [ɛft-'sunz] scans to EHFT-soonz ['ɛft-sunz] @ *2NOB* III, 1, 12

egal EE-guhl ['i-gəl]

egally EE-guh-lee ['i-gə-li]

Egeon *(CE)* ee-JEE-uhn [i-'ʤi-ən] or i-__-__ [ɪ-__-__]

Egeus *(MID)* ee-JEE-uhs [i-'ʤi-əs] or i-__-__ [ɪ-__-__]

Eglamour *(2GEN)* EHG-luh-mawr ['ɛg-lə-mɔɚ] or __-__- moor [__-__-mʊɚ]

eglantine EHG-luhn-teyen ['ɛg-lən-taɪn]

egregious i-GREE-juhs [ɪ-'gri-ʤəs]

eke EEK [ik]

Elbe EHLB [ɛlb]

Elbow *(MM)* EHL-boh ['ɛl-boʊ]

eld EHLD [ɛld]

elflocks EHLF-lahks ['ɛlf-lɑks]

eliads EHL-yuhdz ['ɛl-jədz]

Elinor, Queen *(KJ)* EHL-i-nawr ['ɛl-ɪ-nɔɚ] or __-__-ner [__-__-nɚ]

ell EHL [ɛl]

Elsinore EHL-si-nawr ['ɛl-sɪ-nɔɚ]

Eltham EHL-tuhm ['ɛl-təm] or __-thuhm [__-θəm]

elvish-marked EHL-vish-mahrkt ['ɛl-vɪʃ-mɑɚkt]

EE i be/ I ɪ bit/ EH ɛ bet/ AA æ bat/ OO u boot / OO ʊ book/ AW ɔ bought/ AH ɑ father/ ER ɝ bird/
UH ʌ cup/ AY eɪ bay/ EYE aɪ bite/ OY ɔɪ boy/ OH oʊ boat/ OW aʊ how/ YOO ɪu duke/ EAR ɪɚ
beer/ AIR ɛɚ bear/ OOR ʊɚ tour/ AWR ɔɚ bore/ AHR ɑɚ bar/ NG ŋ king/ SH ʃ ship/ ZH ʒ vision/
TH θ thirty/ TH ð then/ CH ʧ child/ J ʤ just/ For complete list, see Key to Pronunciation p. 2.

Ely EE-lee ['i-li]
    Ely, Bishop of *(HV)*

Elysium i-LIZ-ee-uhm [ɪ-'lɪz-i-əm] scans to ___-LIZ-yuhm
    [___-'lɪz-jəm] or ___-LIZH-___-___ [___-'lɪʒ-___-___] scans
    to ___-LIZH-yuhm [___-'lɪʒ-jəm] e.g. @ *HV* IV, 1, 260

embargements ehm-BAHRJ-muhnts [ɛm-'bɑɚʤ-mənts]

embassade EHM-buh-sahd ['ɛm-bə-sɑd]

embassage EHM-buh-sij ['ɛm-bə-sɪʤ]

embattailed scans to ehm-BAA-t(uh)l-id [ɛm-'bæ-tl̩-ɪd]

embayed ehm-BAYD [ɛm-'beɪd]

embolden ehm-BOHL-d(uh)n [ɛm-'boʊl-dn̩]

embowel ehm-BOWL [ɛm-'baʊl]

embrasures ehm-BRAY-zherz [ɛm-'breɪ-ʒɚz]

Emilia i-MEEL-ee-uh [ɪ-'mil-i-ə] scans to __-MEEL-yuh
    [__-'mil-jə] or __-MIL-__-__ [__-'mɪl-__-__] scans to
    __-MIL-yuh [__-'mɪl-jə]
    Emilia *(CE)*
    Emilia *(OTH)* scans e.g. @ V, 3, 92
    Emilia *(2NOB)* scans e.g. @ II, 5, 49
    Emilia *(WT)* scans e.g. @ II, 2, 15

Emmanuel i-MAAN-yo͞o-ehl [ɪ-'mæn-ju-ɛl]

emperor EHM-puh-rer ['ɛm-pə-rɚ] scans to EHM-prer
    ['ɛm-prɚ] e.g. @ *A&C* IV, 14, 90

empery EHM-puh-ree ['ɛm-pə-ri]

empirics scans to EHM-pi-riks ['ɛm-pɪ-rɪks]

empiricutic ehm-PI-ri-KYO͞O-tik [ɛm-pɪ-rɪ-'kju-tɪk]

empoison ehm-POY-zuhn [ɛm-'pɔɪ-zən]

emulous EHM-yuh-luhs ['ɛm-jə-ləs] scans to EHM-luhs
    ['ɛm-ləs] e.g. @ *T&C* II, 3, 224

enactures ehn-AAK-cherz [ɛn-'æk-tʃɚz]

Enceladus ehn-SEHL-uh-duhs [ɛn-'sɛl-ə-dəs]

enchafed in-CHAYFT [ɪn-'tʃeɪft]

endart ehn-DAHRT [ɛn-'dɑɚt]

endite ehn-DEYET [ɛn-'daɪt]

Endymion ehn-DIM-ee-uhn [ɛn-'dɪm-i-ən]

enew i-NYOO [ɪ-'nɪu]

enfeoffed ehn-FEEFT [ɛn-'fift]

enfranched ehn-FRAANCH-id [ɛn-'fræntʃ-ɪd] or in-___-___
    [ɪn-___-___]

enfranchise ehn-FRAAN-cheyez [ɛn-'fræn-tʃaɪz] or in-__-__
    [ɪn-__-__]

enfranchisement ehn-FRAAN-chuhz-muhnt [ɛn-'fræn-tʃəz-mənt]
    or ___-FRAAN-cheyez-___ [___-'fræn-tʃaɪz-___]

enfreed ehn-FREED [ɛn-'frid]

engild ehn-GILD [ɛn-'gɪld]

enginer EHN-ji-ner ['ɛn-dʒɪ-nɚ]

engirt ehn-GERT [ɛn-'gɝt]

englut ehn-GLUHT [ɛn-'glʌt]

enjailed ehn-JAYLD [ɛn-'dʒeɪld] or in-___ [ɪn-___]

enjoin ehn-JOYN [ɛn-'dʒɔɪn] scans to EHN-joyn ['ɛn-dʒɔɪn]
    @ *AW* III, 5, 90

enlard ehn-LAHRD [ɛn-'lɑɚd]

Enobarbus see "Domitius Enobarbus"

---

enow i-NOW [ɪ-'nɑʊ]

ensconce ehn-SKAHNS [ɛn-'skɑns]

ensear ehn-SEAR [ɛn-'sɪɚ]

ensign EHN-sin ['ɛn-sɪn]

enskied in-SKEYED [ɪn-'skaɪd] or ehn-____ [ɛn-___]

ensure ehn-SHOOR [ɛn-'ʃʊɚ]

entrails EHN-traylz ['ɛn-treɪlz]

envenom ehn-VEHN-uhm [ɛn-'vɛn-əm]

environ ehn-VEYE-ruhn [ɛn-'vaɪ-rən]

Ephesian i-FEE-zhuhn [ɪ-'fi-ʒən]

Ephesus EHF-i-suhs ['ɛf-ɪ-səs]

epicure EHP-i-kyo͞or ['ɛp-ɪ-kʊɚ]

Epicurean EHP-i KYO͞O-ree-uhn [ɛp-ɪ-'kjʊ-ri-ən] scans to
____-__-KYO͞O-ryuhn [__-__-'kʊ-rjən] @ *A&C* II, 1, 24

epicurism scans to eh-PI-kyo͞o-rizm [ɛ-'pɪ-kjʊ-rɪzm]

Epicurus EH-pi-KYO͞O-ruhs [ɛ-pɪ-'kjʊ-rəs]

Epidamnum EHP-i-DAAM-nuhm [ɛp-ɪ-'dæm-nəm]

Epidaurus EHP-i-DAW-ruhs [ɛp-ɪ-'dɔ-rəs]

epistle i-PIS-uhl [ɪ-'pɪs-əl]

Epistrophus i-PIS-truh-fuhs [ɪ-'pɪs-trə-fəs]

epitaph EHP-i-taaf ['ɛp-ɪ-tæf]

epithet EHP-i-theht ['ɛp-ɪ-θɛt]

epitheton i-PITH-uh-tahn [ɪ-'pɪθ-ə-tɑn]

equinoctial EH-kwuh-NAHK-shuhl [ɛ-kwə-'nɑk-ʃəl]

equipage EHK-wuh-pij ['ɛk-wə-pɪʤ]

equivocal i-KWIV-uh-k(uh)l [ɪ-ˈkwɪv-ə-kl̩]

equivocation i-KWIV-uh-KAY-shuhn [ɪ-kwɪv-ə-ˈkeɪ-ʃən]

equivocator i-KWIV-uh-KAY-ter [ɪ-ˈkwɪv-ə-keɪ-tɚ]

ere AIR [ɛɚ] scans @ *1HVI* I, 3, 88, perhaps EH-er [ˈɛ-ɚ]

Erebus EH-ruh-buhs [ˈɛ-rə-bəs]

ergo ER-goh [ˈɝ-goʊ] or AIR-___ [ˈɛɚ-___]

Ermengard ER-muhn-gahrd [ˈɝ-mən-gɑɚd]

erned ERND [ɝnd]

Eros *(A&C)* EH-rahs [ˈɛ-rɑs] or ___-rohs [___-roʊs]

Erpingham ER-ping-uhm [ˈɝ-pɪŋ-əm] or ___-___-haam
      [___-___-hæm]
    Erpingham, Sir Thomas *(HV)*

err ER [ɝ]

errant EH-ruhnt [ˈɛ-rənt]

erst ERST [ɝst]

erudition scans to AIR-yuh-DI-shee-uhn [ɛɚ-jə-ˈdɪ-ʃi-ən]

eryngoes i-RING-gohz [ɪ-ˈrɪŋ-goʊz]

Escalus EHS-kuh-luhs [ˈɛs-kə-ləs]
    Escalus *(MM)*
    Escalus, Prince of Verona *(R&J)* vuh-ROH-nuh [və-ˈroʊ-nə]

Escanes *(PER)* EHS-kuh-neez [ˈɛs-kə-niz]

escapend i-SKAY-puhnd [ɪ-ˈskeɪ-pənd]

eschewed ehs-CHOOD [ɛs-ˈtʃud]

escoted eh-SKAHT-id [ɛ-ˈskɑt-ɪd]

EE i be/ I ɪ bit/ EH ɛ bet/ AA æ bat/ OO u boot / OO ʊ book/ AW ɔ bought/ AH ɑ father/ ER ɝ bird/
UH ʌ cup/ AY eɪ bay/ EYE aɪ bite/ OY ɔɪ boy/ OH oʊ boat/ OW aʊ how/ YOO ɪu duke/ EAR ɪɚ
beer/ AIR ɛɚ bear/ OOR ʊɚ tour/ AWR ɔɚ bore/ AHR ɑɚ bar/ NG ŋ king/ SH ʃ ship/ ZH ʒ vision/
TH θ thirty/ TH ð then/ CH tʃ child/ J dʒ just/ For complete list, see Key to Pronunciation p. 2.

103

esill AY-suhl ['eɪ-səl] or EE-__ ['i-__]

especial i-SPEHSH-uhl [ɪ-'spɛʃ-əl] scans to __-__-ee-uhl [__-__-i-əl] @ *HAM* IV, 7, 97

esperance EHS-puh-ruhns ['ɛs-pə-rəns] scans to ___-___-ruhns-ay [___-___-rəns-eɪ] @ *1HIV* V, 2, 96

espial i-SPEYE-uhl [ɪ-'spaɪ-əl] scans to I-speyel ['ɪ-spaɪl] @ *1HVI* I, 4, 8

espouse i-SPOWZ [ɪ-'spaʊz]

espy i-SPEYE [ɪ-'spaɪ]

esquire EHS-kweyer ['ɛs-kwaɪɚ] scans to ehs-KWEYER [ɛs-'kwaɪɚ] e.g. @ *HV* I, 1, 14

Essex, Earl of *(KJ)* EHS-iks ['ɛs-ɪks]

estridge EHS-trij ['ɛs-trɪʤ]

eterne i-TERN [ɪ-'tɝn]

eternized i-TER-neyezd [ɪ-'tɝ-naɪzd]

Ethiop / Ethiope EE-thee-ohp ['i-θi-oʊp] scans to EE-thyohp ['i-θjoʊp] e.g. @ *PER* II, 2, 20

Ethiopian always scans to EE-thee-OH-pyuhn [i-θi-'oʊ-pjən]

Etna EHT-nuh ['ɛt-nə]

Eton EE-t(uh)n ['i-tn̩]

eunuch YOO-nuhk ['ju-nək]

Euphrates scans to YOO-fray-teez ['ju-freɪ-tiz]

Euriphile yoo-RI-fi-lee [jʊ-'rɪ-fɪ-li]

Europa yoo-ROH-puh [jʊ-'roʊ-pə]

Evans, Sir Hugh *(MW)* EH-vuhnz HYOO ['ɛ-vənz] [hju]

evitate EH-vi-tayt ['ɛ-vɪ-teɪt]

ewe Y$\overline{OO}$ [ju]

ewer Y$\overline{OO}$-er ['ju-ɚ] scans to Y$\overline{OO}$R ['juɚ] e.g. @ *SHR* II, 1, 350

exact (adj) ig-ZAAKT [ɪg-'zækt] scans to EHG-zaakt ['ɛg-zækt] e.g. @ *1HIV* IV, 1, 46

excess always scans to ik-SEHS [ɪk-'sɛs]

exchequer ehks-CHEHK-er [ɛks-'tʃɛk-ɚ]

exclaim (n) always scans to iks-KLAYM [ɪks-'kleɪm]

execrable EHKS-i-kruh-b(uh)l ['ɛks-ɪ-krə-bļ]

execrations EHK-si-KRAY-shuhnz [ɛk-sɪ-'kreɪ-ʃənz]

executor ig-ZEHK-yuh-ter [ɪg-'zɛk-jə-tɚ] scans to EHK-si-ky$\overline{oo}$-ter ['ɛk-sɪ-kju-tɚ] @ *HV* I, 2, 203

exequies EHKS-uh-kweez ['ɛks-ə-kwiz]

Exeter EHK-si-ter ['ɛk-sɪ-tɚ] scans to EHK-ster ['ɛk-stɚ] Exeter, Duke of *(HV)* scans @ IV, 8, 52

exhale ehks-HAYL [ɛks-'heɪl]

exhort ig-ZAWRT [ɪg-'zɔɚt]

exigent EHK-suh-juhnt ['ɛk-sə-dʒənt]

exile EHK-seyel ['ɛk-saɪl] scans to ehg-ZEYEL [ɛg-'zaɪl] e.g. @ *2GEN* III, 2, 3

exorciser EHK-sawr-seyez-er ['ɛk-sɔɚ-saɪz-ɚ]

expiate EHKS-pee-ayt ['ɛks-pi-eɪt]

exploit (n) always scans to ehks-PLOYT [ɛks-'plɔɪt]

expositor ehks-PAHZ-i-tawr [ɛks-'pɑz-ɪ-tɔɚ]

EE i be/ I ɪ bit/ EH ɛ bet/ AA æ bat/ $\overline{OO}$ u boot / $\overline{OO}$ ʊ book/ AW ɔ bought/ AH ɑ father/ ER ɝ bird/ UH ʌ cup/ AY eɪ bay/ EYE aɪ bite/ OY ɔɪ boy/ OH oʊ boat/ OW ɑʊ how/ Y$\overline{OO}$ ɪu duke/ EAR ɪɚ beer/ AIR ɛɚ bear/ $\overline{OO}$R ʊɚ tour/ AWR ɔɚ bore/ AHR ɑɚ bar/ NG ŋ king/ SH ʃ ship/ ZH ʒ vision/ TH θ thirty/ <u>TH</u> ð then/ CH tʃ child/ J dʒ just/ For complete list, see Key to Pronunciation p. 2.

expostulate ik-SPAHS-chuh-layt [ɪk-'spɑs-tʃə-leɪt]

expostulation ik-SPAHS-chuh-LAY-shuhn [ɪk-spɑs-tʃə-'leɪ-ʃən]

exposture ik-SPAHS-cher [ɪk-'spɑs-tʃɚ] or __-SPOHS-__ [__-'spoʊs-__]

expressure ehks-PREH-sho͞or [ɛks-'prɛ-ʃʊɚ]

expulsed ehks-PUHLST [ɛks-'pʌlst]

exquisite ik-SKWIZ-it [ɪk-'skwɪz-ɪt] scans to EHK-skwi-zit ['ɛk-skwɪ-zɪt] e.g. @ *R&J* I, 1, 227

exsufflicate ik-SUHF-li-kit [ɪk-'sʌf-lɪ-kɪt]

extant EHK-stuhnt ['ɛk-stənt] or possibly ehk-STAANT [ɛk-'stænt] in prose

extemporal ik-STEHM-puh-ruhl [ɪk-'stɛm-pə-rəl] scans to ___-STEHM-pruhl [___-'stɛm-prəl] e.g. @ *1HVI* III, 1, 6

extempore ik-STEHM-puh-ree [ɪk-'stɛm-pə-ri] scans to ___-STEHM-pree [___-'stɛm-pri] @ *SHR* II, 1, 265

exteriorly ehks-TEAR-yer-lee [ɛks-'tɪɚ-jɚ-li]

extermined ehks-TER-mind [ɛks-'tɝ-mɪnd]

extern scans to ik-STERN [ɪk-'stɝn]

extirp ehk-STERP [ɛk-'stɝp]

extirpate scans to iks-TER-payt [ɪks-'tɝ-peɪt]

Exton, Sir Pierce of *(RII)* EHKS-t(uh)n PEARS ['ɛks-tn̩] [pɪɚs]

extraordinary always scans to EHK-struh-AWR-din-eh-ree [ɛk-strə-'ɔɚ-dɪn-ɛ-ri] possibly the same in prose

extraught ehks-TRAWT [ɛks-'trɔt]

extreme ik-STREEM [ɪk-'strim] scans to EHK-streem ['ɛk-strim] e.g. @ *COR* IV, 5, 70

eyases EYE-uhs-iz ['aɪ-əs-ɪz]

eyas-musket EYE-uhs-MUHS-kit ['aɪ-əs-mʌs-kɪt]

eyed EYED [aɪd]

eyne EYEN [aɪn]

eyrie EH-ree ['ɛ-ri] or I-ree ['ɪ-ri]

Fabian *(12th)* FAY-bee-uhn ['feɪ-bi-ən] scans to FAY-byuhn ['feɪ-bjən] @ V, 1, 305

facinerious FAAS-i-NI-ree-uhs [fæs-ɪ-'nɪ-ri-əs]

factionary FAAK-shuhn-eh-ree ['fæk-ʃən-ɛ-ri]

factious FAAK-shuhs ['fæk-ʃəs]

fadge FAAJ [fædʒ]

fagot / faggot FAAG-uht ['fæg-ət]

fain FAYN [feɪn]

falc'ner FAWLK-ner ['fɔlk-nɚ] or FAALK-__ ['fælk-__]

falchion FAWL-chuhn ['fɔl-tʃən]

Falconbridge FAW-kuhn-brij ['fɔ-kən-brɪdʒ] or FAWL-__-__ ['fɔl-__-__] or FAAL-__-__ ['fæl-__-__] or FAHL-__-__ ['fɑl-__-__]
　　Falconbridge, Jacques JAY-kweez ['dʒeɪ-kwiz]

falconer FAWL-kuhn-er ['fɔl-kən-ɚ] or FAAL-__-__ ['fæl-__-__]

fallow FAAL-oh ['fæl-oʊ]

Falstaff FAWL-staaf ['fɔl-stæf]
　　Falstaff, Sir John *(1HIV, 2HIV, MW)*
　　Falstaff, Sir John *(1HVI)*
　　Falstaff's Page *(2HIV)*

EE i be/ I ɪ bit/ EH ɛ bet/ AA æ bat/ OO u boot / OO ʊ book/ AW ɔ bought/ AH ɑ father/ ER ɝ bird/
UH ʌ cup/ AY eɪ bay/ EYE aɪ bite/ OY ɔɪ boy/ OH oʊ boat/ OW aʊ how/ YOO ɪu duke/ EAR ɪɚ
beer/ AIR ɛɚ bear/ OOR ʊɚ tour/ AWR ɔɚ bore/ AHR ɑɚ bar/ NG ŋ king/ SH ʃ ship/ ZH ʒ vision/
TH θ thirty/ TH ð then/ CH tʃ child/ J dʒ just/ For complete list, see Key to Pronunciation p. 2.

familiar fuh-MIL-yer [fə-'mɪl-jɚ] scans to __-__-ee-er
[__-__-i-ɚ] e.g. @ *R&J* III, 3, 6

fancy-monger FAAN-see-MUHNG-ger ['fæn-si-mʌŋ-gɚ] or
__-__-MAHNG-__ [__-__-maŋ-__]

fanes FAYNZ [feɪnz]

Fang *(2HIV)* FAANG [fæŋ]

fantasticoes faan-TAAS-ti-kohz [fæn-'tæs-tɪ-kouz]

fap FAAP [fæp]

farborough FAHR-buh-roh ['fɑɚ-bə-rou]

fardel FAHR-d(uh)l ['fɑɚ-dl̩]

farewell fair-WEHL [fɛɚ-'wɛl] scans to FAIR-wehl ['fɛɚ-wɛl]
e.g. @ *RII* II, 2, 8

farre FAHR [fɑɚ]

farthingale FAHR-<u>th</u>ing-gayl ['fɑɚ-ðɪŋ-geɪl] or __-<u>th</u>in-__
[__-ðɪn-__]

farthings FAHR-<u>th</u>ingz ['fɑɚ-ðɪŋz]

fashion-monger FAA-shuhn-MUHNG-ger ['fæ-ʃən-mʌŋ-gɚ]
or __-__-MAHNG-__ [__-__-maŋ-__]

fashion-monging FAA-shuhn-MUHNG-ging ['fæ-ʃən-'mʌŋ-
gɪŋ] or __-__-MAHNG-__ [__-__-maŋ-__]

fathom FAA-<u>th</u>uhm ['fæ-ðəm]

fatigate FAA-ti-gayt ['fæ-tɪ-geɪt]

Faulconbridge FAWL-kuhn-brij ['fɔl-kən-brɪdʒ] or
FAW-__-__ ['fɔ-__-__]
Faulconbridge, Lady *(KJ)*
Faulconbridge, Robert *(KJ)*

Faustuses FOWS-tuhs-iz ['fɑus-təs-ɪz]

fay FAY [feɪ]

fealty FEE-uhl-tee ['fi-əl-ti] scans to FEEL-tee ['fil-ti]
    e.g. @ *RII* V, 2, 45

feat FEET [fit]

featly FEET-lee ['fit-li]

fecks FEHKS [fɛks]

fedary FEHD-uh-ree ['fɛd-ə-ri] scans to FEHD-ree ['fɛd-ri]
    @ *CYM* III, 2, 21

federary scans to FEHD-ruh-ree ['fɛd-rə-ri] or FEHD-uh-ree
    ['fɛd-ə-ri]

Feeble, Francis *(2HIV)* FEE-b(uh)l FRAAN-sis ['fi-bḷ]
    ['fræn-sɪs]

feeze FEEZ [fiz]

feign FAYN [feɪn]

felicitate fi-LIS-i-tayt [fɪ-'lɪs-ɪ-teɪt]

felicity fi-LIS-i-tee [fɪ-'lɪs-ɪ-ti]

fellies FEH-leez ['fɛ-liz]

fen FEHN [fɛn]

fennel FEHN-uhl ['fɛn-əl]

fenny FEHN-ee ['fɛn-i]

Fenton *(MW)* FEHN-tuhn ['fɛn-tən]

Fer see "le Fer"

Ferdinand FER-di-naand ['fɝ-dɪ-nænd]
    Ferdinand *(TEMP)*
    Ferdinand, King of Navarre *(LLL)* nuh-VAHR [nə-'vɑɚ]

fere FEAR [fɪɚ]

EE i be/ I ɪ bit/ EH ɛ bet/ AA æ bat/ OO u boot / OO ʊ book/ AW ɔ bought/ AH ɑ father/ ER ɝ bird/
UH ʌ cup/ AY eɪ bay/ EYE aɪ bite/ OY ɔɪ boy/ OH oʊ boat/ OW aʊ how/ YOO ɪu duke/ EAR ɪɚ
beer/ AIR ɛɚ bear/ OOR ʊɚ tour/ AWR ɔɚ bore/ AHR ɑɚ bar/ NG ŋ king/ SH ʃ ship/ ZH ʒ vision/
TH θ thirty/ TH ð then/ CH ʧ child/ J ʤ just/ For complete list, see Key to Pronunciation p. 2.

Ferrara fuh-RAH-ruh [fə-'rɑ-rə]

Ferrers scans to feh-RERZ [fɛ-'rɝz]

ferret FEH-rit ['fɛ-rɪt]

ferula FAIR-yōō-luh ['fɛɚ-ju-lə]

fervency FER-vuhn-see ['fɝ-vən-si]

fescue FEHS-kyōō ['fɛs-kju]

Feste *(12th)* FEHS-tee ['fɛs-ti]

festinate FEHS-ti-nit ['fɛs-tɪ-nɪt]

festinately FEHS-ti-nit-lee ['fɛs-tɪ-nɪt-li]

fet FEHT [fɛt]

fetlocks FEHT-lahks ['fɛt-lɑks]

fetter FEHT-er ['fɛt-ɚ]

feverous always scans to FEEV-ruhs ['fiv-rəs]

fia FEE-uh ['fi-ə]

Fidele fi-DAY-lee [fɪ-'deɪ-li] or ___-DEE-___ [___-'di-___]

fidiused FID-ee-uhst ['fɪd-i-əst]

fie FEYE [faɪ]

Fiennes, James, Lord Say *(2HVI)* FEYENZ [faɪnz]

fife / Fife FEYEF [faɪf]

figo FI-goh ['fɪ-goʊ] or FEE-___ ['fi-___]

filberts FIL-berts ['fɪl-bɚts]

filch FILCH [fɪltʃ]

filed FEYELD [faɪld]

filial always scans to FIL-yuhl ['fɪl-jəl]

fillet FIL-it ['fɪl-ɪt]

fillip FIL-ip ['fɪl-ɪp]

finical FIN-i-k(uh)l ['fɪn-ɪ-kl̩]

finny FIN-ee ['fɪn-i]

Finsbury possibly scans to **FINZ**-bree ['fɪnz-bri] or finz-**BREE** [fɪnz-'bri]

firago fuh-**RAH**-goh [fə-'rɑ-goʊ]

fire FEYER [faɪɚ] scans to **FEYE**-er ['faɪ-ɚ] e.g. @ *JC* III, 1, 171 first citation

firk FERK [fɝk]

fishmonger FISH-muhng-ger ['fɪʃ-məŋ-gɚ] or ___-mahng-___ [___-mɑŋ-___]

fisnomy FIZ-nuh-mee ['fɪz-nə-mi]

fistula FIS-chuh-luh ['fɪs-tʃə-lə]

fitchew FITCH-o͞o ['fɪtʃ-u]

Fitzwater, Lord *(RII)* always scans to fits-**WAWT**-er [fɪts-'wɔt-ɚ]

fixure FIK-sher ['fɪk-ʃɚ]

flagon FLAAG-uhn ['flæg-ən]

flamen FLAY-muhn ['fleɪ-mən]

Flaminius *(TIMON)* fluh-**MIN**-ee-uhs [flə-'mɪn-i-əs]

Flanders FLAAN-derz ['flæn-dɚz]

Flavina fluh-**VEE**-nuh [flə-'vi-nə]

Flavius FLAY-vee-uhs ['fleɪ-vi-əs] scans to **FLAY**-vyuhs ['fleɪ-vjəs]

EE i be/ I ɪ bit/ EH ɛ bet/ AA æ bat/ O͞O u boot / O͝O ʊ book/ AW ɔ bought/ AH ɑ father/ ER ɝ bird/ UH ʌ cup/ AY eɪ bay/ EYE aɪ bite/ OY ɔɪ boy/ OH oʊ boat/ OW aʊ how/ YO͞O ɪu duke/ EAR ɪɚ beer/ AIR ɛɚ bear/ O͞OR ʊɚ tour/ AWR ɔɚ bore/ AHR ɑɚ bar/ NG ŋ king/ SH ʃ ship/ ZH ʒ vision/ TH θ thirty/ TH ð then/ CH tʃ child/ J ʤ just/ For complete list, see Key to Pronunciation p. 2.

Flavius *(JC)* scans @ V, 3, 108

Flavius *(TIMON)*

Fleance *(MAC)* **FLEE**-uhns ['fli-əns] possibly scans to FLEENS [flins] @ III, 1, 35

fledge FLEHJ [flɛʤ]

fleer FLEAR [flɪɚ]

fleshment FLEHSH-muhnt ['flɛʃ-mənt]

fleshmonger FLEHSH-muhng-ger ['flɛʃ-məŋ-gɚ] or ___-mahng-___ [___-maŋ-___]

fleur-de-luce FLER-duh-lōōs ['flɝ-də-lus] or **FLOOR**-__-__ ['flʊɚ-__-__]

flewed FLOOD [flud]

flexure FLEHK-sher ['flɛk-ʃɚ]

Flibbertigibbet FLI-ber-tee-JI-bit ['flɪ-bɚ-ti-ʤɪ-bɪt]

Flint FLINT [flɪnt]

flirt-gills FLERT-jilz ['flɝt-ʤɪlz]

Florence FLAW-rehns ['flɔ-rɛns] or **FLAH**-___ ['fla-___] Florence, Duke of *(AW)*

Florentine FLAW-ruhn-teen ['flɔ-rən-tin] or __-__-teyen [__-__-taɪn]

Florentius flaw-REHN-shuhs [flɔ-'rɛn-ʃəs]

Florizel *(WT)* FLAW-ri-zehl ['flɔ-rɪ-zɛl] or **FLAH**-__-__ ['fla-__-__]

flote FLOHT [floʊt]

flouriets scans to **FLOW**-rits ['flaʊ-rɪts] @ *MID* IV, 1, 54

flourish FLUH-rish ['flʌ-rɪʃ] or **FLOO**-___ ['flu-___]

flout FLOWT [flaʊt]

flower-de-luce scans to FLOWR-duh-lōōs ['flaʊɚ-də-lus]
e.g. @ *1HVI* I, 1, 80

Fluellen *(HV)* flōō-EHL-in [flu-'ɛl-ɪn]

flurted FLERT-id ['flɝt-ɪd]

Flute, Francis / Thisbe *(MID)* FLŌŌT [flut] THIZ-bee ['θɪz-bi]

fob FAHB [fɑb]

foh FOH [foʊ]

foin FOYN [fɔɪn]

foison FOY-zuhn ['fɔɪ-zən]

Foix FOYZ [fɔɪz]

font FAHNT [fɑnt]

Fontybell FAHN-ti-behl ['fɑn-tɪ-bɛl]

Fool FŌŌL [ful]
  Fool *(LEAR)*
  Fool *(TIMON)*

fopp'ry FAHP-ree ['fɑp-ri]

fopped FAHPT [fɑpt]

foppery FAHP-uh-ree ['fɑp-ə-ri]

for't FAWRT [fɔrt]

forbade fer-BAAD [fɚ-'bæd] or fawr-___ [fɔɚ-___]

Ford FAWRD [fɔɚd]
  Ford *(MW)*
  Ford, Mistress *(MW)*

fordo fawr-DŌŌ [fɔɚ-'du]

113

forepast FAWR-paast ['fɔɚ-pæst]

fore-spurrer fawr-SPE(r)-rer [fɔɚ-'spɜ-rɚ]

Forester *(LLL)* FAW-ri-ster ['fɔ-rɪ-stɚ] or FAH-__-__ ['fɑ-__-__]

forfeit FAWR-fit ['fɔɚ-fɪt]

forfeiture FAWR-fi-cher ['fɔɚ-fɪ-tʃɚ]

forgetive FAWR-ji-tiv ['fɔɚ-ʤɪ-tɪv]

forlorn fer-LAWRN [fɚ-'lɔɚ-n] scans to FAWR-lawrn ['fɔɚ-lɔɚ-n] e.g. @ *1HVI* I, 2, 19

fornicatress FAWR-ni-KAY-tris [fɔɚ-nɪ-'keɪ-trɪs]

Forres FAW-ris ['fɔ-rɪs] or FAH-___ ['fɑ-___]

Forrest FAW-rist ['fɔ-rist] or FAH-___ ['fɑ-___]

forset-seller FAWR-sit-sehl-er ['fɔɚ-sɪt-sɛl-ɚ] some editions "faucet" FAW-sit ['fɔ-sɪt]

forsooth fawr-SOOTH [fɔɚ-'suθ]

forswear fawr-SWAIR [fɔɚ-'swɛɚ]

forsworn fawr-SWAWRN [fɔɚ-'swɔɚ-n]

Fortinbras *(HAM)* FAWR-tin-brahs ['fɔɚ-tɪn-brɑs] or ___-___-braas [___-___-bræs]

fortnight FAWRT-neyet ['fɔɚt-naɪt]

fortune / Fortune FAWR-chuhn ['fɔɚ-tʃən]

forwhy fawr-HWEYE [fɔɚ-'hwaɪ]

foughten FAW-t(uh)n ['fɔ-tɳ]

foutra FOO-truh ['fu-trə]

fracted FRAAK-tid ['fræk-tɪd]

frampold FRAAM-pohld ['fræm-poʊld]

frampul FRAAM-puhl ['fræm-pəl]

France FRAANS [fræns]
    France, King of *(AW)*
    France, King of *(LEAR)*
    France, Princess of *(LLL)*

Frances / Francis FRAAN-sis ['fræn-sɪs]
    Francis *(1HIV)*
    Francis, Friar *(MADO)* FREYER [fraɪɚ] scans to
        FREYE-er ['fraɪ-ɚ] e.g. @ V, 4, 18

Francisca *(MM)* fraan-SIS-kuh [fræn-'sɪs-kə]

Francisco fraan-SIS-koh [fræn-'sɪs-koʊ]
    Francisco *(HAM)*
    Francisco *(TEMP)*

Frankford FRAANGK-ferd ['fræŋk-fɚd]

Frateretto FRAA-tuh-REH-toh [fræ-tə-'rɛ-toʊ]

fraught FRAWT [frɔt]

fraughtage FRAW-tij ['frɔ-tɪʤ]

fray FRAY [freɪ]

freelier FREE-lee-er ['fri-li-ɚ]

frequent (v) always scans to free-KWEHNT [fri-'kwɛnt]

fret FREHT [frɛt]

Friar FREYER [fraɪɚ] scans to **FREYE**-er ['fraɪ-ɚ]
    e.g. @ *R&J* V, 2, 1

Friar Penker scans to **FREYE**-er **PEHNG**-ker ['fraɪ-ɚ]
    ['pɛŋ-kɚ]

frieze FREEZ [friz]

EE i be/ I ɪ bit/ EH ɛ bet/ AA æ bat/ OO u boot / OO ʊ book/ AW ɔ bought/ AH ɑ father/ ER ɝ bird/
UH ʌ cup/ AY eɪ bay/ EYE aɪ bite/ OY ɔɪ boy/ OH oʊ boat/ OW aʊ how/ YOO ɪu duke/ EAR ɪɚ
beer/ AIR ɛɚ bear/ OOR ʊɚ tour/ AWR ɔɚ bore/ AHR ɑɚ bar/ NG ŋ king/ SH ʃ ship/ ZH ʒ vision/
TH θ thirty/ TH ð then/ CH ʧ child/ J ʤ just/ For complete list, see Key to Pronunciation p. 2.

frippery FRIP-uh-ree ['frɪp-ə-ri]

friskins FRIS-kinz ['frɪs-kɪnz]

Frogmore FRAHG-mawr ['frɑg-mɔɚ]

Froissart FROY-sahrt ['frɔɪ-sɑɚt]

frontier always scans to FRUHN-tear ['frʌn-tɪɚ]

frontlet FRUHNT-lit ['frʌnt-lɪt]

Froth *(MM)* FRAWTH [frɔθ] or FRAHTH [frɑθ]

froward FROH-werd ['froʊ-wɚd]

fructful FRO͞OKT-fool ['frukt-fʊl] or FRUHKT-___
['frʌkt-___]

fructify FRUHK-tuh-feye ['frʌk-tə-faɪ] or FRO͞OK-__-__
['frʊk-__-__]

frush FRUHSH [frʌʃ]

frustrate (adj) (ineffectual) FRUHS-trayt ['frʌs-treɪt]

fubbed FUHBD [fʌbd]

fullam FO͞OL-uhm ['fʊl-əm]

fulsome FO͞OL-suhm ['fʊl-səm]

Fulvia FO͞OL-vee-uh ['fʊl-vi-ə] scans to FO͞OL-vyuh
['fʊl-vjə] e.g. @ *A&C* I, 2, 103

fumiter FYO͞O-mi-ter ['fju-mɪ-tɚ]

fumitory FYO͞O-mi-taw-ree ['fju-mɪ-tɔ-ri]

funeral FYO͞ON-ruhl ['fjun-rəl] scans to FYO͞O-nuh-ruhl
['fju-nə-rəl] e.g. @ *JC* III, 1, 233

furbish FER-bish ['fɝ-bɪʃ]

furlong FER-lawng ['fɝ-lɔŋ]

Furnival FER-ni-vuhl ['fɝ-nɪ-vəl]

furze FERZ [fɝz]

fust FUHST [fʌst]

fustian FUHS-chuhn ['fʌs-tʃən] or ___-tee-uhn [___-ti-ən]

fustilarian FUHS-ti-LAA-ree-uhn [fʌs-tɪ-'læ-ri-ən]

fusty FUHS-tee ['fʌs-ti]

fut FUHT [fʌt] or FŌOT [fʊt]

gabble GAAB-uhl ['gæb-əl]

gaberdine GAAB-er-deen ['gæb-ɚ-din]

gad GAAD [gæd]

Gadshill *(1HIV)* GAADZ-hil ['gædz-hɪl]

gage GAYJ [geɪdʒ]

gainsaid gayn-SAYD [geɪn-'seɪd] or ___-SEHD [___-'sɛd]

gainsay gayn-SAY [geɪn-'seɪ]

Galathe GAAL-uh-thee ['gæl-ə-θi]

Galen GAY-lin ['geɪ-lɪn]

gall GAWL [gɔl]

gallant GAAL-uhnt ['gæl-ənt] possibly scans to guh-LAHNT [gə-'lɑnt] @ *RII* V, 3, 15

Gallia GAAL-ee-uh ['gæl-i-ə] scans to GAAL-yuh ['gæl-jə] e.g. @ *HV* I, 2, 217

Gallian always scans to GAAL-yuhn ['gæl-jən]

galliard GAAL-yerd ['gæl-jɚd]

galliasses GAAL-ee-aas-iz ['gæl-i-æs-ɪz] possibly scans to GAAL-yuhs-iz ['gæl-jəs-ɪz] @ *SHR* II, 1, 380

EE i be/ I ɪ bit/ EH ɛ bet/ AA æ bat/ ŌO u boot / ŌO ʊ book/ AW ɔ bought/ AH ɑ father/ ER ɝ bird/ UH ʌ cup/ AY eɪ bay/ EYE aɪ bite/ OY ɔɪ boy/ OH oʊ boat/ OW aʊ how/ YŌO ɪu duke/ EAR ɪɚ beer/ AIR ɛɚ bear/ ŌOR ʊɚ tour/ AWR ɔɚ bore/ AHR ɑɚ bar/ NG ŋ king/ SH ʃ ship/ ZH ʒ vision/ TH θ thirty/ TH ð then/ CH tʃ child/ J dʒ just/ For complete list, see Key to Pronunciation p. 2.

117

gallimaufry GAAL-i-MAW-free [gæl-ɪ-'mɔ-fri] or __-__-MAH-__ [__-__-'mɑ-__]

Galloway GAAL-uh-way ['gæl-ə-weɪ]

gallowglasses GAAL-oh-glaas-iz ['gæl-ou-glæs-ɪz]

gallowses GAAL-ohz-iz ['gæl-ouz-ɪz]

Gallus *(A&C)* GAAL-uhs ['gæl-əs]

Gam GAAM [gæm]

gambol GAAM-b(uh)l ['gæm-bl̩]

gamester GAYM-ster ['geɪm-stɚ]

gammon GAAM-uhn ['gæm-ən]

gamut GAAM-uht ['gæm-ət]

gangrened GAANG-greend ['gæŋ-grind]

Ganymede GAAN-i-meed ['gæn-ɪ-mid]

gaol JAYL [ʤeɪl]

gaoler / Gaoler JAYL-er ['ʤeɪl-ɚ]
Gaoler *(2NOB)*
Gaoler *(WT)*
Gaoler's Daughter *(2NOB)*

gaping GAY-ping ['geɪ-pɪŋ]

garboils GAHR-boylz ['gɑɚ-bɔɪlz]

Gardiner, afterward Bishop of Winchester *(HVIII)*
GAHRD-ner ['gɑɚd-nɚ]

Gargantua gahr-GAAN-choo-uh [gɑɚ-'gæn-tʃu-ə]

Gargrave, Sir Thomas *(1HVI)* GAHR-grayv ['gɑɚ-greɪv]

gaskins GAAS-kinz ['gæs-kɪnz]

gasted GAAST-id ['gæst-ɪd]

118

gastness GAAST-nis ['gæst-nɪs]

gat GAAT [gæt]

gaud see "gawd"

Gaul GAWL [gɔl]

Gaultier GAW-ter ['gɔ-tɚ]

Gaultree GAWL-tree ['gɔl-tri]

gaunt / Gaunt GAWNT [gɔnt]

gauntlet GAWNT-lit ['gɔnt-lɪt]

gawd GAWD [gɔd]

Gawsey GAW-zee ['gɔ-zi] or ___-see [__-si]

geck GEHK [gɛk]

gelt GEHLT [gɛlt]

geminy JEHM-i-neye ['ʤɛm-ɪ-naɪ]

gennets JEHN-its ['ʤɛn-ɪts]

Genoa JEHN-oh-uh ['ʤɛn-oʊ-ə]

Geoffrey JEHF-ree ['ʤɛf-ri]

George Alow uh-LOH [ə-'loʊ]

George, Duke of Clarence *(RIII)* JAWRJ KLAA-ruhns [ʤɔɚʤ] ['klæ-rəns]

Gerard de Narbon juh-RAHRD duh-NAHR-buhn [ʤə-'raɚd] [də-'naɚ-bən]

germain JER-muhn ['ʤɝ-mən]

germane jer-MAYN [ʤɚ-'meɪn]

---

germans JER-muhnz ['ʤɝ-mənz]

Gertrude *(HAM)* GER-trōōd ['gɝ-trud]

gests JEHSTS [ʤɛsts]

Ghost of Hamlet's Father *(HAM)* GOHST [goʊst]

gi'in GIN [gɪn]

gib GIB [gɪb]

gibber JIB-er ['ʤɪb-ɚ]

gibbet JIB-it ['ʤɪb-ɪt]

gib-cat GIB-kaat ['gɪb-kæt]

gibe JEYEB [ʤaɪb]

giber JEYEB-er ['ʤaɪb-ɚ]

gibing JEYEB-ing ['ʤaɪb-ɪŋ]

gig GIG [gɪg]

giglet / giglot GIG-lit ['gɪg-lɪt]

gild GILD [gɪld]

Gilliams GIL-yuhmz ['gɪl-jəmz]

Gillian scans to JIL-yuhn ['ʤɪl-jən]

gillyvors JIL-ee-vawrz ['ʤɪl-i-vɔɚz]

gimmaled GIM-uhld ['gɪm-əld] or JIM-___ ['ʤɪm-___]

gimmors JIM-erz ['ʤɪm-ɚz]

gin (n) (a snare or trap) JIN [ʤɪn]

gin (v) (to begin) GIN [gɪn]

ging GING [gɪŋ]

Ginn JIN [ʤɪn]

Giraldo juh-**RAHL**-doh [ʤə-'rɑl-doʊ] or __-**RAAL**-__
[__-'ræl-__]

girt GERT [gɝt]

Gis JIS [ʤɪs]

Glamis **GLAHM**-is ['glɑm-ɪs] possibly scans to **GLAHMZ**
[glɑmz] e.g. @ *MAC* I, 5, 20

glanders **GLAAN**-derz ['glæn-dəz]

Glansdale, Sir William *(1HVI)* **GLAANZ**-d(uh)l ['glænz-dl̩]

gleek GLEEK [glik]

Glendower **GLEHN**-dow-er ['glɛn-dɑʊ-ə] scans to **GLEHN**-
dowr ['glɛn-dɑʊə] or glehn-**DOWR** [glɛn-'dɑʊə]
Glendower, Owen *(1HIV)* scans to first syllable stress
e.g. @ V, 5, 40; scans to second syllable stress e.g.
@ I, 3, 101

glikes GLEYEKS [glaɪks]

glister **GLIS**-ter ['glɪs-tə]

globy **GLOH**-bee ['gloʊ-bi]

glose GLOHZ [gloʊz]

Gloucester **GLAHS**-ter ['glɑs-tə] scans to **GLAHS**-i-ter
['glɑs-ɪ-tə] or **GLAH**-sis-ter ['glɑ-sɪs-tə]
Gloucester, Duchess of *(RII)*
Gloucester, Duke of *(RIII)* scans e.g. @ III, 4, 46
Gloucester, Duke of, Humphrey *(1HVI)* scans e.g. @ I, 3, 6
Gloucester, Earl of *(LEAR)*

Gloucestershire **GLAHS**-ter-sher ['glɑs-tə-ʃə] or ___-___-
shear [___-___-ʃɪə]

gloze GLOHZ [gloʊz]

EE i be/ I ɪ bit/ EH ɛ bet/ AA æ bat/ OO u boot / OO ʊ book/ AW ɔ bought/ AH ɑ father/ ER ɝ bird/
UH ʌ cup/ AY eɪ bay/ EYE aɪ bite/ OY ɔɪ boy/ OH oʊ boat/ OW ɑʊ how/ YOO ɪu duke/ EAR ɪə
beer/ AIR ɛə bear/ OOR ʊə tour/ AWR ɔə bore/ AHR ɑə bar/ NG ŋ king/ SH ʃ ship/ ZH ʒ vision/
TH θ thirty/ TH ð then/ CH ʧ child/ J ʤ just/ For complete list, see Key to Pronunciation p. 2.

gnaw NAW [nɔ]

Gneius NEE-uhs ['ni-əs]

gobbets GAH-bits ['gɑ-bɪts]

Gobbo GAH-boh ['gɑ-boʊ]
    Gobbo, Launcelot *(MVEN)* LAHNS-uh-laht ['lɑns-ə-lɑt]
        scans to **LAHNS**-laht ['lɑns-lɑt] or **LAANS**-___-___
        ['læns-___-___] scans to **LAANS**-___ ['læns-___] or
        LAWNS-___-___ ['lɔns-___-___] scans to **LAWNS**-___
        ['lɔns-___]
    Gobbo, Old *(MVEN)*

God 'ield gahd-EELD [gɑd-'ild]

God be w' you GAHD BEYE YOO [gɑd] [baɪ] [ju] or
    GAHD BWEE YOO [gɑd] [bwi] [ju]

God bye you GAHD BEYE YOO [gɑd] [baɪ] [ju] alternate
    spellings include "God b'uy you"

god-den / God-den gōōd-EHN [gʊd-'ɛn]

Goffe, Matthew *(2HVI)* GAHF [gɑf]

gogs-wouns gahgz-WOONZ [gɑgz-'wunz]

Golgotha GAHL-guh-thuh ['gɑl-gə-θə]

Goliases goh-LEYE-uh-siz [goʊ-'laɪ-ə-sɪz]

Goliath guh-LEYE-uhth [gə-'laɪ-əθ]

gondola GAHN-duh-luh ['gɑn-də-lə]

gondolier gahn-duh-LEAR [gɑn-də-'lɪɚ]

Goneril *(LEAR)* GAHN-uh-ruhl ['gɑn-ə-rəl] scans to
    GAHN-ruhl ['gɑn-rəl] @ I, 1, 82

Gonzago guhn-ZAH-goh [gən-'za-goʊ]

Gonzalo *(TEMP)* guhn-ZAH-loh [gən-'za-loʊ] possibly
    GAHN-zuh-loh ['gɑn-zə-loʊ] @ V, 1, 68

good-den / good den gŏŏd-DEHN [gʊd-ˈdɛn]

Goodrig GŎŎD-rig [ˈgʊd-rɪg]

Goodwin GŎŎD-win [ˈgʊd-wɪn]

Goodwin Sands GŎŎD-win SAANDZ [ˈgʊd-wɪn] [sændz]

gorbellied GAWR-behl-eed [ˈgɔɚ-bɛl-id]

Gorboduc GAWR-buh-duhk [ˈgɔɚ-bə-dək]

Gordian always scans to GAWR-dyuhn [ˈgɔɚ-djən]

gorget GAWR-jit [ˈgɔɚ-ʤɪt]

Gorgon GAWR-guhn [ˈgɔɚ-gən]

gormandize GAWR-muhn-deyez [ˈgɔɚ-mən-daɪz]

gosling GAHZ-ling [ˈgɑz-lɪŋ]

goss GAWS [gɔs] or GAHS [gɑs]

Goths GAHTHS [gɑθs] except GOHTS [goʊts]
@ *AYL* III, 3, 7 to make the pun with "goats"

gourd GAWRD [gɔɚd]

gouts GOWTS [gaʊts]

Governor of Harfleur *(HV)* HAHR-fler [ˈhɑɚ-flɚ] or
___-flōō [___-flu]

Gower GOW-er [ˈgaʊ-ɚ]
Gower *(2HIV, HV)*
Gower *(PER)*

graff GRAAF [græf]

gramercy gruh-MER-see [grə-ˈmɝ-si]

grandam / Grandam GRAAN-daam [ˈgræn-dæm]

EE i be/ I ɪ bit/ EH ɛ bet/ AA æ bat/ ŌŌ u boot / ŎŎ ʊ book/ AW ɔ bought/ AH ɑ father/ ER ɝ bird/
UH ʌ cup/ AY eɪ bay/ EYE aɪ bite/ OY ɔɪ boy/ OH oʊ boat/ OW aʊ how/ YŌŌ ɪu duke/ EAR ɪɚ
beer/ AIR ɛɚ bear/ ŌŌR ʊɚ tour/ AWR ɔɚ bore/ AHR ɑɚ bar/ NG ŋ king/ SH ʃ ship/ ZH ʒ vision/
TH θ thirty/ <u>TH</u> ð then/ CH ʧ child/ J ʤ just/ For complete list, see Key to Pronunciation p. 2.

123

Grandpré graand-PRAY [grænd-'preɪ]
    Grandpré *(HV)*

grandsire GRAAND-seyer ['grænd-saɪɚ]

Gratiano GRAH-shee-AH-noh [grɑ-ʃi-'ɑ-noʊ] scans to
    ___-SHYAH-noh [__-'ʃjɑ-noʊ]
    Gratiano *(MVEN)* scans @ I, 1, 58
    Gratiano *(OTH)* scans @ V, 2, 365

Gratii GRAY-shee-eye ['greɪ-ʃi-aɪ]

gratillity gruh-TIL-i-tee [grə-'tɪl-ɪ-ti]

gratis GRAA-tis ['græ-tɪs] or GRAH-___ ['grɑ-___]

gratulate GRAA-chuh-layt ['græ-tʃə-leɪt]

Graymalkin gray-MAWL-kin [greɪ-'mɔl-kɪn]

Grecian GREE-shuhn ['gri-ʃən]

Green *(RII)* GREEN [grin]

greensward GREENZ-werd ['grinz-wɚd]

Greenwich GREHN-ich ['grɛn-ɪtʃ] or GRIN-ij ['grɪn-ɪdʒ]

Gregory GREHG-uh-ree ['grɛg-ə-ri] scans to GREHG-ree
    ['grɛg-ri]
    Gregory *(R&J)*
    Gregory de Cassado scans @ *HVIII* III, 2, 321 duh-kuh-
    SAH-doh [də-kə-'sɑ-doʊ]

Gremio *(SHR)* GREHM-ee-oh ['grɛm-i-oʊ] scans to
    GREHM-yoh ['grɛm-joʊ] e.g. @ I, 1, 96

Grey GRAY [greɪ]
    Grey, Lady, afterward Queen Elizabeth *(3HVI)*
    Grey, Lord *(RIII)*
    Grey, Sir Thomas *(HV)*

griffin GRIF-in ['grɪf-ɪn]

Griffith *(HVIII)* GRIF-ith ['grɪf-ɪθ]

griffon GRIF-uhn ['grɪf-ən]

Grindstone GREYEND-stohn ['graɪnd-stoʊn]

gripe GREYEP [graɪp] or GRIP [grɪp]

grise GREYES [graɪs] or GREYEZ [graɪz]

grisly GRIZ-lee ['grɪz-li]

Grissel GRI-s(uh)l ['grɪ-sl̩]

grize GREYEZ [graɪz]

groat GROHT [groʊt]

grovel GRAHV-uhl ['grɑv-əl] or GRUHV-__ ['grʌv-__]

Grumio *(SHR)* GRO͞OM-ee-oh ['grum-i-oʊ] scans to GRO͞OM-yoh ['grum-joʊ] e.g. @ I, 2, 27

guardage GAHR-dij ['gɑɚ-dɪdʒ]

guardant GAHR-d(uh)nt ['gɑɚ-dn̩t]

gudgeon GUHJ-uhn ['gʌdʒ-ən]

guerdon GER-d(uh)n ['gɝ-dn̩]

Guiana gee-AAN-uh [gi-'æn-ə] or __-AHN-__ [__-'ɑn-__]

Guichard GICH-erd ['gɪtʃ-ɚd]

Guiderius / Polydore *(CYM)* scans to gwi-DI-ryuhs [gwɪ-'dɪ-rjəs] called PAH-li-dawr ['pɑ-lɪ-dɔɚ]

Guildenstern *(HAM)* GIL-d(uh)n-stern ['gɪl-dn̩-stɚn]

guilders GIL-derz ['gɪl-dɚz]

Guildhall GILD-hawl ['gɪld-hɔl] @ *RIII* III, 5, 73 with "Mayor" as one syllable; scans to gild-HAWL [gɪld-'hɔl] @ *RIII* III, 5, 102

EE i be/ I ɪ bit/ EH ɛ bet/ AA æ bat/ O͞O u boot / O͝O ʊ book/ AW ɔ bought/ AH ɑ father/ ER ɝ bird/ UH ʌ cup/ AY eɪ bay/ EYE aɪ bite/ OY ɔɪ boy/ OH oʊ boat/ OW aʊ how/ YO͞O ɪu duke/ EAR ɪə beer/ AIR ɛə bear/ O͞OR ʊə tour/ AWR ɔə bore/ AHR ɑə bar/ NG ŋ king/ SH ʃ ship/ ZH ʒ vision/ TH θ thirty/ T̲H̲ ð then/ CH tʃ child/ J dʒ just/ For complete list, see Key to Pronunciation p. 2.

guile GEYEL [gaɪl]

Guilford GIL-ferd ['gɪl-fɚd]
Guilford, Sir Henry *(HVIII)*

Guiltian GIL-tee-uhn ['gɪl-ti-ən] or ___-shee-___ [___-ʃi-___]

guinea GIN-ee ['gɪn-i]

Guinever GWIN-uh-ver ['gwɪn-ə-vɚ] some editions
"Guinevere" GWIN-uh-vear ['gwɪn-ə-vɪɚ]

guise GEYEZ [gaɪz]

gules GYOOLZ [gjulz]

gundello GUHN-duh-loh ['gʌn-də-loʊ]

gurnet GER-nit ['gɝ-nɪt]

Gurney, James *(KJ)* GER-nee ['gɝ-ni]

Guyenne gee-EHN [gi-'ɛn] or geye-___ [gaɪ-___]

Guynes GEEN [gin]

Guysors jee-ZAWRZ [dʒi-'zɔɚz]

gyve JEYEV [dʒaɪv]

H (the letter) AYCH [eɪtʃ]

Haberdasher *(SHR)* HAAB-er-dash-er ['hæb-ɚ-dæʃ-ɚ]

habiliment huh-BIL-uh-muhnt [hə-'bɪl-ə-mənt]

hackney HAAK-nee ['hæk-ni]

Hagar's HAY-gahrz ['heɪ-gɑɚz]

haggard HAAG-erd ['hæg-ɚd]

haggish HAAG-ish ['hæg-ɪʃ]

halberd HAAL-berd ['hæl-bɚd] or HAWL-___ ['hɔl-___]

halcyon always scans to HAAL-syuhn ['hæl-sjən]

126

hale HAYL [heɪl]

halfpence HAY-puhnts ['heɪ-pənts]

halfpenny HAY-puh-nee ['heɪ-pə-ni]

halidom / holidam / holidame HAAL-i-duhm ['hæl-ɪ-dəm]
scans to HAAL-duhm ['hæl-dəm] @ *SHR* V, 2, 104

hallo huh-LOH [hə-'loʊ] or hah-___ [hɑ-___] possibly scans
to HAH-loh ['hɑ-loʊ] @ *12th* I, 5, 258

halloed / hallooed huh-LOHD [hə-'loʊd] or hah-___
[hɑ-___]

halloing huh-LOO-ing [hə-'lu-ɪŋ] or ___-LOH-___
[___-'loʊ-___] scans to HAAL-wing ['hæl-wɪŋ] or
HAHL-___ ['hɑl-___] @ *2GEN* V, 4, 13

Hallowmas HAAL-oh-muhs ['hæl-oʊ-məs] or __-__-maas
[__-__-mæs]

Hames HAAMZ [hæmz] or HAYMZ [heɪmz]

Hamlet *(HAM)* HAAM-lit ['hæm-lɪt]

handkercher HAANG-ker-cher ['hæŋ-kɚ-tʃɚ]

handkerchief HAANG-ker-chif ['hæŋ-kɚ-tʃɪf]

Hannibal HAAN-uh-b(uh)l ['hæn-ə-bl̩]

hap HAAP [hæp]

haply HAAP-lee ['hæp-li]

harbinger HAHR-bin-jer ['hɑɚ-bɪn-dʒɚ]

Harcourt *(2HIV)* HAHR-kawrt ['hɑɚ-kɔɚt] or ___-kert
[___-kɚt]

hardiment HAHR-di-muhnt ['hɑɚ-dɪ-mənt]

EE i be/ I ɪ bit/ EH ɛ bet/ AA æ bat/ OO u boot / OO ʊ book/ AW ɔ bought/ AH ɑ father/ ER ɝ bird/
UH ʌ cup/ AY eɪ bay/ EYE aɪ bite/ OY ɔɪ boy/ OH oʊ boat/ OW aʊ how/ YOO ɪu duke/ EAR ɪə
beer/ AIR ɛə bear/ OOR ʊə tour/ AWR ɔə bore/ AHR ɑə bar/ NG ŋ king/ SH ʃ ship/ ZH ʒ vision/
TH θ thirty/ TH ð then/ CH tʃ child/ J dʒ just/ For complete list, see Key to Pronunciation p. 2.

hardocks HAHR-dahks ['hɑɚ-dɑks]

harebell HAIR-behl ['hɛɚ-bɛl]

Harfleur HAHR-fler ['hɑɚ-flɚ] or ___-floo [___-flu]

Ha'rford-West HAHR-ferd-wehst ['hɑɚ-fɚd-wɛst]

harlot HAHR-luht ['hɑɚ-lət]

harlotry HAHR-luh-tree ['hɑɚ-lə-tri]

Harpier HAHR-pear ['hɑɚ-pɪɚ] or ___-per [___-pɚ]

harrow HAA-roh ['hæ-roʊ]

Hastings HAYS-tingz ['heɪs-tɪŋz]
    Hastings, Lord *(2HIV)*
    Hastings, Lord William *(3HVI, RIII)*

haught HAWT [hɔt]

hautboy HOH-boy ['hoʊ-bɔɪ] or OH-___ ['oʊ-___]

haver (a possessor) HAAV-er ['hæv-ɚ]

havior HAYV-yer ['heɪv-jɚ]

havoc HAAV-uhk ['hæv-ək]

hawthorn HAW-thawrn ['hɔ-θɔɚn]

he'ld HEELD [hild]

hebona huh-BOH-nuh [hə-'boʊ-nə] or __-BUH-__ [__-'bʌ-__]
  or __-BAH-__ [__-'bɑ-__] possibly scans to HEHB-nuh
  ['hɛb-nə] @ *HAM* I, 5, 62 if "cursed" two syllables

Hecate HEHK-it ['hɛk-ɪt] scans to HEHK-i-tee ['hɛk-ɪ-ti]
    Hecate *(MAC)*
    Hecate scans @ *1HVI* III, 2, 64

Hector HEHK-ter ['hɛk-tɚ] or possibly ___-tawr [___-tɔɚ]
    Hector *(T&C)*

Hecuba HEHK-yuh-buh ['hɛk-jə-bə] or __-yoo-__ [__-jʊ-__]
  scans to HEHK-buh ['hɛk-bə] @ *CYM* IV, 2, 313

heigh HAY [heɪ]

heigh-ho HAY-hoh ['heɪ-hoʊ] or hay-HOH [heɪ-'hoʊ]

heighth HEYETTH [haɪtθ] or HEYETH [haɪθ]

heinous HAY-nuhs ['heɪ-nəs]

heir AIR [ɛɚ]

Helen HEHL-in ['hɛl-ɪn]
Helen *(CYM)*
Helen *(T&C)*

Helena HEHL-i-nuh ['hɛl-ɪ-nə]
Helena *(AW)*
Helena *(MID)*

Helenus *(T&C)* HEHL-i-nuhs ['hɛl-ɪ-nəs]

Helias scans to HEEL-yuhs ['hil-jəs] @ *T&C* Pro, 16

Helicanus *(PER)* HEH-li-KAY-nuhs [hɛ-lɪ-'keɪ-nuhs] also
called "Helicane" HEH-li-kayn ['hɛ-lɪ-keɪn] e.g. @ II, Cho, 17

Helicons HEH-li-kuhnz ['hɛ-lɪ-kənz]

Hellespont HEHL-i-spahnt ['hɛl-ɪ-spɑnt]

hempen HEHM-puhn ['hɛm-pən]

henceforth HEHNS-fawrth ['hɛns-fɔɚθ] scans to hehns-
FAWRTH [hɛns-'fɔɚθ] e.g. @ *2HVI* V, 1, 80

Henry HEHN-ree ['hɛn-ri] scans to HEHN-uh-ree ['hɛn-ə-ri]
Henry, Earl of Richmond, afterward Henry VII *(3HVI, RIII)*
scans e.g. @ *3HVI* I, 1, 107
Henry, King IV *(RII, 1HIV, 2HIV)* scans e.g. @ *RII* IV, 1, 112
Henry, King V *(2HIV, HV)*
Henry, King VI *(1HVI, 2HVI, 3HVI)* scans e.g. @ *1HVI*
II, 5, 82

EE i be/ I ɪ bit/ EH ɛ bet/ AA æ bat/ OO u boot / OO ʊ book/ AW ɔ bought/ AH ɑ father/ ER ɚ bird/
UH ʌ cup/ AY eɪ bay/ EYE aɪ bite/ OY ɔɪ boy/ OH oʊ boat/ OW aʊ how/ YOO ɪu duke/ EAR ɪɚ
beer/ AIR ɛɚ bear/ OOR ʊɚ tour/ AWR ɔɚ bore/ AHR ɑɚ bar/ NG ŋ king/ SH ʃ ship/ ZH ʒ vision/
TH θ thirty/ TH ð then/ CH ʧ child/ J ʤ just/ For complete list, see Key to Pronunciation p. 2.

129

Henry, King VIII *(HVIII)*
Henry, Prince of Wales, also called "Hal" *(1HIV, 2HIV)*
Henry, Prince *(KJ)*

hent HEHNT [hɛnt]

Henton see "Nicholas Henton"

Herbert HER-bert ['hɝ-bət]
Herbert, Sir Walter *(RIII)*
Herbert, William, Earl of Pembroke *(3HVI)* PEHM-brŏŏk
['pɛm-brʊk] or PEHM-brohk ['pɛm-broʊk]

Herculean scans to her-KYŌŌL-yuhn [hɝ-'kjul-jən]

Hercules HER-kyŏŏ-leez ['hɝ-kju-liz] scans to HER-kleez
['hɝ-kliz] or her-KLEEZ [hə-'kliz] @ *2NOB* I, 1, 66

Hereford / Herford HER-ferd ['hɝ-fəd]

Herefordshire HER-ferd-sher ['hɝ-fəd-ʃə] or __-__-shear
[__-__-ʃɪə]

heresy HEH-ri-see ['hɛ-rɪ-si]

heretic HEH-ri-tik ['hɛ-rɪ-tɪk]

Hermes HER-meez ['hɝ-miz]

Hermia *(MID)* HER-mee-uh ['hɝ-mi-ə] scans to HER-
myuh ['hɝ-mjə] e.g. @ I, 1, 46

Hermione *(WT)* her-MEYE-i-nee [hə-'maɪ-ɪ-ni] scans to
__-MEYE-nee [__-'maɪ-ni] e.g. @ V, 3, 28

Herne HERN [hɝn]

Hero HI-roh ['hɪ-roʊ]
Hero *(MADO)*

Herod HEH-ruhd ['hɛ-rəd]

Hesperides heh-SPEH-ri-deez [hɛ-'spɛ-rɪ-diz]

Hesperus HEHS-puh-ruhs ['hɛs-pə-rəs]

hest HEHST [hɛst]

hie HEYE [haɪ]

Hiems HEYE-uhmz ['haɪ-əmz]

hight HEYET [haɪt]

highway / high way HEYE-way ['haɪ-weɪ] scans to heye-WAY [haɪ-'weɪ] e.g. @ *MVEN* V, 1, 263

hilding HILD-ing ['hɪld-ɪŋ]

hilloa hi-LOH [hɪ-'loʊ]

hilt HILT [hɪlt]

Hinckley HINGK-lee ['hɪŋk-li]

hind HEYEND [haɪnd]

Hipparchus hi-PAHR-kuhs [hɪ-'pɑɚ-kəs]

Hippolyta hi-PAH-li-tuh [hɪ-'pɑ-lɪ-tə]
Hippolyta *(MID)*
Hippolyta *(2NOB)*

Hiren HEYE-ruhn ['haɪ-rən]

Hirtius HER-shuhs ['hɝ-ʃəs]

Hisperia his-PI-ree-uh [hɪs-'pɪ-ri-ə]

hither HITH-er ['hɪð-ɚ]

hitherward HITH-er-werd ['hɪð-ɚ-wɚd]

hoar HAWR [hɔɚ]

Hob HAHB [hɑb]

Hobbididence HAH-bi-DI-d(uh)ns [hɑ-bɪ-'dɪ-dn̩s]

Hobgoblin HAHB-gahb-lin ['hɑb-gɑb-lɪn]

EE i be/ I ɪ bit/ EH ɛ bet/ AA æ bat/ OO u boot / OO ʊ book/ AW ɔ bought/ AH ɑ father/ ER ɝ bird/ UH ʌ cup/ AY eɪ bay/ EYE aɪ bite/ OY ɔɪ boy/ OH oʊ boat/ OW aʊ how/ YOO ɪu duke/ EAR ɪɚ beer/ AIR ɛɚ bear/ OOR ʊɚ tour/ AWR ɔɚ bore/ AHR ɑɚ bar/ NG ŋ king/ SH ʃ ship/ ZH ʒ vision/ TH θ thirty/ TH ð then/ CH tʃ child/ J dʒ just/ For complete list, see Key to Pronunciation p. 2.

131

hoise HOYZ [hɔɪz]

Holborn HOHL-bern ['hoʊl-bən] or HOH-___ ['hoʊ-___]

holidam / holidame HAAL-i-duhm ['hæl-ɪ-dəm]

holily HOH-li-lee ['hoʊ-lɪ-li]

holla (an interjection) hoh-LAH [hoʊ-'lɑ] or huh-___ [hə-___]

Hollander HAHL-uhn-der ['hɑl-ən-dɚ]

hollo HAH-loh ['hɑ-loʊ] possibly scans to huh-LOH
   [hə-'loʊ] e.g. @ *COR* I, 8, 7

holloed HAHL-ohd ['hɑl-oʊd]

Holmedon HOHM-duhn ['hoʊm-dən]

Holofernes *(LLL)* HAHL-oh-FER-neez [hɑl-oʊ-'fɝ-niz] or
   ___-uh-___-___ [___-ə-___-___]

holp HOHLP [hoʊlp]

Holy-rood scans to HOHL-rōōd ['hoʊl-rud]

homage HAH-mij ['hɑ-mɪdʒ] or AH-___ ['ɑ-___]

homager HAHM-ij-er ['hɑm-ɪdʒ-ɚ] or AHM-___-___
   ['ɑm-___-___]

Hoppedance HAHP-daans ['hɑp-dæns]

Horace HAW-ruhs ['hɔ-rəs]

Horatio *(HAM)* huh-RAY-shyoh [hə-'reɪ-ʃjoʊ] scans to
   ___-___-shee-oh [___-___-ʃi-oʊ] e.g. @ I, 2, 180

Horner, Thomas *(2HVI)* HAWR-ner ['hɔɚ-nɚ]

horologe HAW-ruh-lohj ['hɔ-rə-loʊdʒ]

horrider HAW-ri-der ['hɔ-rɪ-dɚ] or HAH-___-___ ['hɑ-___-___]

Hortensio *(SHR)* hawr-TEHN-shee-oh [hɔɚ-'tɛn-ʃi-oʊ]
   scans to ___-TEHN-shyoh [___-'tɛn-ʃjoʊ] e.g. @ I, 2, 63 later

posing as "Litio" LI-shee-oh [ˈlɪ-ʃi-ou] scans to LI-shyoh [ˈlɪ-ʃjou] e.g. @ II, 1, 60

Hortensius *(TIMON)* hawr-TEHN-see-uhs [hɔɚ-ˈtɛn-si-əs] or possibly scans to ___-TEHN-shyuhs [___-ˈtɛn-ʃjəs]

Hostilius hahs-TIL-ee-uhs [hɑs-ˈtɪl-i-əs] scans to ___-TIL-yuhs [___-ˈtɪl-jəs] @ *COR* II, 3, 235, possibly scans to HAHS-til-___ [ˈhɑs-tɪl-___] @ *TIMON* III, 2, 62

hour OWR [ɑuɚ] scans to OW-er [ˈɑu-ɚ] e.g. @ *CE* III, 1, 122

house (v) HOWZ [hɑuz]

housewifery hows-WEYE-fuh-ree [hɑus-ˈwaɪ-fə-ri] or scans to HOWS-wif-ree [hɑus-ˈwɪf-ri] @ *OTH* II, 1, 112

hovel HUHV-uhl [ˈhʌv-əl] or **HAHV-**___ [ˈhɑv-___]

howbeit always scans to how-BEET [hɑu-ˈbit]

howe'er how-AIR [hɑu-ˈɛɚ]

howlet HOW-lit [ˈhɑu-lɪt]

howsoe'er HOW-soh-air [ˈhɑu-sou-ɛɚ]

howsoever HOW-soh-ehv-er [ˈhɑu-sou-ɛv-ɚ]

howsome'er HOW-suhm-air [ˈhɑu-səm-ɛɚ]

hoxes HAHKS-iz [ˈhɑks-ɪz]

Hoy-day HOY-day [ˈhɔɪ-deɪ]

hugger-mugger HUHG-er-MUHG-er [ˈhʌg-ɚ-mʌg-ɚ]

Hugh Rebeck HYOO REE-behk [hju] [ˈri-bɛk]

humane HYOO-mayn [ˈhju-meɪn] scans to hyoo-MAYN [hju-ˈmeɪn] e.g. @ *MAC* III, 4, 76

humblebee HUHM-buhl-bee [ˈhʌm-bəl-bi]

EE i be/ I ɪ bit/ EH ɛ bet/ AA æ bat/ OO u boot / ŎŎ ʊ book/ AW ɔ bought/ AH ɑ father/ ER ɚ bird/ UH ʌ cup/ AY eɪ bay/ EYE aɪ bite/ OY ɔɪ boy/ OH ou boat/ OW ɑu how/ YOO ɪu duke/ EAR ɪɚ beer/ AIR ɛɚ bear/ OOR ʊɚ tour/ AWR ɔɚ bore/ AHR ɑɚ bar/ NG ŋ king/ SH ʃ ship/ ZH ʒ vision/ TH θ thirty/ TH ð then/ CH tʃ child/ J dʒ just/ For complete list, see Key to Pronunciation p. 2.

Hume, John *(2HVI)* HY$\overline{OO}$M [hjum]

Humphrey HUHM-free [ˈhʌm-fri] scans to HUHM-fuh-ree [ˈhʌm-fə-ri]
    Humphrey of Gloucester, afterward Duke *(2HIV, HV, 1HVI, 2HVI)* scans e.g. @ *2HVI* I, 1, 160 GLAHS-ter [ˈglɑs-tɚ] scans to GLAHS-i-ter [ˈglɑs-ɪ-tɚ] or GLAH-sis-ter [ˈglɑ-sɪs-tɚ] e.g. @ *1HVI* I, 3, 6
    Humphrey, Lord Stafford *(2HVI)* STAAF-erd [ˈstæf-ɚd]

Hungerford HUHNG-ger-ferd [ˈhʌŋ-gɚ-fɚd]

Huntingdon HUHNT-ing-duhn [ˈhʌnt-ɪŋ-dən]

hurricano huh-ri-KAY-noh [hə-rɪ-ˈkeɪ-nou]

huswife / huswive HUHZ-if [ˈhʌz-ɪf] or HUHS-weyef [ˈhʌs-waɪf]

Hybla HEYE-bluh [ˈhaɪ-blə]

Hydra HEYE-druh [ˈhaɪ-drə]

hyen HEYE-uhn [ˈhaɪ-ən] or heye-EEN [haɪ-ˈin]

Hymen HEYE-muhn [ˈhaɪ-mən] or ___-mehn [___-mɛn]
    Hymen *(AYL, 2NOB)*

Hymenaeus HEYE-muh-NEE-uhs [haɪ-mə-ˈni-əs]

hyperbole heye-PER-buh-lee [haɪ-ˈpɝ-bə-li]

hyperbolical HEYE-per-BAH-li-k(uh)l [haɪ-pɚ-ˈbɑ-lɪ-kl̩]

Hyperion heye-PI-ree-uhn [haɪ-ˈpɪ-ri-ən] scans to ___-PI-ryuhn [___-ˈpɪ-rjən] e.g. @ *HAM* III, 4, 57

Hyrcan elides with "th" to form <u>THER</u>-kuhn [ˈðɝ-kən]

Hyrcania scans to her-KAY-nyuh [hɚ-ˈkeɪ-njə]

Hyrcanian always elides with "the" to form <u>ther</u>-KAY-nyuhn [ðɚ-ˈkeɪ-njən]

hyssop HIS-uhp ['hɪs-əp]

I'ld EYELD [aɪld]

i'th ITH [ɪð]

Iachimo *(CYM)* YAHK-i-moh ['jɑk-ɪ-moʊ] scans to YAHK-moh ['jɑk-moʊ] @ II, 5, 14

Iago *(OTH)* ee-AH-goh [i-'ɑ-goʊ] scans to YAH-goh ['jɑ-goʊ] e.g. @ V, 2, 155

Icarus IK-uh-ruhs ['ɪk-ə-rəs]

Iden, Alexander *(2HVI)* EYE-d(uh)n AAL-ig-ZAAN-der ['aɪ-dn̩] [æl-ɪg-'zæn-dɚ]

ides EYEDZ [aɪdz]

idolatrous scans to eye-DAHL-truhs [aɪ-'dɑl-trəs]

ignis fatuus IG-nuhs FAACH-wuhs ['ɪg-nəs] ['fætʃ-wəs]

ignominy IG-nuh-min-ee ['ɪg-nə-mɪn-i]

ignomy IG-nuh-mee ['ɪg-nə-mi]

Ilion IL-ee-uhn ['ɪl-i-ən] scans to IL-yuhn ['ɪl-jən] or possibly EYEL-__-__ ['aɪl-__-__] scans to EYEL-__ ['aɪl-__] e.g. @ T&C II, 2, 109

Ilium IL-ee-uhm ['ɪl-i-əm] scans to IL-yuhm ['ɪl-jəm] or possibly EYEL-__-__ ['aɪl-__-__] scans to EYEL-__ ['aɪl-__] e.g. @ T&C I, 1, 97

illustrate (adj) i-LUHS-trit [ɪ-'lʌs-trɪt]

illustrated (part) scans to i-LUHS-tray-tid [ɪ-'lʌs-treɪ-tɪd]

Illyria i-LI-ree-uh [ɪ-'lɪ-ri-ə] scans to __-LI-ryuh [__-'lɪ-rjə] @ *12th* I, 2, 2

EE i be/ I ɪ bit/ EH ɛ bet/ AA æ bat/ OO u boot / OO ʊ book/ AW ɔ bought/ AH ɑ father/ ER ɝ bird/
UH ʌ cup/ AY eɪ bay/ EYE aɪ bite/ OY ɔɪ boy/ OH oʊ boat/ OW aʊ how/ YOO ɪu duke/ EAR ɪɚ
beer/ AIR ɛɚ bear/ OOR ʊɚ tour/ AWR ɔɚ bore/ AHR ɑɚ bar/ NG ŋ king/ SH ʃ ship/ ZH ʒ vision/
TH θ thirty/ TH ð then/ CH tʃ child/ J dʒ just/ For complete list, see Key to Pronunciation p. 2.

Illyrian i-LEA-ryuhn [ɪ-ˈlɪ-rjən]

imbar im-BAHR [ɪm-ˈbɑɚ]

imbrue im-BR$\overline{OO}$ [ɪm-ˈbru]

immanity i-MAAN-i-tee [ɪ-ˈmæn-ɪ-ti]

immask i-MAASK [ɪ-ˈmæsk]

immoment im-MOH-muhnt [ɪm-ˈmoʊ-mənt]

immure i-MY$\overline{OO}$R [ɪ-ˈmjʊɚ]

Imogen *(CYM)* IM-uh-jin [ˈɪm-ə-ʤɪn] scans to IM-jin [ˈɪm-ʤɪn] e.g. @ V, 1, 10

impare (adj) scans to IM-pair [ˈɪm-pɛɚ]

impartment im-PAHRT-muhnt [ɪm-ˈpɑɚt-mənt]

impasted im-PAYST-id [ɪm-ˈpeɪst-ɪd]

imperator IM-puh-RAH-tawr [ɪm-pə-ˈrɑ-tɚ] or __-__-__-ter [__-__-__-tɚ]

imperceiverant IM-per-SEEV-uh-ruhnt [ɪm-pɚ-ˈsiv-ə-rənt] or __-__-SEHV-__-__ [__-__-ˈsɛv-__-__]

imperious im-PI-ree-uhs [ɪm-ˈpɪ-ri-əs] scans to __-PI-ryuhs [__-ˈpɪ-rjəs] e.g. @ *A&C* IV, 15, 23

impeticos im-PEHT-i-kohz [ɪm-ˈpɛt-ɪ-koʊz]

impious im-PEE-uhs [ɪm-ˈpi-əs] or __-PEYE-__ [__-ˈpaɪ-__] scans to IM-pyuhs [ˈɪm-pjəs] e.g. @ *1HVI* V, 1, 2

implacable im-PLAAK-uh-b(uh)l [ɪm-ˈplæk-ə-bl̩] or __-PLAYK-__-__ [__-ˈpleɪk-__-__]

implorators scans to im-PLAWR-terz [ɪm-ˈplɔɚ-tɚz]

import (n) always scans to im-PAWRT [ɪm-ˈpɔɚt]

import (v) im-PAWRT [ɪm-ˈpɔɚt]

importunacy IM-pawr-TYŌŌN-uh-see [ɪm-pɔɚ-'tɪun-ə-si]
scans to ___-___-TYŌŌN-see [___-___-'tɪun-si]
@ *TIMON* II, 2, 41

importunate im-PAWR-chuh-nit [ɪm-'pɔɚ-tʃə-nɪt]

importune im-PAWR-tyōn [ɪm-'pɔɚ-tɪun] or ___-___-
chuhn [___-___-tʃən]

importunity im-pawr-TYŌŌN-i-tee [ɪm-pɔɚ-'tɪun-ɪ-ti]

imposthume im-PAHS-tyōōm [ɪm-'pɑs-tjum]

imprese IM-preez ['ɪm-priz] or ___-prehs [___-prɛs]

impress (n) im-PREHS [ɪm-'prɛs]

impress (v) im-PREHS [ɪm-'prɛs] scans to IM-prehs
['ɪm-prɛs] @ *LEAR* V, 3, 50

impressure im-PREHSH-er [ɪm-'prɛʃ-ɚ]

imprimis im-PREYE-mis [ɪm-'praɪ-mɪs]

impudency IM-pyuh-duhn-see ['ɪm-pjə-dən-si]

impugn im-PYŌŌN [ɪm-'pjun]

in't INT [ɪnt]

incarnadine in-KAHR-nuh-deyen [ɪn-'kɑɚ-nə-daɪn] or
__-__-__-deen [__-__-__-din]

incidency IN-si-dehn-see ['ɪn-sɪ-dɛn-si]

inclips in-KLIPS [ɪn-'klɪps]

incony in-KUHN-ee [ɪn-'kʌn-i] possibly scans to INK-nee
['ɪnk-ni] or INGK-___ ['ɪŋk-___] @ *LLL* III, 1, 127

Inde IND [ɪnd] in *TEMP*, probably EYEND [aɪnd] in *LLL*,
and either in *AYL*

EE i be/ I ɪ bit/ EH ɛ bet/ AA æ bat/ ŌŌ u boot / ŎŎ ʊ book/ AW ɔ bought/ AH ɑ father/ ER ɝ bird/
UH ʌ cup/ AY eɪ bay/ EYE aɪ bite/ OY ɔɪ boy/ OH oʊ boat/ OW aʊ how/ YŌŌ ɪu duke/ EAR ɪɚ
beer/ AIR ɛɚ bear/ ŌŌR ʊɚ tour/ AWR ɔɚ bore/ AHR ɑɚ bar/ NG ŋ king/ SH ʃ ship/ ZH ʒ vision/
TH θ thirty/ TH ð then/ CH tʃ child/ J dʒ just/ For complete list, see Key to Pronunciation p. 2.

indenture in-DEHN-cher [ɪn-ˈdɛn-tʃɚ]

India IN-dee-uh [ˈɪn-di-ə] scans to IN-dyuh [ˈɪn-djə]
   e.g. @ *T&C* I, 1, 96

indict in-DEYET [ɪn-ˈdaɪt]

indictment in-DEYET-muhnt [ɪn-ˈdaɪt-mənt]

indigest IN-di-jehst [ˈɪn-dɪ-ʤɛst]

indign in-DEYEN [ɪn-ˈdaɪn]

indissoluble scans to in-DI-sahl-YOO-b(uh)l [ɪn-ˈdɪ-sɑl-ju-bl̩]

indite in-DEYET [ɪn-ˈdaɪt]

indrenched in-DREHNCHT [ɪn-ˈdrɛntʃt]

indubitate in-DYOO-bi-tit [ɪn-ˈdɪu-bɪ-tɪt]

indue in-DYOO [ɪn-ˈdɪu]

inexecrable in-EHK-si-kruh-b(uh)l [ɪn-ˈɛk-sɪ-krə-bl̩]

inexorable in-EHK-si-ruh-b(uh)l [ɪn-ˈɛk-sɪ-rə-bl̩]

infamonize in-FAA-muh-neyez [ɪn-ˈfæ-mə-naɪz]

infer in-FER [ɪn-ˈfɝ]

ingener IN-jin-er [ˈɪn-ʤɪn-ɚ]

ingenious in-JEEN-yuhs [ɪn-ˈʤin-jəs]

ingot ING-guht [ˈɪŋ-gət]

inheritrix in-HEH-ri-triks [ɪn-ˈhɛ-rɪ-trɪks]

injurious in-JOO-ree-uhs [ɪn-ˈjʊ-ri-əs] scans to __-JOO-ryuhs
   [__-ˈʤʊ-rjəs] e.g. @ *MID* III, 2, 195

inkle ING-k(uh)l [ˈɪŋ-kl̩]

inly IN-lee [ˈɪn-li]

inoculate i-NAHK-yuh-layt [ɪ-ˈnɑk-jə-leɪt]

insanie in-SAYN-ee [ɪn-ˈseɪn-i]

insatiate always scans to in-SAY-shuht [ɪn-ˈseɪ-ʃət]

insisture in-SIS-cher [ɪn-ˈsɪs-tʃɚ] or __-__-chŏŏr [__-__-tʃʊɚ]

intendment in-TEHND-muhnt [ɪn-ˈtɛnd-mənt]

intenible scans to in-TEHN-b(uh)l [ɪn-ˈtɛn-bl̩]

inter in-TER [ɪn-ˈtɝ]

inter'gatory in-TER-guh-TAW-ree [ɪn-ˈtɝ-gə-tɔ-ri]

intercessors IN-ter-SEHS-erz [ɪn-tɚ-ˈsɛs-ɚz]

interim IN-tuh-ruhm [ˈɪn-tə-rəm]scans to IN-truhm [ˈɪn-trəm] e.g. @ *OTH* I, 3, 258

intermit IN-ter-mit [ˈɪn-tɚ-mɪt]

interposer IN-ter-POHZ-er [ɪn-tɚ-ˈpouz-ɚ]

interpreter in-TER-pri-ter [ɪn-ˈtɝ-prɪ-tɚ]

interrogatories in-tuh-RAHG-uh-TAW-reez [ɪn-tə-ˈrɑg-ə-tɔ-riz] scans to ___-TER-guh-TAW-___ [___-ˈtɝ-gə-tɔ-___] @ *CYM* V, 5, 392

intertissued IN-ter-TI-shŏŏd [ɪn-tɚ-ˈtɪ-ʃud]

intervallums IN-ter-VAAL-uhmz [ɪn-tɚ-ˈvæl-əmz]

intestate in-TEHS-tit [ɪn-ˈtɛs-tɪt]

intestine in-TEHS-tin [ɪn-ˈtɛs-tɪn]

intil in-TIL [ɪn-ˈtɪl]

intituled in-TICH-ŏŏld [ɪn-ˈtɪtʃ-uld] or __-TIT-yŏŏld [__-ˈtɪt-juld]

intrenchant in-TREHN-chuhnt [ɪn-ˈtrɛn-tʃənt]

EE i be/ I ɪ bit/ EH ɛ bet/ AA æ bat/ ŌŌ u boot / ŎŎ ʊ book/ AW ɔ bought/ AH ɑ father/ ER ɝ bird/ UH ʌ cup/ AY eɪ bay/ EYE aɪ bite/ OY ɔɪ boy/ OH ou boat/ OW ɑu how/ YŌŌ ɪu duke/ EAR ɪɚ beer/ AIR ɛɚ bear/ ŎŎR ʊɚ tour/ AWR ɔɚ bore/ AHR ɑɚ bar/ NG ŋ king/ SH ʃ ship/ ZH ʒ vision/ TH θ thirty/ TH ð then/ CH tʃ child/ J ʤ just/ For complete list, see Key to Pronunciation p. 2.

139

intrinse in-TRINZ [ɪn-'trɪnz] or __-TRINS [__-'trɪns]

intrinsicate in-TRIN-si-kit [ɪn-'trɪn-sɪ-kɪt]

inundation in-uhn-DAY-shuhn [ɪn-ən-'deɪ-ʃən]

inure i-NYOŌR [ɪ-'njʊɚ]

invectively in-VEHK-tiv-lee [ɪn-'vɛk-tɪv-li]

inveigled in-VAY-guhld [ɪn-'veɪ-gəld]

Inverness in-ver-NEHS [ɪn-və-'nɛs]

inviolable always scans to in-VEYE-luh-b(uh)l [ɪn-'vaɪ-lə-bļ]

inward (the interior or a confidant) IN-werd ['ɪn-wɚd]

inwards (the bowels or innards) IN-erdz ['ɪn-ɚdz]

Io EYE-oh ['aɪ-oʊ]

Ionia eye-OH-nee-uh [aɪ-'oʊ-ni-ə]

Ionian scans to and elides with "the" to form t͟heye-OH-nyuhn [ðaɪ-'oʊ-njən]

Ipswich IP-switch ['ɪp-swɪtʃ] or ___-sij [__-sɪʤ]

Iras *(A&C)* EYE-ruhs ['aɪ-rəs]

ire EYER [aɪɚ]

ireful EYER-fuhl ['aɪɚ-fəl]

Ireland EYER-luhnd ['aɪɚ-lənd] scans to EYE-ruh-luhnd ['aɪ-rə-lənd] e.g. @ *1HVI* I, 1, 192

Iris EYE-ris ['aɪ-rɪs]
   Iris *(TEMP)*

iron EYERN [aɪɚn] scans to EYE-ruhn ['aɪ-rən] e.g. @ *MID* II, 1, 196

irregulous scans to i-REHG-luhs [ɪ-'rɛg-ləs]

irreparable i-REHP-uh-ruh-b(uh)l [ɪ-'rɛp-ə-rə-bļ]

irrevocable i-REHV-uh-kuh-b(uh)l [ɪ-'rɛv-ə-kə-b̩l]

Isabel *(HV)* IZ-uh-behl ['ɪz-ə-bɛl]

Isabella *(MM)* IZ-uh-BEHL-uh [ɪz-ə-'bɛl-ə] also called
   "Isabel" IZ-uh-behl ['ɪz-ə-bɛl] scans to IZ-behl ['ɪz-bɛl]
   @ II, 2, 67

Isbel IZ-behl ['ɪz-bɛl]

Iscariot is-KAA-ree-uht [ɪs-'kæ-ri-ət]

Isidore IZ-uh-dawr ['ɪz-ə-dɔɚ]

Isis EYE-sis ['aɪ-sɪs]

Isle of Man EYEL uhv MAAN ['aɪl] [əv] [mæn]

issue ISH-o͞o ['ɪʃ-u]

iterance scans to I-truhns ['ɪ-trəns]

iteration it-uh-RAY-shuhn [ɪt-ə-'reɪ-ʃən]

Ithaca ITH-i-kuh ['ɪθ-ɪ-kə]

i-wis / iwis i-WIS [ɪ-'wɪs]

jackanapes JAAK-uh-nayps ['ʤæk-ə-neɪps]

Jacob JAY-kuhb ['ʤeɪ-kəb]

Jamy *(HV)* JAY-mee ['ʤeɪ-mi]

Janus JAY-nuhs ['ʤeɪ-nəs]

Japhet JAY-feht ['ʤeɪ-fɛt]

Jaquenetta *(LLL)* JAAK-wuh-NEH-tuh [ʤæk-wə-'nɛ-tə]

Jaques JAY-kweez ['ʤeɪ-kwiz] or JAY-kwis ['ʤeɪ-kwɪs]
   possibly scan to JAYKS [ʤeɪks] or JAAKS [ʤæks]
   when it's the last word in verse line

Jaques *(AYL)*
Jaques de Boys *(AYL)* JAYKS [ʤeɪks] or JAAKS [ʤæks]
    duh-**BOYZ** [də-'bɔɪz] or ___-**BOYS** [___-bɔɪs]
Jaques le Grand luh GRAAND [lə] [grænd]

Jasons JAY-s(uh)nz ['ʤeɪ-sn̩z]

jaunce JAWNS [ʤɔns]

jauncing JAWN-sing ['ʤɔn-sɪŋ]

Jephtha JEHF-tuh ['ʤɛf-tə]

Jephthah JEHF-thuh ['ʤɛf-θə]

jerkin JER-kin ['ʤɝ-kɪn]

Jeronimy juh-RAH-nuh-mee [ʤə-'rɑ-nə-mi]

Jerusalem juh-R$\overline{OO}$-suh-luhm [ʤə-'ru-sə-ləm]

jesses JEHS-iz ['ʤɛs-ɪz]

Jessica *(MVEN)* JEHS-i-kuh ['ʤɛs-ɪ-kə] scans to JEHS-kuh
    ['ʤɛs-kə] @ V, 1, 21

Jesu JAY-zy$\overline{oo}$ ['ʤeɪ-zju] or ___-sy$\overline{oo}$ [___-sju] or ___-z$\overline{oo}$
    [___-zu] or ___-s$\overline{oo}$ [___-su] or YAY-___ ['jeɪ-___]

jewel J$\overline{OO}$-uhl ['ʤu-əl] scans to J$\overline{OO}$L [ʤul]
    e.g. @ *KJ* V, 1, 40

Jewess J$\overline{OO}$-is ['ʤu-ɪs]

Jewry J$\overline{OO}$-ree ['ʤu-ri]

Jezebel JEHZ-uh-behl ['ʤɛz-ə-bɛl]

Job JOHB [ʤoʊb]

jocund JAH-kuhnd ['ʤɑ-kənd]

John JAHN [ʤɑn]
    John of Gaunt, Duke of Lancaster *(RII)* GAWNT [gɔnt]
    LAANG-kuhs-ter ['læŋ-kəs-tɚ] or __-kaas-__
    [__-kæs-__]

John, Don *(MADO)*
John, Duke of Bedford *(HV)*
John, Friar *(R&J)*
John, King *(KJ)*

joinder JOYN-der [ˈʤɔɪn-dɚ]

jointress JOYN-truhs [ˈʤɔɪn-trəs]

jointure JOYN-cher [ˈʤɔɪn-tʃɚ]

jollity JAHL-i-tee [ˈʤɑl-ɪ-ti]

Joshua JAHSH-yo͞o-uh [ˈʤɑʃ-ju-ə]

Jourdain, Margery *(2HVI)* jer-DAYN MAHR-juh-ree
[ʤɚ-ˈdeɪn] [ˈmɑɚ-ʤə-ri]

Jove JOHV [ʤoʊv]

Jud-as JO͞OD-aas [ˈʤud-æs]

Judas JO͞O-duhs [ˈʤu-dəs]

Jude JO͞OD [ʤud]

Judean scans to JO͞O-dyuhn [ˈʤu-djən]

judicious jo͞o-DISH-uhs [ʤu-ˈdɪʃ-əs]

Julia *(2GEN)* JO͞OL-yuh [ˈʤul-jə] scans to JO͞OL-ee-uh
[ˈʤul-i-ə] e.g. @ V, 4, 99

Juliet JO͞OL-yeht [ˈʤul-jɛt] scans to JO͞OL-ee-eht [ˈʤul-i-ɛt]
Juliet *(MM)* also called "Julietta" jo͞ol-YEHT-uh
[ʤul-ˈjɛt-ə]
Juliet *(R&J)* scans e.g. @ V, 3, 73, also called "Jule"
JO͞OL [ʤul] @ I, 3, 43

Julio Romano JO͞O-lee-oh ro-MAHN-oh [ˈʤu-li-oʊ]
[roʊ-ˈmɑn-oʊ]

Julius Caesar JŌŌL-yuhs SEE-zer ['ʤul-jəs] ['si-zɚ]
Julius Caesar *(JC)*

July jōō-LEYE [ʤʊ-'laɪ] scans to JŌŌ-leye ['ʤu-laɪ]
e.g. @ *HVIII* I, 1, 154

Junius JŌŌN-yuhs ['ʤun-jəs]
Junius Brutus *(COR)* BRŌŌ-tuhs ['bru-təs]

Juno JŌŌ-noh ['ʤu-noʊ]
Juno *(TEMP)*

Jupiter JŌŌ-pi-ter ['ʤu-pɪ-tɚ] possibly scans to JŌŌP-ter ['ʤup-tɚ] @ *CYM* II, 3, 125

jure JŌŌR [ʤʊɚ]

Justeius juhs-TEE-uhs [ʤəs-'ti-əs]

justicer JUHS-ti-ser ['ʤʌs-tɪ-sɚ]

justle JUHS-uhl ['ʤʌs-əl]

justs JUHSTS [ʤʌsts] (archaic form of "jousts")

juvenal JŌŌ-vuh-nuhl ['ʤu-və-nəl]

kam KAAM [kæm]

Kated KAYT-id ['keɪt-ɪd]

Katharine KAATH-uh-rin ['kæθ-ə-rɪn] scans to KAATH-rin ['kæθ-rɪn]
Katharine *(LLL)* scans @ V, 2, 47

Katherine KAATH-uh-rin ['kæθ-ə-rɪn] scans to KAATH-rin ['kæθ-rɪn]
Katherine *(HV)*
Katherine *(HVIII)*
Katherine *(SHR)* scans @ II, 1, 184, also called
"Katherina" KAATH-uh-REE-nuh [kæθ-ə-'ri-nə] or
KAAT-__-__-__ [kæt-__-__-__] and "Kate" KAYT
[keɪt]

kecksies KEHKS-eez ['kɛks-iz]

Keech KEECH [kitʃ]

keel KEEL [kil]

Keisar KEYE-zer ['kaɪ-zɚ]

ken / kenn KEHN [kɛn]

Kent KEHNT [kɛnt]
    Kent, Earl of *(LEAR)* disguised as "Caius" KEYE-uhs
    ['kaɪ-əs] or **KAY-___** ['keɪ-___]

Kentishman KEHNT-ish-muhn ['kɛnt-ɪʃ-mən]

kern KERN [kɝn]

kersey KER-zee ['kɝ-zi]

Ketly KEHT-lee ['kɛt-li]

kibe KEYEB [kaɪb]

kickshaws KIK-shawz ['kɪk-ʃɔz]

Kildare kil-DAIR [kɪl-'dɛɚ]

killen KIL-uhn ['kɪl-ən]

Killingworth KIL-ing-werth ['kɪl-ɪŋ-wɚθ]

kiln-hole KILN-hohl ['kɪln-hoʊl]

Kimbolton KIM-uhl-tuhn ['kɪm-əl-tən] or **KIM-bohl-___**
    ['kɪm-boʊl-___]

kine KEYEN [kaɪn]

kinred KIN-rid ['kɪn-rɪd]

kirtle KER-t(uh)l ['kɝ-tl̩]

kissing-comfits KIS-ing-KUHM-fits ['kɪs-ɪŋ-kʌm-fɪts]

EE i be/ I ɪ bit/ EH ɛ bet/ AA æ bat/ OO u boot / OO ʊ book/ AW ɔ bought/ AH ɑ father/ ER ɝ bird/
UH ʌ cup/ AY eɪ bay/ EYE aɪ bite/ OY ɔɪ boy/ OH oʊ boat/ OW aʊ how/ YOO ɪu duke/ EAR ɪɚ
beer/ AIR ɛɚ bear/ OOR ʊɚ tour/ AWR ɔɚ bore/ AHR ɑɚ bar/ NG ŋ king/ SH ʃ ship/ ZH ʒ vision/
TH θ thirty/ TH ð then/ CH tʃ child/ J ʤ just/ For complete list, see Key to Pronunciation p. 2.

145

knapped NAAPT [næpt]

knave NAYV [neɪv]

knoll NOHL [noʊl]

koth-a KOHTH-uh [ˈkouθ-ə] variant of "quoth-a"
   KWOHTH-uh [ˈkwouθ-ə] which is a variant of "quoth he"
   KWOHTH-hee [ˈkwouθ-hi]

La Far luh FAHR [lə] [fɑɚ]

Laban LAY-buhn [ˈleɪ-bən]

Labeo scans to LAY-byoh [ˈleɪ-bjoʊ]

Labienus LAA-bi-EE-nuhs [læ-bɪ-ˈi-nəs]

labyrinth LAAB-uh-rinth [ˈlæb-ə-rɪnθ]

Lacedaemon LAAS-i-DEE-muhn [læs-ɪ-ˈdi-mən]

Lacies LAY-seez [ˈleɪ-siz]

lade LAYD [leɪd]

lading LAYD-ing [ˈleɪd-ɪŋ]

Lady Brach BRAACH [brætʃ]

Laertes lay-AIR-teez [leɪ-ˈɛɚ-tiz] or __-ER-__ [__-ˈɝ-__]
   Laertes *(HAM)*

Lafew *(AW)* luh-FYO͞O [lə-ˈfju]

lakin LAY-kin [ˈleɪ-kɪn]

Lambert's LAAM-berts [ˈlæm-bɚts]

lambkins LAAM-kinz [ˈlæm-kɪnz]

lamentable luh-MEHN-tuh-b(uh)l [lə-ˈmɛn-tə-bl̩] scans to
   LAAM-uhn-__-__ [ˈlæm-ən-__-__] e.g. @ *RII* V, 1, 44

lamentings luh-MEHNT-ingz [lə-ˈmɛnt-ɪŋz]

Lammas Eve LAA-muhs EEV [ˈlæ-məs] [iv]

Lammastide LAA-muhs-teyed ['læ-məs-taɪd]

Lamord luh-MAWRD [lə-'mɔɚd]

lampass LAAM-puhs ['læm-pəs]

Lancaster LAANG-kuhs-ter ['læŋ-kəs-tɚ] or __-kaas-__
[__-kæs-__]
Lancaster, John, Prince of *(1HIV, 2HIV)*

lanched LAANCHT [læntʃt]

Langley LAANG-lee ['læŋ-li]

Langton LAANG-tuhn ['læŋ-tən]

languor LAANG-ger ['læŋ-gɚ]

lanthorn LAANT-hawrn ['lænt-hɔɚn] or LAAN-tern
['læn-tɚn]

Lapland LAAP-laand ['læp-lænd]

largess always scans to LAHR-jehs ['lɑɚ-dʒɛs]

'larum LAH-ruhm ['lɑ-rəm] or LAA-__ ['læ-__]

lascivious luh-SIV-ee-uhs [lə-'sɪv-i-əs] scans to __-SIV-yuhs
[__-'sɪv-jəs] e.g. @ *RIII* I, 1, 13

lath LAATH [læθ]

latten bilbo LAA-t(uh)n BIL-boh ['læ-tn̩] ['bɪl-boʊ]

latter LAAT-er ['læt-ɚ]

lattice LAAT-is ['læt-ɪs]

laud LAWD [lɔd]

Launce *(2GEN)* LAWNS [lɔns] or LAANS [læns] or
LAHNS [lɑns]

EE i be/ I ɪ bit/ EH ɛ bet/ AA æ bat/ O͞O u boot / O͝O ʊ book/ AW ɔ bought/ AH ɑ father/ ER ɝ bird/
UH ʌ cup/ AY eɪ bay/ EYE aɪ bite/ OY ɔɪ boy/ OH oʊ boat/ OW aʊ how/ YO͞O ɪu duke/ EAR ɪɚ
beer/ AIR ɛɚ bear/ O͞OR ʊɚ tour/ AWR ɔɚ bore/ AHR ɑɚ bar/ NG ŋ king/ SH ʃ ship/ ZH ʒ vision/
TH θ thirty/ T̲H̲ ð then/ CH tʃ child/ J dʒ just/ For complete list, see Key to Pronunciation p. 2.

147

laund LAWND [lɔnd]

Laurence, Friar LAW-ruhns ['lɔ-rəns]
Laurence, Friar *(R&J)*

Lavatch *(AW)* luh-VAACH [lə-'vætʃ] or ___-VAHCH
[___-'vɑtʃ]

lave LAYV [leɪv]

Lavinia *(TITUS)* luh-VIN-ee-uh [lə-'vɪn-i-ə] scans to
___-VIN-yuh [__-'vɪn-jə] e.g. @ I, 1, 55

lavolt luh-VOHLT [lə-'voʊlt]

lavoltas luh-VOHL-tuhz [lə-'voʊl-təz]

lazar LAA-zer ['læ-zɚ] or LAY-__ ['leɪ-__]

Lazarus LAAZ-uh-ruhs ['læz-ə-rəs]

Le Beau *(AYL)* luh BOH [lə] [boʊ], Folio spelling "Le Beu"
suggests luh BY$\overline{\text{OO}}$ [lə] [bju]

Le Bon luh BOHN [lə] [boʊn]

Le Fer luh FAIR [lə] [fɛɚ]

Le Port Blanc luh pawrt BLAANGK [lə] [pɔɚt] [blæŋk]

Le Roy luh ROY [lə] [rɔɪ]

Leah LEE-uh ['li-ə]

Leander lee-AAN-der [li-'æn-dɚ]

Lear, King of Britain *(LEAR)* LEAR [lɪɚ]

leas LEEZ [liz]

leasing (lying) LEEZ-ing ['liz-ɪŋ]

leathern LEH<u>TH</u>-ern ['lɛð-ɚn]

leavy LEE-vee ['li-vi]

Leda LEE-duh ['li-də]

leet LEET [lit]

legate / Legate LEHG-it ['lɛg-ɪt]

legative LEHG-uh-tiv ['lɛg-ə-tɪv]

legerity luh-JEH-ri-tee [lə-'dʒɛ-rɪ-ti]

legitimation luh-JIT-uh-MAY-shuhn [lə-dʒɪt-ə-'meɪ-ʃən]

Leicester LEHS-ter ['lɛs-tɚ]

Leicestershire LEHS-ter-sher ['lɛs-tɚ-ʃɚ] or ___-___-shear
  [___-___-ʃɪɚ]

leiger LEH-jer ['lɛ-dʒɚ] or LEE-___ ['li-___]

leisure LEE-zher ['li-ʒɚ] or LEH-___ ['lɛ-___]

leman LEHM-uhn ['lɛm-ən] or LEEM-___ ['lim-___]

Lena, Popilius *(JC)* LEE-nuh, always scans to poh-PI-lyuhs
  ['li-nə] [pou-'pɪ-ljəs]

lenity LEHN-i-tee ['lɛn-ɪ-ti]

Lennox *(MAC)* LEHN-uhks ['lɛn-əks]

lenten LEHN-tuhn ['lɛn-tən]

Leonardo *(MVEN)* scans to lee-NAHR-doh [li-'nɑɚ-dou]

Leonati lee-uh-NAY-teye [li-ə-'neɪ-taɪ]

Leonato *(MADO)* LEE-uh-NAH-toh [li-ə-'nɑ-tou]

Leonine *(PER)* LEE-uh-neyen ['li-ə-naɪn]

Leontes *(WT)* lee-AHN-teez [li-'ɑn-tiz] also called "Sicilia"
  si-SIL-ee-uh [sɪ-'sɪl-i-ə] scans to ___-SIL-yuh [___-'sɪl-yuh]
  @ I, 2, 217

Lepidus, M. Aemilius *(A&C, JC)* see "M. Aemilius Lepidus"

EE i be/ I ɪ bit/ EH ɛ bet/ AA æ bat/ OO u boot / OO ʊ book/ AW ɔ bought/ AH ɑ father/ ER ɝ bird/
UH ʌ cup/ AY eɪ bay/ EYE aɪ bite/ OY ɔɪ boy/ OH ou boat/ OW aʊ how/ YOO ɪu duke/ EAR ɪɚ
beer/ AIR ɛɚ bear/ OOR ʊɚ tour/ AWR ɔɚ bore/ AHR ɑɚ bar/ NG ŋ king/ SH ʃ ship/ ZH ʒ vision/
TH θ thirty/ TH ð then/ CH tʃ child/ J dʒ just/ For complete list, see Key to Pronunciation p. 2.

lest LEHST [lɛst]

Lestrale LEH-strahl [ˈlɛ-strɑl] scans to leh-STRAHL [lɛ-ˈstrɑl]
@ *HV* IV, 8, 95

lethe / Lethe LEE-thee [ˈli-θi]

leviathan / Leviathan luh-VEYE-uh-thuhn [lə-ˈvaɪ-ə-θən]

levy LEHV-ee [ˈlɛv-i]

Lewis LOOS [lus] scans to LOO-is [ˈlu-ɪs]
Lewis XI *(3HVI)* scans @ III, 3, 169 and possibly III, 3, 23
Lewis, the Dauphin *(HV)* DAW-fin [ˈdɔ-fɪn]
Lewis, the Dauphin *(KJ)* some editions "Dolphin"
DAHL-fin [ˈdɑl-fɪn]

libbard's LIB-erdz [ˈlɪb-ɚ-dz]

libertine LIB-er-teen [ˈlɪb-ɚ-tin] or ___-___-teyen
[___-___-taɪn]

Libya LIB-ee-uh [ˈlɪb-i-ə] scans to LIB-yuh [ˈlɪb-jə]
e.g. @ *WT* V, 1, 165

licentious leye-SEHN-shuhs [laɪ-ˈsɛn-ʃəs] scans to ___-___-
shee-uhs [__-__-ʃi-əs] @ *CE* II, 2, 130

Lichas LEYE-kuhs [ˈlaɪ-kəs]

lictors LIK-terz [ˈlɪk-tɚz]

lief LEEF [lif]

liege LEEJ [lidʒ]

lieger LEE-jer [ˈli-dʒɚ]

lien (part) (to be at rest in a horizontal position) LEYEN
[laɪn]

liest LEYEST [laɪst]

lieu LOO [lu]

lieutenantry lōō-TEHN-uhn-tree [lu-'tɛn-ən-tri] scans to ___-TEHN-tree [___-'tɛn-tri] @ *A&C* III, 11, 39

lieve LEEV [liv]

Ligarius *(JC)* li-GEH-ree-uhs [lɪ-'gɛ-ri-əs] scans to ___-GEH-ryuhs [___-'gɛ-rjəs] e.g. @ II, 1, 215

liggens LIG-uhnz ['lɪg-ənz]

limbeck LIM-behk ['lɪm-bɛk]

Limbo LIM-boh ['lɪm-boʊ]

Limbo Patrum LIM-boh PAA-truhm ['lɪm-boʊ] ['pæ-trəm]

lime LEYEM [laɪm]

Limehouse (a section of London) LIM-uhs ['lɪm-əs]

limekiln LEYEM-kiln ['laɪm-kɪln]

limned LIMD [lɪmd]

Lincoln, Bishop of *(HVIII)* LING-kuhn ['lɪŋ-kən]

Lincolnshire LING-kuhn-sher ['lɪŋ-kən-ʃɚ] or ___-___-shear [___-___-ʃɪɚ]

lineal LIN-ee-uhl ['lɪn-i-əl] scans to LIN-yuhl ['lɪn-jəl] e.g. @ *2HIV* IV, 5, 45

lineally scans to LIN-yuh-lee ['lɪn-jə-li]

lineament LIN-ee-uh-muhnt ['lɪn-i-ə-mənt] scans to LIN-yuh-___ ['lɪn-jə-___] e.g. @ *R&J* I, 3, 83

Lingard LING-gahrd ['lɪŋ-gɑɚd]

lings LINGZ [lɪŋz]

linsey-woolsey LIN-zee-WŎŎL-zee ['lɪn-zi-wʊl-zi]

EE i be/ I ɪ bit/ EH ɛ bet/ AA æ bat/ ŌŌ u boot / ŎŎ ʊ book/ AW ɔ bought/ AH ɑ father/ ER ɝ bird/ UH ʌ cup/ AY eɪ bay/ EYE aɪ bite/ OY ɔɪ boy/ OH oʊ boat/ OW aʊ how/ YŌŌ ɪu duke/ EAR ɪɚ beer/ AIR ɛɚ bear/ ŌŌR ʊɚ tour/ AWR ɔɚ bore/ AHR ɑɚ bar/ NG ŋ king/ SH ʃ ship/ ZH ʒ vision/ TH θ thirty/ TH ð then/ CH tʃ child/ J dʒ just/ For complete list, see Key to Pronunciation p. 2.

Lionel LEYE-uh-n(uh)l [ˈlaɪ-ə-n̩]

lither LITH-er [ˈlɪð-ɚ]

litigious li-TIJ-uhs [lɪ-ˈtɪʤ-əs]

Litio see "Hortensio"

live (adv) (gladly, willingly) LEEV [liv] or possibly LEEF [lif]

livelong LIV-lawng [ˈlɪv-lɔŋ]

Livia LIV-ee-uh [ˈlɪv-i-ə]

loach LOHCH [loʊʧ]

loath LOHTH [loʊθ]

loathe LOHTH [loʊð]

loathly LOHTH-lee [ˈloʊð-li] or LOHTH-___ [ˈloʊθ-___]

loathness LOHTH-nis [ˈloʊð-nɪs] or LOHTH-__ [ˈloʊθ-__]

lockram LAHK-ruhm [ˈlɑk-rəm]

lodestar LOHD-stahr [ˈloʊd-stɑɚ]

Lodovico (OTH) LOH-doh-VEE-koh [loʊ-doʊ-ˈvi-koʊ] or ___- duh-___-___ [___-də-___-___]

Lodowick LOH-duh-wik [ˈloʊ-də-wɪk] or LAH-___-___ [ˈlɑ-___-___]

loggets LAHG-its [ˈlɑg-ɪts]

Lombardy LAHM-bahr-dee [ˈlɑm-bɑɚ-di]

Longaville (LLL) LAWNG-uh-vil [ˈlɔŋ-ə-vɪl] or ___-___-veyel [___-___-vaɪl] @ IV, 3, 128 and V, 2, 53 for rhyme

loofed LUHFT [lʌft]

lop LAHP [lɑp]

Lord Mayor of London LUHN-duhn [ˈlʌn-dən]

152

Lord Mayor of London *(HVIII)*
Lord Mayor of London *(RIII)*

Lorenzo *(MVEN)* luh-**REHN**-zoh [lə-'rɛn-zoʊ] or
loh-___-___ [loʊ-___-___]

Lorraine scans to **LOH**-rayn ['loʊ-reɪn]

louse (v) (to have lice) LOWZ [laʊz]

lout LOWT [laʊt]

Louvre L$\overline{OO}$V-er ['luv-ɚ] or ___-ruh [___-rə] possibly
LUHV-er ['lʌv-ɚ] @ *HV* II, 4, 132

Lovel / Lovell **LUHV**-uhl ['lʌv-əl]
Lovel, Lord *(RIII)*
Lovell, Sir Thomas *(HVIII)*

love-monger **LUHV**-muhng-ger ['lʌv-mən-gɚ] or
___-mahng-___ [___-maŋ-___]

lower / low'r / lour (to frown) LOWR [laʊɚ]

lown (a man of low station) L$\overline{OO}$N [lun] and possibly
LOWN [laʊn] @ *OTH* II, 3, 87 for rhyme

lozel LOH-z(uh)l ['loʊ-zl̩]

lubber **LUHB**-er ['lʌb-ɚ]

Luccicos l$\overline{oo}$-**CHEE**-kuhs [lu-'tʃi-kəs]

Luce L$\overline{OO}$S [lus]
Luce *(CE)*

Lucentio l$\overline{oo}$-**SEHN**-shee-oh [lu-'sɛn-ʃi-oʊ] scans to
___- **SEHN**-shyoh [___-'sɛn-ʃjoʊ]
Lucentio *(SHR)* scans @ II, 1, 101 later posing as
"Cambio" **KAAM**-bee-oh ['kæm-bi-oʊ] scans to
KAAM-byoh ['kæm-bjoʊ] @ IV, 4, 105

EE i be/ I ɪ bit/ EH ɛ bet/ AA æ bat/ $\overline{OO}$ u boot / $\overline{OO}$ ʊ book/ AW ɔ bought/ AH ɑ father/ ER ɚ bird/
UH ʌ cup/ AY eɪ bay/ EYE aɪ bite/ OY ɔɪ boy/ OH oʊ boat/ OW aʊ how/ Y$\overline{OO}$ ɪu duke/ EAR ɪɚ
beer/ AIR ɛɚ bear/ $\overline{OO}$R ʊɚ tour/ AWR ɔɚ bore/ AHR ɑɚ bar/ NG ŋ king/ SH ʃ ship/ ZH ʒ vision/
TH θ thirty/ <u>TH</u> ð then/ CH tʃ child/ J dʒ just/ For complete list, see Key to Pronunciation p. 2.

luces LŌOS-iz ['lus-ɪz]

Lucetta *(2GEN)* lōo-SEHT-uh [lu-'sɛt-ə]

Luciana *(CE)* LŌO-see-AH-nuh [lu-si-'ɑ-nə]

Lucianus LŌO-shee-AY-nuhs [lu-ʃi-'eɪ-nəs] or __-see-__-__
    [__-si-__-__] or __-__-AH-__ [__-__-'ɑ-__]

Lucifer LŌO-si-fer ['lu-sɪ-fɚ]

Lucilius lōo-SIL-ee-uhs [lu-'sɪl-i-əs] scans to ___-SIL-yuhs
    [__-'sɪl-jəs]
    Lucilius *(JC)* scans @ V, 3, 106
    Lucilius *(TIMON)*

Lucina lōo-SEYE-nuh [lu-'saɪ-nə]

Lucio LŌO-see-oh ['lu-si-oʊ] or lōo-SEE-___ [lu-'si-___] in
    prose, scans to LŌO-syoh ['lu-sjoʊ] or LŌO-shyoh
    ['lu-ʃjoʊ]
    Lucio *(MM)* scans @ I, 2, 171

Lucius LŌO-shuhs ['lu-ʃəs] scans to LŌO-shee-uhs ['lu-ʃi-əs]
    Lucius *(JC)*
    Lucius *(TIMON)* scans @ III, 4, 2
    Lucius *(TITUS)* scans @ IV, 4, 78
    Lucius Pella PEH-luh ['pɛ-lə]

lucre LŌO-ker ['lu-kɚ]

Lucrece lōo-KREES [lu-'kris] scans to LŌO-krees ['lu-kris]
    e.g. @ *TITUS* IV, 1, 64

Lucretia's lōo-KREE-shuhz [lu-'kri-ʃəz]

Lucullus *(TIMON)* lōo-KUHL-uhs [lu-'kʌl-əs]

Lucy, Sir William *(1HVI)* LŌO-see ['lu-si]

Lud LUHD [lʌd]

Ludlow LUHD-loh ['lʌd-loʊ]

Luna LŌO-nuh ['lu-nə]

lunes LŌŌNZ [lunz]

Lupercal LŌŌ-per-kaal ['lu-pɚ-kæl]

lustre LUHS-ter ['lʌs-tɚ]

Lycaonia LEYE-kay-OH-nee-uh [laɪ-keɪ-'oʊ-ni-ə]

Lychorida *(PER)* leye-KAW-ri-duh [laɪ-'kɔ-rɪ-də]

Lycurguses leye-KER-guhs-iz [laɪ-'kɝ-gəs-ɪz]

Lydia LI-dee-uh ['lɪ-di-ə]

lym LIM [lɪm]

Lymoges, Duke of Austria *(KJ)* li-MOH-zhiz [lɪ-'moʊ-ʒɪz]
     possibly scans to LI-moh-__ ['lɪ-moʊ-__] @ III, 1, 114 or
     li-MOHZH [lɪ-'moʊʒ] if headless line

Lynn LIN [lɪn]

Lysander *(MID)* leye-SAAN-der [laɪ-'sæn-dɚ]

Lysimachus *(PER)* leye-SIM-uh-kuhs [laɪ-'sɪm-ə-kəs]

M. Aemilius Lepidus MAHR-kuhs ee-MIL-i-uhs ['mɑɚ-kəs]
     [i-'mɪl-ɪ-əs] or i-__-__-__ [ɪ-__-__-__] LEH-pi-duhs
     ['lɛ-pɪ-dəs] scans to leh-PI-__ [lɛ-'pɪ-__]
     M. Aemilius Lepidus *(A&C)*
     M. Aemilius Lepidus *(JC)* scans @ III, 2, 264

Mab MAAB [mæb]

Macbeth maak-BEHTH [mæk-'bɛθ]
     Macbeth *(MAC)* may have rhymed @ I, 1, 7 to "heath"
     Macbeth, Lady *(MAC)*

Maccabaeus MAAK-uh-BEE-uhs [mæk-ə-'bi-əs]

Macdonwald maak-DAHN-uhld [mæk-'dɑn-əld]

EE i be/ I ɪ bit/ EH ɛ bet/ AA æ bat/ ŌŌ u boot / ŎŎ ʊ book/ AW ɔ bought/ AH ɑ father/ ER ɝ bird/
UH ʌ cup/ AY eɪ bay/ EYE aɪ bite/ OY ɔɪ boy/ OH oʊ boat/ OW aʊ how/ YŌŌ ɪu duke/ EAR ɪɚ
beer/ AIR ɛɚ bear/ ŌŌR ʊɚ tour/ AWR ɔɚ bore/ AHR ɑɚ bar/ NG ŋ king/ SH ʃ ship/ ZH ʒ vision/
TH θ thirty/ TH ð then/ CH tʃ child/ J dʒ just/ For complete list, see Key to Pronunciation p. 2.

Macduff maak-DUHF [mæk-'dʌf]
Macduff *(MAC)*
Macduff, Lady *(MAC)*

Macedon MAAS-i-dahn ['mæs-ɪ-dɑn]

Machiavel MAAK-ee-uh-vehl ['mæk-i-ə-vɛl] scans to
___-yuh-vehl [___-jə-vɛl] e.g. @ *1HVI* V, 4, 74

machinations MAAK-uh-NAY-shuhnz [mæk-ə-'neɪ-ʃənz]

Macmorris *(HV)* muhk-MAW-ris [mək-'mɔ-rɪs] or
maak-___-___ [mæk-___-___]

maculate MAAK-yuh-lit ['mæk-jə-lɪt]

maculation MAAK-yuh-LAY-shuhn [mæk-jə-'leɪ-ʃən]

madding MAAD-ing ['mæd-ɪŋ]

Madeira muh-DI-ruh [mə-'dɪ-rə]

madrigals MAAD-ri-g(uh)lz ['mæd-rɪ-gl̩z]

Maecenas *(A&C)* mee-SEE-nuhs [mi-'si-nəs] or mi-___-___
[mɪ__-__]

magistrates MAAJ-i-strayts ['mædʒ-ɪ-streɪts]

magnanimity MAAG-ni-NIM-i-tee [mæg-nɪ-'nɪm-ɪ-ti]

magnanimous maag-NAAN-uh-muhs [mæg-'næn-ə-məs]

magnifico maag-NIF-i-koh [mæg-'nɪf-ɪ-koʊ]

Magnus MAAG-nuhs ['mæg-nəs]

Mahomet MAY-uh-meht ['meɪ-ə-mɛt]

Mahu MAH-hoō ['mɑ-hu]

Maidenhead / maidenhead MAY-d(uh)n-hehd ['meɪ-dn̩-hɛd]

maidenliest MAY-d(uh)n-lee-ist ['meɪ-dn̩-li-ɪst]

Maine MAYN [meɪn]

maintain mayn-TAYN [meɪn-'teɪn] scans to MAYN-tayn ['meɪn-teɪn] e.g. @ *1HVI* I, 1, 71

malapert MAAL-uh-pert ['mæl-ə-pɚt]

Malcolm *(MAC)* MAAL-kuhm ['mæl-kəm]

maledictions MAAL-i-DIK-shuhnz [mæl-ɪ-'dɪk-ʃənz]

malefactor MAAL-uh-faak-ter ['mæl-ə-fæk-tɚ]

malkin MAWL-kin ['mɔl-kɪn]

Mall MAWL [mɔl] or MAHL [mɑl]

mallicholy MAAL-i-kah-lee ['mæl-ɪ-kɑ-li]

mallows MAAL-ohz ['mæl-ouz]

malmsey MAHM-zee ['mɑm-zi]

Malvolio *(12th)* maal-VOH-lee-oh [mæl-'vou-li-ou] scans to __-VOH-lyoh [__-'vou-ljou] e.g. @ V, 1, 268

Mamillius *(WT)* muh-MIL-ee-uhs [mə-'mɪl-i-əs] scans to __-MIL-yuhs [__-'mɪl-jəs] @ I, 2, 210

mammet MAAM-it ['mæm-ɪt]

mammocked MAAM-uhkt ['mæm-əkt]

mamm'ring MAAM-ring ['mæm-rɪŋ]

manage MAAN-ij ['mæn-ɪdʒ]

mandragora maan-DRAAG-uh-ruh [mæn-'dræg-ə-rə]

manikin MAAN-i-kin ['mæn-ɪ-kɪn]

Manningtree MAAN-ing-tree ['mæn-ɪŋ-tri]

mansionry MAAN-chuhn-ree ['mæn-tʃən-ri]

EE i be/ I ɪ bit/ EH ɛ bet/ AA æ bat/ OO u boot / OO ʊ book/ AW ɔ bought/ AH ɑ father/ ER ɝ bird/
UH ʌ cup/ AY eɪ bay/ EYE aɪ bite/ OY ɔɪ boy/ OH ou boat/ OW ɑu how/ YOO ɪu duke/ EAR ɪɚ
beer/ AIR ɛɚ bear/ OOR ʊɚ tour/ AWR ɔɚ bore/ AHR ɑɚ bar/ NG ŋ king/ SH ʃ ship/ ZH ʒ vision/
TH θ thirty/ TH ð then/ CH tʃ child/ J dʒ just/ For complete list, see Key to Pronunciation p. 2.

Mantua MAAN-chōō-wuh ['mæn-tʃu-wə] scans to **MAAN**-chwuh ['mæn-tʃwə] or **MAAN**-tyōō-uh ['mæn-tju-ə] scans to **MAAN**-tyuh ['mæn-tjə] e.g. @ *R&J* III, 3, 169

Mantuan MAAN-chōō-wuhn ['mæn-tʃu-wən]

mapp'ry MAAP-ree ['mæp-ri]

mar MAHR [maɚ]

Marcade *(LLL)* MAHR-kuh-dee ['maɚ-kə-di]

Marcellus mahr-SEHL-uhs [maɚ-'sɛl-əs]
   Marcellus *(HAM)*

Marchioness MAHR-shuh-nis ['maɚ-ʃə-nɪs]

marchpane MAHRCH-payn ['maɚtʃ-peɪn]

Marcians MAHR-shuhnz ['maɚ-ʃənz]

Marcus MAHR-kuhs ['maɚ-kəs]
   Marcus Crassus **KRAAS**-uhs ['kræs-əs]
   Marcus Octavius scans to ahk-**TAYV**-yuhs [ak-'teɪv-jəs]

Mardian *(A&C)* MAHR-dee-uhn ['maɚ-di-ən] scans to **MAHR**-dyuhn ['maɚ-djən] @ I, 5, 8

Margarelon *(T&C)* MAHR-guh-reh-luhn ['maɚ-gə-rɛ-lən]

Margaret MAHR-guh-rit ['maɚ-gə-rɪt] scans to **MAHR**-grit ['maɚ-grɪt]
   Margaret *(1HVI)* scans e.g. @ V, 3, 51
   Margaret *(2HVI)*
   Margaret *(3HVI)* scans e.g. @ I, 1, 228
   Margaret *(MADO)*
   Margaret *(RIII)* scans e.g. @ I, 2, 93

margent MAHR-juhnt ['maɚ-ʤənt]

Margery MAHR-juh-ree ['maɚ-ʤə-ri]

Maria muh-REYE-uh [mə-'raɪ-ə]
   Maria *(LLL)* possibly __-REE-__ [__-'rɪ-__]
   Maria *(12th)*

Marian MAA-ree-uhn ['mæ-ri-ən] scans to MAA-ryuhn ['mæ-rjən] or MEH-__-_ ['mɛ-__-__] scans to MEH-__ ['mɛ-__] e.g. @ *CE* III, 1, 31

Mariana MEH-ri-AA-nuh [mɛ-rɪ-'æ-nə] or MAA-__-__-__ [mæ-__-__-__]
Mariana *(AW)*
Mariana *(MM)*

Marina *(PER)* muh-REE-nuh [mə-'ri-nə]

marjoram MAHR-juh-ruhm ['mɑɚ-ʤə-rəm]

Mark Antony *(A&C)* MAHRK AAN-tuh-nee [mɑɚk] ['æn-tə-ni] scans to AANT-nee ['ænt-ni] e.g. @ II, 1, 39; also called "Antonio" scans to aan-TOHN-yoh [æn-'toʊn-joʊ] @ II, 2, 7, and "Antonius" scans to aan-TOHN-yuhs [æn-'toʊn-jəs] e.g. @ I, 1, 56 (for the name in JC, see "Antonius, Marcus")

Marle MAHRL [mɑɚl]

marmoset MAHR-muh-seht ['mɑɚ-mə-sɛt]

Marquess MAHR-kwis ['mɑɚ-kwɪs]

Marquis MAHR-kwis ['mɑɚ-kwɪs]

marriage MAA-rij ['mæ-rɪʤ] scans to MAA-ree-ij ['mæ-ri-ɪʤ] e.g. @ *R&J* IV, 1, 11

Mars MAHRZ [mɑɚz]

Marseilles mahr-SAYLZ [mɑɚ-'seɪlz] scans to mahr-SEHL-uhs [mɑɚ-'sɛl-əs] e.g. @ *AW* IV, 4, 9 (if French pronunciation is preferred in prose mahr-SAY [mɑɚ-'seɪ])

Marshal MAHR-sh(uh)l ['mɑɚ-ʃl̩] scans to MAHR-uh-sh(uh)l ['mɑɚ-ə-ʃl̩] e.g. @ *1HIV* IV, 4, 2
Marshal *(PER)*

EE i be/ I ɪ bit/ EH ɛ bet/ AA æ bat/ OO u boot / OO ʊ book/ AW ɔ bought/ AH ɑ father/ ER ɝ bird/ UH ʌ cup/ AY eɪ bay/ EYE aɪ bite/ OY ɔɪ boy/ OH oʊ boat/ OW aʊ how/ YOO ɪu duke/ EAR ɪɚ beer/ AIR ɛɚ bear/ OOR ʊɚ tour/ AWR ɔɚ bore/ AHR ɑɚ bar/ NG ŋ king/ SH ʃ ship/ ZH ʒ vision/ TH θ thirty/ <u>TH</u> ð then/ CH ʧ child/ J ʤ just/ For complete list, see Key to Pronunciation p. 2.

Marshal, Lord *(RII)*

Marshalsea MAHR-sh(uh)l-see ['mɑɚ-ʃḷ-si]

Mar-text, Sir Oliver *(AYL)* **MAHR**-tehkst **AH**-li-ver ['mɑɚ-tɛkst] ['ɑ-lɪ-vɚ]

martial / Martial MAHR-sh(uh)l ['mɑɚ-ʃḷ]

Martino mahr-TEE-noh [mɑɚ-'ti-noʊ]

Martius *(TITUS)* MAHR-shuhs ['mɑɚ-ʃəs]

martlemas MAHR-t(uh)l-muhs ['mɑɚ-tḷ-məs]

martlet MAHRT-lit ['mɑɚt-lɪt]

Marullus *(JC)* muh-RUHL-uhs [mə-'rʌl-əs]

Masham MAASH-uhm ['mæʃ-əm] or MAAS-___ ['mæs-___]

masque MAASK [mæsk]

masquers MAASK-erz ['mæsk-ɚz]

massy MAAS-ee ['mæs-i]

masterdom MAAS-ter-duhm ['mæs-tɚ-dəm]

mastic MAAS-tik ['mæs-tɪk]

mastiff MAAS-tif ['mæs-tɪf]

matin MAA-tin ['mæ-tɪn]

mattock MAAT-uhk ['mæt-ək]

Mauchus MAW-kuhs ['mɔ-kəs]

Maud MAWD [mɔd]

Maudlin MAWD-lin ['mɔd-lɪn]

maugre MAW-ger ['mɔ-gɚ]

Mauritania MAW-ri-TAY-nee-uh [mɔ-rɪ-'teɪ-ni-ə]

maw MAW [mɔ]

mawkin MAW-kin ['mɔ-kɪn]

Mayor
> of Coventry *(3 HVI)* KUHV-uhn-tree ['kʌv-ən-tri]
> of London *(1HVI)*
> of Saint Albans *(2HVI)* AWL-buhnz ['ɔl-bənz]
> of York *(3HVI)*

mazzard MAAZ-erd ['mæz-ɚd]

meacock MEE-kahk ['mi-kɑk]

mead MEED [mid]

meanwhile always scans to meen-HWEYEL [min-'hwaɪl]

Mede MEED [mid]

Medea mi-DEE-uh [mɪ-'di-ə]

Media MEE-dee-uh ['mi-di-ə] scans to MEE-dyuh ['mi-djə]
> @ *A&C* III, 6, 14

medicinable / med'cinable MEHD-sin-uh-b(uh)l
> ['mɛd-sɪn-ə-bļ] possibly scans to ___-sin-b(uh)l
> [__-sɪn-bļ] e.g. @ *T&C* III, 3, 44

medicinal scans to MEHD-si-n(uh)l ['mɛd-sɪ-nļ]

meditance MEHD-i-tuhns ['mɛd-ɪ-təns]

Mediterranean MEHD-i-tuh-RAY-nee-uhn [mɛd-ɪ-tə-'reɪ-ni-ən]
> possibly scans to MEHD-tuh-ray-nyuhn ['mɛd-tə-reɪ-njən]
> @ *TEMP* I, 2, 234

medlar MEHD-ler ['mɛd-lɚ]

meed MEED [mid]

meiny MAY-nee ['meɪ-ni]

Meisen MEYE-s(uh)n ['maɪ-sņ]

EE i be/ I ɪ bit/ EH ɛ bet/ AA æ bat/ OO u boot / OO ʊ book/ AW ɔ bought/ AH ɑ father/ ER ɝ bird/
UH ʌ cup/ AY eɪ bay/ EYE aɪ bite/ OY ɔɪ boy/ OH oʊ boat/ OW aʊ how/ YOO ɪu duke/ EAR ɪɚ
beer/ AIR ɛɚ bear/ OOR ʊɚ tour/ AWR ɔɚ bore/ AHR ɑɚ bar/ NG ŋ king/ SH ʃ ship/ ZH ʒ vision/
TH θ thirty/ TH ð then/ CH tʃ child/ J dʒ just/ For complete list, see Key to Pronunciation p. 2.

Meleager MEH-lee-**AY**-jer [mɛ-li-'eɪ-ʤɚ]

Melford MEHL-ferd ['mɛl-fɚd]

mell MEHL [mɛl]

mellifluous muh-**LIF**-lo͞o-uhs [mə-'lɪf-lu-əs]

Melun *(KJ)* muh-**LŌON** [mə-'lun]

Menaphon MEHN-uh-fuhn ['mɛn-ə-fən]

Menas MEEN-uhs ['min-əs]
  Menas *(A&C)*

Menecrates muh-**NEHK**-ruh-teez [mə-'nɛk-rə-tiz]
  Menecrates *(A&C)*

Menelaus MEHN-uh-**LAY**-uhs [mɛn-ə-'leɪ-əs]
  Menelaus *(T&C)*

Menenius Agrippa *(COR)* muh-**NEE**-nee-uhs uh-**GRIP**-uh
  [mə-'ni-ni-əs] [ə-'grɪp-ə] scans to ___-**NEE**-nyuhs
  [___-'ni-njəs] @ III, 3, 7

Menon MEE-nahn ['mi-nɑn]

Menteith mehn-**TEETH** [mɛn-'tiθ]
  Menteith *(MAC)*

Mephistophilus MEHF-uh-**STAHF**-i-luhs [mɛf-ə-'stɑf-ɪ-ləs]

mercatante mer-kuh-**TAHN**-tay [mɚ-kə-'tɑn-teɪ]

Mercatio mer-**KAY**-shee-oh [mɚ-'keɪ-ʃi-oʊ]

mercer / Mercer *(TIMON)* MER-ser ['mɝ-sɚ]

Mercurial mer-**KYO͞O**-ree-uhl [mɚ-'kjʊ-ri-əl]

Mercury MER-kyuh-ree ['mɝ-kjə-ri]

Mercutio *(R&J)* mer-**KYO͞O**-shee-oh [mɚ-'kju-ʃi-oʊ] scans
  to ___-**KYO͞O**-shyoh [___-'kju-ʃjoʊ] e.g. @ I, 2, 68

mere (only or absolute) MEAR [mɪɚ]

mered (to mark a boundary) scans to **MI**-rid ['mɪ-rɪd]

meritorious MEH-ri-**TAW**-ree-uhs [mɛ-rɪ-'tɔ-ri-əs]

Merlin MER-lin ['mɝ-lɪn]

Merops MEH-rahps ['mɛ-rɑps] or ___-rohps [___-roʊps]

Merriman MEH-ri-muhn ['mɛ-rɪ-mən]

mervailous scans to mer-**VAYL**-uhs [mɚ-'veɪl-əs]

Mesena mi-**SEE**-nuh [mɪ-'si-nə] Folio spelling, most editions
    "Misena"

Mesopotamia scans to MEHS-uh-puh-**TAYM**-yuh
    [mɛs-ə-pə-'teɪm-jə]

Messala *(JC)* meh-**SAH**-luh [mɛ-'sɑ-lə] or __-**SAY**-__
    [__-'seɪ-__]

Messaline MEHS-uh-leen ['mɛs-ə-lin]

Messina muh-**SEEN**-uh [mə-'sin-ə] possibly scans to
    MEH-sin-___ ['mɛ-sɪn-___] @ *MADO* V, 4, 123

metamorphose MEHT-uh-**MAWR**-fohz [mɛt-ə-'mɔɚ-foʊz]

Metamorphosis MEHT-uh-**MAWR**-fuh-sis [mɛt-ə-'mɔɚ-fə-sɪs]

mete MEET [mit]

metheglin muh-**THEHG**-lin [mə-'θɛg-lɪn]

methought mi-**THAWT** [mɪ-'θɔt]

mettle MEH-t(uh)l ['mɛ-tl̩]

Metullus Cimber *(JC)* mi-**TEHL**-uhs **SIM**-ber [mɪ-'tɛl-əs]
    ['sɪm-bɚ]

mew MYOO [mju]

EE i be/ I ɪ bit/ EH ɛ bet/ AA æ bat/ OO u boot / OO ʊ book/ AW ɔ bought/ AH ɑ father/ ER ɝ bird/
UH ʌ cup/ AY eɪ bay/ EYE aɪ bite/ OY ɔɪ boy/ OH oʊ boat/ OW aʊ how/ YOO ɪu duke/ EAR ɪɚ
beer/ AIR ɛɚ bear/ OOR ʊɚ tour/ AWR ɔɚ bore/ AHR ɑɚ bar/ NG ŋ king/ SH ʃ ship/ ZH ʒ vision/
TH θ thirty/ TH ð then/ CH tʃ child/ J dʒ just/ For complete list, see Key to Pronunciation p. 2.

mewling MYOO-ling ['mju-liŋ]

Michael, Sir *(1HIV)* MEYE-kuhl ['maɪ-kəl]

Michaelmas MIK-uhl-muhs ['mɪk-əl-məs]

micher MICH-er ['mɪtʃ-ɚ]

miching mallecho MICH-ing MAAL-uh-koh ['mɪtʃ-ɪŋ] ['mæl-ə-koʊ]

mickle MIK-uhl ['mɪk-əl]

Milan MI-luhn ['mɪ-lən] possibly scans to mi-LAAN [mɪ-'læn] or __-LAHN [__-'lɑn] @ *TEMP* II, 1, 128

Milan, Duke of *(2GEN)* MI-luhn ['mɪ-lən]

milch MILCH [mɪltʃ]

Milford MIL-ferd ['mɪl-fɚd]

Milo MEYE-loh ['maɪ-loʊ]

Minerva mi-NER-vuh [mɪ-'nɝ-və]

minikin MIN-i-kin ['mɪn-ɪ-kɪn]

minim MIN-uhm ['mɪn-əm]

minim-rest MIN-uhm-rehst ['mɪn-əm-rɛst]

minimus MIN-uh-muhs ['mɪn-ə-məs]

minion MIN-yuhn ['mɪn-jən] scans to MIN-ee-uhn ['mɪn-i-ən] e.g. @ *KJ* II, 1, 392

ministration MIN-i-STRAY-shuhn [mɪn-ɪ-'streɪ-ʃən]

Minola, Baptista *(SHR)* MIN-uh-luh baap-TIS-tuh ['mɪn-ə-lə] [bæp-'tɪs-tə]

Minos MEYE-nahs ['maɪ-nɑs] or ___-nohs [___-noʊs]

Minotaurs MIN-uh-tawrz ['mɪn-ə-tɔɚz]

minstrelsy MIN-struhl-see ['mɪn-strəl-si]

minutely (continual) MIN-it-lee ['mɪn-ɪt-li]

mirable MI-ruh-b(uh)l ['mɪ-rə-bl̩]

Miranda *(TEMP)* mi-RAAN-duh [mɪ-'ræn-də]

miry MEYE-ree ['maɪ-ri]

Misanthropos mi-SAAN-throh-pahs [mɪ-'sæn-θroʊ-pɑs] or
__-ZAAN-__-__ [__-'zæn-__-__]

mischievous MIS-chi-vuhs ['mɪs-tʃɪ-vəs]

misconster mis-KAHN-ster [mɪs-'kɑn-stɚ]

misconst'red mis-KAHN-sterd [mɪs-'kɑn-stɚd]

misconstrue always scans to mis-KAHN-strōō
[mɪs-'kɑn-stru]

miscreant MIS-kree-uhnt ['mɪs-kri-ənt]

miscreate MIS-kree-ayt ['mɪs-kri-eɪt]

misprise see "misprize"

misprised (mistaken) scans to MIS-preyezd ['mɪs-praɪzd]
@ *MID* III, 2, 74

misprision mis-PRIZH-uhn [mɪs-'prɪʒ-ən]

misprize / misprise (to undervalue) mis-PREYEZ [mɪs-'praɪz]

Mithridates MITH-ri-DAY-teez [mɪθ-rɪ-'deɪ-tiz]

Mitigation MI-ti-GAY-shuhn [mɪ-tɪ-'geɪ-ʃən]

mobled MOH-blid ['moʊ-blɪd] or MOH-b(uh)ld ['moʊ-bl̩d]
or MAH-___ ['mɑ-___]

Mockwater MAHK-waw-ter ['mɑk-wɔ-tɚ] or MUHK-__-__
['mʌk-__-__] or MAYK-__-__ ['meɪk-__-__]

Modena moh-DEE-nuh [moʊ-'di-nə]

modicum MAHD-i-kuhm ['mɑd-ɪ-kəm]

Modo MOH-doh ['moʊ-doʊ]

moe MOH [moʊ]

moi'ty MOY-tee ['mɔɪ-ti]

moiety MOY-i-tee ['mɔɪ-ɪ-ti] scans to MOY-tee ['mɔɪ-ti]
    e.g. @ *WT* III, 2, 38

mollification MAHL-uh-fi-KAY-shuhn [mɑl-ə-fɪ-'keɪ-ʃən]

mome MOHM [moʊm]

momentany MOH-muhn-tuhn-ee ['moʊ-mən-tən-i]

Monarcho muh-NAHR-koh [muh-'nɑɚ-koʊ] or mah-__-__
    [mɑ-__-__]

'mong MUHNG [mʌŋ]

'mongst MUHNGST [mʌŋst]

Monmouth MAHN-muhth ['mɑn-məθ]

Monsieur mahn-SOO-er [mɑn-'su-ɚ] (if French pronuncia-
    tion is preferred mi-SYER [mɪ-'sjɚ])

monstrous MAHN-struhs ['mɑn-strəs] scans to MAHNS-
    tuh-ruhs ['mɑns-tə-rəs] e.g. @ *OTH* II, 3, 207

monstruosity MAHN-stroo-AH-si-tee [mɑn-stru-'ɑ-sɪ-ti]

Montacute, Thomas, Earl of Salisbury *(HVIII)* MAHN-tuh-
    kyoot ['mɑn-tə-kjut]

Montague MAHN-tuh-gyoo ['mɑn-tə-gju]
    Montague *(R&J)*
    Lady Montague *(R&J)*

Montano *(OTH)* mahn-TAAN-oh [mɑn-'tæn-oʊ] or
    __-TAHN-__ [__-'tɑn-__]

montant MAHN-tuhnt ['mɑn-tənt]

Montferrat mahnt-fuh-**RAAT** [mɑnt-fə-'ræt]

Montgomery, Sir John *(3HVI)* muhnt-**GUHM**-ree [mənt-'gʌm-ri] scans to __-__-uh-ree [__-__-ə-ri] @ IV, 7, 40

Montjoy *(HV)* **MAHNT**-joy ['mɑnt-ʤɔɪ] scans to mahnt-**JOY** [mɑnt-'ʤɔɪ] @ III, 5, 61

moor / Moor MO͝OR [mʊɚ]

Moorfields **MO͝OR**-feeldz ['mʊɚ-fildz]

mop (n) (a grimace) MAHP [mɑp]

mop (v) (to make a face) MAHP [mɑp]

mope (v) (to be gloomy) MOHP [moʊp]

Mopsa *(WT)* **MAHP**-suh ['mɑp-sə]

Mordake **MAWR**-dayk ['mɔɚ-deɪk] possibly **MER**-dahk ['mɝ-dɑk] in keeping with "Murdocke," original name in Holinshed

More MAWR [mɔɚ]

Morisco muh-**RIS**-koh [mə-'rɪs-koʊ]

Morocco, Prince of *(MVEN)* muh-**RAH**-koh [mə-'rɑ-koʊ]

mort MAWRT [mɔɚt]

Mortimer **MAWR**-ti-mer ['mɔɚ-tɪ-mɚ]
Mortimer, Edmund, Earl of March *(1HIV, 1HVI)*
MAHRCH [mɑɚʧ]
Mortimer, Lady *(1HIV)*
Mortimer, Sir Hugh *(3HVI)*
Mortimer, Sir John *(3HVI)*

mortise **MAWR**-tis ['mɔɚ-tɪs]

EE i be/ I ɪ bit/ EH ɛ bet/ AA æ bat/ O͞O u boot / O͝O ʊ book/ AW ɔ bought/ AH ɑ father/ ER ɝ bird/ UH ʌ cup/ AY eɪ bay/ EYE aɪ bite/ OY ɔɪ boy/ OH oʊ boat/ OW ɑʊ how/ YO͞O ɪu duke/ EAR ɪɚ beer/ AIR ɛɚ bear/ O͝OR ʊɚ tour/ AWR ɔɚ bore/ AHR ɑɚ bar/ NG ŋ king/ SH ʃ ship/ ZH ʒ vision/ TH θ thirty/ TH ð then/ CH ʧ child/ J ʤ just/ For complete list, see Key to Pronunciation p. 2.

Morton MAWR-t(uh)n [ˈmɔɚ-tn̩]
  Morton *(2HIV)*
  Morton, John, Bishop of Ely *(RIII)* **EE**-lee [ˈi-li]

mose MOHZ [moʊz]

mote MOHT [moʊt]

Moth MAWTH [mɔθ] or MAHTH [maθ]
  Moth *(LLL)* probably MOHT [moʊt] as in "mote" (a speck)
  Moth *(MID)*

motley MAHT-lee [ˈmat-li]

mought MOWT [maʊt] or MAWT [mɔt]

Mouldy, Ralph *(2HIV)* MOHLD-ee [ˈmoʊld-i]

mounched MUHNCHT [mʌntʃt]

Mounsieur Basimecu MOWN-sear **BAAZ**-i-muh-kōō
  [ˈmaʊn-sɪɚ] [ˈbæz-ɪ-mə-ku]

mountant MOWN-tuhnt [ˈmaʊn-tənt]

Mountanto mown-**TAHN**-toh [maʊn-ˈtan-toʊ]

mountebank MOWN-tuh-baangk [ˈmaʊn-tə-bæŋk]

mouth (n) MOWTH [maʊθ]

mouth (v) MOW<u>TH</u> [maʊð]

mow (n) (grimace) MOW [maʊ]

mow (v) (to cut down) MOH [moʊ]

Mowbray MOH-bray [ˈmoʊ-breɪ] or ___-bree [___-bri]
  Mowbray, John, Duke of Norfolk *(3HVI)* **NAWR**-fuhk
    [ˈnɔɚ-fək]
  Mowbray, Lord *(2HIV)*
  Mowbray, Thomas, Duke of Norfolk *(RII)*

moy MOY [mɔɪ]

Moyses MOY-zehz [ˈmɔɪ-zɛz]

Mugs MUHGZ [mʌgz]

muleter MYO͞OL-ter [ˈmjul-tɚ]

Muliteus scans to MYO͞O-li-tyuhs [ˈmju-lɪ-tjəs]

mulled MUHLD [mʌld]

Mulmutius muhl-MYO͞O-shuhs [məl-ˈmju-ʃəs]

multipotent muhl-TIP-uh-tuhnt [məl-ˈtɪp-ə-tənt]

multitudinous always scans to muhl-ti-TYO͞OD-nuhs [məl-tɪ-ˈtɪud-nəs]

muniments MYO͞O-ni-muhnts [ˈmju-nɪ-mənts]

mure MYO͞OR [mjʊɚ]

murk MERK [mɝk]

murrain MUH-rin [ˈmʌ-rɪn] or ME(r)-___ [ˈmɝ-___]

murrion MUH-rin [ˈmʌ-rɪn] or ME(r)-___ [ˈmɝ-___]

murther MER-ther [ˈmɝ-ðɚ]

muscadel MUHS-kuh-dehl [ˈmʌs-kə-dɛl]

Muscovites MUHS-kuh-veyets [ˈmʌs-kə-vaɪts]

Muscovits MUHS-kuh-vits [ˈmʌs-kə-vɪts]

Muscovy MUHS-kuh-vee [ˈmʌs-kə-vi]

mushrumps MUHSH-ruhmps [ˈmʌʃ-rəmps]

musit MYO͞O-zit [ˈmju-zɪt]

Muskos MUHS-kohs [ˈmʌs-koʊs]

muss MUHS [mʌs]

EE i be/ I ɪ bit/ EH ɛ bet/ AA æ bat/ O͞O u boot / O͞O ʊ book/ AW ɔ bought/ AH ɑ father/ ER ɝ bird/ UH ʌ cup/ AY eɪ bay/ EYE aɪ bite/ OY ɔɪ boy/ OH oʊ boat/ OW aʊ how/ YO͞O ɪu duke/ EAR ɪɚ beer/ AIR ɛɚ bear/ O͞OR ʊɚ tour/ AWR ɔɚ bore/ AHR ɑɚ bar/ NG ŋ king/ SH ʃ ship/ ZH ʒ vision/ TH θ thirty/ TH ð then/ CH tʃ child/ J dʒ just/ For complete list, see Key to Pronunciation p. 2.

169

mustachio muh-STAA-shee-oh [mə-'stæ-ʃi-oʊ] or
  __-STAH-__-__ [__-'stɑ-__-__] or __-STAA-shyoh
  [__-'stæ-ʃjoʊ] or __-STAH-shyoh [__-'stɑ-ʃjoʊ]

Mustardseed *(MID)* MUHS-terd-seed ['mʌs-tɚd-sid]

muster MUHS-ter ['mʌs-tɚ]

mutine MYOO͞-tin ['mju-tɪn]

mutineer MYOO͞-t(uh)n-ear ['mju-tn̩-ɪɚ]

Mutius *(TITUS)* MYOO͞-shuhs ['mju-ʃəs] scans to
  MYOO͞-shee-uhs ['mju-ʃi-əs] @ I, 1, 392

Myrmidons MER-mi-dahnz ['mɝ-mɪ-dɑnz] or __-__- duhnz
  [__-__-dənz]

Mytilen MIT-i-lehn ['mɪt-ɪ-lɛn]

Mytilene MIT-i-LEE-nee [mɪt-ɪ-'li-ni]

Mytilin MIT-i-lin ['mɪt-ɪ-lɪn]

Naiades NEYE-aadz ['naɪ-ædz]

Naples NAY-p(uh)lz ['neɪ-pl̩z]

narcissus / Narcissus nahr-SIS-uhs [nɑɚ-'sɪs-əs]

Nathaniel *(LLL)* nuh-THAAN-yuhl [nə-'θæn-jəl]

naught NAWT [nɔt]

Navarre see "Ferdinand"

nave NAYV [neɪv]

nay NAY [neɪ]

nayward NAY-werd ['neɪ-wɚd]

Nazarite NAAZ-uh-reyet ['næz-ə-raɪt]

ne NEE [ni]

ne'er NAIR [nɛɚ]

ne'ertheless NAIR-<u>th</u>uh-lehs ['nɛɚ-ðə-lɛs]

neaf NEEF [nif]

Neapolitan NEE-uh-PAHL-i-tuhn [ni-ə-'pɑl-ɪ-tən]

neatherd NEET-herd ['nit-hɚd]

neb NEHB [nɛb]

Nebuchadnezzar NEHB-uh-kuhd-NEHZ-er
[nɛb-ə-kəd-'nɛz-ɚ]

necessitied nuh-SEHS-i-teed [nə-'sɛs-ɪ-tid]

Nedar NEED-er ['nid-ɚ] or NEHD-__ ['nɛd-__]

needle NEE-d(uh)l ['ni-dļ] scans to one syllable NEELD
[nild] or NEEL [nil] e.g. @ *MID* III, 2, 204

neele NEEL [nil]

neeze NEEZ [niz]

neglection ni-GLEHK-shuhn [nɪ-'glɛk-ʃən]

neif NEEF [nif]

neigh NAY [neɪ]

Nell *(CE)* NEHL [nɛl]

Nemean always scans to NEE-myuhn ['ni-mjən]

Nemesis NEHM-i-sis ['nɛm-ɪ-sɪs]

Neoptolemus NEE-uhp-TAHL-i-muhs [ni-əp-'tɑl-ɪ-məs]

Neptune NEHP-tyōōn ['nɛp-tɪun]

Nereides NI-ree-idz ['nɪ-ri-ɪdz] or NI-ree-i-deez ['nɪ-ri-ɪ-diz]

Nerissa *(MVEN)* nuh-RIS-uh [nə-'rɪs-ə]

Nero NI-roh ['nɪ-roʊ]

EE i be/ I ɪ bit/ EH ɛ bet/ AA æ bat/ ŌŌ u boot / ŎŎ ʊ book/ AW ɔ bought/ AH ɑ father/ ER ɝ bird/
UH ʌ cup/ AY eɪ bay/ EYE aɪ bite/ OY ɔɪ boy/ OH oʊ boat/ OW aʊ how/ YŌŌ ɪu duke/ EAR ɪɚ
beer/ AIR ɛɚ bear/ ŌŌR ʊɚ tour/ AWR ɔɚ bore/ AHR ɑɚ bar/ NG ŋ king/ SH ʃ ship/ ZH ʒ vision/
TH θ thirty/ <u>TH</u> ð then/ CH tʃ child/ J dʒ just/ For complete list, see Key to Pronunciation p. 2.

171

Nervii NER-vee-eye ['nɝ-vi-aɪ]

Nessus NEHS-uhs ['nɛs-əs]

Nestor NEHS-ter ['nɛs-tɚ] or ___-tawr [___-tɔɚ]
Nestor *(T&C)*

nether NE<u>TH</u>-er ['nɛð-ɚ]

Nevil NEH-vuhl ['nɛ-vəl] or ___-vil [___-vɪl]
Nevil, John, Marquess of Montague *(3HVI)* MAHN-tuh-
gyoo ['mɑn-tə-gju]
Nevil, Ralph, Earl of Westmoreland *(3HVI)* WEHST-mer-
luhnd ['wɛst-mɚ-lənd]
Nevil, Richard, Earl of Salisbury *(2HVI)* SAWLZ-buh-ree
['sɔlz-bə-ri] scans to SAWLZ-bree ['sɔlz-bri] e.g. @ I, 3, 72
Nevil, Richard, Earl of Warwick *(2HVI, 3HVI)* WAW-rik
['wɔ-rɪk] or WAH-__ ['wɑ-__]

Newgate NYOO-gayt ['nɪu-geɪt] or ___-guht [___-gət]

newsmonger NYOOZ-muhng-ger ['nɪuz-məŋ-gɚ] or ___-
mahng-___ [___-mɑŋ-___]

newt NYOOT [nɪut]

new-trothed scans to nyoo-TRO<u>H</u>TH-id [nɪu-'trouð-ɪd]

Nicander neye-KAAN-der [naɪ-'kæn-dɚ]

Nicanor *(COR)* neye-KAY-ner [naɪ-'keɪ-nɚ]

Nicholas Henton scans to NIK-luhs HEHN-t(uh)n ['nɪk-ləs]
['hɛn-tn̩] @ *HVIII* I, 2, 147

niggard NIG-erd ['nɪg-ɚd]

Nilus NEYE-luhs ['naɪ-ləs]

ninny / Ninny NI-nee ['nɪ-ni]

Ninus NEYEN-uhs ['naɪn-əs] or NIN-__ ['nɪn-__]

Niobe NEYE-oh-bee ['naɪ-ou-bi] or ___- uh-___ [___-ə-___]
in the plural scans to NEYE-bees ['naɪ-biz] @ *T&C* V, 10, 19

172

Nob NAHB [nɑb]

noblesse NOH-blehs ['noʊ-blɛs]

noddle NAH-d(uh)l ['nɑ-dl̩]

noddy NAH-dee ['nɑ-di]

noes NOHZ [noʊz]

noisome NOY-suhm ['nɔɪ-səm]

nole NOHL [noʊl]

nonage NAH-nij ['nɑ-nɪʤ]

nonce NAHNS [nɑns]

nonino nah-nee-NOH [nɑ-ni-'noʊ]

nonpareil nahn-puh-REHL [nɑn-pə-'rɛl] or ___-___-RAYL [___-___-'reɪl]

nook-shotten noͦok-SHAH-t(uh)n [nʊk-'ʃɑ-tn̩]

Norbery, Sir John scans to nawr-BREE [nɔɚ-'bri]

Norfolk, Duke of NAWR-fuhk ['nɔɚ-fək]
Norfolk, Duke of *(HVIII)*
Norfolk, Duke of *(RIII)*

Normandy NAWR-muhn-dee ['nɔɚ-mən-di]

Northampton nawr-THAAMP-t(uh)n [nɔɚ-'θæmp-tn̩] or nawrth-HAAMP-___ [nɔɚθ-'hæmp-___]

Northamptonshire nawr-THAAMP-t(uh)n-sher [nɔɚ-'θæmp-tn̩-ʃɚ] or nawrth-HAAMP-___-___ [nɔɚθ-'hæmp-___-___] or ___-___-___-shear [___-___-___-ʃɪɚ]

Northumberland nawr-THUHM-ber-luhnd [nɔɚ-'θʌm-bɚ-lənd]

Northumberland, Earl of *(RII, 1HIV, 2HIV)* possibly
   scans to nawr-**THUM**-bluhnd [nɔɚ-'θʌm-blənd]
   @ *1HIV* V, 5, 37
Northumberland, Lady *(2HIV)*

Norweyan nawr-**WAY**-uhn [nɔɚ-'weɪ-ən]

notary **NOHT**-uh-ree ['noʊt-ə-ri] scans to **NOHT**-ree
   ['noʊt-ri] @ *MVEN* I, 3, 140

not'st (to observe) NOHTST [noʊtst]

nought NAWT [nɔt]

novice **NAH**-vis ['nɑ-vɪs]

novum **NOH**-vuhm ['noʊ-vəm]

noyance **NOY**-uhns ['nɔɪ-əns]

nullity **NUHL**-i-tee ['nʌl-ɪ-ti]

Numa **NYOO**-muh ['nɪu-mə]

nuncio scans to **NUHN**-syoh ['nʌn-sjoʊ]

nuncle **NUHNG**-k(uh)l ['nʌŋ-kl̩]

nuptial **NUHP**-shuhl ['nʌp-ʃəl] scans to **NUHP**–shee-uhl
   ['nʌp-ʃi-əl] e.g. @ *TEMP* V, 1, 308

Nurse NERS [nɝs]
   Nurse *(R&J)*
   Nurse *(TITUS)*

Nym NIM [nɪm]
   Nym *(HV, MW)*

nymph NIMF [nɪmf]
   Nymphs *(TEMP)*

O (an interjection) OH [oʊ]

o' (abbreviation for "of" or "on") uh [ə]

o'er AWR [ɔɚ]

o'th UH<u>TH</u> [ʌð]

Oatcake, Hugh OHT-kayk HY$\overline{OO}$ ['oʊt-keɪk] [hju]

oathable OH<u>TH</u>-uh-b(uh)l ['oʊð-ə-bl̩]

oath OHTH [oʊθ]

oaths OH<u>TH</u>Z [oʊðz]

ob. (abbreviation for "obolus") AHB-uh-luhs ['ɑb-ə-ləs]

obduracy AHB-dy$\overline{oo}$-ruh-see ['ɑb-djʊ-rə-si]

obdurate ahb-DY$\overline{OO}$-rit [ɑb-'djʊ-rɪt] scans to AHB-dy$\overline{oo}$-___ ['ɑb-dju-___] @ *2GEN* IV, 2, 119

obeisance scans to oh-BAY-uh-suhns [oʊ-'beɪ-ə-səns] if the line @ *SHR* Ind, 1, 107 is an Epic Caesura, or possibly OH-bay-suhns ['oʊ-beɪ-səns]

Oberon *(MID)* OH-buh-rahn ['oʊ-bə-rɑn]

Obidicut oh-BID-i-kuht [oʊ-'bɪd-ɪ-kət]

oblations oh-BLAY-shuhnz [oʊ-'bleɪ-ʃənz]

obliquy / obloquy AHB-luh-kwee ['ɑb-lə-kwi]

obscure (adj) ahb-SKY$\overline{OO}$R [ɑb-'skjʊɚ] scans to AHB-sky$\overline{oo}$r ['ɑb-skjʊɚ] e.g. @ *HAM* IV, 5, 211

obsequies AHB-si-kweez ['ɑb-sɪ-kwiz]

obsequious ahb-SEE-kwee-uhs [ɑb-'si-kwi-əs] or uhb-___-___-___ [əb-___-___-___]

obsequiously scans to ahb-SEE-kwuhs-lee [ɑb-'si-kwəs-li]

observants (n) AHB-zer-vuhnts ['ɑb-zɚ-vənts]

obstinacy always scans to AHB-stin-AY-see [ɑb-stɪn-'eɪ-si]

EE i be/ I ɪ bit/ EH ɛ bet/ AA æ bat/ $\overline{OO}$ u boot / $\overline{OO}$ ʊ book/ AW ɔ bought/ AH ɑ father/ ER ɝ bird/ UH ʌ cup/ AY eɪ bay/ EYE aɪ bite/ OY ɔɪ boy/ OH oʊ boat/ OW aʊ how/ Y$\overline{OO}$ ɪu duke/ EAR ɪɚ beer/ AIR ɛɚ bear/ $\overline{OO}$R ʊɚ tour/ AWR ɔɚ bore/ AHR ɑɚ bar/ NG ŋ king/ SH ʃ ship/ ZH ʒ vision/ TH θ thirty/ <u>TH</u> ð then/ CH tʃ child/ J ʤ just/ For complete list, see Key to Pronunciation p. 2.

175

occident AHK-suh-duhnt ['ɑk-sə-dənt] or __-__-dehnt [__-__-dɛnt]

ocean OH-shuhn ['oʊ-ʃən] scans to OH-shee-uhn ['oʊ-ʃi-ən] e.g. @ *HV* III, 1, 14

Octavia *(A&C)* ahk-TAYV-ee-uh [ɑk-'teɪv-i-ə] scans to ___-TAY-vyuh [___-'teɪ-vjə] e.g. @ II, 2, 119

Octavius ahk-TAYV-ee-uhs [ɑk-'teɪv-i-əs] scans to __-TAY-vyuhs [__-'teɪ-vjəs]
Octavius Caesar *(A&C)*
Octavius Caesar *(JC)* scans @ III, 1, 276

ocular scans to AHK-ler ['ɑk-lə-]

odoriferous OH-duh-RIF-uh-ruhs [oʊ-də-'rɪf-ə-rəs] scans to __-__-RIF-ruhs [__-__-'rɪf-rəs] @ *KJ* III, 4, 26

'od's / 'ods / od's (corruption of "God's") AHDZ [ɑdz]

'ods nouns (corruption of "God's wounds") AHDZ NO͞ ONZ [ɑdz] [nunz]

oeillades uh-YAHDZ [ə-'jɑdz] or IL-ee-yuhdz ['ɪl-i-jədz] @ *MW* I, 3, 54

oes OHZ [oʊz]

offal AWF-uhl ['ɔf-əl]

offendress uh-FEHN-dris [ə-'fɛn-drɪs]

Old Shepherd SHEHP-erd ['ʃɛp-ə-d]
Old Shepherd *(1HVI)*
Old Shepherd *(WT)*

Oliver *(AYL)* AH-li-ver ['ɑ-lɪ-və-]

Olivia *(12th)* oh-LIV-ee-uh [oʊ-'lɪv-i-ə] scans to __-LIV-yuh [__-'lɪv-jə] e.g. @ I, 1, 20

Olympus oh-LIM-puhs [oʊ-'lɪm-pəs] or uh-___-___ [ə-___-___]

omittance oh-MI-tuhns [oʊ-'mɪ-təns]

oneyers WUHN-yerz ['wʌn-jɚz]

ope OHP [oʊp]

operance AHP-uh-ruhns ['ɑp-ə-rəns]

operant always scans to AHP-ruhnt ['ɑp-rənt]

Ophelia *(HAM)* oh-FEEL-yuh [oʊ-'fil-jə] scans to __-__-ee-uh [__-__-i-ə] e.g. @ IV, 5, 158

opinion uh-PIN-yuhn [ə-'pɪn-jən] scans to __-__-ee-yuhn [__-__-i-jən] e.g. @ *1HIV* V, 4, 47

opportune always scans to ah-PAWR-tyo͞on [ɑ-'pɔɚ-tɪun]

opprobriously scans to uh-PROH-bruhs-lee [ə-'proʊ-brəs-li]

oppugnancy uh-PUHG-nuhn-see [ə-'pʌg-nən-si]

oracle AW-ruh-k(uh)l ['ɔ-rə-kl̩] scans to AWR-k(uh)l ['ɔɚ-kl̩] @ *WT* III, 2, 126

orator AW-ruh-ter ['ɔ-rə-tɚ] or AH-__-__ ['ɑ-__-__]

ordain awr-DAYN [ɔɚ-'deɪn] scans to AWR-dayn ['ɔɚ-deɪn] @ *TITUS* V, 3, 22

ordinance AWR-d(uh)n-uhns ['ɔɚ-dn̩-əns]

ordinant AWR-d(uh)n-uhnt ['ɔɚ-dn̩-ənt]

ordnance AWRD-nuhns ['ɔɚd-nəns]

ordure AWR-jer ['ɔɚ-ʤɚ]

orgulous AWR-gyuh-luhs ['ɔɚ-gjə-ləs]

orisons AW-ri-zuhnz ['ɔ-rɪ-zənz]

Orlando *(AYL)* awr-LAAN-doh [ɔɚ-'læn-doʊ]

EE i be/ I ɪ bit/ EH ɛ bet/ AA æ bat/ O͞O u boot / O͞O ʊ book/ AW ɔ bought/ AH ɑ father/ ER ɝ bird/ UH ʌ cup/ AY eɪ bay/ EYE aɪ bite/ OY ɔɪ boy/ OH oʊ boat/ OW aʊ how/ YO͞O ɪu duke/ EAR ɪə beer/ AIR ɛə bear/ O͞OR ʊə tour/ AWR ɔə bore/ AHR ɑə bar/ NG ŋ king/ SH ʃ ship/ ZH ʒ vision/ TH θ thirty/ T̲H̲ ð then/ CH ʧ child/ J ʤ just/ For complete list, see Key to Pronunciation p. 2.

Orleans AWR-lee-uhnz ['ɔɚ-li-ənz] scans to AWR-lyuhnz
['ɔɚ-ljənz] or ___-leenz [___-linz]
Orleans, Duke of *(HV)* scans @ *HV* II, 4, 5

Orodes ah-ROH-deez [ɑ-'roʊ-diz]

Orpheus always scans to AWR-fyuhs ['ɔɚ-fjəs] or __-fyōōs
[__-fjus]

Orsino *(12th)* awr-SEE-noh [ɔɚ-'si-noʊ]

ort AWRT [ɔɚt]

orthography awr-THAHG-ruh-fee [ɔɚ-'θɑg-rə-fi]

osier OH-zher ['oʊ-ʒɚ]

osprey AHS-pree ['ɑs-pri] or ___-pray [___-preɪ]

Osric *(HAM)* AHZ-rik ['ɑz-rɪk] or AHS-___ ['ɑs-___]

Ossa AH-suh ['ɑ-sə]

ostent always scans to ah-STEHNT [ɑ-'stɛnt]

ostler / Ostler *(1HIV)* AHS-ler ['ɑs-lɚ]

Oswald *(LEAR)* AHZ-wawld ['ɑz-wɔld]

Othello *(OTH)* oh-THEHL-oh [oʊ-'θɛl-oʊ]

Ottoman AH-tuh-muhn ['ɑ-tə-mən]

Ottomites AH-tuh-meyets ['ɑ-tə-maɪts]

ouches OWCH-iz ['aʊtʃ-ɪz]

ought AWT [ɔt]

ounce OWNTS [aʊnts]

ouphs OWFS [aʊfs] or ŌŌFS [ufs]

ousel ŌŌ-zuhl ['u-zəl]

outdure OWT-dyōōr ['aʊt-djʊɚ]

Overdone, Mistress *(MM)* OH-ver-duhn ['oʊ-vɚ-dən]

overscutched OH-ver-skuhcht ['ou-vɚ-skətʃt]

Ovid AH-vid ['ɑ-vɪd]

Ovidius Naso oh-VID-ee-uhs NAY-zoh [ou-'vɪd-i-əs]
['neɪ-zou]

Owen OH-in ['ou-in]

Oxford AHKS-ferd ['ɑks-fɚd]

Oxfordshire AHKS-ferd-sher ['ɑks-fɚd-ʃɚ] or __-__-shear
[__-__-ʃɪɚ]

oxlips AHKS-lips ['ɑks-lɪps]

oyes oh-YEHZ [ou-'jɛz] or ___-YEHS [___-'jɛs] scans to
OH-yehz ['ou-jɛz] or OH-yehs ['ou-jɛs] @ *MW* V, 5, 39

Pacorus PAAK-uh-ruhs ['pæk-ə-rəs]

paction PAAK-shuhn ['pæk-ʃən]

paddock / Paddock PAAD-uhk ['pæd-ək]

Padua PAA-dyo͞o-uh ['pæ-dju-ə] scans to PAA-dywuh
['pæ-djwə] or ___-jo͞o-uh [___-ʤu-ə] scans to ___-jwuh
[___-ʤwə] e.g. @ *MVEN* III, 4, 49

Page PAYJ [peɪʤ]
    Page *(MW)*
    Page, Anne *(MW)*
    Page, Mistress *(MW)*
    Page, William *(MW)*

Palamades PAAL-uh-MEE-deez [pæl-ə-'mi-diz]

Palamon *(2NOB)* PAAL-uh-muhn ['pæl-ə-mən] scans to
PAAL-muhn ['pæl-mən] or __-__-mahn [__-__-mɑn] scans
to __-mahn [__-mɑn] e.g. @ V, 3, 51

EE i be/ I ɪ bit/ EH ɛ bet/ AA æ bat/ O͞O u boot / O͝O ʊ book/ AW ɔ bought/ AH ɑ father/ ER ɝ bird/
UH ʌ cup/ AY eɪ bay/ EYE aɪ bite/ OY ɔɪ boy/ OH ou boat/ OW aʊ how/ YO͞O ɪu duke/ EAR ɪɚ
beer/ AIR ɛɚ bear/ O͞OR ʊɚ tour/ AWR ɔɚ bore/ AHR ɑɚ bar/ NG ŋ king/ SH ʃ ship/ ZH ʒ vision/
TH θ thirty/ TH ð then/ CH tʃ child/ J ʤ just/ For complete list, see Key to Pronunciation p. 2.

179

Palatine PAAL-uh-teyen ['pæl-ə-taɪn]

Palestine PAAL-i-steyen ['pæl-ɪ-staɪn]

palfrey PAWL-free ['pɔl-fri]

palisadoes PAAL-i-SAY-dohz [pæl-ɪ-'seɪ-douz]

Pallas PAAL-uhs ['pæl-əs] or ___-aas [___-æs]

palliament scans to PAAL-yuh-muhnt ['pæl-jə-mənt]

palmer PAHM-er ['pɑm-ɚ]

palsy PAWL-zee ['pɔl-zi]

palter PAWL-ter ['pɔl-tɚ]

paltry PAWL-tree ['pɔl-tri]

paly PAY-lee ['peɪ-li]

Pandar PAAN-der ['pæn-dɚ]

Pandarus PAAN-duh-ruhs ['pæn-də-rəs]
   Pandarus *(T&C)* also called "Pandar" PAAN-der ['pæn-dɚ]

pander / Pander *(PER)* PAAN-der ['pæn-dɚ]

Pandulph, Cardinal *(KJ)* PAAN-duhlf ['pæn-dəlf]

pannier PAAN-yer ['pæn-jɚ] or ___-ee-er [___-i-ɚ]

Pannonians paa-NOH-nyuhnz [pæ-'nou-njənz] or
   puh-__-__ [pə-__-__]

Pansa PAAN-zuh ['pæn-zə] or ___-suh [___-sə]

pantaloon paan-tuh-LOON [pæn-tə-'lun]

Pantheon scans to PAAN-thyuhn ['pæn-θjən] @ *TITUS* I, 1,
   245 and paan-THEE-uhn [pæn-'θi-ən] or ___-THEE-ahn
   [___-'θi-ɑn] @ *TITUS* I, 1, 336

Panthino *(2GEN)* paan-THEE-noh [pæn-'θi-nou]

pantler PAANT-ler ['pænt-lɚ]

Papal Legate *(1HVI)* PAY-puhl LEHG-it ['peɪ-pəl] ['lɛg-ɪt]

Paphlagonia PAAF-luh-GOH-nee-uh [pæf-lə-'gou-ni-ə]

Paphos PAY-fohs ['peɪ-foʊs]

papist PAY-pist ['peɪ-pɪst]

Paracelsus PAA-ruh-SEHL-suhs [pæ-rə-'sɛl-səs]

paragon PAA-ruh-gahn ['pæ-rə-gɑn] or PEH-__-__ ['pɛ-__-__]

paramour PAA-ruh-mōōr ['pæ-rə-mʊɚ] or PEH-___-___
   ['pɛ-___-___]

parapets PAA-ruh-pehts ['pæ-rə-pɛts]

paraquito PAA-ruh-KEE-toh [pæ-rə-'ki-toʊ]

Parca PAHR-kuh ['pɑɚ-kə]

pard PAHRD [pɑɚd]

Paris PAA-ris ['pæ-rɪs]
   Paris *(R&J)*
   Paris *(T&C)*

Paris-ward PAA-ris-werd ['pæ-rɪs-wɚd]

paritors PAA-ri-tawrz ['pæ-rɪ-tɔɚz] or __-__terz [__-__tɚz]

Park-ward PAHRK-werd ['pɑɚk-wɚd]

parle PAHRL [pɑɚl]

parley PAHR-lee ['pɑɚ-li]

parlous PAHR-luhs ['pɑɚ-ləs]

parmacity PAHR-muh-SI-tee [pɑɚ-mə-'sɪ-ti]

Parolles *(AW)* puh-ROHL-iz [pə-'roʊl-ɪz] or __-__-eez
   [__-__-iz] or __-RAHL-is [__-'rɑl-ɪs]

EE i be/ I ɪ bit/ EH ɛ bet/ AA æ bat/ OO u boot / OO ʊ book/ AW ɔ bought/ AH ɑ father/ ER ɝ bird/
UH ʌ cup/ AY eɪ bay/ EYE aɪ bite/ OY ɔɪ boy/ OH oʊ boat/ OW aʊ how/ YOO ɪu duke/ EAR ɪɚ
beer/ AIR ɛɚ bear/ OOR ʊɚ tour/ AWR ɔɚ bore/ AHR ɑɚ bar/ NG ŋ king/ SH ʃ ship/ ZH ʒ vision/
TH θ thirty/ TH ð then/ CH tʃ child/ J dʒ just/ For complete list, see Key to Pronunciation p. 2.

Parthia PAHR-thee-uh ['pɑɚ-θi-ə] scans to **PAHR**-thyuh ['pɑɚ-θjə] e.g. @ *A&C* II, 3, 32

Parthian always scans to **PAHR**-thyuhn ['pɑɚ-θjən]

partisan PAHR-ti-zuhn ['pɑɚ-tɪ-zən] or __-__-zaan [__-__-zæn]

Partlet PAHRT-lit ['pɑɚt-lɪt]

pash PAASH [pæʃ]

passado puh-SAH-doh [pə-'sɑ-doʊ]

passant PAAS-uhnt ['pæs-ənt]

passy measures pavin PAAS-ee MEHZH-erz PAA-vin ['pæs-i] ['mɛʒ-ɚ-z] ['pæ-vɪn]

pastern PAAS-tern ['pæs-tɚ-n]

pasty (a pie) PAAS-tee ['pæs-ti]

Patchbreech PAACH-brich ['pætʃ-brɪtʃ] or ___-breech [___-brɪtʃ]

pate PAYT [peɪt]

patens PAA-t(uh)nz ['pæ-tn̩z]

patent PAAT-uhnt ['pæt-ənt] or PAYT-___ ['peɪt-___]

patience / Patience PAY-shuhns ['peɪ-ʃəns] scans to PAY-shee-uhns ['peɪ-ʃi-əns]
Patience *(HVIII)* scans @ IV, 2, 165

patrician puh-TRI-shuhn [pə-'tri-ʃən] scans to __-__-shee-uhn [__-__-ʃi-ən] @ *COR* V, 6, 82

patrimony PAA-tri-moh-nee ['pæ-trɪ-moʊ-ni]

Patroclus *(T&C)* puh-TROHK-luhs [pə-'troʊk-ləs] or ___-TRAHK-___ [___-'trɑk-___]

Paulina *(WT)* paw-LEYE-nuh [pɔ-'laɪ-nə] (paw-LEE-nuh [pɔ-'li-nə] is sometimes heard)

paunch / Paunch PAWNCH [pɔntʃ]

pax PAAKS [pæks]

peascod PEEZ-kahd ['piz-kɑd]

pease PEEZ [piz]

Peaseblossom *(MID)* PEEZ-blah-suhm ['piz-blɑ-səm]

pedant / Pedant PEH-d(uh)nt ['pɛ-dn̩t]
   Pedant *(SHR)*, later posing as Vincentio vin-SEHN-shee-oh
   [vɪn-'sɛn-ʃi-ou] scans to ___-SEHN-shyoh
   [___-'sɛn-ʃjou] @ I, 1, 192

pedantical puh-DAAN-ti-k(uh)l [pə-'dæn-tɪ-kl̩]

pedlar PEHD-ler ['pɛd-lɚ]

Pedro, Don, Prince of Arragon *(MADO)* PAY-droh AA-ruh-
   gahn ['peɪ-drou] ['æ-rə-gɑn]

Peesel PI-s(uh)l [pɪ-sl̩] or ___-z(uh)l [___-zl̩] or PEE-s(uh)l
   ['pi-sl̩] or ___-z(uh)l [___-zl̩]

Pegasus PEHG-uh-suhs ['pɛg-ə-səs]

peise PEEZ [piz] or PAYZ [peɪz]

peize PEEZ [piz]

pelf PEHLF [pɛlf]

Pelion PEE-lee-uhn ['pi-li-ən] scans to PEE-lyuhn ['pi-ljən]
   @ *HAM* V, 1, 240

Peloponnesus pehl-OH-puh-NEE-suhs [pɛl-ou-pə-'ni-səs]

Pelops PEE-lahps ['pi-lɑps]

Pembroke PEHM-brook ['pɛm-brʊk] or ___-brohk
   [___-brouk]

Pembroke, Earl of *(KJ)*

pence PEHNS [pɛns]

Pendragon pehn-DRAAG-uhn [pɛn-'dræg-ən]

penetrative PEHN-i-tray-tiv ['pɛn-ɪ-treɪ-tɪv]

penitential PEHN-i-TEHN-shuhl [pɛn-ɪ-'tɛn-ʃəl]

penner PEHN-er ['pɛn-ɚ]

pennons PEHN-uhnz ['pɛn-ənz]

pennyworth PEHN-ee-werth ['pɛn-i-wɚθ] or PEHN-erth
   ['pɛn-ɚθ]

Pentapolis pehn-TAA-puh-luhs [pɛn-'tæ-pə-ləs]

Pentecost PEHN-ti-kahst ['pɛn-tɪ-kɑst]

Penthesilea PEHN-theh-si-LEE-uh [pɛn-θɛ-sɪ-'li-ə]

penurious scans to peh-NYO͞OR-yuhs [pɛ-'njʊɚ-jəs]

penury PEHN-yo͞o-ree ['pɛn-jʊ-ri] scans to PEHN-ree
   ['pɛn-ri] e.g. @ *R&J* V, 1, 49

Pepin PEHP-in ['pɛp-ɪn]

per se per-SAY [pɚ-'seɪ] or __-SEE [__-'si]

peradventure per-aad-VEHN-cher [pɚ-æd-'vɛn-tʃɚ]

Percy PER-see ['pɝ-si]
   Percy, Henry *(RII, 1HIV)* also called "Hotspur" HAHT-sper
      ['hɑt-spɚ]
   Percy, Henry, Earl of Northumberland *(RII, 1HIV, 2HIV)*
      nawr-THUHM-ber-luhnd [nɔɚ-'θʌm-bɚ-lənd]
   Percy, Lady *(1HIV, 2HIV)*
   Percy, Thomas, Earl of Worcester *(1HIV)* WO͞OS-ter
      ['wʊs-tɚ] scans to WO͞O-sis-ter ['wu-sɪs-tɚ] @ I, 3, 15
   Percy, Henry, Earl of Northumberland *(3HVI)*

perdie per-DEE [pɚ-'di]

Perdita *(WT)* PER-di-tuh [ˈpɝ-dɪ-tə]

perdition per-DISH-uhn [pɚ-ˈdɪʃ-ən]

perdu per-DYOO [pɚ-ˈdɪu] possibly scans to PER-dyoo [ˈpɝ-dɪu] @ *LEAR* IV, 7, 35

perdurable per-DYOO-ruh-b(uh)l [pɚ-ˈdɪu-rə-bl̩] scans to PER-dyoo-__-__ [ˈpɝ-dɪu-__-__] @ *HV* IV, 5, 8

perdurably scans to PER-dyoo-ruh-blee [ˈpɝ-dɪu-rə-bli]

perdy per-DEE [pɚ-ˈdi]

peregrinate PEH-ri-gri-nayt [ˈpɛ-rɪ-grɪ-neɪt]

peremptory puh-REHMP-tuh-ree [pə-ˈrɛmp-tə-ri] scans to PEH-ruhmp-taw-ree [ˈpɛ-rəmp-tɔ-ree] e.g. @ *LLL* IV, 3, 221 and PREHMP-tuh-ree [ˈprɛmp-tə-ri] @ *1HIV* I, 3, 17, and possibly PREHMP-tree [ˈprɛmp-tri] @ *2HVI* III, 1, 8

perfect (v) always scans to PER-fehkt [ˈpɝ-fɛkt]

perfecter PER-fehk-ter [ˈpɝ-fɛk-tɚ]

perfidious per-FID-ee-uhs [pɚ-ˈfɪd-i-əs] scans to __-FID-yuhs [__-ˈfɪd-jəs] @ *TEMP* I, 2, 68

perfit PER-fit [ˈpɝ-fɪt]

perfume (n) PER-fyoom [ˈpɝ-fjum] e.g. @ *HAM* I, 3, 9 and per-FYOOM [pɚ-ˈfjum] e.g. @ *SHR* I, 1, 172

perfume (v) per-FYOOM [pɚ-ˈfjum] scans to PER-fyoom [ˈpɝ-fjum] @ *2HIV* III, 1, 12

periapts PEH-ree-ahpts [ˈpɛ-ri-ɑpts]

Pericles *(PER)* PEH-ri-kleez [ˈpɛ-rɪ-kliz] possibly scans to peh-RI-__ [pɛ-ˈrɪ-__] @ II, 3, 81

Perigenia PEH-ri-JEEN-yuh [pɛ-rɪ-ˈdʒin-jə]

EE i be/ I ɪ bit/ EH ɛ bet/ AA æ bat/ OO u boot / OO ʊ book/ AW ɔ bought/ AH ɑ father/ ER ɝ bird/ UH ʌ cup/ AY eɪ bay/ EYE aɪ bite/ OY ɔɪ boy/ OH oʊ boat/ OW aʊ how/ YOO ɪu duke/ EAR ɪɚ beer/ AIR ɛɚ bear/ OOR ʊɚ tour/ AWR ɔɚ bore/ AHR ɑɚ bar/ NG ŋ king/ SH ʃ ship/ ZH ʒ vision/ TH θ thirty/ TH ð then/ CH tʃ child/ J dʒ just/ For complete list, see Key to Pronunciation p. 2.

Perigort scans to PAIR-gawrt [ˈpɛɚ-gɔɚt]

perilous scans to PAIR-luhs [ˈpɛɚ-ləs] e.g. @ *HV* Pro, 22

perishen PEH-ri-shun [ˈpɛ-rɪ-ʃən]

periwig PEH-ri-wig [ˈpɛ-rɪ-wɪg]

perjure (n) or (v) PER-jer [ˈpɝ-ʤɚ]

Perk, Gilbert PAHRK [pɑɚk]

Perkes PAHRKS [pɑɚks]

peroration PEH-ruh-RAY-shuhn [pɛ-rə-ˈreɪ-ʃən]

perpend per-PEHND [pɚ-ˈpɛnd]

perpetuity per-pi-TYOO-i-tee [pə-pɪ-ˈtɪu-ɪ-ti] scans to
    ___-___-TYOO-tee [___-___-ˈtɪu-ti] @ *CYM* V, 4, 6

Perseus PER-see-uhs [ˈpɝ-si-əs] scans to PER-syuhs
    [ˈpɝ-sjəs] e.g. @ *T&C* I, 3, 42

persever per-SEHV-er [pə-ˈsɛv-ɚ]

perseverance per-SEHV-uh-ruhns [pə-ˈsɛv-ə-rəns] scans to
    ___-SEHV-ruhns [___-ˈsɛv-rəns] e.g. @ *MAC* IV, 3, 93

Persia PER-zhuh [ˈpɝ-ʒə]

persistive per-SIS-tiv [pə-ˈsɪs-tɪv]

personated PER-suhn-ay-tid [ˈpɝ-sən-eɪ-tɪd]

perspective always scans to PER-spehk-tiv [ˈpɝ-spɛk-tɪv]

perspicuous per-SPIK-yoo-uhs [pə-ˈspɪk-ju-əs]

pertaunt-like PAIR-tawnt-leyek [ˈpɛɚ-tɔnt-laɪk] or
    PER-__-__ [ˈpɝ-__-__]

perturbation per-ter-BAY-shuhn [pə-tə-ˈbeɪ-ʃən]

perusal puh-ROO-z(uh)l [pə-ˈru-zl̩]

pestiferous pehs-TIF-uh-ruhs [pɛs-'tɪf-ə-rəs] scans to
___-TIF-ruhs [___-'tɪf-rəs] @ *1HVI* III, 1, 15

petar pi-TAHR [pɪ-'tɑɚ]

Peter of Pomfret *(KJ)* PAHM-frit ['pɑm-frɪt] or PUHM-___
['pʌm-___]

Peto PEE-toh ['pi-toʊ]
Peto *(1HIV, 2HIV)*

Petrarch PEE-trahrk ['pi-trɑɚk] or PEH-___ ['pɛ-___]

Petruchio pi-TRŌO-kee-oh [pɪ-'tru-ki-oʊ] scans to
___-TRŌO-kyoh [___-'tru-kjoʊ] or ___-___-chee -___
[___-___-tʃi-___] scans to ___-TRŌO-chyoh [___-'tru-tʃjoʊ]
Petruchio *(SHR)* scans e.g. @ I, 2, 128

pettitoes PEH-tee-tohz ['pɛ-ti-toʊz]

Phaeton FAY-i-tuhn ['feɪ-ɪ-tən]

phantasime faan-TAAZ-uhm [fæn-'tæz-əm]

phantasma faan-TAAZ-muh [fæn-'tæz-mə]

Pharamond FAA-ruh-mahnd ['fæ-rə-mɑnd] or ___-___-muhnd
[___-___-mənd]

Pharaoh FEH-roh ['fɛ-roʊ] or FAY-___ ['feɪ-___] or
FAA-___ ['fæ-___]

Pharsalia fahr-SAYL-yuh [fɑɚ-'seɪl-jə]

Pheazar FEE-zer ['fi-zɚ]

Phebe *(AYL)* FEE-bee ['fi-bi]

Phebes (v) FEE-beez ['fi-biz]

pheese FEEZ [fiz]

EE i be/ I ɪ bit/ EH ɛ bet/ AA æ bat/ ŌO u boot / ŌO ʊ book/ AW ɔ bought/ AH ɑ father/ ER ɝ bird/
UH ʌ cup/ AY eɪ bay/ EYE aɪ bite/ OY ɔɪ boy/ OH oʊ boat/ OW aʊ how/ YŌO ɪu duke/ EAR ɪɚ
beer/ AIR ɛɚ bear/ ŌOR ʊɚ tour/ AWR ɔɚ bore/ AHR ɑɚ bar/ NG ŋ king/ SH ʃ ship/ ZH ʒ vision/
TH θ thirty/ TH ð then/ CH tʃ child/ J ʤ just/ For complete list, see Key to Pronunciation p. 2.

Phibbus FIB-uhs ['fɪb-əs]

Philadelphos FIL-uh-DEHL-fuhs [fɪl-ə-'dɛl-fəs] or
___-___-___-fahs [__-__-__-fɑs]

Philario *(CYM)* scans to fi-LAHR-yoh [fɪ-'lɑɚ-joʊ]

Philarmonus FIL-ahr-MOHN-uhs [fil-ɑɚ-'moʊn-əs]

Philemon fi-LEE-muhn [fɪ-'li-mən] or feye-___-___
[faɪ-___-___]
Philemon *(PER)*

Philip FI-lip ['fɪ-lɪp]
Philip the Bastard *(KJ)*
Philip, King *(KJ)*

Philippan fi-LIP-uhn [fɪ-'lɪp-ən]

Philippe (female name in 2HVI) FI-lip ['fɪ-lip]

Philippi fi-LIP-eye [fɪ-'lɪp-aɪ]

Phillida FIL-i-duh ['fɪl-ɪ-də]

Philo *(A&C)* FEYE-loh ['faɪ-loʊ]

Philomel / Philomele FIL-uh-mehl ['fɪl-ə-mɛl]

Philomela FIL-uh-MEE-luh [fɪl-ə-'mi-lə]

Philostrate *(MID)* FI-luh-strayt ['fɪ-lə-streɪt]

Philoten FI-luh-tin ['fɪ-lə-tɪn] or FEYE-__-__ ['faɪ-__-__]

Philotus *(TIMON)* fi-LOH-tuhs [fɪ-'loʊ-təs] or feye-___-___
[faɪ-___-___]

phlegmatic flehg-MAAT-ik [flɛg-'mæt-ɪk]

Phoebe FEE-bee ['fi-bi]

Phoebus FEE-buhs ['fi-bəs]

Phoenicia fi-NEE-shuh [fɪ-'ni-ʃə] or fuh-__-__ [fə-__-__]

Phoenicians fi-NEE-shuhnz [fɪ-'ni-ʃənz] or fuh-__-__ [fə-__-__]

Phoenix FEE-niks ['fi-nɪks]

Photinus FOH-ti-nuhs ['foʊ-tɪ-nəs] or FAH-__-__ ['fɑ-__-__]

Phrygia FRIJ-ee-uh ['frɪdʒ-i-ə] scans to FRIJ-yuh ['frɪdʒ-jə] e.g. @ *T&C* Pro, 7

Phrygian always scans to FRIJ-yuhn ['frɪdʒ-jən]

Phrynia *(TIMON)* FRI-nee-uh ['frɪ-ni-ə]

Picardy PIK-er-dee ['pɪk-ɚ-di]

Pickt-hatch PIKT-haach ['pɪkt-hætʃ]

pied PEYED [paɪd]

piedness PEYED-nuhs ['paɪd-nəs]

pight PEYET [paɪt]

Pigrogromitus PI-groh-GRAHM-i-tuhs [pɪ-groʊ-'grɑm-ɪ-təs]

Pilate PEYE-luht ['paɪ-lət]

Pilch PILCH [pɪltʃ]

pilcher PILCH-er ['pɪltʃ-ɚ]

Pillicock PIL-i-kahk ['pɪl-ɪ-kɑk]

pillory PIL-uh-ree ['pɪl-ə-ri]

Pimpernell PIM-per-nehl ['pɪm-pɚ-nɛl]

Pinch, Doctor *(CE)* PINCH [pɪntʃ]

Pindarus *(JC)* PIN-duh-ruhs ['pɪn-də-rəs]

pinion PIN-yuhn ['pɪn-jən]

EE i be/ I ɪ bit/ EH ɛ bet/ AA æ bat/ OO u boot / OO ʊ book/ AW ɔ bought/ AH ɑ father/ ER ɝ bird/
UH ʌ cup/ AY eɪ bay/ EYE aɪ bite/ OY ɔɪ boy/ OH oʊ boat/ OW aʊ how/ YOO ɪu duke/ EAR ɪɚ
beer/ AIR ɛɚ bear/ OOR ʊɚ tour/ AWR ɔɚ bore/ AHR ɑɚ bar/ NG ŋ king/ SH ʃ ship/ ZH ʒ vision/
TH θ thirty/ TH ð then/ CH tʃ child/ J dʒ just/ For complete list, see Key to Pronunciation p. 2.

pinnace PIN-uhs ['pɪn-əs]

pioned PEYE-uhn-id ['paɪ-ən-ɪd]

pioner PEYE-uh-ner ['paɪ-ə-nɚ] scans to PEYE-ner
['paɪ-nɚ] @ *OTH* III, 3, 346

pippin PIP-in ['pɪp-ɪn]

Pirithous *(2NOB)* peye-RI-thoh-uhs [paɪ-'rɪ-θou-əs] scans to
PEYE-ri-thuhs ['paɪ-rɪ-θəs] or __-__-thōos [__-__-θus]
e.g. @ I, 1, 207

Pisa PEE-zuh ['pi-zə]

Pisanio *(CYM)* pi-ZAHN-ee-oh [pɪ-'zɑn-i-ou] scans to
__-ZAHN-yoh [__-'zɑn-jou] e.g. @ III, 5, 56

pish PISH [pɪʃ]

pismires PIS-meyerz ['pɪs-maɪɚz] or PIZ-__ ['pɪz-__]

Pistol PIS-t(uh)l ['pɪs-tl̩]
Pistol *(2HIV, HV, MW)*

pitchy PICH-ee [pɪtʃ-i]

pith PITH [pɪθ]

Pittie-ward PIT-ee-werd ['pɪt-i-wɚd] or possibly PEHT-__-__
['pɛt-__-__] many emendations including "Petty-ward"

Pius PEYE-uhs ['paɪ-əs]

pizzle PIZ-uhl ['pɪz-əl]

Placentio scans to pluh-SEHN-shyoh [plə-'sɛn-ʃjou]

plaguy PLAY-gee ['pleɪ-gi]

plaints PLAYNTS [pleɪnts]

planched PLAANCH-id ['plæntʃ-ɪd]

plantage PLAAN-tij ['plæn-tɪdʒ]

Plantagenet plaan-TAAJ-uh-nit [plæn-'tædʒ-ə-nɪt] scans to
___-TAAJ-nit [___-'tædʒ-nɪt]
Plantagenet, Edward, Earl of Warwick *(RIII)* **WAW**-rik
['wɔ-rɪk] or **WAH-**___ ['wɑ-___]
Plantagenet, Richard, afterwards Duke of Gloucester, and
Richard III *(2HVI, 3HVI, RIII)* **GLAHS**-ter ['glɑs-tɚ]
scans to **GLAHS**-i-ter ['glɑs-ɪ-tɚ] or **GLAH**-sis-ter
['glɑ-sɪs-tɚ] @ *RIII* III, 4, 46
Plantagenet, Richard, afterwards Duke of York *(1HVI,*
2HVI, 3HVI) scans @ *3HVI* III, 1, 140, possibly
scans to PLAAN-tuh-**JEHN**-it [plæn-tə-'dʒɛn-ɪt]
@ *1HVI* III, 1, 149

plantain PLAAN-tuhn ['plæn-tən] possibly plaan-**TAYN**
[plæn-'teɪn] @ *LLL* III, 1, 66, 67

plash PLAASH [plæʃ]

Plashy PLAASH-ee ['plæʃ-i]

plated PLAY-tid ['pleɪ-tɪd]

plats PLAATS [plæts]

plausive PLAW-ziv ['plɔ-zɪv] or ___-siv [___-sɪv]

Plautus PLAW-tuhs ['plɔ-təs]

play-feres PLAY-fearz ['pleɪ-fɪɚz]

pleached PLEECHT [plitʃt]

plebeians pli-BEE-uhnz [plɪ-'bi-ənz] scans to **PLEHB**-yuhnz
['plɛb-jənz] e.g. @ *COR* I, 9, 7 and possibly scans to
PLEH-bee-uhnz ['plɛ-bi-ənz] @ *A&C* IV, 12, 34 (if "to
the" elides to one syllable)

plebeii PLEE-bee-eye ['pli-bi-aɪ] or **PLEH-**___-___ ['plɛ-___-___]

plebs PLEHBZ [plɛbz]

EE i be/ I ɪ bit/ EH ɛ bet/ AA æ bat/ O͞O u boot / O͝O ʊ book/ AW ɔ bought/ AH ɑ father/ ER ɝ bird/
UH ʌ cup/ AY eɪ bay/ EYE aɪ bite/ OY ɔɪ boy/ OH oʊ boat/ OW aʊ how/ YO͞O ɪu duke/ EAR ɪɚ
beer/ AIR ɛɚ bear/ O͞OR ʊɚ tour/ AWR ɔɚ bore/ AHR ɑɚ bar/ NG ŋ king/ SH ʃ ship/ ZH ʒ vision/
TH θ thirty/ T̲H̲ ð then/ CH tʃ child/ J dʒ just/ For complete list, see Key to Pronunciation p. 2.

pleurisy PLOO-ri-see ['plʊ-rɪ-si]

plied PLEYED [plaɪd]

plies PLEYEZ [plaɪz]

plight PLEYET [plaɪt]

plummet PLUHM-it ['plʌm-ɪt]

plurisy PLOO-ri-see ['plʊ-rɪ-si]

Plutus PLOO-tuhs ['plu-təs]

Po POH [poʊ]

pocky PAHK-ee ['pɑk-i]

poesy POH-i-zee ['poʊ-ɪ-zi] or ___-___-see [___-___-si] scans
   to **POH**-zee ['poʊ-zi] or ___-see [___-si] @ *SHR* I, 1, 36

Poictiers poy-TEARZ [pɔɪ-'tɪɚ-z]

Poins POYNZ [pɔɪnz]
   Poins *(1HIV, 2HIV)*

point-devise POYNT-di-veyes ['pɔɪnt-dɪ-vaɪs]

Poitiers poy-TEARZ [pɔɪ-'tɪɚ-z] scans to **POY**-tearz ['pɔɪ-tɪɚ-z]
   @ *KJ* I, 1, 11

Polacks POH-laaks ['poʊ-læks]

poleaxe POHL-aaks ['poʊl-æks]

pole-clipt POHL-klipt ['poʊl-klɪpt]

Polemon pah-LEH-muhn [pɑ-'lɛ-mən] or ___-LEE-___
   [___-li-___]

politic PAH-li-tik ['pɑ-lɪ-tɪk]

politicly PAHL-uh-tik-lee ['pɑl-ə-tɪk-li] scans to **PAHL**-tik-lee
   ['pɑl-tɪk-li] @ *SHR* IV, 1, 175

Polixenes puh-LIKS-uh-neez [pə-'lɪks-ə-niz] scans to
   ___-LIKS-neez [___-'lɪks-niz]

Polixenes *(WT)* scans e.g. @ I, 2, 351 also called "Bohemia"
boh-**HEE**-mee-uh [boʊ-'hi-mi-ə] scans to
___-**HEE**-myuh [___-'hi-mjə] e.g. @ IV, 4, 581

pollaxe **POHL**-aaks ['poʊl-æks]

polled **POHLD** [poʊld]

Polonius *(HAM)* puh-**LOH**-nyuhs [pə-'loʊ-njəs] possibly
___-___-nee-uhs [___-___-ni-əs] in prose

poltroons scans to **POHL**-trōōnz ['poʊl-trunz]

Polydamas pah-**LID**-uh-muhs [pɑ-'lɪd-ə-məs]

Polyxena puh-**LIKS**-uh-nuh [pə-'lɪks-ə-nə] or pah-__-__-__
[pɑ-__-__-__] or poh-__-__-__ [poʊ-__-__-__]

pomander **POH**-maan-der ['poʊ-mæn-dɚ]

pomegranate **PAHM**-graan-it ['pɑm-græn-ɪt] scans to
___-**GRAAN**-___ [___-'græn-___] @ *R&J* III, 5, 4

pomewater **POHM**-waw-ter ['poʊm-wɔ-tɚ]

Pomfret **PAHM**-frit ['pɑm-frɪt] or **PUHM**-___ ['pʌm-___]

Pomgarnet **PAHM**-gahr-nit ['pɑm-gaɚ-nɪt]

pommel **PAHM**-uhl ['pɑm-əl]

Pompey **PAHM**-pee ['pɑm-pi]
Pompey *(MM)*

Pompion **PUHMP**-ee-uhn ['pʌmp-i-ən] or **PUHMP**-yuhn
['pʌmp-jən]

poniard **PAHN**-yerd ['pɑn-jɚd]

Pont **PAHNT** [pɑnt]

Pontic **PAHN**-tik ['pɑn-tɪk]

EE i be/ I ɪ bit/ EH ɛ bet/ AA æ bat/ ŌŌ u boot / ŌŌ ʊ book/ AW ɔ bought/ AH ɑ father/ ER ɝ bird/
UH ʌ cup/ AY eɪ bay/ EYE aɪ bite/ OY ɔɪ boy/ OH oʊ boat/ OW aʊ how/ YŌŌ ɪu duke/ EAR ɪə
beer/ AIR ɛə bear/ ŌŌR ʊə tour/ AWR ɔɚ bore/ AHR aɚ bar/ NG ŋ king/ SH ʃ ship/ ZH ʒ vision/
TH θ thirty/ TH ð then/ CH ʧ child/ J ʤ just/ For complete list, see Key to Pronunciation p. 2.

Ponton de Santrailles PAHN-tuhn duh-SAAN-trayl-eez
['pɑn-tən] [də-'sæn-treɪl-iz]

popingay PAHP-in-gay ['pɑp-ɪn-geɪ] some editions "popinjay"
PAHP-in-jay ['pɑp-ɪn-ʤeɪ]

popish POHP-ish ['poʊp-ɪʃ]

pop'rin PAHP-rin ['pɑp-rɪn]

porpentine / Porpentine PAWR-puhn-teyen ['pɔɚ-pən-taɪn]

porringer PAW-rin-jer ['pɔ-rɪn-ʤɚ] or PAH-___-___
['pɑ-___-___]

portage PAWR-tij ['pɔɚ-tɪʤ]

portance PAWR-t(uh)ns ['pɔɚ-tn̩s]

portcullised pawrt-KUHL-ist [pɔɚt-'kʌl-ɪst]

portent always scans to pawr-TEHNT [pɔɚ-'tɛnt]

portentous pawr-TEHN-tuhs [pɔɚ-'tɛn-təs]

Porter *(MAC)* PAWR-ter ['pɔɚ-tɚ]

Portia PAWR-shuh ['pɔɚ-ʃə] scans to PAWR-shee-uh ['pɔɚ-ʃi-ə]
Portia *(JC)*
Portia *(MVEN)* scans e.g. @ I, 1, 66

portraiture PAWR-tri-cho͞or ['pɔɚ-trɪ-ʧʊɚ] or ___-___-cher
[___-___-ʧɚ]

posset PAHS-it ['pɑs-ɪt]

postern POH-stern ['poʊ-stɚn] or PAH-___ ['pɑ-___]

posthaste pohst-HAYST [poʊst-'heɪst]

Posthumus Leonatus *(CYM)* pahs-TYO͞O-muhs LEE-oh-
NAH-tuhs [pɑs-'tɪu-məs] [li-oʊ-'nɑ-təs] scans to PAHS-
tyo͞o-___ ['pɑs-tɪu-___] @ IV, 2, 320 and possibly PAHS-
tymuhs ['pɑs-tjməs] @ I, 1, 41

posy POH-zee ['poʊ-zi]

194

potations poh-TAY-shuhnz [pou-'teɪ-ʃənz]

potch PAHCH [pɑtʃ]

potentate POH-t(uh)n-tayt ['pou-tn̩-teɪt]

pothecary PAHTH-uh-keh-ree ['pɑθ-ə-kɛ-ri] scans to
____-uh-kree [____-ə-kri] @ *R&J* V, 3, 289

pother PAH<u>TH</u>-er ['pɑð-ɚ]

Potpan PAHT-paan ['pɑt-pæn]

pottle PAH-t(uh)l ['pɑ-tl̩]

poulter POHL-ter ['poul-tɚ]

poultice POHL-tis ['poul-tɪs]

Poultney POHLT-nee ['poult-ni]

pouncet POWN-sit ['pɑun-sɪt]

pox PAHKS [pɑks]

Poysam POY-suhm ['pɔɪ-səm]

practic PRAAK-tik ['præk-tɪk]

practisants PRAAK-ti-suhnts ['præk-tɪ-sənts]

praemunire PREE-myōō-NEYE-ree [pri-mju-'naɪ-ri]

praetor PREE-ter ['pri-tɚ]

Prague PRAHG [prɑg]

prank PRAANGK [præŋk]

Prat PRAAT [præt]

prate PRAYT [preɪt]

prater PRAY-ter ['preɪ-tɚ]

EE i be/ I ɪ bit/ EH ɛ bet/ AA æ bat/ ŌŌ u boot / ŌŌ ʊ book/ AW ɔ bought/ AH ɑ father/ ER ɝ bird/ UH ʌ cup/ AY eɪ bay/ EYE aɪ bite/ OY ɔɪ boy/ OH ou boat/ OW ɑu how/ YŌŌ ɪu duke/ EAR ɪɚ beer/ AIR ɛɚ bear/ ŌŌR ʊɚ tour/ AWR ɔɚ bore/ AHR ɑɚ bar/ NG ŋ king/ SH ʃ ship/ ZH ʒ vision/ TH θ thirty/ <u>TH</u> ð then/ CH tʃ child/ J dʒ just/ For complete list, see Key to Pronunciation p. 2.

prattle PRAA-t(uh)l ['præ-tl̩]

prayer (one who offers a petition to heaven) PRAIR [prɛɚ]
scans to **PRAY**-er ['preɪ-ɚ] e.g. @ *R&J* I, 5, 105

prayer (a petition to heaven) PRAIR [prɛɚ] scans to **PRAY**-er
['preɪ-ɚ] e.g. @ *TITUS* III, 1, 75

preambulate pree-AAM-byo͞o-layt [pri-'æm-bju-leɪt]

precedence scans to pri-SEE-duhns [prɪ-'si-dəns]

precedent (adj) pri-SEE-duhnt [prɪ-'si-dənt]

precedent (n) PREHS-i-duhnt ['prɛs-ɪ-dənt]

precept PREE-sehpt ['pri-sɛpt]

preceptial pree-SEHP-chuhl [pri-'sɛp-tʃəl]

precinct scans to pree-SINGKT [pri-'sɪŋkt]

precipitance pri-SIP-i-tuhns [prɪ-'sɪp-ɪ-təns]

precisian pri-SIZH-uhn [prɪ-'sɪʒ-ən]

preeminence pree-EHM-i-nuhns [pri-'ɛm-ɪ-nəns]

preferment pri-FER-muhnt [prɪ-'fɝ-mənt]

preformed scans to pree-FAWRM-id [pri-'fɔɚm-ɪd]

prejudicates pri-JO͞O-di-kayts [prɪ-'ʤu-dɪ-keɪts]

prelate PREHL-it ['prɛl-ɪt]

premised scans to pri-MEYEZ-id [prɪ-'maɪz-ɪd]

prenominate pree-NAHM-i-nit [pri-'nɑm-ɪ-nɪt] scans to __-
NAHM-nit [__-'nɑm-nɪt] @ *HAM* II, 1, 43

prentice PREHN-tis ['prɛn-tɪs]

prenzie PREHN-zee ['prɛn-zi]

prerogative pri-RAHG-uh-tiv [prɪ-'rɑg-ə-tɪv]

presage (n) PREH-sij ['prɛ-sɪʤ] scans to pri-SAYJ [prɪ-'seɪʤ] @ *RII* II, 2, 142

presage (v) pri-SAYJ [prɪ-'seɪʤ]

prescience PREH-shee-uhns ['prɛ-ʃi-əns] or PREE-__-__ ['pri-__-__] scans to pri-SHEE-__ ['prɪ-'ʃi-__] @ *T&C* I, 3, 199

prescript PREE-skript ['pri-skrɪpt]

presentment pri-ZEHNT-muhnt [prɪ-'zɛnt-mənt]

prest PREHST [prɛst]

presurmise pree-ser-MEYEZ [pri-sɚ-'maɪz]

pretense PREE-tehns ['pri-tɛns] scans to pri-TEHNS [prɪ-'tɛns] e.g. @ *MAC* II, 3, 127

Priam PREYE-uhm ['praɪ-əm]
Priam *(T&C)* possibly scans to PREYEM [praɪm] @ Pro, 15; also called "Priamus" PREYE-uhm-uhs ['praɪ-əm-əs]

Priapus preye-AY-puhs [praɪ-'eɪ-pəs]

pricket PRIK-it ['prɪk-ɪt]

primer PREYEM-er ['praɪm-ɚ]

primero pri-MEH-roh [prɪ-'mɛ-rou]

primest PREYEM-ist ['praɪm-ɪst]

primogenity PREYE-moh-JEHN-i-tee [praɪ-mou-'ʤɛn-ɪ-ti]

primy PREYE-mee ['praɪ-mi]

princox PRIN-kahks ['prɪn-kɑks] or PRING -__ ['prɪŋ-__]

prioress PREYE-uh-ris ['praɪ-ə-rɪs]

EE i be/ I ɪ bit/ EH ɛ bet/ AA æ bat/ OO u boot / OO ʊ book/ AW ɔ bought/ AH ɑ father/ ER ɚ bird/ UH ʌ cup/ AY eɪ bay/ EYE aɪ bite/ OY ɔɪ boy/ OH ou boat/ OW aʊ how/ YOO ɪu duke/ EAR ɪɚ beer/ AIR ɛɚ bear/ OOR ʊɚ tour/ AWR ɔɚ bore/ AHR ɑɚ bar/ NG ŋ king/ SH ʃ ship/ ZH ʒ vision/ TH θ thirty/ TH ð then/ CH ʧ child/ J ʤ just/ For complete list, see Key to Pronunciation p. 2.

priory PREYE-uh-ree ['praɪ-ə-ri] scans to PREYE-ree ['praɪ-ri] @ *CE* V, 1, 37

Priscian PRISH-ee-uhn ['prɪʃ-i-ən]

prithee PRI-<u>thee</u> ['prɪ-ði]

prived scans to PREYE-vid ['praɪ-vɪd]

privilege PRIV-lij ['prɪv-lɪdʒ] scans to PRIV-uh-lij ['prɪv-ə-lɪdʒ] e.g. @ *MID* I, 1, 41

privily PRIV-i-lee ['prɪv-ɪ-li]

privity PRIV-i-tee ['prɪv-ɪ-ti]

privy PRIV-ee ['prɪv-i]

probal PROH-b(uh)l ['proʊ-bl̩]

proceed pruh-SEED [prə-'sid] scans to PROH-seed ['proʊ-sid] e.g. @ *2HVI* I, 3, 147

proconsul proh-KAHN-s(uh)l [proʊ-'kan-sl̩]

procreant PROH-kree-uhnt ['proʊ-kri-ənt]

Procrus PROH-kris ['proʊ-krɪs]

Proculeius *(A&C)* PROH-kyōō-LEE-uhs [proʊ-kju-'li-əs]

procurator PRAHK-yuh-ray-ter ['prɑk-jə-reɪ-tɚ]

prodigal PRAHD-i-guhl ['prɑd-ɪ-gəl] scans to PRAHD-guhl ['prɑd-gəl] @ *MVEN* II, 5, 15

prodigious pruh-DIJ-uhs [prə-'dɪdʒ-əs] or proh-___-___ [proʊ-___-___]

proditor PRAH-di-ter ['prɑ-dɪ-tɚ]

proface proh-FAYS [proʊ-'feɪs]

profanation PRAH-fuh-NAY-shuhn [prɑ-fə-'neɪ-ʃən] scans to ___-___-___-shee-uhn [___-___-___-ʃi-ən] @ *MM* II, 2, 128

proffer PRAHF-er ['prɑf-ɚ]

198

profound pruh-FOWND [prə-'faʊnd] scans to PROH-fownd ['proʊ-faʊnd] e.g. @ *HAM* IV, 1, 1

progenitors proh-JEHN-i-terz [proʊ-'ʤɛn-ɪ-tɚz]

progeny PRAHJ-i-nee ['praʤ-ɪ-ni]

Progne PRAHG-nee ['prag-ni]

prognostication prahg-NAH-sti-KAY-shuhn [prag-na-stɪ-'keɪ-ʃən]

prolixious proh-LIK-shuhs [proʊ-'lɪk-ʃəs]

prolixity proh-LIK-si-tee [proʊ-'lɪk-sɪ-ti]

prologue / Prologue PROH-lahg ['proʊ-lag]

Promethean always scans to proh-MEE-thyuhn [proʊ-'mi-θjən] or pruh-___-___ [prə-__-__]

Prometheus scans to proh-MEE-thyuhs [proʊ-'mi-θjəs] or pruh-___-___ [prə-___-___]

prompture PRAHMP-cher ['pramp-ʧɚ]

promulgate scans to pruh-MOOL-gayt [prə-'mʊl-geɪt]

propagate PRAH-puh-gayt ['pra-pə-geɪt]

propend proh-PEHND [proʊ-'pɛnd]

propension proh-PEHN-shuhn [proʊ-'pɛn-ʃən]

prophecy (n) PRAHF-i-see ['praf-ɪ-si]

prophesier PRAHF-i-seye-er ['praf-ɪ-saɪ-ɚ]

prophesy (v) PRAHF-i-seye ['praf-ɪ-saɪ]

prophetess PRAHF-i-tis ['praf-ɪ-tɪs]

propinquity proh-PING-kwi-tee [proʊ-'pɪŋ-kwɪ-ti]

EE i be/ I ɪ bit/ EH ɛ bet/ AA æ bat/ OO u boot / OO ʊ book/ AW ɔ bought/ AH ɑ father/ ER ɝ bird/ UH ʌ cup/ AY eɪ bay/ EYE aɪ bite/ OY ɔɪ boy/ OH oʊ boat/ OW aʊ how/ YOO ɪu duke/ EAR ɪɚ beer/ AIR ɛɚ bear/ OOR ʊɚ tour/ AWR ɔɚ bore/ AHR ɑɚ bar/ NG ŋ king/ SH ʃ ship/ ZH ʒ vision/ TH θ thirty/ TH ð then/ CH ʧ child/ J ʤ just/ For complete list, see Key to Pronunciation p. 2.

Propontic pruh-PAHN-tik [prə-'pɑn-tɪk]

propugnation PROH-puhg-NAY-shuhn [proʊ-pəg-'neɪ-ʃən]

prorogue pruh-ROHG [prə-'roʊg] or proh-___ [proʊ-___]

proselytes PRAH-suh-leyets ['prɑ-sə-laɪts]

Proserpina proh-SER-pi-nuh [proʊ-'sɝ-pɪ-nə]

Proserpine PRAH-ser-peyen ['prɑ-sɚ-paɪn]

Prospero *(TEMP)* PRAHS-puh-roh ['prɑs-pə-roʊ] scans to
  PRAHS-proh ['prɑs-proʊ] e.g. @ I, 2, 20 also called
  "Prosper" PRAHS-per ['prɑs-pɚ] @ II, 2, 2

protest (n) always scans to proh-TEHST [proʊ-'tɛst]

Proteus PROH-tee-uhs ['proʊ-ti-əs] scans to PROH-tyuhs
  ['proʊ-tjəs]
  Proteus *(2GEN)* scans e.g. @ I, 1, 56

protractive proh-TRAAK-tiv [proʊ-'træk-tɪv]

provand PRAHV-uhnd ['prɑv-ənd]

provender PRAHV-uhn-der ['prɑv-ən-dɚ]

proverbed PRAH-verbd ['prɑ-vɚbd]

providently PRAHV-i-duhnt-lee ['prɑv-ɪ-dənt-li]

Provincial proh-VIN-shuhl [proʊ-'vɪn-ʃəl]

proviso pruh-VEYE-zoh [prə-'vaɪ-zoʊ]

Provost *(MM)* PROH-vohst ['proʊ-voʊst]

prowess PROW-is ['praʊ-ɪs] scans to PROWS [praʊs]
  @ *MAC* V, 8, 41

Prudence PROO-d(uh)ns ['pru-dn̩s]

prun'st PROONST [prunst]

Psalmist SAHM-ist ['sɑm-ɪst]

psalteries SAWL-tuh-reez ['sɔl-tə-riz]

Ptolemy TAHL-uh-mee ['tɑl-ə-mi] possibly scans to
TAHL-mee ['tɑl-mi] @ *A&C* I, 4, 6; in plural scans to
TAHL-meez ['tɑl-miz] @ *A&C* III, 12, 18

Publicola puhb-LIK-uh-luh [pəb-'lɪk-ə-lə]

Publius PUHB-lee-uhs ['pʌb-li-əs] scans to PUHB-lyuhs
['pʌb-ljəs]
Publius *(JC)*
Publius *(TITUS)* scans @ IV, 3, 25

Puck (Robin Goodfellow) *(MID)* PUHK [pʌk] RAH-bin
GŎŎD-feh-loh ['rɑ-bɪn] ['gʊd-fɛ-loʊ]

pudder PUHD-er ['pʌd-ɚ]

pudency PYŌŌ-d(uh)n-see ['pju-dn̩-si]

pugging PUHG-ing ['pʌg-ɪŋ]

puisny PYŌŌ-nee ['pju-ni]

puissance PYŌŌ-i-suhns ['pju-ɪ-səns] scans to PYŌŌ-suhns
['pju-səns] or PWEE-suhns ['pwi-səns] e.g. @ *2HIV* II, 3, 52

puissant always scans to PYŌŌ-suhnt ['pju-sənt] or
PWEE-suhnt ['pwi-sənt]

puling PYŌŌL-ing ['pjul-ɪŋ]

pulsidge PUHL-sij ['pʌl-sɪdʒ]

pumpion PUHMP-yuhn ['pʌmp-jən]

punto PUHN-toh ['pʌn-toʊ] or PŎŎN-___ ['pʊn-___]

punto reverso PUHN-toh or PŎŎN-___ ri-VER-soh
['pʌn-toʊ] or ['pʊn-___] [rɪ-'vɝ-soʊ]

pur PER [pɝ]

---

purblind PER-bleyend [ˈpɚ-blaɪnd]

purgation per-GAY-shuhn [pɚ-ˈɡeɪ-ʃən]

purgative scans to PERG-tiv [ˈpɚɡ-tɪv]

purlieus PERL-yo͞oz [ˈpɚl-juz]

purport per-PAWRT [pɚ-ˈpɔɚt]

purpose (v) PER-puhs [ˈpɚ-pəs]

pursents per-SEHNTS [pɚ-ˈsɛnts]

pursuivant PER-swi-vuhnt [ˈpɚ-swɪ-vənt]

pursy PER-see [ˈpɚ-si]

purveyor scans to PER-vay-er [ˈpɚ-veɪ-ɚ]

pusillanimity PYO͞O-suh-luh-NIM-i-tee [pju-sə-lə-ˈnɪm-ɪ-ti]

pussel PUH-suhl [ˈpʌ-səl]

puttock PUHT-uhk [ˈpʌt-ək]

Pygmalion's pig-MAYL-yuhnz [pɪɡ-ˈmeɪl-jənz]

pyramides pi-RAAM-i-deez [pɪ-ˈræm-ɪ-diz]

pyramis PI-ruh-mis [ˈpɪ-rə-mɪs]

Pyramus PI-ruh-muhs [ˈpɪ-rə-məs]

Pyrenean PI-ruh-NEE-uhn [pɪ-rə-ˈni-ən]

Pyrrhus PI-ruhs [ˈpɪ-rəs]

Pythagoras pi-THAAG-uh-ruhs [pɪ-ˈθæɡ-ə-rəs]

quaff KWAHF [kwɑf]

quagmire KWAAG-meyer [ˈkwæɡ-maɪɚ]

qualm KWAHM [kwɑm]

qualmish KWAHM-ish [ˈkwɑm-ɪʃ]

quarrelous scans to KWAWR-luhs ['kwɔɚ-ləs]

quat KWAHT [kwɑt]

quatch KWAHCH [kwɑtʃ]

quean KWEEN [kwin]

queasy KWEE-zee ['kwi-zi]

Queen KWEEN [kwin]
  Queen *(CYM)*
  Queen *(RII)*

quell KWEHL [kwɛl]

quern KWERN [kwɜ˞n]

questant KWEHS-tuhnt ['kwɛs-tənt]

questrists KWEHS-trists ['kwɛs-trɪsts]

Queubus KYOO-buhs ['kju-bəs]

Quickly KWIK-lee ['kwɪk-li]
  Quickly, Mistress / Hostess *(1HIV, 2HIV, HV, MW)*

quiddities KWID-i-teez ['kwɪd-ɪ-tiz]

quietus kweye-EE-tuhs [kwaɪ-'i-təs]

quillets KWIL-its ['kwɪl-ɪts]

quillities KWIL-i-teez ['kwɪl-ɪ-tiz]

Quinapalus kwin-AAP-uh-luhs [kwɪn-'æp-ə-ləs]

Quince, Peter / Prologue *(MID)* KWINS [kwɪns]

quintain KWIN-tuhn ['kwɪn-tən]

quintessence kwin-TEHS-uhns [kwɪn-'tɛs-əns] scans to
  KWIN-tuh-suhns ['kwɪn-tə-səns] @ *AYL* III, 2, 133

EE i be/ I ɪ bit/ EH ɛ bet/ AA æ bat/ OO u boot / OO ʊ book/ AW ɔ bought/ AH ɑ father/ ER ɝ bird/
UH ʌ cup/ AY eɪ bay/ EYE aɪ bite/ OY ɔɪ boy/ OH oʊ boat/ OW aʊ how/ YOO ɪu duke/ EAR ɪɚ
beer/ AIR ɛɚ bear/ OOR ʊɚ tour/ AWR ɔɚ bore/ AHR ɑɚ bar/ NG ŋ king/ SH ʃ ship/ ZH ʒ vision/
TH θ thirty/ TH ð then/ CH tʃ child/ J dʒ just/ For complete list, see Key to Pronunciation p. 2.

Quintus KWIN-tuhs ['kwɪn-təs]
   Quintus *(TITUS)*

quire KWEYER [kwaɪɚ]

quittance KWIT-uhns ['kwɪt-əns]

quoif KWOYF [kwɔɪf]

quoit KWOYT [kwɔɪt]

quondam KWAHN-duhm ['kwɑn-dəm] or ___-daam
   [___-dæm]

quotidian kwoh-TID-ee-uhn [kwoʊ-'tɪd-i-ən]

rabblement RAA-b(uh)l-muhnt ['ræ-bl̩-mənt]

Rafe RAYF [reɪf]

Ragozine RAAG-uh-zeen ['ræg-ə-zin]

raiment RAY-muhnt ['reɪ-mənt]

Rainold Lord Cobham REH-nuhld KAHB-uhm ['rɛ-nəld]
   ['kɑb-əm]

Rambures raam-BOORZ [ræm-'bʊɚz] scans to
   RAAM-boorz ['ræm-bʊɚz] @ *HV* III, 5, 43 with
   "Jacques" two syllables

rampallian raam-PAAL-yuhn [ræm-'pæl-jən]

rampired RAAM-peyerd ['ræm-paɪɚd]

Ramston, Sir John scans to raams-TUHN [ræms-'tʌn]

rancor RAANG-ker ['ræŋ-kɚ]

randon RAAN-duhn ['ræn-dən]

rapier RAYP-yer ['reɪp-jɚ]

Rapine RAYP-eyen ['reɪp-aɪn] or ___-in [___-ɪn] or
   RAAP-eyen ['ræp-aɪn] or ___-in [___-ɪn]

rase RAYZ [reɪz]

Ratcliffe, Sir Richard *(RIII)* RAAT-klif ['ræt-klɪf]

ratsbane RAATS-bayn ['ræts-beɪn]

raught RAWT [rɔt]

ravel RAAV-uhl ['ræv-əl]

raven (n) (a black bird) RAYV-uhn ['reɪv-ən]

raven (v) (to devour greedily) RAAV-uhn ['ræv-ən]

Ravenspurgh RAA-vuhn-sperg ['ræ-vən-spɚg] scans to
 RAAVN-sperg ['rævn-spɚg] or RAY-vuhn-sperg
 ['reɪ-vən-spɚg] scans to RAYVN-___ ['reɪvn-___]
 e.g. @ *3HVI* IV, 7, 8

ravin (adj) (ravenous) RAAV-uhn ['ræv-ən]

raze (v) RAYZ [reɪz]

razes (n) RAYZ-iz ['reɪz-ɪz]

razure RAY-zher ['reɪ-ʒɚ]

Readins REHD-inz ['rɛd-ɪnz]

rearward REAR-werd ['rɪɚ-wɚd]

reave REEV [riv]

rebato ri-BAH-toh [rɪ-'bɑ-toʊ]

recant ri-KAANT [rɪ-'kænt]

recantation REE-kaan-TAY-shuhn [ri-kæn-'teɪ-ʃən]

recanter ri-KAANT-er [rɪ-'kænt-ɚ]

receptacle always scans to REE-sehp-tuh-k(uh)l
 ['ri-sɛp-tə-kl̩]

rechate ri-CHAYT [rɪ-'tʃeɪt]

---

recking REHK-ing ['rɛk-ɪŋ]

recognizance ri-KAHG-ni-zuhns [rɪ-'kɑg-nɪ-zəns]

recomforture ri-KUHM-fuh-cher [rɪ-'kʌm-fə-tʃɚ]

recompense REHK-uhm-pehns ['rɛk-əm-pɛns]

recompt ri-KOWNT [rɪ-'kaʊnt] (archaic form of "recount" stems from Latin "computare," to count)

record (n) REH-kerd ['rɛ-kɚd] scans to ruh-KAWRD [rə-'kɔɚd] e.g. @ *RIII* IV, 4, 28

recordation REH-kawr-DAY-shuhn [rɛ-kɔɚ-'deɪ-ʃən]

recourse REE-kawrs ['ri-kɔɚs] scans to ri-KAWRS [rɪ-'kɔɚs] e.g. @ *T&C* V, 3, 55

recreant REHK-ree-uhnt ['rɛk-ri-ənt] scans to REHK-ruhnt ['rɛk-rənt] e.g. @ *KJ* III, 1, 129

recreate (to refresh oneself by diversion) REH-kree-ayt ['rɛ-kri-eɪt]

recure ree-KYŎOR [ri-'kjʊɚ] or ri-___ [rɪ-'___]

rede REED [rid]

redound ri-DOWND [rɪ-'daʊnd]

redress (n) REE-drehs ['ri-drɛs] scans to ri-DREHS [rɪ-'drɛs] e.g. @ *RII* II, 3, 171

redress (v) ri-DREHS [rɪ-'drɛs]

reechy REE-chee ['ri-tʃi]

reeking REEK-ing ['rik-ɪŋ]

reeky REEK-ee ['rik-i]

refelled ri-FEHLD [rɪ-'fɛld]

reflex (n) or (v) ri-FLEHKS [rɪ-'flɛks]

reformation REH-fer-**MAY**-shuhn [rɛ-fə-'meɪ-ʃən] scans to
__-__-___-shee-uhn [__-__-__-ʃi-ən] @ *LLL* V, 2, 859

refractory ri-**FRAAK**-tuh-ree [rɪ-'fræk-tə-ri]

reft REHFT [rɛft]

refuge (v) **REH**-fyo͞oj ['rɛ-fjuʤ] or possibly scans to
reh-**FYO͞OJ** [rɛ-'fjuʤ] @ *RII* V, 5, 26

Regan *(LEAR)* REE-guhn ['ri-gən]

regent / Regent REE-juhnt ['ri-ʤənt]

region REE-juhn ['ri-ʤən] scans to REE-jee-uhn ['ri-ʤi-ən]
e.g. @ *JC* V, 1, 3

regreet (n) ri-**GREET** [rɪ-'grit]

reguerdon ree-**GER**-d(uh)n [rɪ-'gɝ-dn̩]

Reignier RAYN-yer ['reɪn-jɚ]
  Reignier, Duke of Anjou *(1HVI)* AAN-jo͞o ['æn-ʤu] scans
  to aan-**JO͞O** [æn-'ʤu] e.g. @ V, 3, 95

rejoindure ri-**JOYN**-dyo͞or [rɪ-'ʤɔɪn-djʊɚ]

rejourn ree-**JERN** [ri-'ʤɝn]

relume ri-**LO͞OM** [rɪ-'lum]

remediate ri-**MEE**-dee-it [rɪ-'mi-di-ɪt] or scans to
__-**MEE**-dyuht [__-'mi-djət]

remembrancer ri-**MEHM**-bruhns-er [rɪ-'mɛm-brəns-ɚ]

remissness ri-**MIS**-nis [rɪ-'mɪs-nɪs]

remuneration ri-**MYO͞O**-nuh-**RAY**-shuhn [rɪ-mju-nə-'reɪ-ʃən]

rend REHND [rɛnd]

EE i be/ I ɪ bit/ EH ɛ bet/ AA æ bat/ O͞O u boot / O͞O ʊ book/ AW ɔ bought/ AH ɑ father/ ER ɝ bird/
UH ʌ cup/ AY eɪ bay/ EYE aɪ bite/ OY ɔɪ boy/ OH oʊ boat/ OW aʊ how/ YO͞O ɪu duke/ EAR ɪɚ
beer/ AIR ɛɚ bear/ O͞OR ʊɚ tour/ AWR ɔɚ bore/ AHR ɑɚ bar/ NG ŋ king/ SH ʃ ship/ ZH ʒ vision/
TH θ thirty/ TH ð then/ CH tʃ child/ J ʤ just/ For complete list, see Key to Pronunciation p. 2.

renegado REH-ni-GAY-doh [rɛ-nɪ-'geɪ-doʊ] or ___-___-GAH-___ [___-___-'gɑ-___]

renege ri-NEHG [rɪ-'nɛg] or __-NIG [__-'nɪg]

repast ri-PAAST [rɪ-'pæst]

repasture ri-PAAS-cher [rɪ-'pæs-tʃɚ]

repine ri-PEYEN [rɪ-'paɪn]

reprehend reh-pri-HEHND [rɛ-prɪ-'hɛnd]

reprobate REH-pruh-bayt ['rɛ-prə-beɪt]

repugn ri-PYO͞ON [rɪ-'pjun]

repugnancy ri-PUHG-nuhn-see [rɪ-'pʌg-nən-si]

repulse ri-PUHLS [rɪ-'pʌls]

repured ri-PYO͞O-rid [rɪ-'pjʊ-rɪd]

repute ri-PYO͞OT [rɪ-'pjut]

requit ri-KWIT [rɪ-'kwɪt]

requital ri-KWEYE-t(uh)l [rɪ-'kwaɪ-tl̩]

requite ri-KWEYET [rɪ-'kwaɪt] scans to REE-kweyet ['ri-kwaɪt] @ *TIMON* IV, 3, 518

reremice REAR-meyes ['rɪɚ-maɪs]

resorters ri-ZAWR-terz [rɪ-'zɔɚ-tɚz]

respite (n) or (v) REHS-pit ['rɛs-pɪt]

restem ree-STEHM [ri-'stɛm]

restorative ri-STAW-ruh-tiv [rɪ-'stɔ-rə-tɪv]

retires ri-TEYERZ [rɪ-'taɪɚz]

revel REHV-uhl ['rɛv-əl]

reveller REHV-uh-ler ['rɛv-ə-lɚ]

revenue REHV-uh-nyōō ['rɛv-ə-nɪu] scans to ri-VEHN-yōō [rɪ-'vɛn-ju] e.g. @ *A&C* III, 6, 30

reverb ri-VERB [rɪ-'vɝb]

reverberate (adj) scans to ri-VER-brit [rɪ-'vɝ-brɪt]

reversion ri-VER-zhuhn [rɪ-'vɝ-ʒən]

Reynaldo *(HAM)* ri-NAHL-doh [rɪ-'nɑl-doʊ] or __-NAAL-__ [__-'næl-__]

Rheims REEMZ [rimz]

Rhenish REHN-ish ['rɛn-ɪʃ]

Rhesus REE-suhs ['ri-səs]

rheum RŌŌM [rum]

rheumatic rōō-MAAT-ik [ru-'mæt-ɪk] scans to RŌŌ-muh-tik ['ru-mə-tɪk] @ *MID* II, 1, 105

rheumy RŌŌM-ee ['rum-i]

Rhodes ROHDZ [roʊdz]

Rhodope ROHD-uh-pee ['roʊd-ə-pi]

rhubarb RŌŌ-bahrb ['ru-bɑɚb]

Rialto ree-AAL-toh [ri-'æl-toʊ]

ribald RI-buhld ['rɪ-bəld]

riband / ribband RIB-uhnd ['rɪb-ənd]

ribaudred possibly ri-BAW-drid [rɪ-'bɔ-drɪd] if "death is" contracts to one syllable. Many editors emend with "ribald."

Rice ap Thomas REYES aap TAH-muhs [raɪs] [æp] ['tɑ-məs]

EE i be/ I ɪ bit/ EH ɛ bet/ AA æ bat/ ŌŌ u boot / Ō̆Ŏ ʊ book/ AW ɔ bought/ AH ɑ father/ ER ɝ bird/ UH ʌ cup/ AY eɪ bay/ EYE aɪ bite/ OY ɔɪ boy/ OH oʊ boat/ OW aʊ how/ YŌŌ ɪu duke/ EAR ɪɚ beer/ AIR ɛɚ bear/ ŌŌR ʊɚ tour/ AWR ɔɚ bore/ AHR ɑɚ bar/ NG ŋ king/ SH ʃ ship/ ZH ʒ vision/ TH θ thirty/ T̲H̲ ð then/ CH ʧ child/ J ʤ just/ For complete list, see Key to Pronunciation p. 2.

209

Richard RICH-erd [ˈrɪtʃ-ɚd]
    Richard II *(RII)*
    Richard, afterward Duke of Gloucester *(2HVI, 3HVI)*
    Richard, Duke of Gloucester, afterwards King Richard III
        (RIII)
    Richard, Duke of York *(RIII)*

riggish RIG-ish [ˈrɪg-ɪʃ]

rigol RI-guhl [ˈrɪ-gəl]

Rinaldo *(AW)* ri-NAHL-doh [rɪ-ˈnɑl-dou] or ___-NAAL-___
    [___-ˈnæl-___]

rivage RIV-ij [ˈrɪv-ɪʤ]

rivality reye-VAAL-i-tee [raɪ-ˈvæl-ɪ-ti]

rivalled REYE-vuhld [ˈraɪ-vəld]

rive REYEV [raɪv]

rivelled RI-vuhld [ˈrɪ-vəld]

rivo (an exclamation) possibly REE-voh [ˈri-vou]

roan ROHN [roun]

Robin *(MW)* RAH-bin [ˈrɑ-bɪn]

robustious roh-BUHS-chuhs [rou-ˈbʌs-tʃəs]

Roderigo RAH-duh-REE-goh [rɑ-də-ˈri-gou] scans to
    rah-DREE-___ [rɑ-ˈdri-___]
    Roderigo *(OTH)* scans @ I, 1, 182

roe ROH [rou]

Rogero roh-JEH-roh [rou-ˈʤɛ-rou]

rogue ROHG [roug]

roisting ROYST-ing [ˈrɔɪst-ɪŋ]

romage RUHM-ij [ˈrʌm-ɪʤ]

Rome ROHM [roʊm] except ROOM [rum] @ *KJ* III, 1, 180 and *JC* I, 2, 156, and possibly *JC* III, 1, 288, in keeping with Elizabethan pun of contempt

Romeo *(R&J)* ROH-mee-oh ['roʊ-mi-oʊ] scans to ROHM-yoh ['roʊm-joʊ] e.g. @ I, 1, 114

Romish ROH-mish ['roʊ-mɪʃ]

ronyon RUHN-yuhn ['rʌn-jən]

rood ROOD [rud]

rooky ROOK-ee ['rʊk-i]

ropery ROHP-uh-ree ['roʊp-ə-ri]

Rosalind / Rosalinde *(AYL)* RAHZ-uh-lind ['rɑz-ə-lɪnd] except RAHZ-uh-leyend ['rɑz-ə-laɪnd] to accommodate rhymes @ III, 2, 83 and ff

Rosalinda RAHZ-uh-LIN-duh [rɑz-ə-'lɪn-də]

Rosaline RAH-zuh-leyen ['rɑ-zə-laɪn]
Rosaline *(LLL)*

Roscius RAHSH-ee-uhs ['rɑʃ-i-əs] scans to RAHSH-yuhs ['rɑʃ-jəs] @ *3HVI* V, 6, 10

rosemary ROHZ-muh-ree ['roʊz-mə-ri] or ___-meh-___ [___-mɛ-___]

Rosencrantz *(HAM)* ROH-zuhn-KRAANTS ['roʊ-zən-krænts] or ___-z(uh)n-___ [___-zn̩-___]

Ross RAWS [rɔs] or RAHS [rɑs]
Ross *(MAC)*
Ross, Lord *(RII)*

Rossillion roh-SIL-yuhn [roʊ-'sɪl-jən] possibly scans to ROH-sil-__ ['roʊ-sɪl-__] @ *AW* V, 1, 29

EE i be/ I ɪ bit/ EH ɛ bet/ AA æ bat/ OO u boot / OO ʊ book/ AW ɔ bought/ AH ɑ father/ ER ɝ bird/ UH ʌ cup/ AY eɪ bay/ EYE aɪ bite/ OY ɔɪ boy/ OH oʊ boat/ OW aʊ how/ YOO ɪu duke/ EAR ɪɚ beer/ AIR ɛɚ bear/ OOR ʊɚ tour/ AWR ɔɚ bore/ AHR ɑɚ bar/ NG ŋ king/ SH ʃ ship/ ZH ʒ vision/ TH θ thirty/ TH ð then/ CH tʃ child/ J ʤ just/ For complete list, see Key to Pronunciation p. 2.

Rossillion, Bertram, Count of *(AW)* **BER**-truhm
['bɝ-trəm]
Rossillion, Countess of *(AW)*

Rotherham, Thomas, Archbishop of York *(RIII)*
RA<u>TH</u>-uh-ruhm ['rað-ə-rəm]

Rouen ROH-uhn ['rou-ən] scans to ROHN [roun]
e.g. @ *1HVI* III, 2, 17

Rouge-mount ROOZH-mownt ['ruʒ-mount]

roundel ROWN-d(uh)l ['raun-dl̩]

roundure ROWN-jer ['raun-ʤɚ]

rouse ROWZ [rauz]

Roussi roo-SEE [ru-'si]

rout ROWT [raut]

rove ROHV [rouv]

rowel ROWL [raul] or scans to ROW-uhl ['rau-əl]

rowel-head ROW-uhl-hehd ['rau-əl-hɛd]

Rowland ROH-luhnd ['rou-lənd]
Rowland de Boys duh-**BOYZ** [də-'bɔɪz] or __-**BOYS**
[__-'bɔɪs]

roynish ROYN-ish ['rɔɪn-ɪʃ]

ruddock RUHD-uhk ['rʌd-ək]

rudesby ROODZ-bee ['rudz-bi]

rue ROO [ru]

Rugby *(MW)* RUHG-bee ['rʌg-bi]

ruin ROO-in ['ru-ɪn]

ruinate ROO-i-nayt ['ru-ɪ-neɪt]

ruminate ROO-muh-nayt ['ru-mə-neɪt]

Rumor *(2HIV)* RŌO-mer ['ru-mɚ]

runagate RUHN-uh-gayt ['rʌn-ə-geɪt] scans to RUHN-gayt ['rʌn-geɪt] @ *CYM* I, 6, 137

runnion RUHN-yuhn ['rʌn-jən]

Russia RUHSH-uh ['rʌʃ-ə] scans to RUHSH-ee-uh ['rʌʃ-i-ə] @ *MM* II, 1, 127

rustically RUHS-ti-kuh-lee ['rʌs-tɪ-kə-li]

ruth RŌOTH [ruθ]

ruthful RŌOTH-fuhl ['ruθ-fəl]

Rutland RUHT-luhnd ['rʌt-lənd]

ruttish RUHT-ish ['rʌt-ɪʃ]

Rycas REYE-kuhs ['raɪ-kəs]

s. (abbreviation for "shilling") SHIL-ing ['ʃɪl-ɪŋ]

Saba SAH-buh ['sɑ-bə] or SAY-___ ['seɪ-__]

Sackerson SAAK-er-suhn ['sæk-ɚ-sən]

sacring SAYK-ring ['seɪk-rɪŋ]

saffron SAAF-ruhn ['sæf-rən]

Sagittary SAAJ-i-teh-ree ['sædʒ-ɪ-tɛ-ri] scans to SAAJ-i-tree ['sædʒ-ɪ-tri] @ *OTH* I, 1, 157

sain SAYN [seɪn]

Saint Albans SAYNT AWL-buhnz [seɪnt] ['ɔl-bənz]

Saint Denis SAYNT DEHN-is [seɪnt] ['dɛn-ɪs]

Saint Jaques SAYNT JAY-kweez [seɪnt] ['dʒeɪ-kwiz]

Sala SAY-luh ['seɪ-lə] or SAA-___ ['sæ-__]

EE i be/ I ɪ bit/ EH ɛ bet/ AA æ bat/ ŌO u boot / ŌO ʊ book/ AW ɔ bought/ AH ɑ father/ ER ɝ bird/ UH ʌ cup/ AY eɪ bay/ EYE aɪ bite/ OY ɔɪ boy/ OH oʊ boat/ OW aʊ how/ YŌO ɪu duke/ EAR ɪɚ beer/ AIR ɛɚ bear/ ŌOR ʊɚ tour/ AWR ɔɚ bore/ AHR ɑɚ bar/ NG ŋ king/ SH ʃ ship/ ZH ʒ vision/ TH θ thirty/ TH ð then/ CH tʃ child/ J dʒ just/ For complete list, see Key to Pronunciation p. 2.

Salerio *(MVEN)* always scans to suh-**LEH**-ryoh [sə-'lɛ-rjoʊ] or ___-**LI**-___ [___-'lɪ-___]

Salic **SAY**-lik ['seɪ-lɪk] or **SAA**-___ ['sæ-___]

Salisbury **SAWLZ**-buh-ree ['sɔlz-bə-ri] scans to **SAWLZ**-bree ['sɔlz-bri]
   Salisbury *(HV)*
   Salisbury *(RII)*
   Salisbury, Earl of *(KJ)* scans e.g. @ IV, 2, 162

sallet **SAAL**-it ['sæl-ɪt]

sally (n) or (v) **SAAL**-ee ['sæl-i]

Saltiers (possible corruption of "Satyrs") **SAYL**-terz ['seɪl-tɚz] or **SAAL**-___ ['sæl-___]

saltpetre **SAWLT**-pee-ter ['sɔlt-pi-tɚ]

salve **SAAV** [sæv] possibly **SAHL**-vay ['sɑl-veɪ] @ *LLL* III, 1, 65, 67

Samingo suh-**MING**-goh [sə-'mɪŋ-goʊ]

sampire **SAAM**-peyer ['sæm-paɪɚ]

Sampson *(R&J)* **SAMP**-suhn ['sæmp-sən]

sanctuarize scans to **SAANGK**-choo-reyez ['sæŋk-tʃu-raɪz]

Sandal **SAAN**-d(uh)l ['sæn-dl̩]

Sandys, Lord *(HVIII)* **SAANDZ** [sændz] also called "Sir Walter Sandys"

sanguine **SAANG**-gwin ['sæŋ-gwɪn]

sans **SAANZ** [sænz]

sapient scans to **SAY**-pyuhnt ['seɪ-pjənt]

Saracens **SAA**-ruh-suhnz ['sæ-rə-sənz]

sarcenet **SAHRS**-nit ['sɑɚs-nɪt]

Sardians SAHR-dee-uhnz ['sɑɚ-di-ənz] or ___-di-___ [___-dɪ-___]

Sardinia scans to sahr-DI-nyuh [sɑɚ-'dɪ-njə]

Sardis SAHR-dis ['sɑɚ-dɪs]

Sarum SEH-ruhm ['sɛ-rəm]

sate SAYT [seɪt]

satiate scans to SAY-shuht ['seɪ-ʃət]

satiety suh-TEYE-i-tee [sə-'taɪ-ɪ-ti] scans to ___-TEYE-tee [___-'taɪ-ti] @ *SHR* I, 1, 24

satisfice SAAT-is-feyes ['sæt-ɪs-faɪs]

Saturninus *(TITUS)* SAA-ter-NEYE-nuhs [sæ-tɚ-'naɪ-nəs] also called "Saturnine" SAA-ter-neyen ['sæ-tɚ-naɪn]

satyr SAY-ter ['seɪ-tɚ] or SAA-___ ['sæ-___]

saucily SAW-si-lee ['sɔ-sɪ-li]

savor SAY-ver ['seɪ-vɚ]

Savoy suh-VOY [sə-'vɔɪ]

Saxons SAAK-suhnz ['sæk-sənz]

Saxony SAAK-suh-nee ['sæk-sə-ni]

'sblood (corruption of "God's blood") ZBLUHD [zblʌd] or SBLUHD [sblʌd]

scabbard SKAAB-erd ['skæb-ɚd]

scaffoldage SKAAF-uhl-dij ['skæf-əl-dɪʤ]

Scales, Lord Thomas *(2HVI)* SKAYLZ [skeɪlz]

scall SKAWL [skɔl]

EE i be/ I ɪ bit/ EH ɛ bet/ AA æ bat/ O͞O u boot / O͝O ʊ book/ AW ɔ bought/ AH ɑ father/ ER ɝ bird/ UH ʌ cup/ AY eɪ bay/ EYE aɪ bite/ OY ɔɪ boy/ OH oʊ boat/ OW aʊ how/ YO͞O ɪu duke/ EAR ɪɚ beer/ AIR ɛɚ bear/ O͞OR ʊɚ tour/ AWR ɔɚ bore/ AHR ɑɚ bar/ NG ŋ king/ SH ʃ ship/ ZH ʒ vision/ TH θ thirty/ T̲H̲ ð then/ CH ʧ child/ J ʤ just/ For complete list, see Key to Pronunciation p. 2.

215

scambling SKAAM-bling ['skæm-blɪŋ]

scamels SKAAM-uhlz ['skæm-əlz] or SKAYM-___ ['skeɪm-___]

scantling SKAANT-ling ['skænt-lɪŋ]

scaped SKAYPT [skeɪpt]

Scarus *(A&C)* SKEH-ruhs ['skɛ-rəs]

scath SKAATH [skæθ]

scathe SKAY<u>TH</u> [skeɪð]

scathful SKAATH-fuhl ['skæθ-fəl]

sceptre SEHP-ter ['sɛp-tɚ]

'schew SCHOO [stʃu]

sciatica seye-AAT-i-kuh [saɪ-'æt-ɪ-kə]

scimitar SIM-i-ter ['sɪm-ɪ-tɚ] or ___-___-tahr [___-___-taɚ]

scion SEYE-uhn ['saɪ-ən]

sconce SKAHNS [skɑns]

Scone SKOON [skun]

scorpion always scans to SKAWR-pyuhn ['skɔɚ-pjən]

scotch SKAHCH [skɑtʃ]

scour SKOWR [skɑʊɚ]

scourge SKERJ [skɝʤ]

scrimers SKRIM-erz ['skrɪm-ɚz] or SKREEM-__ ['skrim-__]

scrip SKRIP [skrɪp]

scrippage SKRIP-ij ['skrɪp-ɪʤ]

scrivener scans to SKRIV-ner ['skrɪv-nɚ]

Scroop SKRŌŌP [skrup]
  Scroop, Lord *(HV)*
  Scroop, Richard, Archbishop of York *(1HIV, 2HIV)*
  Scroop, Sir Stephen *(RII)*

scrowl SKROHL [skroʊl]

scroyles SKROYLZ [skrɔɪlz]

sculls SKUHLZ [skʌlz]

scullion SKUHL-yuhn [ˈskʌl-jən]

scurril SKE(r)-ruhl [ˈskɜ-rəl] or **SKUH**-ruhl [ˈskʌ-rəl]

scurrility skuh-RIL-i-tee [skə-ˈrɪl-ɪ-ti]

scut SKUHT [skʌt]

scutcheon SKUHCH-uhn [ˈskʌtʃ-ən]

Scylla SIL-uh [ˈsɪl-ə]

scythe SEYE<u>TH</u> [saɪð]

Scythia always scans to SI-thyuh [ˈsɪ-θjə]

Scythian always scans to SI-thyuhn [ˈsɪ-θjən]

'sdeath (corruption of "God's death") ZDEHTH [zdɛθ] or
  SDEHTH [sdɛθ]

se'nnight SEHN-eyet [ˈsɛn-aɪt] or ___-it [___-ɪt]

Sea Captain *(12th)* SEE **KAAP**-t(uh)n [si] [ˈkæp-tn̩]

Seacole, George SEE-kohl [ˈsi-koʊl]

sea-marge SEE-mahrj [ˈsi-mɑɚdʒ]

Sebastian si-BAAS-chuhn [sɪ-ˈbæs-tʃən] or ___-___-tyuhn
  [___-___-tjən]
  Sebastian *(TEMP)*
  Sebastian *(12th)*

EE i be/ I ɪ bit/ EH ɛ bet/ AA æ bat/ ŌŌ u boot / ŌŌ ʊ book/ AW ɔ bought/ AH ɑ father/ ER ɝ bird/
UH ʌ cup/ AY eɪ bay/ EYE aɪ bite/ OY ɔɪ boy/ OH oʊ boat/ OW aʊ how/ YŌŌ ɪu duke/ EAR ɪɚ
beer/ AIR ɛɚ bear/ ŌŌR ʊɚ tour/ AWR ɔɚ bore/ AHR ɑɚ bar/ NG ŋ king/ SH ʃ ship/ ZH ʒ vision/
TH θ thirty/ <u>TH</u> ð then/ CH tʃ child/ J dʒ just/ For complete list, see Key to Pronunciation p. 2.

sectary SEHK-tuh-ree [ˈsɛk-tə-ri]

secure (adj) si-KYŌOR [sɪ-ˈkjʊɚ] scans to SI-kyŏor [ˈsɪ-kjʊɚ] e.g. @ *HAM* I, 5, 61

sedge SEHJ [sɛʤ]

sedgy SEHJ-ee [ˈsɛʤ-i]

seel SEEL [sil]

seely SEE-lee [ˈsi-li]

Seely, Sir Bennet SEE-lee [ˈsi-li]

seld SEHLD [sɛld]

Seleucus *(A&C)* suh-LŌO-kuhs [sə-ˈlu-kəs]

semblable SEHM-bluh-b(uh)l [ˈsɛm-blə-bl̩]

semblably SEHM-bluh-blee [ˈsɛm-blə-bli]

semblance SEHM-bluhns [ˈsɛm-bləns] scans to SEHM-buh-luhns [ˈsɛm-bə-ləns] e.g. @ *CE* V, 1, 359

semblative SEHM-bluh-tiv [ˈsɛm-blə-tɪv]

Semiramis suh-MI-ruh-mis [sə-ˈmɪ-rə-mɪs]

Sempronius sehm-PROH-nee-uhs [sɛm-ˈproʊ-ni-əs] scans to ___-PROH-nyuhs [___-ˈproʊ-njəs]
Sempronius *(TIMON)* scans @ III, 4, 110
Sempronius *(TITUS)* scans @ IV, 3, 10

sempster SEHMP-ster [ˈsɛmp-stɚ]

Seneca SEHN-i-kuh [ˈsɛn-ɪ-kə]

seniory SEEN-yuh-ree [ˈsin-jə-ri]

senna SEHN-uh [ˈsɛn-ə]

Sennois SEH-noyz [ˈsɛ-nɔɪz]

Senoys SEH-noyz [ˈsɛ-nɔɪz]

sententious sehn-TEHN-chuhs [sɛn-'tɛn-tʃəs]

sentinel SEHN-tuh-nuhl ['sɛn-tə-nəl]

Septentrion sehp-TEHN-tri-uhn [sɛp-'tɛn-trɪ-ən] or __-__-__-ahn [__-__-__-ɑn]

sepulchre (n) SEHP-uhl-ker ['sɛp-əl-kɚ] scans to seh-PUHL-__ [sɛ-'pʌl-__] @ *RII* I, 3, 196

sepulchre (v) seh-PUHL-ker [sɛ-'pʌl-kɚ]

sequent SEE-kwuhnt ['si-kwənt]

sequester (n) SEE-kwehs-ter ['sɪ-kwɛs-tɚ]

sequester (v) see-KWEHS-ter [si-'kwɛs-tɚ] scans to SEE-kwehs-___ ['si-kwɛs-___] @ *TITUS* II, 3, 75

sequestration SEE-kwi-STRAY-shuhn [si-kwɪ-'streɪ-ʃən]

sere SEAR [sɪɚ]

serpigo ser-PEYE-goh [sɚ-'paɪ-gou] or __-PEE-__ [__-'pi-__]

servile SER-veyel ['sɝ-vaɪl] or ___-vuhl [___-vəl]

Servilius *(TIMON)* ser-VIL-ee-uhs [sɚ-'vɪl-i-əs] scans to ___-VIL-yuhs [___-'vɪl-jəs] @ III, 4, 77

servitor SER-vuh-ter ['sɝ-və-tɚ]

sessa SEHS-uh ['sɛs-ə]

Sestos SEHS-tuhs ['sɛs-təs] or ___-tohs [___-tous]

Setebos SEHT-i-bahs ['sɛt-ɪ-bɑs]

sev'night / sev'n-night SEHV-neyet ['sɛv-naɪt] or SEHN-neyet ['sɛn-naɪt]

severally SEHV-uh-ruh-lee ['sɛv-ə-rə-li] scans to SEHV-ruh-___ ['sɛv-rə-___] @ *CYM* V, 5, 397

EE i be/ I ɪ bit/ EH ɛ bet/ AA æ bat/ OO u boot / OO ʊ book/ AW ɔ bought/ AH ɑ father/ ER ɝ bird/ UH ʌ cup/ AY eɪ bay/ EYE aɪ bite/ OY ɔɪ boy/ OH ou boat/ OW aʊ how/ YOO ɪu duke/ EAR ɪɚ beer/ AIR ɛɚ bear/ OOR ʊɚ tour/ AWR ɔɚ bore/ AHR ɑɚ bar/ NG ŋ king/ SH ʃ ship/ ZH ʒ vision/ TH θ thirty/ TH ð then/ CH tʃ child/ J dʒ just/ For complete list, see Key to Pronunciation p. 2.

Severn SEHV-ern [ˈsɛv-ɚn]

sexton / Sexton SEHKS-tuhn [ˈsɛks-tən]
Sexton *(MADO)*

Sextus Pompeius *(A&C)* SEHKS-tuhs pahm-PEE-uhs
[ˈsɛks-təs] [pɑm-ˈpi-əs]

Seyton *(MAC)* SEE-t(uh)n [ˈsi-tn̩] or possibly SAY-___
[ˈseɪ-___]

'sfoot (corruption of "Christ's foot") SFOOT [sfʊt]

Shadow, Simon *(2HIV)* SHAA-doh SEYE-muhn [ˈʃæ-doʊ]
[ˈsaɪ-mən]

Shafalus SHAA-fuh-luhs [ˈʃæ-fə-ləs]

Shallow SHAA-loh [ˈʃæ-loʊ]
Shallow *(2HIV, MW)*

shealed SHEELD [ʃild]

shearman SHEAR-muhn [ˈʃɪɚ-mən]

sheath SHEETH [ʃiθ]

sheathe SHEE<u>TH</u> [ʃið]

sheepcote SHEEP-koht [ˈʃip-koʊt] or ___-kaht [___-kɑt]

Sheffield SHEHF-eeld [ˈʃɛf-ild]

shelvy SHEHLV-ee [ˈʃɛlv-i]

shent SHEHNT [ʃɛnt]

Sheriff of Wiltshire *(RIII)* WILT-sher [ˈwɪlt-ʃɚ] or
___-shear [___-ʃɪɚ]

sherris SHEH-ris [ˈʃɛ-rɪs]

shipwrack SHIP-raak [ˈʃɪp-ræk]

shire SHEYER [ʃaɪɚ]

shive SHEYEV [ʃaɪv]

shoal SHOHL [ʃoul]

shog SHAHG [ʃɑg]

shoon SHO͞ON [ʃun]

shotten SHAH-t(uh)n ['ʃɑ-tn̩]

shoughs SHUHFS [ʃʌfs] or SHAHKS [ʃɑks] (form of "shock-dog")

shove-groat SHUHV-groht ['ʃʌv-groʊt]

Shrewsbury SHRO͞OZ-buh-ree ['ʃruz-bə-ri] or SHROHZ-___-___ ['ʃroʊz-___-___] possibly SHRO͞OZ-bree ['ʃruz-bri] or SHROHZ-___ ['ʃroʊz-___] in prose

shrieve SHREEV [ʃriv]

shrift SHRIFT [ʃrɪft]

shrive SHREYEV [ʃraɪv]

shriver SHREYEV-er ['ʃraɪv-ɚ]

shroud SHROWD [ʃraʊd]

Shrove SHROHV [ʃroʊv]

shrow SHROH [ʃroʊ]

shrowd SHROHD [ʃroʊd]

Shylock *(MVEN)* SHEYE-lahk ['ʃaɪ-lɑk]

sib SIB [sɪb]

sibyl / Sibyl SIB-uhl ['sɪb-əl]

Sibylla si-BIL-uh [sɪ-'bɪl-ə]

Sicil SIS-uhl ['sɪs-əl]

EE i be/ I ɪ bit/ EH ɛ bet/ AA æ bat/ O͞O u boot / O͝O ʊ book/ AW ɔ bought/ AH ɑ father/ ER ɝ bird/ UH ʌ cup/ AY eɪ bay/ EYE aɪ bite/ OY ɔɪ boy/ OH oʊ boat/ OW aʊ how/ YO͞O ɪu duke/ EAR ɪɚ beer/ AIR ɛɚ bear/ O͞OR ʊɚ tour/ AWR ɔɚ bore/ AHR ɑɚ bar/ NG ŋ king/ SH ʃ ship/ ZH ʒ vision/ TH θ thirty/ TH ð then/ CH ʧ child/ J ʤ just/ For complete list, see Key to Pronunciation p. 2.

Sicilia si-SIL-ee-uh [sɪ-'sɪl-i-ə] scans to ___-SIL-yuh [___-'sɪl-jə] e.g. @ *WT* I, 2, 146 and scans to SI-sil-___ ['sɪ-sɪl-___] @ *WT* IV, 4, 582

Sicilius always scans to si-SIL-yuhs [sɪ-'sɪl-jəs]

Sicils SIS-uhlz ['sɪs-əlz]

Sicily SIS-uh-lee ['sɪs-ə-li] scans to SIS-lee ['sɪs-li] @ *A&C* II, 6, 7

Sicinius Velutus *(COR)* si-SIN-ee-uhs vuh-LOO-tuhs [sɪ-'sɪn-i-əs] [və-'lu-təs]

sicklied SIK-leed ['sɪk-lid]

sicles SI-k(uh)lz ['sɪ-kl̩z]

Sicyon always scans to SIS-yuhn ['sɪs-jən] or SISH-__ ['sɪʃ-__]

siege SEEJ [siʤ]

Siena see-EHN-uh [si-'ɛn-ə]

sieve SIV [sɪv]

signor SEEN-yawr ['sin-jɚ] scans to seen-YAWR [sin-'jɚ] e.g. @ *MVEN* I, 1, 73 (sometimes spelled "signior")

signory SEEN-yuh-ree ['sin-jə-ri] (sometimes spelled "signiory")

Silence *(2HIV)* SEYE-luhns ['saɪ-ləns]

Silius SIL-yuhs ['sɪl-jəs]

sillily SI-li-lee ['sɪ-lɪ-li]

Silvia *(2GEN)* SIL-vee-uh ['sɪl-vi-ə] scans to SIL-vyuh ['sɪl-vjə] e.g. @ II, 4, 46

Silvius SIL-vee-yuhs ['sɪl-vi-jəs] scans to SIL-vyuhs ['sɪl-vjəs] Silvius *(AYL)* scans e.g. @ III, 5, 123

Simon Catling KAAT-ling ['kæt-lɪŋ]

Simonides *(PER)* seye-**MAHN**-uh-deez [saɪ-'mɑn-ə-dɪz]

simony **SEYE**-muh-nee ['saɪ-mə-ni] or **SIM**-uh-___ ['sɪm-ə-___]

Simpcox, Saunder *(2HVI)* **SIMP**-kahks **SAWN**-der ['sɪmp-kɑks] ['sɔn-dɚ]

Simple *(MW)* **SIM**-p(uh)l ['sɪm-pl̩]

simular **SIM**-yuh-ler ['sɪm-jə-lɚ] or ___-___-lahr [___-___-lɑɚ] scans to **SIM**-ler ['sɪm-lɚ] or ___-lahr [___-lɑɚ] @ *CYM* V, 5, 200

Sinel SI-nuhl ['sɪ-nəl] or **SEYE**-___ ['saɪ-___]

sinew **SIN**-yoo ['sɪn-ju]

sinister **SIN**-i-ster ['sɪn-ɪ-stɚ] scans to si-**NIS**-ter [sɪ-'nɪs-tɚ] e.g. @ *HV* II, 4, 85

sink-a-pace **SINGK**-uh-pays ['sɪŋk-ə-peɪs]

Sinon **SEYE**-nuhn ['saɪ-nən]

sire SEYER [saɪɚ]

sirrah SI-ruh ['sɪ-rə]

sith SITH [sɪθ]

sithence **SITH**-uhns ['sɪθ-əns]

situate **SICH**-oo-wayt ['sɪtʃ-u-weɪt] or ___-___-wit [___-___-wɪt] scans to **SICH**-wit ['sɪtʃ-wɪt] @ *CE* II, 1, 16

Siward, Earl of Northumberland *(MAC)* **SYOO**-erd nawr-**THUHM**-ber-luhnd ['sɪu-ɚ-d] [nɔɚ-'θʌm-bɚ-lənd]

sixpence **SIKS**-puhnts ['sɪks-pənts]

skains-mates **SKAYNZ**-mayts ['skeɪnz-meɪts]

EE i be/ I ɪ bit/ EH ɛ bet/ AA æ bat/ OO u boot / OO ʊ book/ AW ɔ bought/ AH ɑ father/ ER ɝ bird/ UH ʌ cup/ AY eɪ bay/ EYE aɪ bite/ OY ɔɪ boy/ OH oʊ boat/ OW aʊ how/ YOO ɪu duke/ EAR ɪɚ beer/ AIR ɛɚ bear/ OOR ʊɚ tour/ AWR ɔɚ bore/ AHR ɑɚ bar/ NG ŋ king/ SH ʃ ship/ ZH ʒ vision/ TH θ thirty/ TH ð then/ CH tʃ child/ J ʤ just/ For complete list, see Key to Pronunciation p. 2.

223

skein SKAYN [skeɪn]

skimble-skamble SKIM-b(uh)l-SKAAM-b(uh)l ['skɪm-bl̩-skæm-bl̩]

skirr SKER [skɝ]

skittish SKI-tish ['skɪ-tɪʃ]

Skogan SKAH-guhn ['skɑ-gən]

skyey SKEYE-ee ['skaɪ-i]

slake SLAYK [sleɪk]

slaver (v) (to smear with saliva) SLAAV-er ['slæv-ɚ]

slavish SLAY-vish ['sleɪ-vɪʃ]

slay SLAY [sleɪ]

sleave SLEEV [sliv]

sleided SLEED-id ['slid-ɪd]

sleight SLEYET [slaɪt]

Slender *(MW)* SLEHN-der ['slɛn-dɚ]

slew SLOO [slu]

'slid (corruption of "God's eyelid") ZLID [zlɪd] or SLID [slɪd]

'slight (corruption of "God's light") ZLEYET [zlaɪt] or SLEYET [slaɪt]

slily SLEYE-lee ['slaɪ-li]

slish SLISH [slɪʃ]

sloth SLAWTH [slɔθ] or SLAHTH [slɑθ] or SLOHTH [sloʊθ]

slough (skin of a snake) SLUHF [slʌf]

slough (a place of deep mud) SLOO [slu] @ *MW* IV, 5, 58

224

slovenly SLUHV-uhn-lee [ˈslʌv-ən-li]

slovenry SLUHV-uhn-ree [ˈslʌv-ən-ri]

slubber SLUHB-er [ˈslʌb-ɚ]

sluggard SLUHG-erd [ˈslʌg-ɚd]

sluice SLOOS [slus]

Sly, Christopher *(SHR)* SLEYE [slaɪ]

Smalus SMAY-luhs [ˈsmeɪ-ləs]

smatch SMAACH [smætʃ]

smatter SMAAT-er [ˈsmæt-ɚ]

smit SMIT [smɪt]

smote SMOHT [smoʊt]

Smulkin SMUHL-kin [ˈsmʌl-kɪn]

smutched SMUHCHT [smʌtʃt]

snaffle SNAA-f(uh)l [ˈsnæ-fl]

Snare *(2HIV)* SNAIR [snɛɚ]

sneap SNEEP [snip]

sneck SNEHK [snɛk]

Snout, Tom / Wall *(MID)* SNOWT [snɑʊt]

Snug / Lion *(MID)* SNUHG [snʌg]

Socrates SAHK-ruh-teez [ˈsɑk-rə-tiz]

soe'er soh-AIR [soʊ-ˈɛɚ]

soho (a cry of sportsmen) soh-HOH [soʊ-ˈhoʊ]

soilure SOYL-yer [ˈsɔɪl-jɚ]

---

sojourn (n) SOH-jern ['soʊ-ʤən]

sojourn (v) SOH-jern ['soʊ-ʤən] scans to soh-JERN [soʊ-'ʤɝn] @ *MID* III, 2, 171

sojourner SOH-jer-ner ['soʊ-ʤə-nə-] or soh-JER-ner [soʊ-'ʤɝ-nə-]

Sol SAHL [sɑl]

solace SAHL-is ['sɑl-ɪs]

Solanio *(MVEN)* suh-LAHN-ee-oh [sə-'lɑn-i-oʊ]

sold'rest SAHD-rist ['sɑd-rɪst]

solder SAHD-er ['sɑd-ə-]

soldier SOHL-jer ['soʊl-ʤə-] scans to SOHL-jee-er ['soʊl-ʤi-ə-] e.g. @ *COR* I, 1, 111

solemnized SAH-lehm-neyezd ['sɑ-lɛm-naɪzd] scans to suh-LEHM-neye-zid [sə-'lɛm-naɪ-zɪd] e.g. @ *LLL* II, 1, 42

solidares SAH-luh-dairz ['sɑ-lə-dɛə-z]

Solinus *(CE)* suh-LEYE-nuhs [sə-'laɪ-nəs]

Solomon SAHL-uh-muhn ['sɑl-ə-mən]

Solon SOH-lahn ['soʊ-lɑn] or ___-luhn [___-lən]

solus SOH-luhs ['soʊ-ləs]

Solyman SAHL-i-muhn ['sɑl-ɪ-mən]

Somervile *(3HVI)* SUHM-er-vil ['sʌm-ə-vɪl]

Somme SAHM [sɑm]

sonance SOH-nuhns ['soʊ-nəns]

sonties SAHN-teez ['sɑn-tiz]

sooth SOOTH [suθ]

soothe SOOTH [suð]

Soothsayer SO͞OTH-say-er ['suθ-seɪ-ɚ] scans to SO͞OTH-sair
['suθ-sɛɚ]
Soothsayer *(A&C)*
Soothsayer *(CYM)* scans @ V, 5, 426
Soothsayer *(JC)*

sop SAHP [sɑp]

sophister SAHF-is-ter ['sɑf-ɪs-tɚ]

Sophy SOH-fee ['soʊ-fi]

sorel SAW-ruhl ['sɔ-rəl]

sortance SAWR-t(uh)ns ['sɔɚ-tn̩s]

Sossius SOH-shuhs ['soʊ-ʃəs]

Soto SOH-toh ['soʊ-toʊ]

sottish SAHT-ish ['sɑt-ɪʃ]

sound (to swoon) SO͞OND [sund] variant of "swoon"
SWO͞ON [swun]

souse SOWS [saʊs]

Southam SUHTH-uhm ['sʌð-əm] or SOWTH-uhm
['saʊð-əm]

Southampton sowth-HAAMP-tuhn [saʊθ-'hæmp-tən]

Southwark SUHTH-erk ['sʌð-ɚk]

Southwell, John *(2HVI)* SUHTH-uhl ['sʌð-əl] or
SOWTH-wuhl ['saʊθ-wəl]

sovereign SAHV-uh-rin ['sɑv-ə-rɪn] scans to SAHV-rin
['sɑv-rɪn] e.g. @ *KJ* V, 1, 4

sowl SOWL [saʊl]

EE i be/ I ɪ bit/ EH ɛ bet/ AA æ bat/ O͞O u boot / O͞O ʊ book/ AW ɔ bought/ AH ɑ father/ ER ɝ bird/
UH ʌ cup/ AY eɪ bay/ EYE aɪ bite/ OY ɔɪ boy/ OH oʊ boat/ OW aʊ how/ YO͞O ɪu duke/ EAR ɪɚ
beer/ AIR ɛɚ bear/ O͞OR ʊɚ tour/ AWR ɔɚ bore/ AHR ɑɚ bar/ NG ŋ king/ SH ʃ ship/ ZH ʒ vision/
TH θ thirty/ TH ð then/ CH ʧ child/ J ʤ just/ For complete list, see Key to Pronunciation p. 2.

227

sow-skin SOW-skin ['sɑu-skɪn]

Sowter SŌŌ-ter ['su-tɚ] or SOW-__ ['sɑu-__]

Sparta SPAHR-tuh ['spɑɚ-tə]

spavin SPAAV-in ['spæv-ɪn]

Speed *(2GEN)* SPEED [spid]

speken SPEEK-uhn ['spik-ən]

sperr SPER [spɝ] some editions "spar" SPAHR [spɑɚ]

spherical SFI-ri-k(uh)l ['sfɪ-rɪ-k]]

sphery SFI-ree ['sfɪ-ri]

Sphinx SFINGKS [sfɪŋks]

spigot SPIG-uht ['spɪg-ət]

spilth SPILTH [spɪlθ]

Spinii SPI-nee-eye ['spɪ-ni-aɪ] or SPEYE-__-__ ['spaɪ-__-__]

spiritualty scans to SPEAR-chool-tee ['spɪɚ-tʃul-ti]

spital SPI-t(uh)l ['spɪ-t]]

splay SPLAY [spleɪ]

spleeny SPLEEN-ee [splin-i]

splenitive SPLEHN-i-tiv ['splɛn-ɪ-tiv]

spousal SPOW-zuhl ['spɑu-zəl]

sprat SPRAAT [spræt]

springe SPRINJ [sprɪndʒ]

spriting SPREYET-ing ['spraɪt-ɪŋ]

spur SPER [spɝ]

Spurio SPYŌŌ-ree-oh ['spjʊ-ri-oʊ]

Squele SKWEEL [skwil]

squier SKWEYER [skwaɪɚ]

squiny SKWIN-ee [ˈskwɪn-i]

squire SKWEYER [skwaɪɚ]

Stafford STAAF-erd [ˈstæf-ɚd]
    Stafford, Humphrey, Duke of Buckingham *(2HVI)*
        BUHK-ing-uhm [ˈbʌk-ɪŋ-əm]
    Stafford, Lord Humphrey *(3HVI)*
    Stafford, Sir Humphrey *(2HVI)*
    Stafford, William *(2HVI)*

Staffordshire STAAF-erd-sher [ˈstæf-ɚd-ʃɚ] or __-__-shear [__-__-ʃɪɚ]

staider STAYD-er [ˈsteɪd-ɚ]

Staines STAYNZ [steɪnz]

stanchless STAWNCH-lis [ˈstɔntʃ-lɪs] or STAANCH-__ [ˈstæntʃ-__]

staniel STAAN-yuhl [ˈstæn-jəl]

Stanley STAAN-lee [ˈstæn-li]
    Stanley, John *(2HVI)*
    Stanley, Lord, Earl of Derby *(RIII)* DAHR-bee [ˈdɑɚ-bi]
        or DER-__ [ˈdɝ-__]
    Stanley, Sir William *(3HVI)*

stanzo STAAN-zoh [ˈstæn-zoʊ]

stark-nak'd stahrk-NAYKT [stɑɚk-ˈneɪkt]

Starveling, Robin / Moonshine *(MID)* STAHRV-ling [ˈstɑɚv-lɪŋ]

Statilius stuh-TIL-yuhs [stə-ˈtɪl-jəs]

statist STAY-tist [ˈsteɪ-tɪst]

---

statue STAACH-ōō ['stætʃ-u] scans to **STAA**-chōō-uh ['stæ-tʃu-ə] e.g. @ *JC* II, 2, 76

staunch STAWNCH [stɔntʃ] or STAHNCH [stantʃ]

stave STAYV [steɪv]

stead STEHD [stɛd]

stealth STEHLTH [stɛlθ]

stelled STEHL-id ['stɛl-ɪd]

stepdame STEHP-daym ['stɛp-deɪm]

Stephano *(MVEN)* steh-**FAH**-noh [stɛ-'fɑ-nou]

Stephano *(TEMP)* **STEH**-fuh-noh ['stɛ-fə-nou]

stigmatic always scans to **STIG**-muh-tik ['stɪg-mə-tɪk]

stigmatical stig-**MAAT**-i-k(uh)l [stɪg-'mæt-ɪ-kl̩]

stile STEYEL [staɪl]

stilly STIL-ee ['stɪl-i]

stithy STI<u>TH</u>-ee ['stɪð-i]

stoccadoes stuh-**KAH**-dohz [stə-'kɑ-douz]

Stokesly STOHKS-lee ['stouks-li]

stomacher STUHM-uh-ker ['stʌm-ə-kɚ] scans to **STUHM**-ker ['stʌm-kɚ] @ *CYM* III, 4, 84

stonish STAHN-ish ['stan-ɪʃ]

stoup STŌŌP [stup]

stover STOH-ver ['stou-vɚ]

Strachy STRAYCH-ee ['streɪtʃ-i]

strappado struh-**PAH**-doh [strə-'pɑ-dou] or ___-**PAY**-___ [___-'peɪ-___]

strategem STRAAT-uh-juhm ['stræt-ə-dʒəm]

Strato *(JC)* **STRAY**-tʊh [ˈstreɪ-toʊ]

strawy **STRAW**-ee [ˈstrɔ-i]

strew **STROO** [stru]

strewments **STROO**-muhnts [ˈstru-mənts]

stricture **STRIK**-cher [ˈstrɪk-tʃɚ]

stroken **STROHK**-uhn [ˈstroʊk-ən]

strond / Strond STRAHND [strɑnd] often emended to
  "strand" STRAAND [strænd]

strooken **STROOK**-uhn [ˈstrʊk-ən]

strossers **STRAWS**-erz [ˈstrɔs-ɚz] or **STRAHS**-__ [ˈstrɑs-__]

strove STROHV [stroʊv]

strow STROH [stroʊ]

strown STROHN [stroʊn]

strucken **STRUHK**-uhn [ˈstrʌk-ən]

Stygian scans to **STIJ**-yuhn [ˈstɪdʒ-jən]

Styx STIKS [stɪks]

subcontracted scans to **SUHB**-kuhn-traakt-id
  [ˈsʌb-kən-trækt-ɪd]

suborn suh-**BAWRN** [sə-ˈbɔɚn]

subornation suhb-awr-**NAY**-shuhn [səb-ɔɚ-ˈneɪ-ʃən]

subsequent scans to suhb-**SEE**-kwehnt [səb-ˈsi-kwɛnt]

substractors suhb-**STRAAK**-terz [sʌb-ˈstræk-tɚz]

subtile **SUH**-t(uh)l [ˈsʌ-tl̩] or **SUHB**-___ [ˈsʌb-__]

EE i be/ I ɪ bit/ EH ɛ bet/ AA æ bat/ OO u boot / ŌŌ ʊ book/ AW ɔ bought/ AH ɑ father/ ER ɝ bird/
UH ʌ cup/ AY eɪ bay/ EYE aɪ bite/ OY ɔɪ boy/ OH oʊ boat/ OW aʊ how/ YOO ɪu duke/ EAR ɪɚ
beer/ AIR ɛɚ bear/ OOR ʊɚ tour/ AWR ɔɚ bore/ AHR ɑɚ bar/ NG ŋ king/ SH ʃ ship/ ZH ʒ vision/
TH θ thirty/ TH ð then/ CH tʃ child/ J dʒ just/ For complete list, see Key to Pronunciation p. 2.

subtile-witted SUH-t(uh)l-WIT-id ['sʌ-tl̩-wɪt-ɪd] or
  SUHB-__-__-__ ['sʌb-__-__-__]

subtilly always scans to SUHT-lee ['sʌt-li]

successantly suhk-SEHS-uhnt-lee [sək-'sɛs-ənt-li]

succor SUHK-er ['sʌk-ɚ]

sue SŌŌ [su] or SYŌŌ [sɪu]

Suffolk SUHF-uhk ['sʌf-ək]
  Suffolk, Duke of *(HVIII)*

Sulla SUH-luh ['sʌ-lə]

sully SUHL-ee ['sʌl-i]

sumpter SUHMP-ter ['sʌmp-tɚ]

sunder SUHN-der ['sʌn-dɚ]

sup SUHP [sʌp]

superfluity SŌŌ-per-FLŌŌ-i-tee [su-pɚ-'flu-ɪ-ti] or
  syōō-__-__-__-__ [sɪu-__-__-__-__]

supernal sōō-PER-nuhl [su-'pɝ-nəl] or syōō-__-__
  [sɪu-__-__]

suppliance suh-PLEYE-uhns [sə-'plaɪ-əns]

suppliant SUHP-lee-uhnt ['sʌp-li-ənt] scans to SUHP-lyuhnt
  ['sʌp-ljənt] e.g. @ *AW* V, 3, 134

supplyant suh-PLEYE-uhnt [sə-'plaɪ-ənt]

supplyment suh-PLEYE-muhnt [sə-'plaɪ-mənt]

supportance suh-PAWR-tuhns [sə-'pɔɚ-təns]

supposal suh-POH-z(uh)l [sə-'pou-zl̩]

supreme sōō-PREEM [su-'prim] or syōō-___ [sɪu-___]
  scans to SŌŌ-preem ['su-prim] or SYŌŌ-___ ['sɪu-___]
  e.g. @ *RIII* III, 7, 118

sur-additon SER-uh-di-shuhn ['sɝ-ə-dɪ-ʃən]

surcease always scans to ser-SEES [sɚ-'sis]

surety (n) SHŌO-ri-tee ['ʃʊ-rɪ-ti] scans to SHŌOR-tee ['ʃʊɚ-ti] e.g. @ *HV* V, 2, 356

surety (v) always scans to SHŌOR-tee ['ʃʊɚ-ti]

surfeit SER-fit ['sɝ-fɪt]

surplice SER-plis ['sɝ-plɪs]

sur-reined SER-raynd ['sɝ-reɪnd]

Surrey SUH-ree ['sʌ-ri] or SE(r)-___ ['sɝ-___]
    Surrey, Duke of *(RII)*
    Surrey, Earl of *(2HIV)*
    Surrey, Earl of *(HVIII)*
    Surrey, Earl of *(RIII)*

survey (n) SER-vay ['sɝ-veɪ] scans to ser-VAY [sɚ-'veɪ] e.g. @ *AW* V, 3, 16

survey (v) ser-VAY [sɚ-'veɪ]

surveyor ser-VAY-er [sɚ-'veɪ-ɚ] scans to SER-vay-er ['sɝ-veɪ-ɚ] @ *HVIII* I, 1, 222

suspect (n) always scans to suh-SPEHKT [sə-'spɛkt]

suspiration suhs-pi-RAY-shuhn [səs-pɪ-'reɪ-ʃən]

suspire suh-SPEYER [sə-'spaɪɚ]

sutler SUHT-ler ['sʌt-lɚ]

Sutton Co'fil' SUH-t(uh)n KOH-fil ['sʌ-tn̩] ['koʊ-fɪl]

swain SWAYN [sweɪn]

sware SWAIR [swɛɚ]

EE i be/ I ɪ bit/ EH ɛ bet/ AA æ bat/ ŌO u boot / ŌO ʊ book/ AW ɔ bought/ AH ɑ father/ ER ɝ bird/ UH ʌ cup/ AY eɪ bay/ EYE aɪ bite/ OY ɔɪ boy/ OH oʊ boat/ OW aʊ how/ YŌO ɪu duke/ EAR ɪɚ beer/ AIR ɛɚ bear/ ŌOR ʊɚ tour/ AWR ɔɚ bore/ AHR ɑɚ bar/ NG ŋ king/ SH ʃ ship/ ZH ʒ vision/ TH θ thirty/ TH ð then/ CH tʃ child/ J dʒ just/ For complete list, see Key to Pronunciation p. 2.

swart SWAWRT [swɔɚt]

swarth SWAWRTH [swɔɚθ]

swarthy SWAWR-<u>thee</u> ['swɔɚ-ði] or ___-thee [___-θi]

swashers SWAH-sherz ['swɑ-ʃɚz]

swath (n) (swaddling clothes) SWAWTH [swɔθ] or
   SWAHTH [swɑθ]

swath (n) (the stroke of a scythe) SWAWTH [swɔθ] or
   SWAHTH [swɑθ]

Sweno SWEE-noh ['swi-noʊ]

swinge SWINJ [swɪnʤ]

swinish SWEYE-nish ['swaɪ-nɪʃ]

Swinstead SWIN-stehd ['swɪn-stɛd]

Swithold SW<u>ITH</u>-uhld ['swɪð-əld] or SWITH-___ [swɪθ-___]
   or SWIT-___ ['swɪt-___]

Switzers SWIT-serz ['swɪt-sɚz]

swoln / swol'n SWOHLN [swoʊln]

swoon SWO͞ON [swun]

sword SAWRD [sɔɚd]

sworder SAWRD-er ['sɔɚd-ɚ]

swound SWOWND [swaʊnd] most editions alter to
   "swoond" SWO͞OND [swund]

'swounds (corruption of "God's wounds") ZO͞ONDZ [zundz]

Sycorax SIK-uh-raaks ['sɪk-ə-ræks] scans to SIK-raaks
   ['sɪk-ræks] @ *TEMP* I, 2, 258

syllogism SIL-uh-ji-zuhm ['sɪl-ə-ʤɪ-zəm]

synod SIN-uhd ['sɪn-əd] or ___-ahd [___-ɑd]

Syracusa SI-ruh-KY$\overline{OO}$-zuh [sɪ-rə-'kju-zə]

Syracuse SI-ruh-kyōoz ['sɪ-rə-kjuz]

Syracusian SI-ruh-KY$\overline{OO}$-zhuhn [sɪ-rə-'kju-ʒən]

Syria SI-ree-uh ['sɪ-ri-ə] scans to SI-ryuh ['sɪ-rjə]
  e.g. @ *A&C* III, 1, 18

T (the letter) TEE [ti]

tabor TAY-ber ['teɪ-bɚ]

tabourines TAA-buh-reenz ['tæ-bə-rinz]

taciturn TAAS-i-tern ['tæs-ɪ-tɚn]

taffeta TAAF-i-tuh ['tæf-ɪ-tə]

taffety TAAF-i-tee ['tæf-ɪ-ti]

taincture TAYNGK-cher ['teɪŋk-tʃɚ]

taint TAYNT [teɪnt]

Talbonites TAWL-buh-neyets ['tɔl-bə-naɪts] or TAAL-__-__
  ['tæl-__-__]

Talbot TAWL-buht ['tɔl-bət] or TAAL-___ ['tæl-___]
  Talbot, John *(1HVI)*
  Talbot, Lord, Earl of Shrewsbury *(1HVI)*

Tamora *(TITUS)* TAAM-uh-ruh ['tæm-ə-rə] scans to
  TAAM-ruh ['tæm-rə] e.g. @ I, 1, 318

Tamworth TAAM-werth ['tæm-wɚθ]

tanlings TAAN-lingz ['tæn-lɪŋz]

taper TAY-per ['teɪ-pɚ]

tapster / Tapster TAAP-ster ['tæp-stɚ]

EE i be/ I ɪ bit/ EH ɛ bet/ AA æ bat/ $\overline{OO}$ u boot / $\overline{OO}$ ʊ book/ AW ɔ bought/ AH ɑ father/ ER ɝ bird/
UH ʌ cup/ AY eɪ bay/ EYE aɪ bite/ OY ɔɪ boy/ OH oʊ boat/ OW aʊ how/ Y$\overline{OO}$ ɪu duke/ EAR ɪɚ
beer/ AIR ɛɚ bear/ $\overline{OOR}$ ʊɚ tour/ AWR ɔɚ bore/ AHR ɑɚ bar/ NG ŋ king/ SH ʃ ship/ ZH ʒ vision/
TH θ thirty/ TH ð then/ CH tʃ child/ J dʒ just/ For complete list, see Key to Pronunciation p. 2.

235

Tarentum tuh-REHN-tuhm [tə-'rɛn-təm]

targe TAHRJ [tɑɚʤ] in plural scans to one syllable
TAHRJZ [tɑɚʤz] @ *A&C* II, 6, 39

Tarpeian tahr-PEE-uhn [tɑɚ-'pi-ən]

Tarquin TAHR-kwin ['tɑɚ-kwɪn]

tarre TAHR [tɑɚ]

tarriance TAA-ree-uhns ['tæ-ri-əns]

Tartar TAHR-ter ['tɑɚ-tɚ]

tattling TAA-t(uh)l-ing ['tæ-tl̩-ɪŋ]

Taurus TAW-ruhs ['tɔ-rəs]
Taurus *(A&C)*

tawny TAW-nee ['tɔ-ni]

Tearsheet TAIR-sheet ['tɛɚ-ʃit]
Tearsheet, Doll *(2HIV)*

teat TEET [tit]

Telamon scans to TEHL-muhn ['tɛl-mən]

Telamonius TEHL-uh-MOH-nee-uhs [tɛl-ə-'moʊ-ni-əs]

Tellus TEHL-uhs ['tɛl-əs]

temperality TEHM-puh-RAAL-i-tee [tɛm-pə-'ræl-ɪ-ti]

temporal TEHM-puh-ruhl ['tɛm-pə-rəl]

Tenantius tuh-NAAN-shuhs [tə-'næn-ʃəs]

tench TEHNCH [tɛntʃ]

tendance TEHN-duhns ['tɛn-dəns]

Tenedos TEHN-uh-dohs ['tɛn-ə-doʊs] or ___-___-dahs
[___-___-dɑs] or ___-___-duhs [___-___-dəs]

tenure TEHN-yer ['tɛn-jɚ] or ___-yo͞or [___-jʊɚ]

236

tercel TER-suhl [ˈtɝ-səl]

Tereus TEAR-yōōs [ˈtɪɚ-jus] or ___-yuhs [__-jəs]

termagant / Termagant TER-muh-guhnt [ˈtɝ-mə-gənt]

terrene TEH-reen [ˈtɛ-rin]

terrestrial tuh-REHS-tree-uhl [tə-ˈrɛs-tri-əl] scans to
  ___-REHS-truhl [__-ˈrɛs-trəl] @ *RII* III, 2, 41

tertian TER-shuhn [ˈtɝ-ʃən]

tester TEHS-ter [ˈtɛs-tɚ]

testerned TEHS-ternd [ˈtɛs-tɚnd]

testril TEHS-truhl [ˈtɛs-trəl]

tetchy TEHCH-ee [ˈtɛtʃ-i]

tetter TEHT-er [ˈtɛt-ɚ]

Tewksbury / Tewkesbury TYŌŌKS-buh-ree [ˈtɪuks-bə-ri]

Thaisa *(PER)* thay-I-suh [θeɪ-ˈɪ-sə] scans to THAY-i-___
  [ˈθeɪ-ɪ-__] e.g. @ V, 1, 212

Thaliard *(PER)* THAAL-yerd [ˈθæl-jɚd]

Thames TEHMZ [tɛmz]

Thane THAYN [θeɪn]

Tharsus TAHR-suhs [ˈtaɚ-səs]

Thasos THAY-sahs [ˈθeɪ-sɑs] or ___-sohs [__-soʊs]

theatre THEE-uh-ter [ˈθi-ə-tɚ] scans to THEE-ter [ˈθi-tɚ]
  @ *KJ* II, 1, 375

Theban THEE-buhn [ˈθi-bən]

EE i be/ I ɪ bit/ EH ɛ bet/ AA æ bat/ ŌŌ u boot / ŌŌ ʊ book/ AW ɔ bought/ AH ɑ father/ ER ɝ bird/
UH ʌ cup/ AY eɪ bay/ EYE aɪ bite/ OY ɔɪ boy/ OH oʊ boat/ OW aʊ how/ YŌŌ ɪu duke/ EAR ɪɚ
beer/ AIR ɛɚ bear/ ŌŌR ʊɚ tour/ AWR ɔɚ bore/ AHR ɑɚ bar/ NG ŋ king/ SH ʃ ship/ ZH ʒ vision/
TH θ thirty/ TH ð then/ CH tʃ child/ J ʤ just/ For complete list, see Key to Pronunciation p. 2.

237

Thebes THEEBZ [θibz] scans to **THEE**-buhs ['θi-bəs]
@ *2NOB* I, 2, 15

thee T͟HEE [ði]

thence T͟HEHNS [ðɛns]

theoric **THEE**-uh-rik ['θi-ə-rɪk] possibly scans to **THEE**-rik
['θi-rɪk] @ *OTH* I, 1, 24

thereat t͟heh-**RAAT** [ðɛ-'ræt]

Thersites ther-**SEYE**-teez [θɚ-'saɪ-tiz]
Thersites *(T&C)*

Theseus **THEE**-see-uhs ['θi-si-əs] scans to **THEE**-syuhs
['θi-sjəs]
Theseus *(MID)* scans @ I, 1, 20
Theseus *(2NOB)*

Thessalian scans to theh-**SAYL**-yuhn [θɛ-'seɪl-jən]

Thessaly **THEHS**-uh-lee ['θɛs-ə-li] possibly scans to
THEHS-lee ['θɛs-li] @ *A&C* IV, 13, 2

Thetis **THEE**-tis ['θi-tɪs]

thews THYŌOZ [θɪuz]

Thidias *(A&C)* **THID**-ee-uhs ['θɪd-i-əs] scans to **THID**-yuhs
['θɪd-jəs] @ III, 13, 73

thine T͟HEYEN [ðaɪn]

Thisbe **THIZ**-bee ['θɪz-bi]

thither **THI**-t͟her ['θɪ-ðɚ]

thitherward **THI**-t͟her-werd ['θɪ-ðɚ-wɚd]

Thoas **THOH**-uhs ['θou-əs]

Thomas **TAH**-muhs ['tɑ-məs]
Thomas *(MM)*
Thomas of Clarence *(2HIV)*

thorough (prep) or (adv) (through) THUH-roh ['θʌ-roʊ] or THE(r)-roh ['θɜ-roʊ]

Thracian THRAY-shuhn ['θreɪ-ʃən]

thrall THRAWL [θrɔl]

thrasonical thruh-SAHN-i-kuhl [θrə-'sɑn-ɪ-kəl] or thray-__-__-__ [θreɪ-__-__-__]

threepence THRUH-puhnts ['θrʌ-pənts] or THRI-___ ['θrɪ-___] or THREE-___ ['θri-___]

threepenny THREHP-uh-nee ['θrɛp-ə-ni]

thrice THREYES [θraɪs]

throe THROH [θroʊ]

throstle THRAH-s(uh)l ['θrɑ-sl̩]

throughfare THROO-fair ['θru-fɛɚ]

throughly THROO-lee ['θru-li]

thrum THRUHM [θrʌm]

Thump, Peter *(2HVI)* THUHMP [θʌmp]

Thurio *(2GEN)* THYOO-ree-oh ['θjʊ-ri-oʊ] scans to THYOOR-yoh ['θjʊɚ-joʊ] e.g. @ II, 6, 39

thwack THWAAK [θwæk]

thwart THWAWRT [θwɔɚt]

thyme TEYEM [taɪm]

Tib TIB [tɪb]

Tiber TEYE-ber ['taɪ-bɚ]

Tiberio teye-BI-ree-oh [taɪ-'bɪ-ri-oʊ]

EE i be/ I ɪ bit/ EH ɛ bet/ AA æ bat/ OO u boot / OO ʊ book/ AW ɔ bought/ AH ɑ father/ ER ɝ bird/ UH ʌ cup/ AY eɪ bay/ EYE aɪ bite/ OY ɔɪ boy/ OH oʊ boat/ OW aʊ how/ YOO ɪu duke/ EAR ɪɚ beer/ AIR ɛɚ bear/ OOR ʊɚ tour/ AWR ɔɚ bore/ AHR ɑɚ bar/ NG ŋ king/ SH ʃ ship/ ZH ʒ vision/ TH θ thirty/ TH ð then/ CH ʧ child/ J ʤ just/ For complete list, see Key to Pronunciation p. 2.

ticed TEYEST [taɪst]

Tiger TEYE-ger ['taɪ-gɚ]

tilly-fally TIL-ee-FAAL-ee ['tɪl-i-fæl-i]

tilth TILTH [tɪlθ]

tiltyard TILT-yahrd ['tɪlt-jɑɚd]

Timandra *(TIMON)* ti-MAAN-druh [tɪ-'mæn-drə]

Timbria scans to TIM-bruh ['tɪm-brə]

Timon TEYE-muhn ['taɪ-mən]
   Timon *(TIMON)*

tinct TINGKT [tɪŋkt]

tincture TINGK-cher ['tɪŋk-tʃɚ]

tirra-lyra TI-ruh-LI-ruh ['tɪ-rə-lɪ-rə]

tirrits TI-rits ['tɪ-rɪts]

tis TIZ [tɪz]

tisick / Tisick TIZ-ik ['tɪz-ɪk]

Titan TEYE-t(uh)n ['taɪ-tn̩]

Titania *(MID)* ti-TAHN-yuh [tɪ-'tɑn-jə] scans to
   __-__-ee-uh [__-__-i-ə] e.g. @ II, 1, 60 (ti-TAYN-yuh
   [tɪ-'teɪn-jə] and teye-__-__ [taɪ-__-__] are sometimes heard)

tithe TEYE*TH* [taɪð]

Titinius *(JC)* ti-TI-nee-uhs [tɪ-'tɪ-ni-əs] scans to __-TI-nyuhs
   [__-'tɪ-njəs] e.g. @ IV, 2, 52

tittles TI-t(uh)lz ['tɪ-tl̩z]

Titus TEYE-tuhs ['taɪ-təs]
   Titus *(TIMON)*
   Titus Andronicus *(TITUS)* aan-DRAHN-i-kuhs
     [æn-'drɑn-ɪ-kəs]
   Titus Lartius *(COR)* LAHR-shuhs ['lɑɚ-ʃəs]

to't TOOT [tut]

toaze TOHZ [touz] or TOWZ [tɑuz]

tod (n) or (v) TAHD [tɑd]

tofore too-FAWR [tu-'fɔɚ] or tuh-___ [tə-___]

toge TOHG [toug]

toged scans to TOH-gid ['tou-gɪd]

Toledo tuh-LEE-doh [tə-'li-dou]

Tomyris TAHM-uh-ris ['tɑm-ə-rɪs]

Topas TOH-paaz ['tou-pæz] or ___-paas [___-pæs]

topmast TAHP-muhst ['tɑp-məst] or ___-maast [___-mæst]

topsail TAHP-s(uh)l ['tɑp-sl̩] or ___-sayl [___-seɪl]

tortive TAWR-tiv ['tɔɚ-tɪv]

Toryne TAH-rin ['tɑ-rɪn] or TOH-___ ['tou-___]

tost TAWST [tɔst]

Touchstone *(AYL)* TUHCH-stohn ['tʌtʃ-stoun]

Touraine always scans to TOO-rayn ['tu-reɪn]

tourney TER-nee ['tɝ-ni]

Tours TOOR [tuɚ]

touse TOWZ [tɑuz]

toward (adj) TAWRD [tɔɚd] scans to TOH-erd ['tou-ɚd]
@ *3HVI* II, 2, 66

toward (adv) TAWRD [tɔɚd] scans to TOH-erd ['tou-ɚd]
e.g. @ *HAM* I, 1, 77

---

toward (prep) TAWRD [tɔɚd] scans to **TOH**-erd ['toʊ-ɚd] e.g. @ *2HVI* II, 1, 195

towardly TAWRD-lee ['tɔɚd-li] or possibly **TOH**-erd-lee ['toʊ-ɚd-li] @ *TIMON* III, 1, 32

towards (adv) TAWRDZ [tɔɚdz] @ *R&J* I, 5, 122

towards (prep) TAWRDZ [tɔɚdz] scans to **TOH**-erdz ['toʊ-ɚdz] e.g. @ *RIII* IV, 5, 17

traduced truh-DYOOST [trə-'dɪust]

traducement truh-DYOOS-muhnt [trə-'dɪus-mənt]

tragedian truh-JEE-dee-uhn [trə-'ʤi-di-ən]

traitress TRAY-truhs ['treɪ-trəs]

traject TRAA-jehkt ['træ-ʤɛkt]

Tranio *(SHR)* **TRAH**-nee-oh ['trɑ-ni-oʊ] scans to **TRAH**-nyoh ['trɑ-njoʊ] e.g. @ I, 1, 17 later posing as "Lucentio" loo-**SEHN**-shee-oh [lu-'sɛn-ʃi-oʊ] scans to ___-**SEHN**-shyoh [___-'sɛn-ʃjoʊ]

translate always scans to traanz-**LAYT** [trænz-'leɪt]

transportance traans-**PAWR**-tuhns [træns-'pɔɚ-təns]

Transylvanian TRAAN-sil-**VAY**-nyuhn [træn-sɪl-'veɪ-njən]

travail (n) truh-**VAYL** [trə-'veɪl] scans to **TRAAV**-uhl ['træv-əl] or ___-ayl [___-eɪl] e.g. @ *HVIII* V, 1, 71

travail (v) truh-**VAYL** [trə-'veɪl] scans to **TRAAV**-uhl ['træv-əl] or ___-ayl [___-eɪl] e.g. @ *AW* II, 3, 157

Travers *(2HIV)* **TRAAV**-erz ['træv-ɚz]

traverse (adv) or (v) truh-**VERS** [trə-'vɝs]

traversed TRAAV-erst ['træv-ɚst]

treachers TREHCH-erz ['trɛtʃ-ɚz]

treatise TREE-tis ['tri-tɪs]

Trebonius *(JC)* tri-BOH-nee-uhs [trɪ-'boʊ-ni-əs] scans to
___-BOH-nyuhs [___-'boʊ-njəs] e.g. @ I, 3, 148

tremor cordis TREH-mer KAWR-dis ['trɛ-mɚ] ['kɔɚ-dɪs]

trencher TREHN-cher ['trɛn-tʃɚ]

Tressel *(RIII)* TREHS-uhl ['trɛs-əl]

treys TRAYZ [treɪz]

tribunal treye-BYOON-uhl [traɪ-'bjun-əl]

tribune TRIB-yoon ['trɪb-jun]

trice TREYES [traɪs]

tricksy TRIK-see ['trɪk-si]

trier TREYER [traɪɚ]

Trigon TREYE-guhn ['traɪ-gən]

Trinculo *(TEMP)* TRING-kyuh-loh ['trɪŋ-kjə-loʊ]

tripartite scans to TREYE-pahr-teyet ['traɪ-pɑɚ-taɪt]

Tripoli scans to TRIP-lee ['trɪp-li]

Tripolis TRIP-uh-lis ['trɪp-ə-lɪs]

Triton TREYE-t(uh)n ['traɪ-tn̩]

triumphers treye-UHMF-erz [traɪ-'ʌmf-ɚ-z]

triumvirate treye-UHM-vuh-rit [traɪ-'ʌm-və-rɪt]

triumviry treye-UHM-vuh-ree [traɪ-'ʌm-və-ri]

trod TRAHD [trɑd]

Troien TROY-uhn ['trɔɪ-ən]

Troilus TROY-luhs ['trɔɪ-ləs] scans to TROY-uh-luhs
['trɔɪ-ə-ləs] or possibly TROH-luhs ['troʊ-ləs] scans to
TROH-uh-luhs ['troʊ-ə-ləs]
Troilus *(T&C)* scans e.g. @ IV, 4, 31

troll TROHL [troʊl]

tropically TROH-pik-lee ['troʊ-pɪk-li] as in "trope" or
TRAA-__-__ ['træ-__-__] if punning on "Mousetrap"
@ *HAM* III, 2, 229

troth TROHTH [troʊθ] or TRAHTH [trɑθ]

troublous TRUHB-luhs ['trʌb-ləs]

trough TRAWF [trɔf] or TRAHF [trɑf]

trow TROH [troʊ]

Troy TROY [trɔɪ]

Troyan see "Troien"

truckle-bed TRUHK-uhl-behd ['trʌk-əl-bɛd]

trudge TRUHJ [trʌʤ]

trull TRUHL [trʌl]

trumpery TRUHM-puh-ree ['trʌm-pə-ri] scans to
TRUHM-pree ['trʌm-pri] e.g. @ *TEMP* IV, 1, 186

truncheon TRUHN-chuhn ['trʌn-tʃən]

Tubal *(MVEN)* TYOO-b(uh)l ['tɪu-bl̩]

tucket TUHK-it ['tʌk-ɪt]

Tullus Aufidius *(COR)* TUH-luhs aw-FID-ee-uhs ['tʌ-ləs]
[ɔ-'fɪd-i-əs] scans to __-FID-yuhs [__-'fɪd-jəs] e.g. @ I, 1, 224

Tully TUHL-ee ['tʌl-i]

tumult TYOO-muhlt ['tɪu-məlt]

tun-dish TUHN-dish ['tʌn-dɪʃ]

Tunis TYOO-nis [ˈtɪu-nɪs]

tupping TUHP-ing [ˈtʌp-ɪŋ]

turfy TER-fee [ˈtɝ-fi]

Turlygod TER-li-gahd [ˈtɝ-lɪ-gɑd]

Turph TERF [tɝf]

turpitude TER-pi-tyōōd [ˈtɝ-pɪ-tɪud]

turqoise TER-koyz [ˈtɝ-kɔɪz]

turquoise TER-koyz [ˈtɝ-kɔɪz] or ___-kwoyz [___-kwɔɪz]

Tuscan TUHS-kuhn [ˈtʌs-kən]

tush TUHSH [tʌʃ]

tut TUHT [tʌt]

twain TWAYN [tweɪn]

twere TWER [twɝ]

twiggen TWIG-uhn [ˈtwɪg-ən]

twit TWIT [twɪt]

'twixt TWIKST [twɪkst]

twopences TUHP-uhnts-iz [ˈtʌp-ənts-ɪz]

Tybalt *(R&J)* TIB-uhlt [ˈtɪb-əlt]

Tyburn TEYE-bern [ˈtaɪ-bɚn]

Tyke TEYEK [taɪk]

Typhon TEYE-fahn [ˈtaɪ-fɑn]

Tyre TEYER [taɪɚ] possibly scans to TEYE-er [ˈtaɪ-ɚ]
   @ *PER* II, 3, 81

EE i be/ I ɪ bit/ EH ɛ bet/ AA æ bat/ OO u boot / OO ʊ book/ AW ɔ bought/ AH ɑ father/ ER ɝ bird/
UH ʌ cup/ AY eɪ bay/ EYE aɪ bite/ OY ɔɪ boy/ OH oʊ boat/ OW aʊ how/ YOO ɪu duke/ EAR ɪɚ
beer/ AIR ɛɚ bear/ OOR ʊɚ tour/ AWR ɔɚ bore/ AHR ɑɚ bar/ NG ŋ king/ SH ʃ ship/ ZH ʒ vision/
TH θ thirty/ TH ð then/ CH tʃ child/ J dʒ just/ For complete list, see Key to Pronunciation p. 2.

Tyrian always scans to TI-ryuhn ['tɪ-rjən]

Tyrrel, Sir James *(RIII)* TI-ruhl ['tɪ-rəl]

Tyrus TEYE-ruhs ['taɪ-rəs]

'ud's UHDZ [ʌdz]

Ulysses yo͞o-LIS-eez [ju-'lɪs-iz]
   Ulysses *(T&C)*

umber UHM-ber ['ʌm-bɚ]

umbrage UHM-brij ['ʌm-brɪʤ]

Umfrevile uhm-FREHV-uhl [əm-'frɛv-əl] possibly scans to
   UHM-fruh-vuhl ['ʌm-frə-vəl]

unaneled uhn-uh-NEELD [ən-ə-'nild]

unchary uhn-CHEH-ree [ən-'ʧɛ-ri] or __-CHAA-__
   [__-'ʧæ-__]

uncleanly uhn-KLEHN-lee [ən-'klɛn-li]

unclew uhn-KLO͞O [ən-'klu]

uncouth (unfamiliar) UHN-ko͞oth ['ʌn-kuθ]

unction UHNGK-shuhn ['ʌŋk-ʃən]

unctuous scans to UHNGK-chuhs ['ʌŋk-ʧəs]

under-skinker UHN-der-SKING-ker ['ʌn-dɚ-skɪŋ-kɚ]

undescried uhn-di-SKREYED [ən-dɪ-'skraɪd]

uneath uhn-EETH [ən-'iθ]

unfeignedly uhn-FAYN-id-lee [ən-'feɪn-ɪd-li]

unfrequented always scans to UHN-free-kwehnt-id
   ['ʌn-fri-kwɛnt-ɪd]

ungenitured uhn-JEHN-i-cherd [ən-'ʤɛn-ɪ-ʧɚd]

unhouseled uhn-HOW-zuhld [ən-'haʊ-zəld]

unlineal scans to uhn-LIN-yuhl [ən-'lɪn-jəl]

unmitigable uhn-MIT-i-guh-b(uh)l [ən-'mɪt-ɪ-gə-bļ]

unplausive uhn-PLAW-ziv [ən-'plɔ-zɪv]

unrecuring uhn-ri-KYOO-ring [ən-rɪ-'kjʊ-rɪŋ]

unseminared uhn-SEHM-i-nahrd [ən-'sɛm-ɪ-naɚd]

unstaid uhn-STAYD [ən-'steɪd]

unstanch uhn-STAWNCH [ən-'stɔntʃ] or ___-STAANCH [___-'stæntʃ]

untoward scans to UHN-tawrd ['ʌn-tɔɚd] @ *SHR* IV, 5, 78 and uhn-TOH-erd [ən-'toʊ-ɚd] @ *KJ* I, 1, 243

unwappered uhn-WAHP-erd [ən-'wɑp-ɚd]

unwonted uhn-WAWNT-id [ən-'wɔnt-ɪd] or ___-WOHNT-___ [___-'woʊnt-___]

upon uh-PAHN [ə-'pɑn] scans to UH-pahn ['ʌ-pɑn] e.g. @ *12th* V, 1, 93

Urchinfield ER-chin-feeld ['ɝ-tʃɪn-fild]

Ursa Major ER-suh MAY-jer ['ɝ-sə] ['meɪ-ʤɚ]

Ursula ER-suh-luh ['ɝ-sə-lə] scans to ERS-luh ['ɝs-lə] Ursula *(MADO)* scans @ III, 1, 34, also called "Ursley" ERS-lee ['ɝs-li] @ III, 1, 4

Urswick, Christopher *(RIII)* ERZ-ik ['ɝz-ɪk] or ERS-___ ['ɝs-___]

usance YOO-zuhns ['ju-zəns]

usurer YOO-zhuh-rer ['ju-ʒə-rɚ]

usurp yoo-ZERP [ju-'zɝp] or ___-SERP [___-'sɝp]

EE i be/ I ɪ bit/ EH ɛ bet/ AA æ bat/ OO u boot / OO ʊ book/ AW ɔ bought/ AH ɑ father/ ER ɝ bird/
UH ʌ cup/ AY eɪ bay/ EYE aɪ bite/ OY ɔɪ boy/ OH oʊ boat/ OW aʊ how/ YOO ɪu duke/ EAR ɪɚ
beer/ AIR ɛɚ bear/ OOR ʊɚ tour/ AWR ɔɚ bore/ AHR ɑɚ bar/ NG ŋ king/ SH ʃ ship/ ZH ʒ vision/
TH θ thirty/ TH ð then/ CH tʃ child/ J ʤ just/ For complete list, see Key to Pronunciation p. 2.

247

usurpation YOO-zer-**PAY**-shuhn [ju-zɚ-'peɪ-ʃən] scans to
__-__-__-shee-uhn [__-__-__-ʃi-ən] e.g. @ *KJ* II, 1, 9

usury YOO-zhuh-ree ['ju-ʒə-ri]

ut UHT [ʌt] or OOT [ʊt]

Utis YOO-tis ['ju-tɪs]

vagary VAY-guh-ree ['veɪ-gə-ri]

vails VAYLZ [veɪlz]

vainglory vayn-**GLAW**-ree [veɪn-'glɔ-ri] or **VAYN**-glaw-__
['veɪn-glɔ-__] scans to second syllable stress @ *HVIII* III,
1, 127

valance VAAL-uhns ['væl-əns]

valanced VAAL-uhnst ['væl-ənst]

Valdes VAAL-deez ['væl-diz]

vale VAYL [veɪl]

Valence VAAL-uhns ['væl-əns]

Valencius vuh-**LEHN**-shee-uhs [və-'lɛn-ʃi-əs]

Valentine VAAL-uhn-teyen ['væl-ən-taɪn]
    Valentine *(TITUS)*
    Valentine *(12th)*
    Valentine *(2GEN)* possibly scans to **VAALN**-teyen
       ['væln-taɪn] @ I, 2, 38, also called "Valentinus"
       VAAL-uhn-**TEYE**-nuhs [væl-ən-'taɪ-nəs]

Valentio scans to vuh-**LEHN**-shyoh [və-'lɛn-ʃjoʊ]

Valeria *(COR)* vuh-**LI**-ree-uh [və-'lɪ-ri-ə] scans to
__-**LI**-ryuh [__-'lɪ-rjə] e.g. @ I, 3, 41

Valerius vuh-**LI**-ree-uhs [və-'lɪ-ri-əs] scans to __-**LI**-ryuhs
      [__-'lɪ-rjəs]
    Valerius *(2NOB)*
    Valerius scans @ *2GEN* V, 3, 8

valor / valour VAAL-er ['væl-ɚ]

vant VAANT [vænt]

vantbrace VAANT-brays ['vænt-breɪs]

Vapians VAY-pee-uhnz ['veɪ-pi-ənz]

varlet VAHR-lit ['vɑɚ-lɪt]

varletry VAHR-li-tree ['vɑɚ-lɪ-tri]

varletto vahr-LEHT-oh [vɑɚ-'lɛt-ou]

Varrius VAA-ree-uhs ['væ-ri-əs] scans to VAA-ryuhs ['væ-rjəs]
  Varrius *(A&C)*
  Varrius *(MM)* scans @ IV, 5, 1

Varro VAA-roh ['væ-rou]
  Varro *(JC)*

vassal VAAS-uhl ['væs-əl]

vassalage VAA-suh-lij ['væ-sə-lɪdʒ]

vastidity vaas-TID-uh-tee [væs-'tɪd-ə-ti]

Vaudemont VOH-duh-mahnt ['vou-də-mɑnt]

Vaughan, Sir Thomas *(RIII)* VAWN [vɔn] scans to VAW-uhn ['vɔ-ən] e.g. @ V, 3, 143

vaultages VAWL-tij-iz ['vɔl-tɪdʒ-ɪz]

Vaumond VAW-muhnd ['vɔ-mənd]

vaunt VAWNT [vɔnt]

Vaux VAWKS [vɔks] or VAHKS [vɑks]
  Vaux *(2HVI)*
  Vaux, Sir Nicholas *(HVIII)*

vaward VOW-erd ['vɑu-ɚd] or ___-awrd [___-ɔɚd]

EE i be/ I ɪ bit/ EH ɛ bet/ AA æ bat/ OO u boot / OO ʊ book/ AW ɔ bought/ AH ɑ father/ ER ɝ bird/ UH ʌ cup/ AY eɪ bay/ EYE aɪ bite/ OY ɔɪ boy/ OH ou boat/ OW ɑu how/ YOO ɪu duke/ EAR ɪɚ beer/ AIR ɛɚ bear/ OOR ʊɚ tour/ AWR ɔɚ bore/ AHR ɑɚ bar/ NG ŋ king/ SH ʃ ship/ ZH ʒ vision/ TH θ thirty/ TH ð then/ CH tʃ child/ J dʒ just/ For complete list, see Key to Pronunciation p. 2.

vegetives VEHJ-i-tivz ['vɛʤ-ɪ-tɪvz]

velure veh-LŌOR [vɛ-'lʊɚ]

vendible VEHN-duh-b(uh)l ['vɛn-də-bļ]

venerable VEHN-uh-ruh-b(uh)l ['vɛn-ə-rə-bļ]

venew VEHN-yōō ['vɛn-ju]

veneys VEHN-eez ['vɛn-iz]

venial scans to VEEN-yuhl ['vin-jəl]

Venice, Duke of VEHN-is ['vɛn-ɪs]
    Venice, Duke of *(MVEN)*
    Venice, Duke of *(OTH)*

ventages VEHN-tij-iz ['vɛn-tɪʤ-ɪz]

Ventidius vehn-TID-ee-uhs [vɛn-'tɪd-i-əs] scans to
    ___-TID-yuhs [___-'tid-jəs]
    Ventidius *(A&C)* scans @ II, 3, 31
    Ventidius *(TIMON)* scans @ I, 2, 9

venturous VEHN-chuh-ruhs ['vɛn-tʃə-rəs] scans to
    VEHNCH-ruhs ['vɛntʃ-rəs] e.g. @ *MID* IV, 1, 34

Venus VEE-nuhs ['vi-nəs]

Ver VER [vɝ]

verbatim ver-BAY-tim [vɝ-'beɪ-tɪm]

Verdun ver-DUHN [vɚ-'dʌn]

verdure VER-jer ['vɝ-ʤɚ]

Verger VER-jer ['vɝ-ʤɚ]

Verges *(MADO)* VER-jis ['vɝ-ʤɪs]

verier VEH-ree-er ['vɛ-ri-ɚ] scans to VAIR-yer ['vɛɚ-jɚ]
    @ *WT* I, 2, 66

veriest VEH-ree-ist ['vɛ-ri-ɪst] scans to VAIR-yist ['vɛɚ-jɪst]
    e.g. @ *CYM* V, 3, 77

Vernon VER-nuhn ['vɝ-nən]
   Vernon *(1HVI)*
   Vernon, Sir Richard *(1HIV)*

Verolles vuh-RAH-luhs [və-'rɑ-ləs] or __-ROH-leez [__-'rou-liz]

Verona vuh-ROH-nuh [və-'rou-nə]

Veronesa VEH-ruh-NEHS-uh [vɛ-rə-'nɛs-ə]

versal VER-suhl ['vɝ-səl]

vestal / Vestal VEHS-t(uh)l ['vɛs-tl̩]

vesture VEHS-cher ['vɛs-tʃɚ]

via VEE-uh ['vi-ə] or VEYE-__ ['vaɪ-__]

vial VEYEL [vaɪl] scans to VEYE-uhl ['vaɪ-əl] e.g. @ *A&C* I, 3, 63

viand VEYE-uhnd ['vaɪ-ənd]

Vicar VIK-er ['vɪk-ɚ]

vicegerent veyes-JI-ruhnt [vaɪs-'dʒɪ-rənt]

Viceroy VEYES-roy ['vaɪs-rɔɪ]

victual VI-t(uh)l ['vɪ-tl̩]

victuallers VIT-lerz ['vɪt-lɚz]

videlicet vi-DEHL-i-seht [vɪ-'dɛl-ɪ-sɛt]

vie VEYE [vaɪ]

vild VEYELD [vaɪld]

villagery VIL-ij-ree ['vɪl-ɪdʒ-ri]

Villiago vil-ee-YAH-goh [vɪl-i-'jɑ-gou]

EE i be/ I ɪ bit/ EH ɛ bet/ AA æ bat/ OO u boot/ OO ʊ book/ AW ɔ bought/ AH ɑ father/ ER ɝ bird/ UH ʌ cup/ AY eɪ bay/ EYE aɪ bite/ OY ɔɪ boy/ OH ou boat/ OW aʊ how/ YOO ɪu duke/ EAR ɪɚ beer/ AIR ɛɚ bear/ OOR ʊɚ tour/ AWR ɔɚ bore/ AHR ɑɚ bar/ NG ŋ king/ SH ʃ ship/ ZH ʒ vision/ TH θ thirty/ TH ð then/ CH tʃ child/ J dʒ just/ For complete list, see Key to Pronunciation p. 2.

251

Vincentio vin-SEHN-shee-oh [vɪn-'sɛn-ʃi-ou] scans to
   ___-SEHN-shyoh [___-'sɛn-ʃjou]
Vincentio *(MM)*
Vincentio *(SHR)* scans @ I, 1, 192

vindicative vin-DIK-uh-tiv [vɪn-'dɪk-ə-tɪv]

vinewd'st VIN-yo͞odst ['vɪn-judst]

Vintner *(1HIV)* VINT-ner ['vɪnt-nɚ]

viol VEYE-uhl ['vaɪ-əl]

Viola *(12th)* VEYE-uh-luh ['vaɪ-ə-lə] scans to VEYE-luh
['vaɪ-lə] @ V, 1, 236

viol-de-gamboys VEYE-uhl-duh-GAAM-boyz
['vaɪ-əl-də-gæm-bɔɪz]

Violênta *(AW)* VEYE-uh-LEHN-tuh [vaɪ-ə-'lɛn-tə]

violently VEYE-luhnt-lee ['vaɪ-lənt-li] scans to
VEYE-uh-lehnt-__ ['vaɪ-ə-lɛnt-__] @ *CE* I, 1, 102

Virgilia *(COR)* ver-JIL-ee-uh [vɚ-'ʤɪl-i-ə]

virginalling VER-jin-uhl-ing ['vɝ-ʤɪn-əl-ɪŋ] or possibly
scans to VER-jin-ling ['vɝ-ʤɪn-lɪŋ]

Virginius ver-JI-nee-uhs [vɚ-'ʤɪ-ni-əs] scans to __-JI-nyuhs
[__-'ʤɪ-njəs] @ *TITUS* V, 3, 50

Virgo VER-goh ['vɝ-gou]

visage VIZ-ij ['vɪz-ɪʤ]

Viscount Rochford VEYE-kownt RAHCH-ferd ['vaɪ-kɑunt]
['rɑtʃ-fɚd]

visor VEYE-zer ['vaɪ-zɚ]

Vitruvio vi-TRO͞O-vee-oh [vɪ-'tru-vi-ou]

viz. (that is) VIZ [vɪz]

vizaments VEYE-zuh-muhnts ['vaɪ-zə-mənts]

vizard VIZ-erd ['vɪz-ɚd] or ___-ahrd [___-ɑɚd]

vizor VEYE-zer ['vaɪ-zɚ]

Volquessen vahl-KEHS-uhn [vɑl-'kɛs-ən]

Volsce VAHLS [vɑls] in plural VAHLS-iz ['vɑls-ɪz]

Volscian VAHL-shuhn ['vɑl-ʃən]

Voltemand *(HAM)* VAHL-ti-maand ['vɑl-tɪ-mænd]

volubility VAHL-yoo-BIL-i-tee [vɑl-ju-'bɪl-ɪ-ti]

voluble VAHL-yuh-b(uh)l ['vɑl-jə-bl̩] possibly scans to
    vahl-YO͞O-___ [vɑl-'ju-___] @ *2NOB* I, 2, 67

Volumnia *(COR)* vuh-LUHM-nee-uh [və-'lʌm-ni-ə]

Volumnius *(JC)* vuh-LUHM-nee-uhs [və-'lʌm-ni-əs] scans to
    ___-LUHM-nyuhs [___-'lʌm-njəs] @ V, 5, 15

vot'ress VOH-tris ['voʊ-trɪs]

votaress VOH-tuh-ris ['voʊ-tə-rɪs]

votarist VOH-tuh-rist ['voʊ-tə-rɪst] scans to VOH-trist
    ['voʊ-trɪst] @ *MM* I, 4, 5

votary VOH-tuh-ree ['voʊ-tə-ri]

vouchsafe vowch-SAYF [vaʊtʃ-'seɪf] scans to VOWCH-sayf
    ['vaʊtʃ-seɪf] @ *LLL* V, 2, 210

vox VAHKS [vɑks]

Vulcan VUHL-kuhn ['vʌl-kən]

waft WAHFT [wɑft] or WAAFT [wæft]

waftage WAHF-tij ['wɑf-tɪdʒ] or WAAFT-___ ['wæf-___]

wafter WAHFT-er ['wɑft-ɚ] or WAAFT-___ ['wæft-___]

EE i be/ I ɪ bit/ EH ɛ bet/ AA æ bat/ O͞O u boot / O͝O ʊ book/ AW ɔ bought/ AH ɑ father/ ER ɝ bird/
UH ʌ cup/ AY eɪ bay/ EYE aɪ bite/ OY ɔɪ boy/ OH oʊ boat/ OW aʊ how/ YO͞O ɪu duke/ EAR ɪə
beer/ AIR ɛə bear/ O͞OR ʊə tour/ AWR ɔə bore/ AHR ɑə bar/ NG ŋ king/ SH ʃ ship/ ZH ʒ vision/
TH θ thirty/ T̲H̲ ð then/ CH tʃ child/ J dʒ just/ For complete list, see Key to Pronunciation p. 2.

wain WAYN [weɪn]

wainropes WAYN-rohps ['weɪn-roʊps]

wainscot WAYN-skuht ['weɪn-skət] or ___-skaht [___-skɑt]

Wallon / Walloon wah-LOON [wɑ-'lun]

wan (adj) (pale) WAHN [wɑn]

wan / wanned (v) (to become pale) WAHN [wɑn] / WAHND [wɑnd]

wane (n) (a decrease) WAYN [weɪn]

wane / waned (v) (to decrease, to lessen) WAYN [weɪn] / WAYND [weɪnd]

wanion WAHN-yuhn ['wɑn-jən]

wanny WAHN-ee ['wɑn-i]

wanton WAHN-tuhn ['wɑn-tən]

wappened WAHP-uhnd ['wɑp-ənd]

warder / Warder WAWR-der ['wɔɚ-dɚ]

ware / Ware WAIR [wɛɚ]

warily WEH-ri-lee ['wɛ-rɪ-li]

warr'st WAWRST [wɔɚst]

warrener WAW-rehn-er ['wɔ-rɛn-ɚ]

warrior WAW-ree-er ['wɔ-ri-ɚ] scans to **WAWR**-yer ['wɔɚ-jɚ] e.g. @ *1HVI* II, 3, 82

Wart, Thomas *(2HIV)* WAWRT [wɔɚt]

Warwick WAW-rik ['wɔ-rɪk] or **WAH-___** ['wɑ-___]
Warwick, Earl of *(2HIV, HV)*

Warwickshire WAW-rik-sher ['wɔ-rɪk-ʃɚ] or __-__-shear [__-__-ʃɪɚ] or **WAH-__-__** ['wɑ-__-__]

Washford WAWSH-ferd ['wɔʃ-fɚd]

wassail WAH-suhl ['wɑ-səl]

wast WUHST [wʌst] or WAHST [wɑst]

Waterford WAW-ter-ferd ['wɔ-tɚ-fɚd]

Waterton, Sir Robert WAW-ter-t(uh)n ['wɔ-tɚ-tn̩]

wawl WAWL [wɔl]

we'ld WEELD [wild]

weal WEEL [wil]

wealsmen WEELZ-muhn ['wilz-mən]

wean WEEN [win]

ween WEEN [win]

weet WEET [wit]

Weird Sisters *(MAC)* WEARD SIS-terz [wɪɚd] ['sɪs-tɚz]
   scans to WEE-erd ['wi-ɚd] or WI-___ ['wɪ-___]
   e.g. @ II, 1, 20

welkin WEHL-kin ['wɛl-kɪn]

wench WEHNCH [wɛntʃ]

wend WEHND [wɛnd]

weraday WEH-ruh-day ['wɛ-rə-deɪ]

wesand WEE-z(uh)nd ['wi-zn̩d]

Westminster WEHST-min-ster ['wɛst-mɪn-stɚ]
   Westminster, Abbot of *(RII)*

Westmoreland WEHST-mer-luhnd ['wɛst-mɚ-lənd]
   Earl of Westmoreland *(1HIV, 2HIV, HV)*

EE i be/ I ɪ bit/ EH ɛ bet/ AA æ bat/ OO u boot / OO ʊ book/ AW ɔ bought/ AH ɑ father/ ER ɝ bird/
UH ʌ cup/ AY eɪ bay/ EYE aɪ bite/ OY ɔɪ boy/ OH oʊ boat/ OW aʊ how/ YOO ɪu duke/ EAR ɪɚ
beer/ AIR ɛɚ bear/ OOR ʊɚ tour/ AWR ɔɚ bore/ AHR ɑɚ bar/ NG ŋ king/ SH ʃ ship/ ZH ʒ vision/
TH θ thirty/ TH ð then/ CH tʃ child/ J dʒ just/ For complete list, see Key to Pronunciation p. 2.

wether WEH<u>TH</u>-er ['wɛð-ɚ]

whales-bone HWAYL-is-bohn ['hweɪl-ɪs-boun]

whate'er hwuht-AIR [hwət-'ɛɚ]

whatsoe'er HWUHT-soh-air ['hwʌt-sou-ɛɚ]

whatsome'er HWUHT-suhm-air ['hwʌt-səm-ɛɚ]

whatsomever HWUHT-suhm-ehv-er ['hwʌt-səm-ɛv-ɚ]

whe'r HWAIR [hwɛɚ]

Wheeson HWEE-suhn ['hwi-sən]

whelk (n) HWEHLK [hwɛlk]

whelked (v) HWEHLKT [hwɛlkt]

whelm HWEHLM [hwɛlm]

whelp HWEHLP [hwɛlp]

whet HWEHT [hwɛt]

whether HWEH<u>TH</u>-er ['hwɛð-ɚ] scans to HWAIR [hwɛɚ]
  e.g. @ *HAM* II, 2, 17

whetstone HWEHT-stohn ['hwɛht-stoun]

whey HWAY [hweɪ]

whiffler HWI-fler ['hwɪ-flɚ]

whilere hweyel-AIR [hwaɪl-'ɛɚ]

whiles HWEYELZ [hwaɪlz]

whilst HWEYELST [hwaɪlst]

whirligig HWER-li-gig ['hwɝ-lɪ-gɪg]

whirring HWE(r)-ring ['hwɝ-rɪŋ]

whist HWIST [hwɪst]

whit HWIT [hwɪt]

Whitefriars scans to hweyet-**FREYE**-erz [hwaɪt-'fraɪ-ɚz]

whither HWI**TH**-er ['hwɪð-ɚ] scans to HWAIR [hwɛɚ] @ *COR* IV, 1, 34

whiting HWEYET-ing ['hwaɪt-ɪŋ]

whiting-time HWEYET-ing-teyem ['hwaɪt-ɪŋ-taɪm]

Whitmore, Walter *(2HVI)* HWIT-mawr WAW-ter ['hwɪt-mɔɚ] ['wɔ-tɚ] (The meaning of the passage in IV, 1 depends on the "Walter"/"water" homonym.)

whitsters HWEYET-sterz ['hwaɪt-stɚz]

Whitsun HWIT-suhn ['hwɪt-sən]

whoremonger HAWR-muhng-ger ['hɔɚ-məŋ-gɚ] or ___-mahng-___ [___-mɑŋ-___]

whoreson HAWR-s(uh)n ['hɔɚ-sn̩]

whorish HAW-rish ['hɔ-rɪʃ]

whosoe'er HO͞O-soh-air ['hu-sou-ɛɚ]

Widow WID-oh ['wɪd-ou]
Widow *(AW)*
Widow *(SHR)*

wield WEELD [wild]

wight WEYET [waɪt]

William *(AYL)* WIL-yuhm ['wɪl-jəm]

Williams, Michael *(HV)* WIL-yuhmz ['wɪl-jəmz]

Willoughby, Lord *(RII)* WIL-uh-bee ['wɪl-ə-bi]

wilt WILT [wɪlt]

Wiltshire WILT-sher ['wɪlt-ʃɚ] or ___-shear [___-ʃɪɚ]

EE i be/ I ɪ bit/ EH ɛ bet/ AA æ bat/ O͞O u boot / O͞O ʊ book/ AW ɔ bought/ AH ɑ father/ ER ɝ bird/ UH ʌ cup/ AY eɪ bay/ EYE aɪ bite/ OY ɔɪ boy/ OH ou boat/ OW ɑu how/ YO͞O ɪu duke/ EAR ɪɚ beer/ AIR ɛɚ bear/ O͞OR ʊɚ tour/ AWR ɔɚ bore/ AHR ɑɚ bar/ NG ŋ king/ SH ʃ ship/ ZH ʒ vision/ TH θ thirty/ TH ð then/ CH ʧ child/ J ʤ just/ For complete list, see Key to Pronunciation p. 2.

Winchester WIN-chehs-ter ['wɪn-tʃɛs-tɚ] or ___-chis-___ [___-tʃɪs-___]

Wincot WING-kuht ['wɪŋ-kət]

wind (n) (a current of air) WIND [wɪnd]

wind (v) (to blow) WIND [wɪnd]

wind (v) (to turn or twist) WEYEND [waɪnd]

windlasses WIND-luhs-iz ['wɪnd-ləs-ɪz]

windring WEYEND-ring ['waɪnd-rɪŋ]

Windsor WIN-zer ['wɪn-zɚ]

Wingham WING-uhm ['wɪŋ-əm]

winnow WIN-oh ['wɪn-ou]

wist WIST [wɪst]

withal with-AWL [wɪð-'ɔl]

withers WITH-erz ['wɪð-ɚ-z]

Wittenberg WI-t(uh)n-berg ['wɪ-tn̩-bɚg]

wittol WI-t(uh)l ['wɪ-tl̩]

wittolly WI-t(uh)l-ee ['wɪ-tl̩-i]

wo't see "woo't"

Wolsey, Cardinal (HVIII) WŎOL-zee ['wul-zi]

wolt WOHLT [woult] or WŎOLT [wult]

womby WŌO-mee ['wu-mi]

Woncot WŎONG-kuht ['wuŋ-kət] or WAHNG-___ ['wɑŋ-___]

wont WAWNT [wɔnt] or WOHNT [wount]

woo't / wo't WŌOT [wut]

woodbine WŎŎD-beyen ['wʊd-baɪn]

Woodeville / Woodville WŎŎD-vil ['wʊd-vɪl] scans to
   WŎŎD-uh-vil ['wʊd-ə-vɪl]
   Woodville, Anthony, Earl Rivers *(RIII)* scans @ I, 1, 67
   Woodville, Richard *(1HVI)*

wooer WŌŌ-er ['wu-ɚ]

woosel WŌŌ-z(uh)l ['wu-zl̩]

Worcester WŎŎS-ter ['wʊs-tɚ]

workyday WERK-ee-day ['wɝk-i-deɪ]

worship WER-ship ['wɝ-ʃɪp]

wor'st WAWRST [wɔɚst]

worsted-stocking WŎŎST-id-STAHK-ing ['wʊst-ɪd-stɑk-ɪŋ]
   or WERST-__-__-__ ['wɝst-__-__-__]

wort (beer) WERT [wɝt]

worts (cabbages) WERTS [wɝts]

wot WAHT [wɑt] or WAWT [wɔt]

wound (n) (a break in the flesh) WŌŌND [wund] possibly
   WOWND [waʊnd] @ *RII* III, 2, 139 and *PER* IV, Cho, 23

wound (v) (turned or twisted) WOWND [waʊnd]

wrack RAAK [ræk]

wrath RAATH [ræθ]

wreak REEK [rik]

wreath (n) REETH [riθ]

wreathe (v) REE_TH_ [rið]

EE i be/ I ɪ bit/ EH ɛ bet/ AA æ bat/ ŌŌ u boot / ŎŎ ʊ book/ AW ɔ bought/ AH ɑ father/ ER ɝ bird/
UH ʌ cup/ AY eɪ bay/ EYE aɪ bite/ OY ɔɪ boy/ OH oʊ boat/ OW aʊ how/ YŌŌ ɪu duke/ EAR ɪɚ
beer/ AIR ɛɚ bear/ ŌOR ʊɚ tour/ AWR ɔɚ bore/ AHR ɑɚ bar/ NG ŋ king/ SH ʃ ship/ ZH ʒ vision/
TH θ thirty/ _TH_ ð then/ CH tʃ child/ J dʒ just/ For complete list, see Key to Pronunciation p. 2.

wrest REHST [rɛst]

writhled RI-thuhld ['rɪ-θəld]

wroath ROHTH [rouθ]

wrought RAWT [rɔt]

Wye WEYE [waɪ]

Xanthippe zaan-**TIP**-ee [zæn-'tɪp-i]

yare YAIR [jɛɚ] or YAHR [jɑɚ]

yaw YAW [jɔ]

yclad ee-**KLAAD** [i-'klæd]

ycleped ee-**KLEEPT** [i-'klipt] scans to ee-**KLIP**-id [i-'klɪp-ɪd]
@ *LLL* V, 2, 591 to make sense of "clipt" in next line

ye YEE [ji]

ye're YER [jɝ]

yea YAY [jeɪ]

Yed YEHD [jɛd]

Yedward YEHD-werd ['jɛd-wɚd]

ye'll YEEL [jil]

yeoman YOH-muhn ['jou-mən]

yerk YERK [jɝk]

yest YEHST [jɛst]

yesty YEHS-tee ['jɛs-ti]

ye've YEEV [jiv]

yew YOO [ju]

yon YAHN [jɑn]

yond YAHND [jɑnd]

yonder YAHND-er [ˈjɑnd-ɚ]

Yorick YAW-rik [ˈjɔ-rɪk]

York YAWRK [jɔɚk]
  York, Duchess of *(RII, RIII)*
  York, Duke of *(HV)*

Yorkshire YAWRK-sher [ˈjɔɚk-ʃɚ] or ___-shear [___-ʃɪɚ]

you'ld YOOLD [juld]

Young Cato *(JC)* KAY-toh [ˈkeɪ-tou]

Young Lucius *(TITUS)* LOO-shuhs [ˈlu-ʃəs]

Young Marcius *(COR)* MAHR-shuhs [ˈmɑɚ-ʃəs]

Young Siward *(MAC)* SYOO-erd [ˈsɪu-ɚd]

younker YUHNG-ker [ˈjʌŋ-kɚ]

y-ravished ee-RAA-vish-id [i-ˈræ-vɪʃ-ɪd]

yslacked ee-SLAAK-id [i-ˈslæk-ɪd]

zealous ZEHL-uhs [ˈzɛl-əs]

zed ZEHD [zɛd]

Zenelophon zeh-NEHL-uh-fahn [zɛ-ˈnɛl-ə-fɑn]

zephyrs ZEHF-erz [ˈzɛf-ɚz]

zounds (corruption of "God's wounds") ZOONDZ [zundz] or possibly ZOWNDZ [zaundz]

EE i be/ I ɪ bit/ EH ɛ bet/ AA æ bat/ OO u boot / OO ʊ book/ AW ɔ bought/ AH ɑ father/ ER ɚ bird/ UH ʌ cup/ AY eɪ bay/ EYE aɪ bite/ OY ɔɪ boy/ OH ou boat/ OW au how/ YOO ɪu duke/ EAR ɪɚ beer/ AIR ɛɚ bear/ OOR ʊɚ tour/ AWR ɔɚ bore/ AHR ɑɚ bar/ NG ŋ king/ SH ʃ ship/ ZH ʒ vision/ TH θ thirty/ TH ð then/ CH ʧ child/ J ʤ just/ For complete list, see Key to Pronunciation p. 2.

latin

ℰ

O that's the Latin word
Love's Labor's Lost III, 1, 129

In an attempt at consistency, the following pronunciations are rendered into what is commonly referred to as "restored" or classical Latin. Many Latin words and phrases have entered the English language. Clearly, it is best to pronounce these in the manner with which the audience is most familiar. Thus, while the letter *c* is always hard in classical Latin pronunciation, names such as Caesar and Cicero should be pronounced as they are commonly sounded in English with the soft *c*. These pronunciations reflect what is called "Anglicized" Latin, which was the form of Latin pronunciation prevalent in Britain until the end of the 19th century, when a movement arose to "restore" or codify Latin pronunciation. To complicate matters further, there is another form of pronunciation, church Latin, which is Italianate in style, and which some may find to be appropriate for ecclesiastical references or greetings. The greatest problem with the classical pronunciation is the use of the *w* for the *v*, producing **WAY**-nee, **WEE**-dee, **WEE**-kee for Caesar's famous quote "Veni, vidi, vici." In this case, we have provided a pronunciation more common for American ears, **VAY**-nee, **VEE**-dee, **VEE**-chee, which is church Latin. Readers should feel free, if they prefer, to use the *v* sound whenever the *w* sound appears. If a pronunciation is other than classical, we have indicated such in parentheses. We have included blunders and those instances

262

where a character's incorrect use of Latin suggests a pronunciation. Finally, it might be good to remember that, in the words of *A Dictionary of Latin Words and Phrases*, "anything goes" in the pronunciation of Latin.

We have alphabetized this section by individual word, phrase, or sentence, used the respelling system exclusively to avoid the confusion that might be engendered by long phonetic transcriptions, and entered all monosyllabic words in lower case letters to present this information as clearly as possible.

Accommodo
   ah-**KAHM**-ah-doh

accusativo
   ah-ko͞o-zuh-**TEE**-woh

Ad Jovem, ad Apollinem, ad martem
   ahd **YOH**-wehm, ahd ah-**PAHL**-i-nehm, ahd **MAHR**-tehm

Ad manes fratrum
   ahd **MAHN**-ays **FRAH**-tro͞om

Adsum
   AHD-so͞om

Aio te, Aeacida, romanos vincere posse
   AH-ee-oh tay, eye-**AH**-kee-duh, roh-**MAHN**-ohs
   WINGK-er-ay **PAHS**-ay

Armigero
   ahr-mi-**JI**-roh

Ave
   AH-vay

Ave-Maries
   AH-vay **MEH**-reez   (church Latin)

EE be/ I bit/ EH bet/ AA bat/ O͞O boot / O͝O book/ AW bought/ AH father/ ER bird/ UH cup/
AY bay/ EYE bite/ OY boy/ OH boat/ OW how/ YO͞O duke/ EAR beer/ AIR bear/ O͞OR tour/
AWR bore/ AHR bar/ NG king/ SH ship/ ZH vision/ TH thirty/ <u>TH</u> then/ CH child/ J just/ For
complete list, see Key to Pronunciation p. 2.

Benedicite
     bay-nay-DEE-chee-tay   (church Latin)

Bis coctus
     bis KAHK-to͞os

bona terra, mala gens
     BAHN-ah TEH-rah, MAH-lah gayns

bone for bene
     BAHN-ay fawr BEHN-ay

Bonos dies (blunder for "bonus dies")
     possibly BOH-nohs DEE-ehs

candidatus
     kahn-di-DAH-to͞os

canus (blunder for "canis")
     possibly KAHN-uhs

caret
     KAHR-eht

caveto (blunder for "cavete")
     possibly kuh-VEH-toh

coelo (blunder for "caelo")
     possibly KEE-loh

Coram (blunder for "quorum")
     possibly KAW-ruhm

cucullus non facit monachum
     ko͞o-KO͞OL-o͞os nahn FAH-kit MAHN-ah-ko͞om

Cum multis aliis
     ko͞om MO͞OL-tees AHL-i-ees

cum privilegio ad imprimendum solum
     ko͞om pree-wi-LAY-gee-yoh ahd im-pri-MEHN-do͞om
     SOH-lo͞om

Custalorum (blunder for "custus rotulorum")
   possibly kuhs-tuh-**LAW**-ruhm

Di faciant laudis summa sit ista tuae
   DEE FAHK-ee-ahnt **LOW**-dis **SOOM**-ah sit **IS**-tah **TOO**-eye

Dii boni
   DEE-ee **BAHN**-ee

Dii deaeque omnes
   DEE-ee day-**EYE**-kway **AHM**-nays

diluculo surgere
   dee-**LOO**-koo-loh soor-**GEH**-ray

Dives
   DEE-wis or **DEYE**-veez (Anglicized Latin)

Ecce signum
   EHK-ay **SIG**-noom

Ego et Rex meus
   EHG-oh eht rayks **MEH**-oos

ergo
   ER-goh

Et bonum quo antiquius eo melius
   eht **BAHN**-oom kwoh ahn-**TEE**-kwi-oos **EH**-oh **MEHL**-i-oos

Et cetera
   eht **KEHT**-eh-ruh

Et opus exegi, quod nec Jovis ira, nec ignis
   eht **AHP**-oos ehks-**AY**-gee, kwahd nehk **YAH**-wis **EE**-rah,
   nehk **IG**-nis

et tu Brute
   eht too **BROO**-tay or possibly scans to broo-**TAY**

EE be/ I bit/ EH bet/ AA bat/ OO boot / OO book/ AW bought/ AH father/ ER bird/ UH cup/
AY bay/ EYE bite/ OY boy/ OH boat/ OW how/ YOO duke/ EAR beer/ AIR bear/ OOR tour/
AWR bore/ AHR bar/ NG king/ SH ship/ ZH vision/ TH thirty/ <u>TH</u> then/ CH child/ J just/ For
complete list, see Key to Pronunciation p. 2.

facere
    FAHK-eh-ray

Facile precor gelida quando pecas omnia sub umbra ruminat
    FAH-ki-lay **PREHK**-awr **GEHL**-i-dah **KWAHN**-doh
    PEHK-ahs **AHM**-nay so͞ob **O͞OM**-brah **RO͞O**-mi-naht

Gallia
    GAAL-ee-yuh or scans to **GAAL**-yuh e.g. @ *1HVI* IV, 7, 48

genitivo hujus
    gehn-i-**TEE**-woh **HO͞O**-yo͞os

Haud credo
    hohd **KRAY**-doh   (spoken so that Dull can misunderstand
    as "old gray doe" @ *LLL* IV, 2, 12)

Hic et ubique
    heek eht o͞o-**BEE**-kway

Hic ibat Simois, hic est Sigeia tellus; Hic steterat Priami regia
celsa senis
    heek **I**-baat **SIM**-oh-is,
    heek ehst si-**GAY**-i-uh **TEHL**-o͞os;
    heek **STEHT**-eh-raht **PREE**-ah-mee **RAY**-gee-ah **KEHL**-
    sah **SEHN**-is

Hic jacet
    heek **YAH**-keht

hic, haec, hoc
    heek, hayk, hahk

Homo
    HOH-moh

honorificabilitudinitatibus
    AHN-eh-ri-fi-**KAA**-bi-li-**TO͞O**-di-ni-**TAA**-ti-buhs (Anglicized
    Latin)

horum, harum, horum
    HAW-ro͞om, **HAH**-ro͞om, **HAW**-ro͞om

Hysterica passio
   hi-**STEH**-ri-kah **PAH**-see-yoh

imitari
   im-i-**TAH**-ree

imprimis
   im-**PREE**-mis

in capite
   in **KAHP**-i-tay

In hac spe vivo
   in hahk spay **WEE**-woh

In limbo Patrum
   in **LIM**-boh **PAH**-trōōm

In terram Salicam mulieres ne succedant
   in **TEH**-rahm **SAHL**-i-kahm mōō-**LEE**-eh-rays nay
   sōōk-**KAY**-dahnt

In via
   in **WEE**-uh or **VEE**-uh or **VEYE**-uh

Integer vitae, scelerisque purus, Non eget Mauri jaculis nec arcu
   in-**TEHG**-er **WEE**-teye skehl-i-**RIS**-kway **PŌŌ**-rōōs,
   nahn **EHG**-eht **MOW**-ree **YAHK**-ōō-lccs nehk **AHRK**-ōō

Invitis nubibus
   in-**WEE**-tōōs **NŌŌ**-bi-bōōs

Ipse
   IP-say

ipso facto
   IP-soh **FAHK**-toh or **FAAK**-toh

Ira furor brevis est
   EE-rah **FŌŌ**-rawr **BREH**-wis ehst

EE be/ I bit/ EH bet/ AA bat/ ŌŌ boot / ŎŎ book/ AW bought/ AH father/ ER bird/ UH cup/
AY bay/ EYE bite/ OY boy/ OH boat/ OW how/ YŌŌ duke/ EAR beer/ AIR bear/ ŌŌR tour/
AWR bore/ AHR bar/ NG king/ SH ship/ ZH vision/ TH thirty/ <u>TH</u> then/ CH child/ J just/ For
complete list, see Key to Pronunciation p. 2.

Item (used to enumerate)
   I-tehm

Lapis
   LAH-pis

Laus deo, bone, intelligo
   lows **DAY**-yoh, **BAHN**-ay, in-**TEHL**-i-goh

Lege, domine
   LEHG-ay, **DAHM**-i-nay

Leo-natus
   LAY-oh-**NAH**-tōōs

Lux tua vita mihi
   lōōks **TŌŌ**-ah **WEE**-tah **MI**-hee

Magni dominator poli, tam lentus audis scelera? tam lentus vides
   MAHG-nee dohm-i-**NAH**-tawr **PAHL**-ee,
   tahm **LEHN**-tōōs **OW**-dees **SKEHL**-eh-rah?
   tahm **LEHN**-tōōs **WID**-ays

manu cita
   MAHN-ōō **KIT**-ah

manus
   MAHN-ōōs

Me pompae provexit apex
   may **PAHM**-peye proh-**WEHK**-sit **AH**-pehks

Medice, te ipsum
   MEHD-i-kay, tay **IP**-sōōm

Mehercle
   may-**HERK**-lay

Memento mori
   meh-**MEHN**-toh **MAW**-ree

Mollis aer
   MAHL-is **AH**-air

268

Mulier
MŌOL-ee-er

ne intelligis, domine
nay in-TEHL-i-gis, DAHM-i-nay

nominativo
noh-min-ah-TEE-woh

Non nobis
nahn NOH-bees

Novi hominen tanquam te
NOH-wee HAHM-i-nehm TAHNG-kwahm tay

obsque hoc nihil est
AHBS-kway hahk NEE-hil ehst

omne bene
AHM-nay BEHN-ay

ostentare
ahs-tehn-TAH-ray

Ovidius Naso
oh-WID-ee-ōōs NAH-soh or oh-VID-ee-uhs NAY-zoh
(Anglicized Latin)

paene gelidus timor occupat artus
PEYE-nay GEHL-i-dōōs TIM-awr AHK-ōō-paht AHR-tōōs

passio
PAHS-ee-oh

pauca
POW-kah

pauca verba
POW-kah WAIR-bah

EE be/ I bit/ EH bet/ AA bat/ ŌŌ boot / ŌŌ book/ AW bought/ AH father/ ER bird/ UH cup/
AY bay/ EYE bite/ OY boy/ OH boat/ OW how/ YŌŌ duke/ EAR beer/ AIR bear/ ŌOR tour/
AWR bore/ AHR bar/ NG king/ SH ship/ ZH vision/ TH thirty/ <u>TH</u> then/ CH child/ J just/ For
complete list, see Key to Pronunciation p. 2.

per se
　　per say

Per Stygia, per manes vehor
　　per **STIG**-ee-ah,　per　**MAHN**-ays　**WEH**-hawr

perge
　　PAIR-gay

pia mater
　　PEE-uh　**MAHT**-er

Praeclarissimus filius noster Henricus Rex Angliae et Heres
Franciae
　　preye-klah-**RIS**-i-mo͞os **FEE**-lee-o͞os **NOH**-ster hehn-**REE**-ko͞os
　　rayks **AHNG**-gli-eye eht **HAY**-rays **FRAHN**-ki-eye

praemunire
　　preye-**MYO͞ON**-i-ray

primo, secundo, tertio
　　PREE-moh,　seh-**KO͝ON**-doh,　**TAIR**-shee-oh

Priscian
　　PRISH-ee-uhn

pro Deum, medius fidius
　　proh　**DAY**-o͞om,　**MEHD**-ee-o͞os　**FID**-ee-o͞os

pueritia
　　po͞o-eh-**RIT**-ee-ah

pulcher
　　PO͝OL-ker

quare
　　KWAH-ray

quasi
　　KWAH-zee

Qui me alit, me extinguit
　　kwee　may　**AH**-lit,　may　ehk-**STING**-gwit

270

Qui passa
    kee **PAAS**-uh

qui, quae, quod
    kee, kay, kahd (to make the pun with keys, case, and cod)

quid for quo
    kwid fawr kwoh

quis
    kwis

Quo usque tandem
    kwoh **O͞OS**-kway **TAHN**-dehm

quoniam
    KWAHN-ee-ahm

Ratolorum (blunder for "Rotulorum")
    possibly raa-tuh-**LAW**-ruhm

Redime te captum quam queas minimo
    REHD-i-may tay **KAHP**-to͞om kwahm **KWAY**-ahs
    MIN-i-moh

respice finem
    REHS-pi-kay **FEE**-nehm

sancta majestas
    SAHNGK-tah mah-**YEHS**-tahs

sanguis
    SAHNG-gwis

satis quid sufficit
    SAHT-is kwid **SO͞O**-fi-kit

Se offendendo (blunder for "de defendendo")
    possibly say **OH**-fehn-dehn-doh

EE be/ I bit/ EH bet/ AA bat/ O͞O boot / O͝O book/ AW bought/ AH father/ ER bird/ UH cup/
AY bay/ EYE bite/ OY boy/ OH boat/ OW how/ YO͞O duke/ EAR beer/ AIR bear/ O͞OR tour/
AWR bore/ AHR bar/ NG king/ SH ship/ ZH vision/ TH thirty/ T̲H̲ then/ CH child/ J just/ For
complete list, see Key to Pronunciation p. 2.

semper idem
 SEHM-pair **EE**-dehm

Sic spectanda fides
 sik spehk-**TAHN**-dah **FID**-ehs

sine
 SEE-nay

singulariter
 sing-go͞o-**LAH**-ri-ter

sit fas aut nefas
 sit fahs awt **NEHF**-ahs

solus
 SOH-luhs

Stuprum
 STO͝OP-ro͞ohm

suum cuique
 SO͝O-o͞om **KWI**-kway

tanta est erga te mentis integritas, regina serenissima
 TAHN-tah ehst **ER**-gah tay **MEHN**-tis in-**TEHG**-ri-tahs,
 ray-**GEE**-nah seh-rehn-**IS**-i-mah

Tantaene animis coelestibus irae
 tahn-**TEYE**-nay **AHN**-i-mees keye-**LEHS**-ti-bo͞os **EE**-reye

Te Deum
 tay **DAY**-o͞om

terra
 TEH-rah

Terras Astrae reliquit
 TEH-rahs **AHS**-treye-uh rehl-**EE**-kwit

tertio
 TER-shee-oh

tremor cordis
TREH-mer **KAWR**-dis

unguem
OŌNG-gwehm

veni, vidi, vici
VAY-nee, **VEE**-dee, **VEE**-chee (church Latin)

Ver
wair

Verba
WAIR-bah

via
WEE-uh or **VEE**-uh or **VEYE**-uh

videlicet
vi-**DEHL**-i-sit (Anglicized Latin)

Video et gaudeo
WID-ay-oh eht **GOW**-day-oh

videsne quis venit
wid-**AYS**-nay kwis **WEHN**-it

Vir sapit qui pauca loquitur
wear **SAHP**-it kwee **POW**-kah **LAH**-kwi-tōōr

viva voce
WEE-wah **WOH**-kay or **VEE**-vah **VOH**-chay or
VOH-chee (church Latin)

vocativo
wohk-ah-**TEE**-woh

vocatur
WOHK-ah-tōōr

vox
wohks

EE be/ I bit/ EH bet/ AA bat/ OŌ boot / ŌO book/ AW bought/ AH father/ ER bird/ UH cup/
AY bay/ EYE bite/ OY boy/ OH boat/ OW how/ YŌO duke/ EAR beer/ AIR bear/ OŌR tour/
AWR bore/ AHR bar/ NG king/ SH ship/ ZH vision/ TH thirty/ T̲H̲ then/ CH child/ J just/ For
complete list, see Key to Pronunciation p. 2.

accents, dialects, and foreign languages

a great feast of language
Love's Labor's Lost V, 1, 35

In some plays, accents are required of characters whose native language is not English. This occurs in both *The Merry Wives of Windsor* and *Henry V*. In the former, Dr. Caius, the physician, speaks English with a French accent and Hugh Evans, the schoolmaster, speaks English with a Welsh accent. The text indicates the French accent with the substitution of *v* for *w,* and *t* or *d* for *th*. Sometimes an extra unstressed vowel sound is added to verbs. The Welsh accent is indicated by the substitution of *p* for *b*, *t* for *d*, and *g* for *k*. The sounds for *v* and *f* are transposed. Also, *s* and *sh* replace *z* and *zh*. In addition, the text indicates that the *w* sound at the beginning of words like *woman* disappears.

The different accents of the four captains in *Henry V* illuminate a central theme in the play. Fluellen, the second largest part, speaks with a Welsh accent. The printed text indicates the use of an Irish accent for MacMorris with the substitution of *ish* for *is* and *Chrish* for *Christ,* and a Scottish accent for Jamy with the repetition of *gud* for *good*. The text also indicates the use of *sall* for *shall* and the substitution of *ay* for *I*. If actors adopt the suggested nationalist accents for these characters, the question then is raised as to what to do with the speech of Gower, the Englishman. We would suggest that, in this one instance, an exception be made to our preference for American speech. The use of an English accent for Gower can accentuate the linguistic differences amongst the characters and point up the competing regional or national interests in both Shakespeare's and Henry's Britain, as well as reflect those of our own world.

In *Henry V*, both Katherine and Alice speak English with a French accent that is indicated with the substitution of *d* for *th* and *wat* for *what*. In turn, Henry's attempt to address Katherine in her native tongue provokes laughter on her part. There is no indication in the text about the accuracy of the Boy's French accent as he interprets between Pistol and the French soldier. However, he does seem to have achieved a basic familiarity with the language while on campaign.

In *Henry IV Part One*, there is no orthographic suggestion as to the adoption of an accent for the part of Glendower. An accent might be employed to excellent effect considering that he is a native speaker of Welsh. In addition, Hotspur seems to insult Glendower with the gibe that "no man speaks better Welsh." Productions have sometimes used a trace of a Spanish accent for Katherine in *Henry VIII*, and a French accent for the Queen in *Richard II* and for Margaret in the *Henry VI* trilogy.

Native speakers should be consulted for the French in *Henry V* and the Welsh exchanges between Glendower and Lady Mortimer in *Henry IV Part One*, as well as for the occasional Spanish and Italian in other plays.

The text of *King Lear* calls for a Somersetshire dialect when Edgar confronts Oswald. The text indicates this with the substitution of *z*'s for *s*'s and *v*'s for *f*'s among others. It is best learned from a native speaker or from a dialect tape.

Questions often arise as to the efficacy of a dialect in the portrayal of the rustic or lower class characters. Our preference is for the use of American speech rather than stage Cockney or generic lower-class English speech. A wide variety of American regional dialects is available. Their usefulness will depend on the setting and location of the stage action.

afterthoughts
&

what's past is prologue
The Tempest II, 1, 247

This section offers brief observations on the poetic diction of each play. Each entry notes the percentage of prose and/or verse in a given play, as well as the amount of rhyming verse, if significant. It also includes a sampling of contractions and of words that expand to fulfill the demands of the meter. Examples of words that require an unusual stress on either their first or second syllables follow. For example, *revenue* is pronounced today with a stress on its first syllable but often requires a stress on its second syllable in Shakespeare. We direct readers to the appropriate sections for accents, dialects, foreign languages, Latin, and words that might present unforseen difficulty.

All's Well That Ends Well
The amount of prose and verse in this play is almost equal. In the gulling of Parolles, the soldiers speak *linsey-woolsy* or *choughs' language* which are nonsense sounds meant to intimidate and frighten. Parolles understands the sounds as belonging to the *Muskos* regiment. This may indicate a Russian flavored pronunciation. *Lustick* is possibly Dutch, while *Mort du vinaigre*! is French. *Capriccio*, which scans to three syllables, is Italianate. The *s* in *rope's* @ IV, 2, 38 stands for "us." Some of the contractions include *I've* for *I have*, *you've* for *you have*, *I'd* for *I would*, and *he'd* for *he*

had. Soldier expands to three syllables @ III, 2, 68. Words with a primary stress on the first syllable include *enjoined* @ III, 5, 90, *perfect* @ IV, 4, 4, and *perspective* @ V, 3, 48. Words with a primary stress on the second syllable include *exploit* @ I, 2, 17, *contract* @ II, 3, 177, and *assay* @ III, 7, 44. See dictionary entry for *baring* @ IV, 1, 47.

Antony and Cleopatra

90 percent of this late play is in verse. There are many epic caesuras and the highest number of shared lines of all of the plays. The text has numerous contractions including *he'd* for *he had*, *th'art* for *thou art*, *th'ast* for *thou hast*, and *I'll* for *I will*. Words that expand include *million, Asia, affections*, and *instruction*. Words with a primary stress on the first syllable include *condemned* @ I, 3, 49, *cement* @ II, 1, 48 and III, 2, 29, and *combating* @ III, 13, 79. Words with a primary stress on the second syllable include *revenue* @ III, 6, 30, *seaside* @ III, 11, 20, *triumphing* @ IV, 8, 16, and *record* @ IV, 9, 8. See dictionary entries for *buffet, prophesy*, and *eat* @ II, 2, 227. Note that *power* often scans to one syllable.

As You Like It

While more than half of the play is in prose, 10 percent of the play is in rhyme, some of which affords comic possibilities, including Celia's reading of Orlando's verse, which forces rhymes like *age/pilgrimage* and *slave/have*. The pronunciation of *Goths* is akin to GOHTS in order to make the pun with *goats*. *Sound* @ V, 2, 26 is often emended to indicate a pronunciation of SWŌŌNED. Words with a primary stress on the first syllable include *antique* @ II, 3, 57 and *upon* @ IV, 3, 150. Words with a primary stress on the second syllable include *exile* @ II, 1, 1, *translate* @ II, 1, 19, and *confines* @ II, 1, 24. *Dials* cans to one or two syllables. Words that expand include *promotion, intermission, observation*, and *reputation. Theatre* expands to three syllables @ II, 7, 137, as does *wrestler* @ II, 3, 70. See dictionary entries for *eat* @ I, 3, 70 and II, 7, 88 (second citation) and *victualled*.

The Comedy of Errors

65 percent of this play is in blank verse with few variants. Slightly more than 20 percent of the verse rhymes. Words that expand include *patience, violently, contagion, Asia,* and *children.* Words with a primary stress on the first syllable include *buffet* @ II, 2, 157 and *travail* @ V, 1, 402. Words with a primary stress on the second syllable include *bedtime* @ I, 2, 28, *sometimes* @ II, 2, 26, and *compact* @ II, 2, 160 and III, 2, 22. *Hour* scans to one or two syllables depending on the meter. Note that *situate* scans to two syllables @ II, 1, 16.

Coriolanus

Approximately 75 percent of this play is in verse. As with other late plays, the verse has many variations including epic caesuras, short lines, and hexameters. Contractions include *I've* for *I have, you've* for *you have,* and *I'd* for *I would.* Words that expand include *malicious, preparation, assembly,* and *violent.* Words with a primary stress on the first syllable include *antique* @ II, 3, 114, *extreme* @ IV, 5, 70, and *cement* @ IV, 6, 86. Words with a primary stress on the second syllable include *record* @ IV, 6, 50 and *increase* @ III, 3, 114. Note that the word *power,* used throughout the play, can have either one or two syllables.

Cymbeline

80 percent of the play is in blank verse. There are numerous contractions, such as *I'm* for *I am, I'll* for *I will,* and *we've* for *we have.* Some of the words that expand are *complexion, soldiers,* and *malefactions.* Words with a primary stress on the first syllable include *exquisite* @ III, 5, 71, *diseased* @ I, 6, 123, and *impious* @ III, 3, 6. Words with a primary stress on the second syllable include *contents* @ II, 2, 27, *maintop* @ IV, 2, 320, and *exiled* @ IV, 4, 26 and V, 4, 59. *Needle* scans to one syllable @ I, 1, 168. *Diamond,* used throughout the play, can be two or three syllables. See "Latin" section for the puns in Act V.

Hamlet

Two-thirds of the play is in blank verse and just under 30 percent is in prose. Contractions include *I'm* for *I am*, *I'll* for *I will*, and *we've* for *we have*. Some of the words that expand are *complexion, soldiers,* and *malefactions*. Words with a primary stress on the first syllable include *complete* @ I, 4, 52, *secure* @ I, 5, 61, and *absurd* @ III, 2, 57. Words with a primary stress on the second syllable include *character* @ I, 3, 59, *exploit* @ IV, 7, 63, and *absent* @ V, 2, 336. *Courage* @ I, 3, 65 is kuh-**RAHJ**. *Tropically* @ III, 2, 229 is either **TROH**-pik-lee in reference to the word *trope* or **TRAA**-pik-lee if punning on *The Mousetrap*, the play within the play. *As's* @ V, 2, 43 may be **AAZ**-iz to pun with "asses." *Chanson* @ II, 2, 409 could perhaps be the French shahn-**SOHN**, though the English **CHAAN**-suhn works equally well in this prose passage. See dictionary entry for *eat* @ IV, 3, 27.

Henry IV Part One

More than 40 percent of the play is in prose; the remainder is in blank verse with a small amount of rhyming verse. *Prisoners*, used throughout the play, scans to either two or three syllables. *Power* usually scans to one syllable. *Glendower* frequently scans to two syllables. Words that expand include *transformation, expedition, determination,* and *suggestion,* as well as *impatience, soldier,* and *physicians*. Words with a primary stress on the first syllable include *frontier* @ I, 3, 19 and *exact* @ IV, 1, 46. Words with a primary stress on the second syllable include *allies* @ I, 1, 16 and *portent(s)* @ II, 3, 59 and V, 1, 20. See dictionary entries for the abbreviations *s., d.,* and *ob.* in II, 4. For a discussion of Glendower, Lady Mortimer, and the use of the Welsh language, see "Accents, Dialects, and Foreign Languages."

Henry IV Part Two

This play features the highest percentage of prose of any of the histories. Words that expand include *rebellion, religion, destruction, foundation, commotion,* and *ocean*. Words with a primary stress on the second syllable include *access* @ IV, 1, 78, *instinct* @ I, 1, 86, and *retail* @ I, 1, 32. Pistol's fantastical language contains a blend of Italian and French. See dictionary entries for *victuallers*, *forgetive*, *gainsaid*, and *eat* @ IV, 5, 164.

Henry V

57 percent of this play is in verse. Contractions include *we're* for *we are*, *you'd* for *you would*, *we'll* for *we will*, and *what's* for *what is*. Some of the words that expand are *invention*, *million*, *convocation*, *ocean*, and *preparation*. Words with a primary stress on the first syllable include *perfected* @ I, 1, 69, *largess* @ IV, Cho, 43, and *Dauphin* @ I, 2, 222 and throughout the play. Words with a primary stress on the second syllable include *exploits* @ I, 2, 121, *assay* @ I, 2, 151, and *sinister* @ II, 4, 85. See dictionary entries for *accompt*, *puissance*, *puissant*, *Louvre*, *Lorraine*, and *executors*. Note that *Lewis* always scans to one syllable, and *Charles* often scans to one syllable. See "Accents, Dialects, and Foreign Languages" for a discussion of the accents used by the "Four Captains."

Henry VI Part One

The play is almost entirely in verse. It contains few variants and has the lowest number of short and shared lines of any of the plays. Contractions include *you've* for *you have*, *we're* for *we are*, and *I'm* for *I am*. Some of the words that expand are *faction*, *proclamation*, *religion*, *apprehension*, *coronation*, *leopard*, *creature*, and *marriage*. Words with a primary stress on the first syllable include *complete* @ I, 2, 83, *forlorn* @ I, 2, 19, and *travail* @ V, 4, 102. Words with a primary stress on the second syllable include *precinct* @ II, 1, 68 and *reflex* @ V, 4, 87. *Charles* always scans to one syllable except @ IV, 4, 26. *Henry* scans to either two or three syllables. *Prisoner*, used throughout the play, scans to two or three syllables. See dictionary entries for *victual* and *Dauphin*.

Henry VI Part Two

82 percent of this play is in blank verse. Contractions include *I'd* for *I would*, *he'd* for *he would*, *t'have* for *to have*, and *he's* for *he is*. Words that expand include *subornation*, *execution*, *ambition*, *patience*, *country*, and *statue*. Words with a primary stress on the

first syllable include *stigmatic* @ V, 1, 215, *forlorn* @ II, 4, 45 and @ III, 2, 77 (if *poisonous* is two syllables), and *corrosive* @ III, 2, 403. Words with a primary stress on the second syllable include *suspect* @ III, 2, 139 and *edict* @ III, 2, 258. *Henry* scans to either two or three syllables. Note that the Elizabethans probably pronounced *Walter* @ IV, 1, 14 as something like "water." It may be necessary to adopt this pronunciation to make complete sense of the passage. See dictionary entries for *Dauphin* and *eat* @ IV, 10, 37.

Henry VI Part Three

The play is almost entirely in verse. Contractions include *you're* for *you are* and *I'd* for *I had*. Words that expand include *rebellion, succession,* and *apprehension*. Words with a primary stress on the first syllable include *Archbishop* @ IV, 3, 53, *horizon* @ IV, 7, 81, and *farewell* @ V, 7, 45. Words with a primary stress on the second syllable include *forecast* @ V, 1, 42 and *crossbow* @ III, 1, 6. See dictionary entries for *recompt* and *desert* @ III, 3, 132.

Henry VIII

More than 95 percent of the play is in verse. There are numerous contractions contained in the text including *and't, in's, t'attach, y'are, be't,* and *t'oppose*. Additional contractions are *I'm* for *I am, they're* for *they are,* and *they'd* for *they would*. Some of the words that expand are *meditations, commission, business,* and *pernicious*. Words with a primary stress on the first syllable include *July* @ I, 1, 154 and *Archbishop* throughout. Words with a primary stress on the second syllable include *discourser* @ I, 1, 41, *advertise* @ II, 4, 176, and *travail* @ V, I, 71.

Julius Caesar

The majority of this play is in verse. Contractions include *I'll* for *I will* and *I'd* for *I had*. Words that expand include *destruction, insurrection,* and *emulation*. Words with a primary stress on the first syllable include *construe* @ I, 2, 45 and I, 3, 34, *upon* @ I, 2, 171, and *mischievous* @ II, 1, 33. Words with a primary stress on the second syllable include *sometimes* @ II, 1, 285, *exploit* @ II, 1, 317 and 318, and *portents* @ II, 2, 80. The word *not'st* @ V, 3,

22 means "to note." *Funeral, soldier,* and *prisoner* scan to two or three syllables. See dictionary entries for *prophesy, statue,* and *wind* @ IV, 1, 32.

King John

This is one of the few plays written entirely in verse. Contractions include *he's* for *he is* and *I'll* for *I shall.* Words that expand include *usurpation, occasion, generation, protection, desolation, minion, ocean,* and *destruction.* Words with a primary stress on the first syllable include *hospitable* @ II, 1, 244, *presage* @ III, 4, 158, *supreme* @ III, 1, 155, and *Milan* @ V, 2, 120. Words with a primary stress on the second syllable include *sunset* @ III, 1, 110 and *seaside* @ V, 7, 91. *Needle* @ V, 2, 157 elides to one syllable. The word *iron,* used throughout the play, is frequently disyllabic. See dictionary entries for *Cordelion, Absey, eat* @ I, 1, 234, and *lien* @ IV, 1, 50.

King Lear

70 percent of the play is in verse. The text has numerous shared lines and hexameters and the most short lines of all the plays. Contractions include *we've* for *we have, I'm* for *I am, be't* for *be it,* and *I'd* for *I would.* Words with a primary stress on the first syllable include *sincere* @ II, 2, 100, *lamentable* @ IV, 1, 5, and *proclaimed* @ IV, 6, 222. Words with a primary stress on the second syllable include *revenue* @ II, 1, 100, *contents* @ II, 4, 33, and *defects* @ IV, 1, 20. See dictionary entries for *champains, fut,* and *sepulchring.* See "Accents, Dialects, and Foreign Languages" for Edgar's dialect in IV, 6.

Love's Labor's Lost

Only 21 percent of this early play is in blank verse. 43 percent is in rhyme. Words that expand include *affections, lamentation,* and *reformation.* Words with a primary stress on the first syllable include *complete* @ I, 1, 133, *profound* @ IV, 3, 163, and *peremptory* @ IV, 3, 221. Words with a primary stress on the second syllable include *sometimes* @ IV, 1, 30, *retails* @ V, 2, 318, and *content* and *contents* @ V, 2, 515. Holofernes's vocabulary is Latinate and effulgent. His pedantry values silent consonants so that words like *debt* are pronounced DEHBT. The text abounds in puns and features *honorificabilitudinitatibus*, the longest word in Shakespeare. See dictionary entries for *ballet* @ I, 2, 103 and *eat* @ IV, 2, 24.

Macbeth

80 percent of the play is in verse. It has a high number of shared lines as well as numerous epic caesuras and short lines. Contractions include *we've* for *we have* and *they've* for *they have*. Some of the words that expand are *execution*, *reflection*, *entrance*, and *monstrous*. Words with a primary stress on the first syllable include *humane* @ III, 4, 76, *largess* @ II, 1, 14, and *obscure* @ II, 3, 55. Words with a primary stress on the second syllable include *th'access* @ I, 5, 42, *pretence* @ II, 3, 127, and *exploits* @ IV, 1, 144. *Weird*, spelled "weyward" in the Folio and used throughout the play, scans to one or two syllables, as does *Glamis*. *Scone*, which is the last word of the play, formerly rhymed with *one*. See dictionary entries for *gripe*, *buffets*, *minutely*, and *eat* @ II, 4, 18.

Measure for Measure

60 percent of the play is in blank verse. There are frequent epic caesuras and short lines. Contractions include *we've* for *we have*, *we're* for *we are*, *I've* for *I have*, *it's* for *it is*, and *th'art* for *thou art*. Words that expand include *commission*, *evasion*, *approbation*, *profanation*, and *Russia*. Words with a primary stress on the first syllable include *unsoiled* @ II, 4, 155, *compelled* @ II, 4, 57, and *chastisement* @ V, 1, 255. Words with a primary stress on the second syllable include *assay* @ I, 4, 76, *access* @ II, 2, 19, and *record* @ II, 2, 40. *Prayer* and *Friar* scan to one or two syllables. Note that *use* is a noun @ I, 3, 26. See dictionary entry for *accompt*.

The Merchant of Venice

Almost three-quarters of the play is in blank verse. 5 percent is in rhyme. Contractions include *you're* for *you are*, *I'm* for *I am*, *you'd* for *you had*, and *I've* for *I have*. Words that expand include *opinion*, *occasions*, *Christian*, and *companions*. Words that have a primary stress on the first syllable include *outside* @ I, 3, 98, *obscure* @ II, 7, 51, and *unthrift* @ V, 1, 16. Words that have a primary stress on the second syllable include *aspect* @ I, 1, 54, *obdurate* @ IV, 1, 8, and *highways* @ V, 1, 263. To get the maximum effect out of the rhyming joke @ V, 1, 305, consider pronouncing *clerk* with the English pronunciation KLAHRK starting at IV, 1, 392. *Le Bon* @ I, 2, 50 is probably "bone." Shylock might play with the word *pirates* as PEYE-raats @ I, 3, 22.

The Merry Wives of Windsor
86 percent of this play is in prose. Within the small amount of verse, some of the contractions are *I'd* for *I had*, *they're* for *they are*, and *we've* for *we have*. Words with a primary stress on the first syllable include *extreme* @ IV, 4, 11 and *unclean* @ IV, 4, 56. Words with a primary stress on the second syllable include *midnight* @ IV, 4, 28, *contents* @ IV, 6, 13, and *charactery* @ V, 5, 71 (if *flowers* is one syllable). See dictionary entry for *buffet*.

A Midsummer Night's Dream
Rhyming verse accounts for 45 percent of this play. Words that expand include *patience, dissension, derision, affection, confusion,* and *imagination*. Words with a primary stress on the first syllable include *rheumatic* @ II, 1, 105 and *misprised* @ III, 2, 74. Words with a primary stress on the second syllable include *edict* @ I, 1, 151, *midnight* @ I, 1, 223, and *compact* @ V, 1, 8. See the dictionary entries for *thorough* @ II, 1, 106, *eat* @ II, 2, 149, and *ballet* @ IV, 1, 212. Note that *childing* @ II, 1, 112 means pregnant or fruitful.

Much Ado About Nothing
Prose accounts for more than 70 percent of this play. Within the verse some of the contractions are *I'd* for *I would*, *we've* for *we have*, *you'll* for *you will*, and *I'm* for *I am*. Words that expand include *affection, complexion, gracious, apparitions, ostentation,* and *patience*. Words that have a primary stress on the first syllable include *betwixt* @ IV, 1, 82 and *unknown* @ IV, 1, 133. Words with a primary stress on the second syllable include *discourse* @ III, 1, 5 and *propose* @ III, 1, 12. See dictionary entries for *victual, pennyworth,* and *eat* @ IV, 1, 192.

Othello

Almost 80 percent of the play in verse. The prose is usually spoken by Iago and Roderigo. It has more epic caesuras than any other play, as well as numerous shared lines and short lines. Contractions include *I'm* for *I am*, *I'd* for *I had*, *we're* for *we are*, and *he's* for *he is*. Words that expand include *estimation, patience, satisfaction,* and *apprehension*. Words with a primary stress on the first syllable include *profane* @ I, 1, 114, *cashiered* @ II, 3, 357, *secure* @ IV, 1, 71, and *antique* @ V, 2, 217. Words with a primary stress on the second syllable include *demonstrate* @ I, 1, 61 and III, 3, 431, *affects* @ I, 3, 263, and *portents* @ V, 2, 45. See dictionary entries for *arithmetician, Moor,* and *close* (adj) @ V, 2, 335.

Pericles

Almost 60 percent of the play is in blank verse. 20 percent is in rhymed verse, an unusually high percentage for a late play. There are a large number of short and shared lines in those parts of the play attributed to Shakespeare. Words that expand are *perfections, companion, marriage, nation,* and *diamond*. Words with a primary stress on the first syllable include *respite* @ I, 1, 117, *entreat* @ II, 4, 45, and *travail* @ III, Cho, 52 and III, 1, 14. Words with a primary stress on the second syllable include *edict* @ I, 1, 112, *access* @ II, 5, 7, and *relapse* @ III, 2, 110.

Richard II

The play is entirely in verse. 20 percent of the verse rhymes and sometimes has the potential for comic effect. For example @ V, 3, 119, *pardonne moi* seems to rhyme with *destroy*, which might indicate the pronunciation. Words which expand include *physician, incision, admonition, succession, proportion, correction,* and *patience*. Words with a primary stress on the first syllable include *complot* @ I, 3, 189, *perspectives* @ II, 2, 18, and *delectable* @ II, 3, 7. Words with a primary stress on the second syllable include *record* @ IV, 1, 230, *contents* @ V, 2, 38 and *sepulchre* @ I, 3, 196. *High way* is two words with the second word in the stressed position @ I, 4, 4. Note that *bounty* expands to three syllables @ II,

3, 67 and *tears* is TAIRZ @ III, 3, 57. See dictionary entry for *eat* @ V, 5, 85.

Richard III
More than 98 percent of this early play is in verse. Contractions include *I'd* for *I had*, *I'm* for *I am*, and *you've* for *you have*. Some of the words that expand are *promotion*, *patient*, and *indignation*. Words with a primary stress on the first syllable include *curtailed* @ I, 1, 18, *excuse* @ I, 2, 84, *accessary* @ I, 2, 191, and *supreme* @ III, 7, 118. Words with a primary stress on the second syllable include *abjects* @ I, 1, 106, *suspects* @ I, 3, 88 and III, 5, 32, and *obdurate* @ I, 3, 346 and III, 1, 39. See dictionary entries for *prophesy* and *characters*.

Romeo and Juliet
71 percent of the play is in blank verse, with slightly over 16 percent in rhyme. The names of the title characters frequently scan to **ROHM**-yoh and **JOOL**-yeht. *Friar* scans to one or two syllables. Contractions include *I'd* for *I would*, *she'd* for *she would*, *I'm* for *I am*, *he's* for *he is,* and *it's* for *it is.* Words that expand include *marriage, invocation, substantial, lamentation,* and *patience.* Words with a primary stress on the first syllable include *confessor* @ II, 6, 21 and III, 3, 49, *unmade* @ III, 3, 70, *before* @ V, 3, 90, and *receptacle* @ IV, 3, 39. *Exile* always stresses on the first syllable except @ III, 3, 43. Words with a primary stress on the second syllable include *access* @ II, Cho, 9, *excess* @ II, 6, 33, and *baptized* @ II, 2, 50. Note the difference in pronunciation between *raven* (a bird) and *ravening* (devouring) @ III, 2, 76. See dictionary entries for *prayers, pennyworth,* and *close* (adj) @ III, 2, 5.

The Taming of the Shrew
72 percent of this early play is in blank verse. Contractions include *we'll* for *we will*, *it's* for *it is, you're* for *you are,* and *you've* for *you have.* Words that expand include *impatient, instructions, patience,* and *million.* Words with a primary stress on the first syllable include *commune* @ I, 1, 101, *largess* @ I, 2, 147, and *extreme*

@ II, 1, 135. Words with a primary stress on the second syllable include *absent* @ Ind, 2, 121, *defects* @ I, 2, 121, and *elsewhere* @ IV, 3, 6. See dictionary entries for *politicly, satiety, extempore,* and *eat* @ IV, 1, 184, first citation.

The Tempest
71 percent of this late play is in verse. There are numerous short and shared lines. The text has frequent contractions including *heard'st, saw'st, canst, hadst, seest, say'st,* and *call'dst.* Other possible contractions include *we're* for *we are, t'have* for *to have,* and *they're* for *they are.* Words that expand include *valiant, vineyard,* and *celebration.* Words with a primary stress on the first syllable include *perfected* @ I, 2, 79, *frustrate* @ III, 3, 10, and *humane* @ I, 2, 346. Words with a primary stress on the second syllable include *extirpate* @ I, 2, 125, *opportune* @ IV, 1, 26, and *solemnized* @ V, 1, 309. See dictionary entries for *aches* and *throughly.*

Timon of Athens
Two-thirds of the play is in blank verse. Almost 20 percent of the lines are short or shared. Contractions include *I'll* for *I will, I've* for *I have, I'd* for *I had, I'm* for *I am,* and *you're* for *you are.* Words that expand include *damnation, factions,* and *valiant.* Words with a primary stress on the first syllable include *austere* @ I, 1, 54, *condemn* @ III, 5, 53, and *detestable* @ IV, 1, 33. Words with a primary stress on the second syllable include *frequents* @ I, 1, 117, *precedent* @ I, 1, 133, and *aspect* @ II, 1, 28. See dictionary entries for *gramercy, triumphers,* and *aches.*

Titus Andronicus
More than 93 percent of the play is in blank verse. There are a few Latin words as well as one anachronistic greeting in French: *bon jour* @ I, 1, 497. Contractions include *they're* for *they are,* and *you're* for *you are. Emperor,* used throughout the play, scans to two or three syllables. Words that expand include *expiation, proclamations, million, impatient, spacious, execution, destruction, patience,* and *Empress.* Words with a primary stress on the first syllable include *abjectly* @ II, 3, 4, *sequestered* @ II, 3, 75, *obscure*

@ II, 3, 77, and *forlorn* @ II, 3, 153. Words with a primary stress on the second syllable include *triumpher* @ I, 1, 173, *conduct* @ IV, 4, 64, and *gramercy* @ I, 1, 498. Some editions substitute "raze" for *race* @ I, 1, 454. See dictionary entry for *prayer* @ III, 1, 75.

Troilus and Cressida

60 percent of the play is in verse. There are numerous epic caesuras and a large number of short and shared lines. The text has many multi-syllabic words that are unique to this play. Contractions include *I'm* for *I am*, *here's* for *here is*, *you're* for *you are,* and *I've* for *I have*. Words that expand include *approbation, oration, execution,* and *genius*. Words with a primary stress on the first syllable include *o'ertop* @ III, 3, 164, *complete* @ III, 3, 180 and IV, 1, 27, and *humane* @ IV, 1, 20 (in an epic caesura line). Words with a primary stress on the second syllable include *canonize* @ II, 2, 202, *characterless* @ III, 2, 180, and *sinister* @ IV, 5, 127. Note that *general* and *surety* can be two or three syllables. See dictionary entries for *dividable, prescience, subsequent,* and *multipotent*.

Twelfth Night

More than 60 percent of the play is in prose and just over 30 percent is in blank verse. Epic caesuras are frequent. Contractions include *I've* for *I have*, *I'd* for *I had,* and *she's* for *she is*. Words that expand include *country, remembrance, creatures, adorations,* and *distraction*. Words with a primary stress on the first syllable include *upon* @ III, 4, 198 and V, 1, 93 and *adverse* @ V, 1, 78. Words with a primary stress on the second syllable include *excess* @ I, 1, 2, *access* @ I, 4, 15, and *discourse* @ I, 4, 24. See dictionary entries for *comptible, champian,* and *convents*.

Two Gentlemen of Verona

More than two-thirds of this early play is in blank verse. Contractions include *I'm* for *I am*, *I'll* for *I will*, *you're* for *you are,* and *there's* for *there is*. Some of the words that expand include *protestation, expedition,* and *correction*. Words with a primary stress on the first syllable include *perfected* @ I, 3, 23, *extreme* @ II, 7, 22 (with *fire* scanning to two syllables), and *lamentable* @

IV, 4, 164. Words with a primary stress on the second syllable include *turmoil* @ II, 7, 37, *allied* @ IV, 1, 49, and *recourse* @ III, 1, 112. See dictionary entries for *throughly, unfrequented, sepulchre* (v), and *Milan*.

The Two Noble Kinsmen

The majority of the play is in blank verse. Contractions include *I'd* for *I would*, *she'd* for *she would*, *I've* for *I have*, *you've* for *you have*, and *I'd* for *I had*. *Iron* often scans to two syllables. Some of the words that expand include *imaginations, sufficient, position*, and *musicians*. Words with a primary stress on the first syllable include *farewell* @ II, 2, 179 and *confessed* @ III, 1, 35. Words with a primary stress on the second syllable include *success* @ V, 3, 69, *record* @ II, 2, 112, *edict* @ III, 6, 145 and 168, and *sinister* @ V, 3, 76. *Moor* @ III, 5, 117 tends towards MAWR and *is* towards IS to make the pun with *Morris*. *Hercules* @ I, 1, 66 is pronounced as ER-kleez. See dictionary entry for *victuals*.

The Winter's Tale

More than 70 percent of this play is in blank verse. Most of the prose occurs when the play shifts to Bohemia. As with other late plays, the verse has many variations including epic caesuras, short lines, and hexameters. Contractions include *I've* for *I have*, *I'd* for *I had*, and *I'll* for *I will*. Words that expand include *confirmation, proclamations, creature*, and *business*. Words with a primary stress on the first syllable include *July* @ I, 2, 168 and *unknown* @ IV, 4, 65 and 484. Words with a primary stress on the second syllable include *allied* @ I, 2, 338, *something* @ II, 2, 25, and *contract* @ IV, 4, 410. See dictionary entries for *gaoler* and *Saltiers*.

references

We turned o'er many books together
The Merchant of Venice IV, 1, 155

Abbott, E. A. *A Shakespearian Grammar*. New York: Dover Publications, 1966.

The American Heritage Dictionary of the English Language, 3rd Edition. Boston: Houghton Mifflin, 1992.

Allen, W. Sidney. *Vox Latina*. Cambridge: Cambridge University Press, 1965.

Attridge, Derek. *Poetic Rhythm: An Introduction*. Cambridge: Cambridge University Press, 1995.

Barton, John. *Playing Shakespeare*. London and New York: Methuen, 1984.

Berry, Cicely. *The Actor and the Text*. New York: Applause, 1992.

———. *Text in Action*. London: Virgin Publishing, 2001.

Cercignani, Fausto. *Shakespeare's Words and Elizabethan Pronunciation*. Oxford: Clarendon Press, 1981.

Colaianni, Louis. *Shakespeare's Names: A New Pronouncing Dictionary*. New York: Quite Specific Media Group, 1999.

Coye, Dale F. *Pronouncing Shakespeare's Words*. Westport, Conn.: Greenwood Press, 1998.

Dobson, E. J. *English Pronunciation, 1500–1700.* 2 vols. Oxford: Clarendon Press, 1968.

Ehrlich, Eugene. *Amo, Amas, Amat and More: How to Use Latin to Your Own Advantage and to the Astonishment of Others.* New York: Harper & Row, 1985.

Irvine, Theodora Ursula. *How to Pronounce the Names in Shakespeare.* Ann Arbor, Michigan: Gryphon Books, 1971.

Jones, Daniel. *English Pronouncing Dictionary,* 15th Edition. Edited by Peter Roach and James Hartmann. Cambridge: Cambridge University Press, 1997.

———. *Everyman's English Pronouncing Dictionary.* Extensively revised and edited by A.C. Gimson. London and Melbourne: J.M. Dent & Sons, 1986.

Kermode, Frank. *Shakespeare's Language.* New York: Farrar, Straus and Giroux, 2001.

Kökeritz, Helge. *Shakespeare's Names: A Pronouncing Dictionary.* New Haven: Yale University Press, 1959.

———. *Shakespeare's Pronunciation.* New Haven: Yale University Press, 1953.

McDonald, Russ. *The Bedford Companion to Shakespeare.* Boston and New York: Bedford Books of St. Martin's Press, 1996.

McLean, Margaret Prendergast. *Good American Speech.* New York: E.P. Dutton and Co., 1946.

Merriam-Webster's Collegiate Dictionary, 10th Edition. Springfield, Mass.: Merriam-Webster, 1993.

Morwood, James. *A Dictionary of Latin Words and Phrases.* Oxford and New York: Oxford University Press, 1998.

The Oxford English Dictionary, 2nd Edition. 20 vols. Oxford: Clarendon, 1989.

The Oxford Universal Dictionary, 3rd Edition. Oxford: Clarendon, 1944.

A Pronouncing Dictionary of American English. Editors John Samuel Kenyon and Thomas Albert Knott. Springfield, Mass.: G&C Merriam Co., 1953.

The Reader's Encyclopedia of Shakespeare. Editors Oscar James Campbell and Edward G. Quinn. New York: MJF Books, 1966.

Reading Shakespeare's Dramatic Language — A Guide. Editors Sylvia Adamson, Lynette Hunter, Lynne Magnusson, Ann Thompson, and Katie Wales. London: Thomson Learning, 2001.

Schmidt, Alexander. *Shakespeare Lexicon and Quotation Dictionary*. 2 Vols. New York: Dover Publications, 1971.

Shakespeare, William. *The First Folio of Shakespeare 1623*. Prepared and Introduced by Doug Moston. New York: Applause Books, 1995.

Shakespeare, William. *William Shakespeare: The Complete Works*. General Editor, Alfred Harbage. New York: The Viking Press, 1969.

Skinner, Edith. *Speak With Distinction*. Edited by Lilene Mansell. Revised by Timothy Monich and Lilene Mansell. New York: Applause, 1990.

Spain, Delbert. *Shakespeare Sounded Soundly*. Santa Barbara, California: Garland-Clarke Editions/Capra Press, 1988.

Tarlinskaja, Marina. *Shakespeare's Verse*. New York: Peter Lang, 1987.

Webster's Third New International Dictionary of the English Language. Springfield, Mass.: Merriam, 1961.

Wilkinson, L. P. *Golden Latin Artistry*. Cambridge: Cambridge University Press, 1963.

Wright, George T. *Shakespeare's Metrical Art*. Berkeley, California: University of California Press, 1988.

Other editions of Shakespeare consulted include *The Riverside Shakespeare* and *The Oxford Shakespeare,* as well as individual volumes in the following series: The Arden, Folger, Kittredge, New American Library, The New Cambridge, New Clarendon, New Penguin, and New Swan.

LOUIS SCHEEDER is a Master Teacher at New York University's Tisch School of the Arts and is the founder and director of The Classical Studio, an advanced training program in the Department of Drama. He has directed on, off, and off-off Broadway and at regional theaters in the United States and Canada. He has worked at the Royal Shakespeare Company, was associated with the Manitoba Theatre Centre, served as producer of the Folger Theatre Group, and teaches and coaches privately in New York City.

SHANE ANN YOUNTS teaches voice and text classes in the Graduate Acting Program of New York University, where she specializes in the texts of Shakespeare. She also teaches private classes and coaches actors for theater, film, and television at her Manhattan studio. She has served as voice consultant for Broadway, and off-Broadway productions, and at regional theaters including the Guthrie Theater, The Public Theater, and The Pearl Theatre. She has taught at The Public Theater's Summer Shakespeare Lab, the Guthrie Experience, The Juilliard School (Drama Division), the American Academy of Dramatic Arts, and NYU's Classical Studio.